GREGG SHORTHAND FOR COLLEGES

SPEED BUILDING

Diamond Jubilee Series

14.50

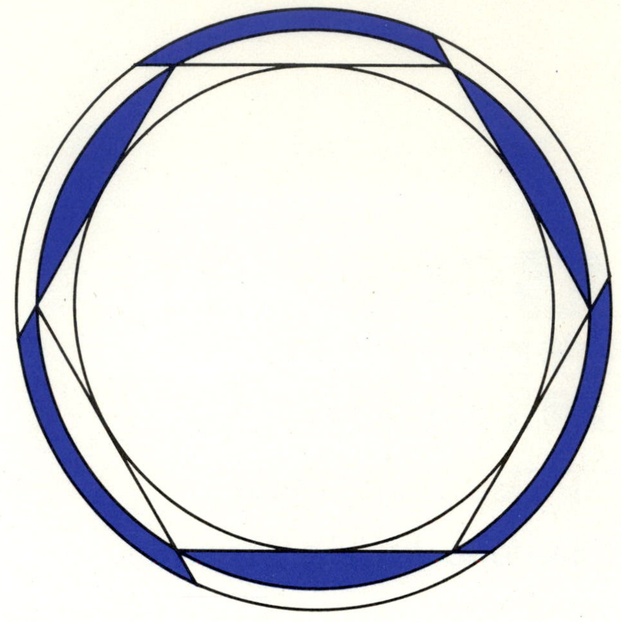

Robert L. Grubbs
Executive Vice President
Robert Morris College

Estelle Popham
Former Chairman, Department of
Business Education
Hunter College

Shorthand written by
Charles Rader

GREGG SHORTHAND FOR COLLEGES

SPEED BUILDING

Diamond Jubilee Series

Gregg Division | McGraw-Hill Book Company

New York | St. Louis | Dallas | San Francisco
Auckland | Düsseldorf | Johannesburg | Kuala Lumpur
London | Mexico | Montreal | New Delhi | Panama | Paris
São Paulo | Singapore | Sydney | Tokyo | Toronto

Art Director	Frank Medina
Designer	Barbara Bert
Shorthand Production Supervisor	Charles Rader
Editorial Staff	Jerome Edelman, Arlene Berkowitz, Mary Buchanan, Karen Corsi
Photographs	Sebastian Milito Cover, 12, 30 Peter Roth 210, 238, 327, 371 Jeremiah Bean 54 Leo de Wys, Inc. 49, 102, 216, 272 Curt Kaufman/Leo de Wys, Inc. 307 Jay Hoops/Leo de Wys, Inc. 160 [right] Stanley Rosenthal/Leo de Wys, Inc. 188 Editorial Photocolor Archives 160 [left] Peter Vadnai from Editorial Photocolor Archives 80 Dan O'Neill from Editorial Photocolor Archives 132 Daniel Brody/Editorial Photocolor Archives 358 Ted Speigel/Black Star 244 Dennis Brack/Black Star 330 Martin S. Dworkin—DPI 300 Linda Moser—DPI 149 Chris Reeburg—DPI 388 Ted Grant—DPI 416
Compositor	King Typographic Service
Printer	R. R. Donnelley & Sons Company

Library of Congress Cataloging in Publication Data

Grubbs, Robert Lowell.
Gregg shorthand for colleges, speed building.

(Diamond jubilee series)

1. Shorthand—Gregg. I. Popham, Estelle L., joint author. II. Title.

Z56.G833G78 653'.4272 75-28308
ISBN 0-07-025080-4

GREGG SHORTHAND FOR COLLEGES, Speed Building
Diamond Jubilee Series

1 2 3 4 5 6 7 8 9 0 DODO 7 8 4 3 2 1 0 9 8 7 6

Preface

Gregg Shorthand for Colleges, Speed Building, Diamond Jubilee Series, is tailored to meet the needs of advanced shorthand students. It is carefully designed to provide students with opportunities to refine both dictation and transcription skills. In most cases, *Gregg Shorthand for Colleges, Speed Building,* will be used after students have completed *Gregg Shorthand for Colleges, Transcription.*

Objectives

Gregg Shorthand for Colleges, Speed Building, has the following main objectives:

1 To help students achieve speed, accuracy, and endurance levels in writing shorthand that will enable them to write with precision for reasonable periods of time.

2 To help students create a reserve of shorthand power that will enable them to shift easily from comfortable cruising rates of dictation to the higher levels of skill demanded in brief, emergency spurts in dictation rates.

3 To help students continue to stock their minds with an ever-increasing vocabulary of shorthand outlines they can write accurately, quickly, and without conscious direction.

4 To help students confidently approach new or unfamiliar words and to construct their outlines according to principle.

5 To help students blend the different primary skills into effective and efficient transcription power.

6 To help students make spelling, capitalization, and punctuation decisions without time-wasting interruptions in the flow of typing.

7 To help students make effective self-appraisals of their progress in the transcription of contemporary business dictation material.

Organization

Gregg Shorthand for Colleges, Speed Building, is lesson-planned, like the other volumes in the college Diamond Jubilee Series. It is organized into two parts consisting of sixteen units of five lessons each. Part 1 consists of two units: an intensive review of brief forms and of shorthand writing principles. Part 2 includes fourteen units of skill-building materials for in- and out-of-class practice in taking and transcribing dictation.

Each of the units in Part 2 is organized for drill and practice purposes around the correspondence of a department or division of a contemporary corporation.

At the beginning of each unit there is a short note to the student that provides information about the general activities and responsibilities of this department or division. The student is supplied also with the name and title of the manager, director, or supervisor who initiates and receives communications.

The departments for which correspondence and drill routines have been prepared include Credit, Sales, Personnel Services, Purchasing, Public Information, Health Services, Advertising, Administrative Services, Production, General Counsel, Financial Services, Environmental Control, Transportation Services, and Research and Development.

Cycle of Emphasis

The units in Part 2 are designed to cycle emphasis on vocabulary, decision making in transcription, dictation speed building, reading and writing practice, transcription speed building, and transcription quizzes.

VOCABULARY

Units 3 through 16 contain shorthand vocabulary reviews that cover all the major principles of Gregg Shorthand. Each unit is organized as follows:

- First lesson: Word families
- Second lesson: Word beginnings and endings
- Third lesson: Brief forms
- Fourth lesson: Word-building principles
- Fifth lesson: Phrasing

The vocabulary of contemporary business is emphasized in each of the lessons in Units 3 through 16. Specialized words and phrases are defined in the Business Vocabulary Builder.

DECISION MAKING IN TRANSCRIPTION

In the first and third lessons of each unit in Part 2, transcription skill-building aids are provided for the student. These aids review spelling, grammar, punctuation, capitalization, and general directions for taking and transcribing dictation effectively and efficiently.

In the second and fourth lessons of each unit, transcription-typing paragraphs are given in shorthand. These short paragraphs contain examples of the transcription pointers emphasized in the preceding lesson. They provide decision-making situations for students to resolve while typing from shorthand copy. The paragraphs may be used also for short, timed transcription spurts of one or two minutes. A cumulative transcription word count is printed to the right of each line of shorthand to enable students to quickly compute their words-a-minute score in the timed writings.

DICTATION SPEED BUILDING

Shorthand students need to develop comfortable cruising speeds in writing shorthand from dictation. Dictation material is presented in a format designed for two basic skill-building dictation patterns.

In the first and third lessons of each unit in Part 2, material set in type is provided for progressive dictation routines. Progressive dictation is designed to force the students' speed in writing shorthand. The progressive-dictation paragraphs are counted for dictation in 1-minute intervals at progressively increasing speeds. Speeds range from a low of 50 words a minute in Lesson 11 to a high of 140 words a minute in Lesson 80.

In the second and fourth lessons, material set in type is provided for stair-step dictation. Stair-step dictation may be described as progressive dictation in reverse. It provides good opportunities for students to build speed, endurance, and a method of attack on new words. Complete directions for the administration of stair-step dictation are contained in the *Instructor's Handbook* accompanying *Gregg Shorthand for Colleges, Speed Building.*

READING AND WRITING PRACTICE

Each lesson in this text contains more than 600 words of connected practice material appropriate to a specific department or division of a modern corporation. The letters, memos, and other communications are modern and representative of the style and language of the contemporary business world. Short, long, and medium-length letters are provided in each lesson.

TRANSCRIPTION SPEED BUILDING

In the fifth lesson of each unit in Part 2, shorthand is provided for transcription timed writings of 3-, 5-, or 10-minute durations. This shorthand material can be used for improving students' transcription skills and for self-appraisal by the students. A cumulative transcription word count is printed to the right of each line of shorthand to enable students to quickly compute their words-a-minute score in the timed writings.

TRANSCRIPTION QUIZZES

At the end of the fifth lesson in each unit of Part 2, a short paragraph is given in shorthand. All punctuation marks have been eliminated from these paragraphs, and students are to supply the appropriate punctuation while typing from the running shorthand material. The quiz paragraphs are designed to provide opportunities for applying the punctuation pointers emphasized in the previous lessons of the unit.

Supporting Materials

Instructor's Handbook for Gregg Shorthand for Colleges, Speed Building, Diamond Jubilee Series Besides offering suggestions on the use of the materials in the program, this handbook provides 80 supplementary dictation letters on topics related to those in each unit. Inside addresses for these letters are given on pages 445-447 of the text.

Tapes for Gregg Shorthand for Colleges, Speed Building, Diamond Jubilee Series The tapes consist of 40 cassettes and feature a variety of dictation skill-building routines.

Student's Transcript of Gregg Shorthand for Colleges, Speed Building, Diamond Jubilee Series This transcript offers the student a counted key to all of the shorthand in the text, which will prove useful to the student in out-of-class practice.

Workbook for Gregg Shorthand for Colleges, Speed Building, Diamond Jubilee Series The drills and exercises in this workbook are related to the corresponding lessons in the text. Additional practice in developing shorthand writing skills and in improving efficiency in decision making may thus be offered to the student.

Acknowledgments

The authors are indebted to many fellow teachers and to the students in their own classes for helpful suggestions, comments, and criticisms.

Robert L. Grubbs

Estelle Popham

Contents

Unit 1	Brief-Form Review	12
Unit 2	Shorthand Theory Review	30
Unit 3	Credit Department	52
Unit 4	Sales Department	78
Unit 5	Personnel Services	106
Unit 6	Purchasing	132
Unit 7	Public Information	160
Unit 8	Health Services	188
Unit 9	Advertising	216
Unit 10	Administrative Services	244
Unit 11	Production	272
Unit 12	General Counsel	300
Unit 13	Financial Services	330
Unit 14	Environmental Control	358
Unit 15	Transportation Services	388
Unit 16	Research and Development	416
Appendix		444

1 BRIEF-FORM AND WRITING-PRINCIPLE REVIEW

Unit 1

BRIEF-FORM REVIEW

In Unit 1 you will be presented with an intensive review of brief forms and brief-form derivatives. By following the procedures accompanying the brief-form charts and by reading and writing the brief-form letters, you will improve your ability to take and transcribe dictation. Since brief forms and their derivatives account for nearly half of all dictation, the more they are automatized, the more efficient your shorthand skill will become.

LESSON 1

Building Brief-Form Skill

In most advanced college shorthand classes, there is usually a diversity of backgrounds ranging from those who were in a shorthand class only weeks ago to those who learned shorthand years ago. It is likely that such a range of previous experience may be found in this shorthand class, and you may be anywhere in the group from one extreme to the other. Each of you, however, will have the same objective—to build dictation speed to the highest possible rate. Thus you will realize the importance of Unit 1, which provides a rapid, intensive review of brief forms and their derivatives which comprise 45 percent of dictation. The letters in this unit are intentionally overloaded with brief forms to provide you with maximum exposure through concentrated review. (Beginning with Unit 3 the materials will be more closely related to actual business operations and serve as better models of current business communication.)

1 BRIEF-FORM REVIEW

The following chart contains approximately the first half of the brief forms. Read it aloud, checking the key below if there is any doubt about an outline. Then reread across the page, forward and backward, and up and down, until you can read the list fluently and accurately in any direction. When you have achieved this goal, cover the shorthand outlines and write each word in shorthand from the key or from live or taped dictation.

Reading goal: 2 minutes or less.

Writing goal: 2½ minutes or less; not more than one error.

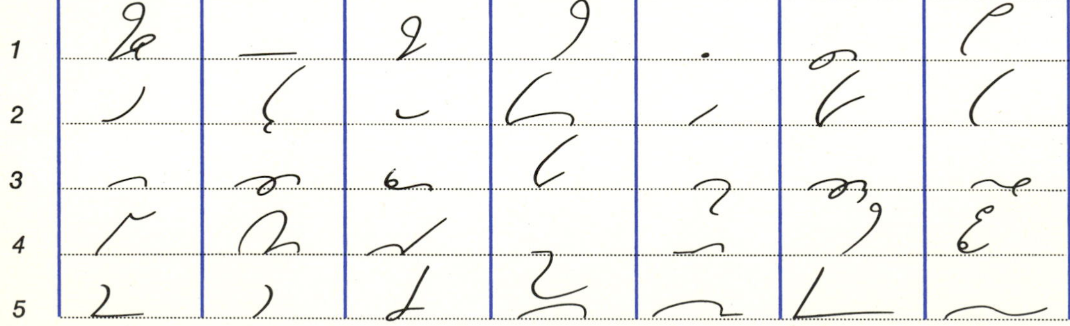

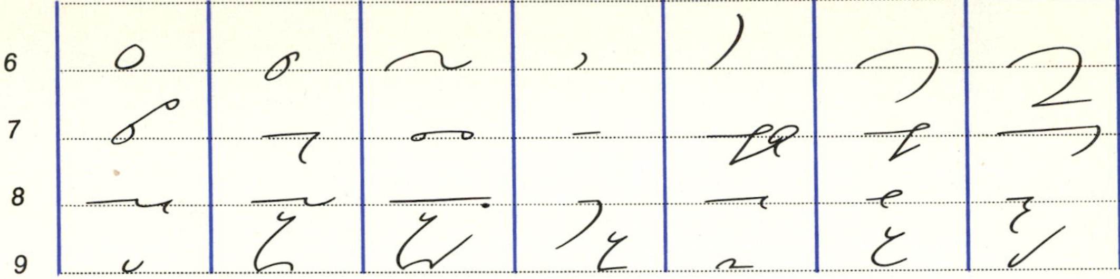

1 Advertise, am, after, advantage, a–an, acknowledge, about.
2 And, business, are–our–hour, big, at–it, between, be–by.
3 Can, character, circular, but, company, characters, correspond–correspondence.
4 During, difficult, could, envelope, enclose, ever–every, experience.
5 From, for, general, good, gone, gentlemen, glad.
6 I, how–out, great, his–is, have, govern, government.
7 Idea, importance–important, immediate, in–not, merchandise, merchant, manufacture.
8 Mrs., Mr., morning, never, must, next, newspaper.
9 Of, object, objected, opinion, one–won, opportunity, order.

Reading and Writing Practice

2

[132]

3

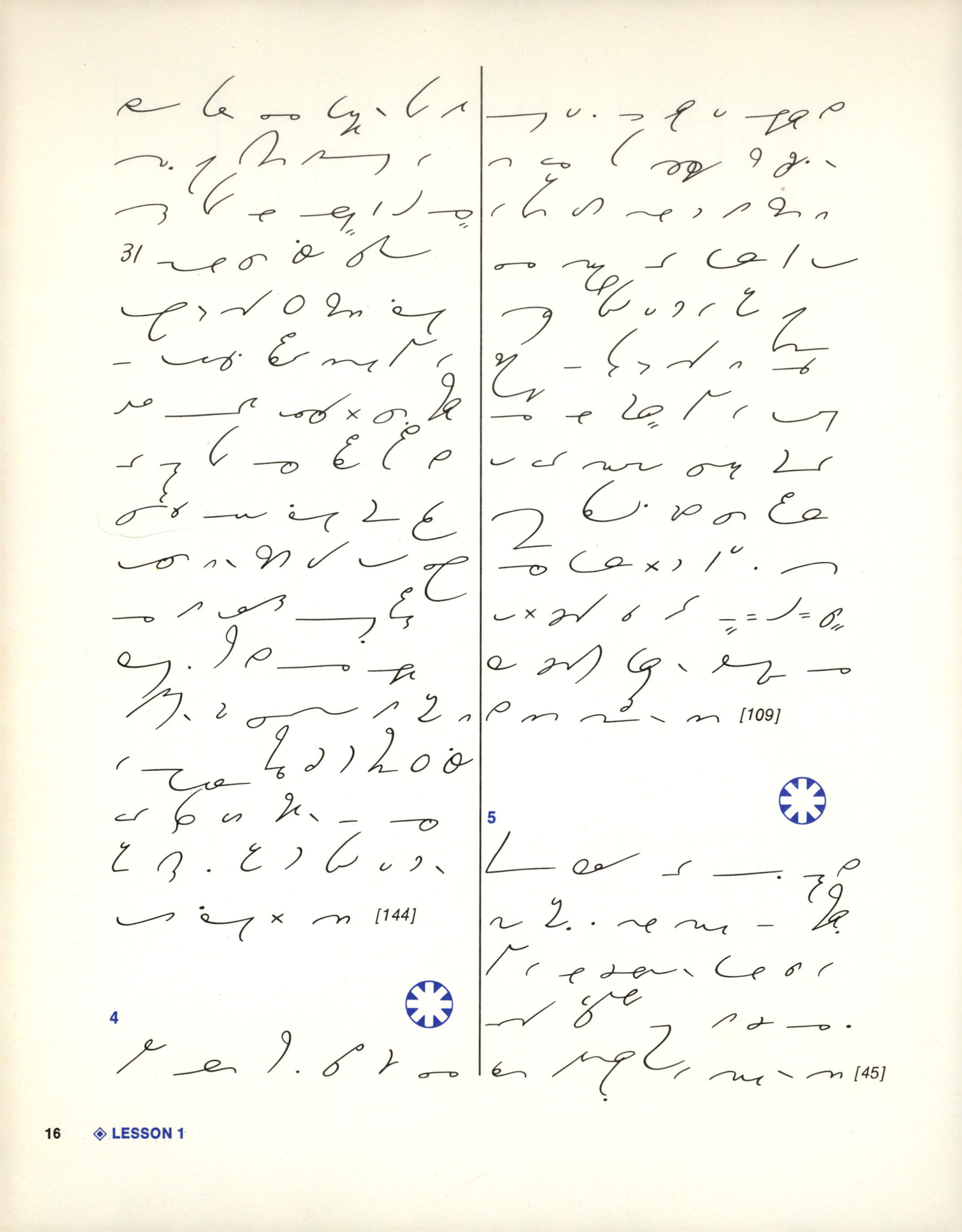

31

[144]

4

[109]

5

[45]

Building Brief-Form Skill

6 BRIEF-FORM REVIEW *(Concluded)*

Here are the rest of the brief forms. Again, read the chart from left to right and from right to left, and then from top to bottom and from bottom to top, until you can read it correctly and fluently. Cover the shorthand outlines and write each word in shorthand from the key or from live or taped dictation.

Reading goal: 2 minutes or less.

Writing goal: 2½ minutes or less; not more than one error.

10

11

12

13

14

15

16

17

18

19

10 Over, organize, part, ordinary, particular, probably, present.

11 Publication–publish, purpose, put, public, progress, question, quantity.

12 Responsible, railroad, railroads, request, regular, regard, recognize.

13 Satisfactory–satisfy, shall, send, short, several, situation, should.

14 State, speak, street, soon, such, subject, success.
15 Thank, that, them, the, their–there, suggest, than.
16 Those, under, time, throughout, they, thing–think, this.
17 Value, upon, use, was, very, well–will, were–year.
18 Which, with, wish, why, what, when, where.
19 World, would, yesterday, work, worth, you–your, yet.

Reading and Writing Practice

7

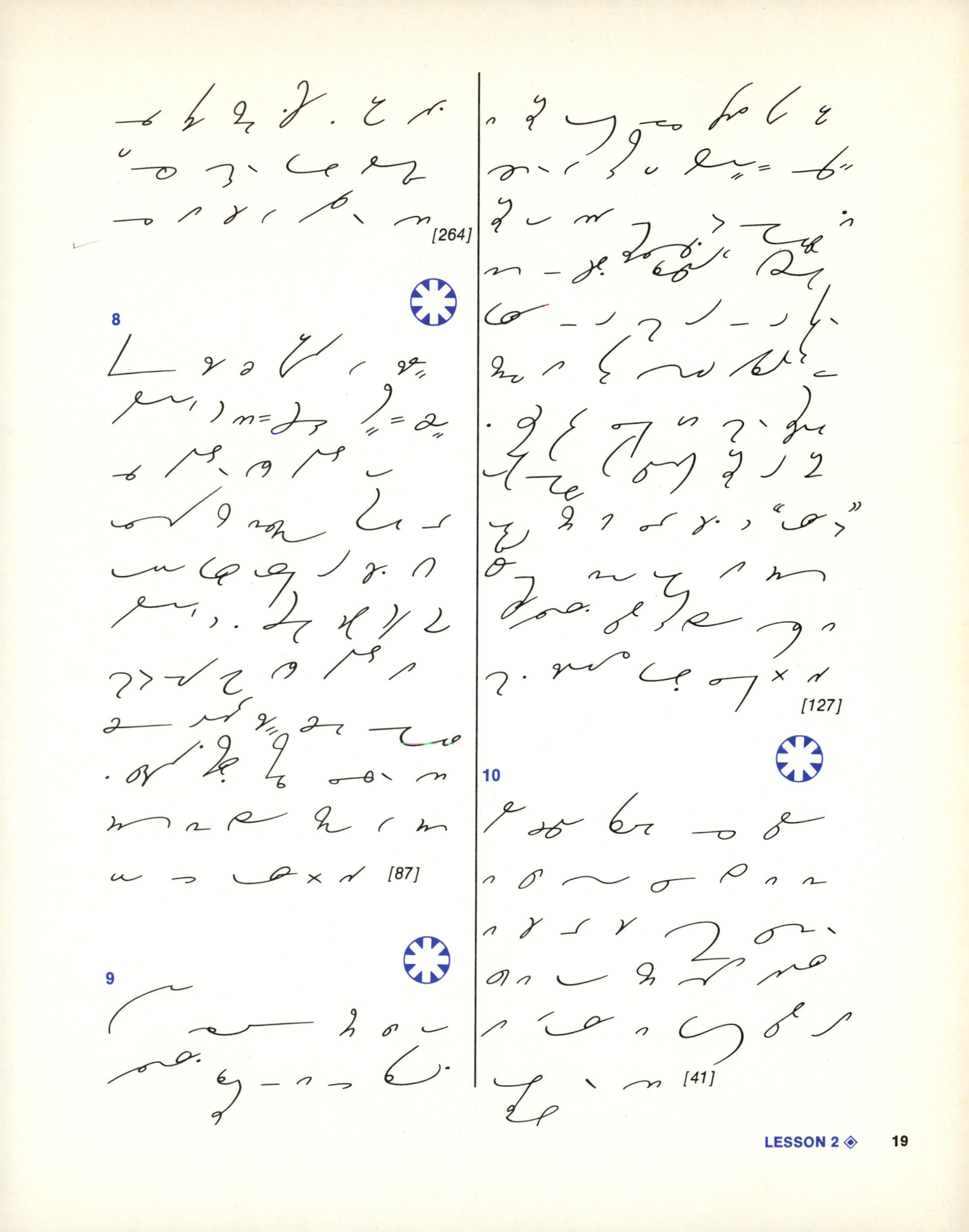

[264]

8

[87]

9

[127]

10

[41]

Building Brief-Form Skill

11 BRIEF FORMS AND DERIVATIVES

Even though you have reviewed the brief forms, you can now profitably devote time to reading and writing brief forms and derivatives.

Reading goal: 4 minutes or less.

Writing goal: 5 minutes; not more than one error.

1

2

3

4

5

6

7

8

9

10

11

12

13

14

15

16

17

1 Use, uses, useful, usefully, usefulness, used.

2 Undergo, underpaid, underrate, underground, understand, understood.

3 There, therefore, thereby; time, timed, timely.

4 Success, successful, successfully; suggest, suggestion, suggested.

5 State, stated, statement, restate, estate, stately.

6 Soon, sooner, soonest; speak, speaks, speaker.

7 Short, shortly, shorter, shorten, shorthand, shortness.

8 Satisfactory–satisfy, satisfied, satisfactorily, satisfaction, dissatisfied, dissatisfaction.

9 Responsible, responsibility, responsibilities; send, sending, sender.

10 Regular, regularly, irregular; request, requested, requesting.

11 Recognize, recognizes, recognition; regarded, regardless, regarding.

12 Publication–publish, publications–publishes, publisher; question, questioned, questionable.

13 Progress, progressed, progressive; public, publicly, republic.

14 Present, presented, presently, presentation, represent, representative.

15 Part, parted, department, apartment, partner, partnership.

16 Over, overcome, overdue, overcoat, overtime, overwork.

17 Organize, organization, organized, organizer, disorganized, reorganize.

Reading and Writing Practice

12

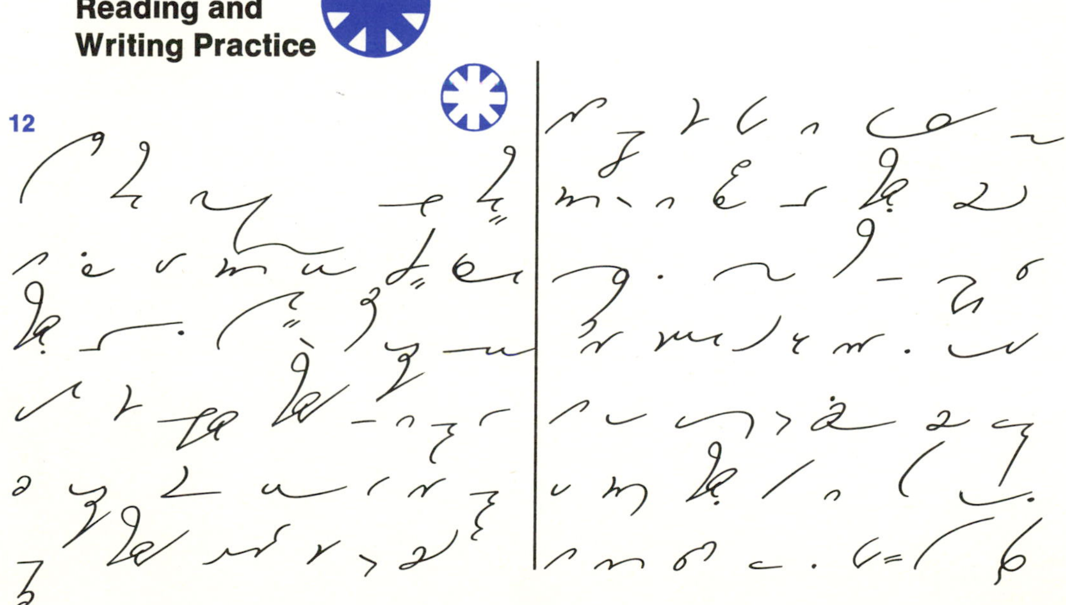

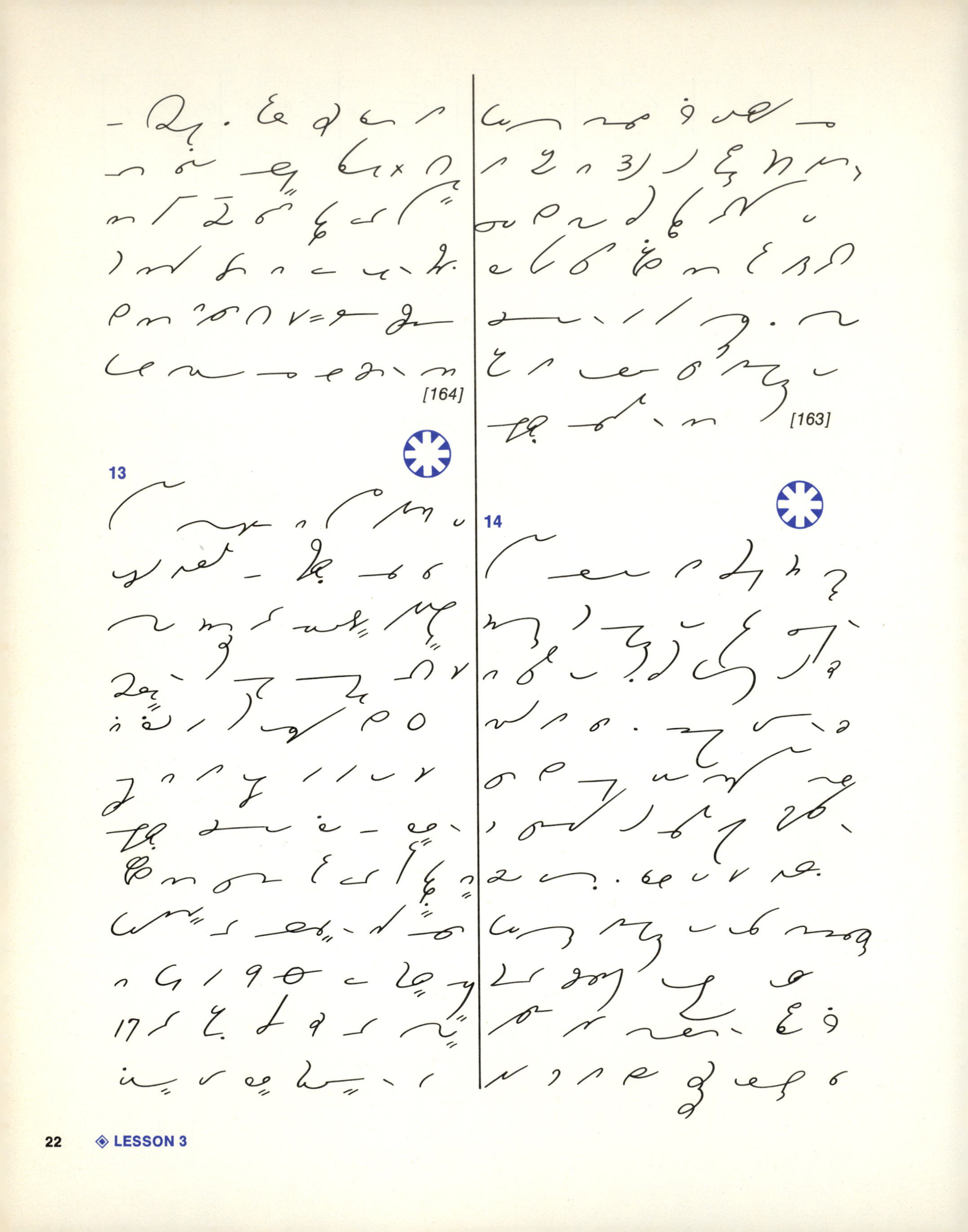

[164]

[163]

13

14

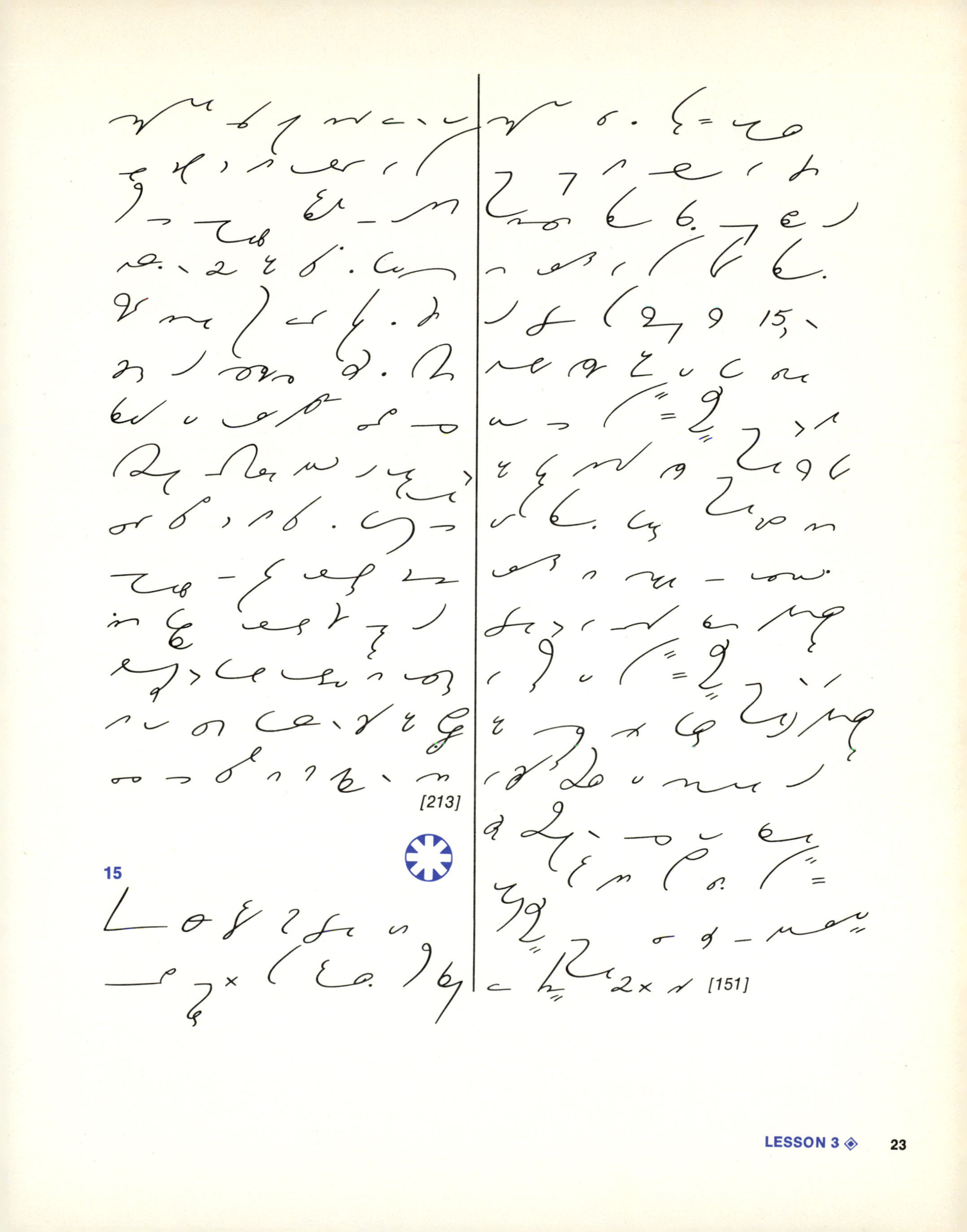

[213]

15

[151]

LESSON 

Building Brief-Form Skill

16 BRIEF FORMS AND DERIVATIVES *(Continued)*

This chart contains 48 brief forms and derivatives. Read the entire list until you can read fluently and then write each word in shorthand until you can meet the goal.

Reading goal: 40 seconds.

Writing goal: 45 seconds; no errors.

1 Time, timeless, sometime; value, valuable, valueless.

2 Worth, worthiest, worthless, trustworthy, noteworthy, newsworthy.

3 Where, whereabouts, elsewhere, somewhere, nowhere, whereas.

4 Well–will, welcome, welfare, wills, willed, willingness.

5 Work, workable, worked, worker, workmanship, workmen.

6 Over, overestimate, overtaken, overcast, overflow, overstate.

7 Wish, wished, wishfully; year, years, yearly.

8 Out, outside, outlined, outlasted, outcast, outcome.

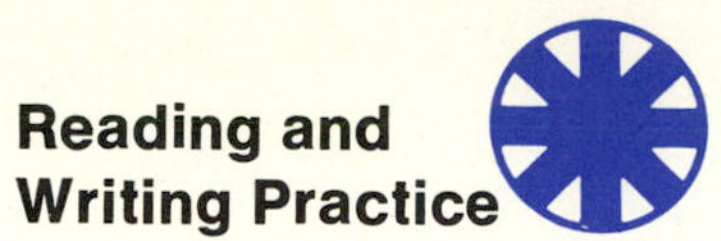

Reading and Writing Practice

17

[110]

18

[106]

19

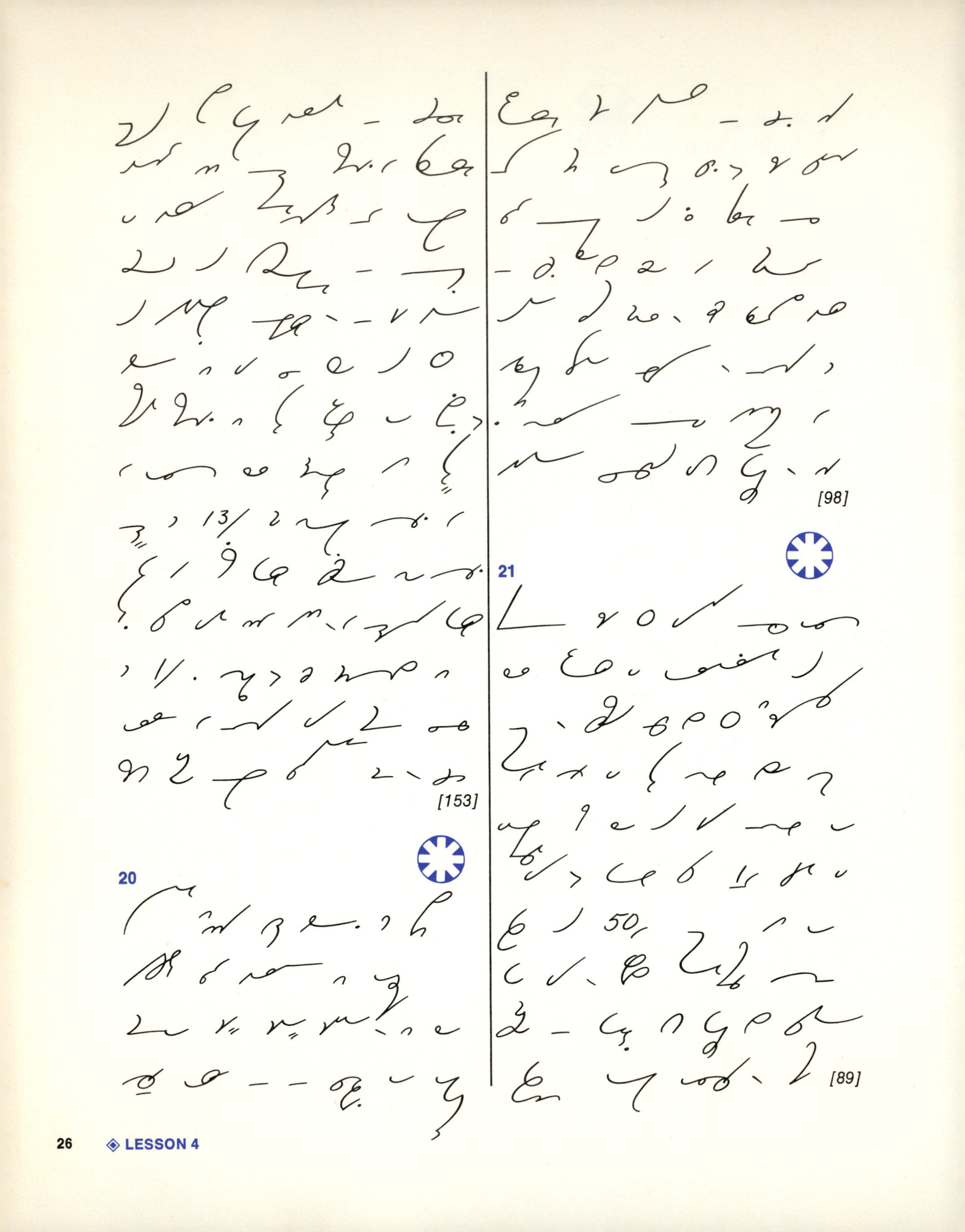

[153]

20

[98]

21

[89]

Building Brief-Form Skill

22 BRIEF FORMS AND DERIVATIVES *(Concluded)*

This chart contains 60 brief forms and derivatives. Read until fluency is acquired, and then write within the time limits.

Reading goal: 50 seconds.

Writing goal: 55 seconds.

1 Opinion, opinionated, opinions; order, disorder, reorder.

2 Manufacture, manufacturing, manufacturers; great, greatness, greatly.

3 Govern, governed, government, governmental, governor, governing.

4 Ever–every, everyone, everybody, everywhere, everlasting, evergreen.

5 Important–importance, self-importance, unimportant; however, somehow, anyhow.

6 How–out, outcome, outlay, output, layout, outmoded.
7 Ordinary, ordinarily, extraordinary; foregone, put, puts.
8 Object, objected, objection, objectionable, objective, objectively.
9 Glad, gladly, gladness; good, goods, goodness.
10 Part, imparted, departure, participated, particle, parties.

Reading and Writing Practice

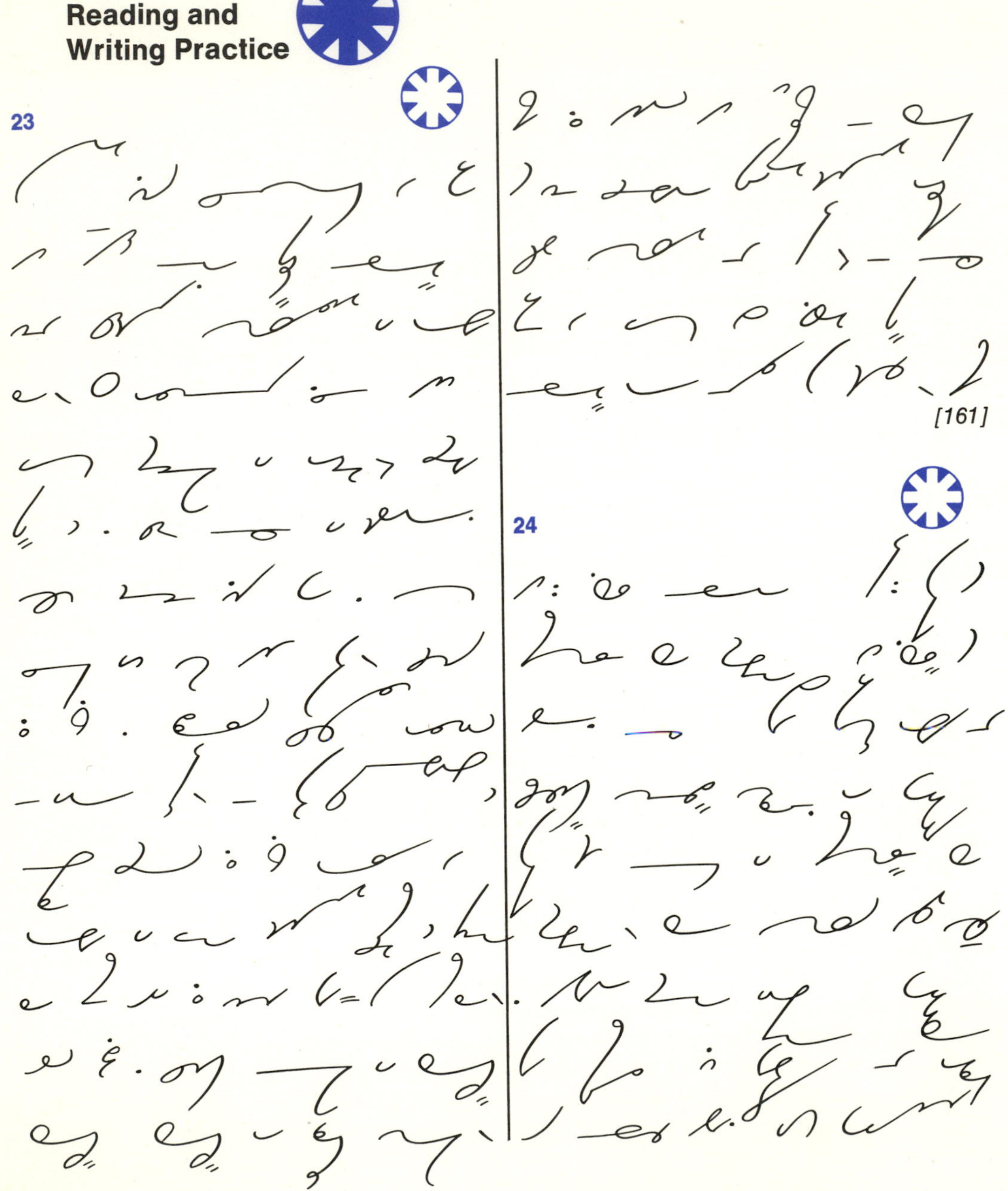

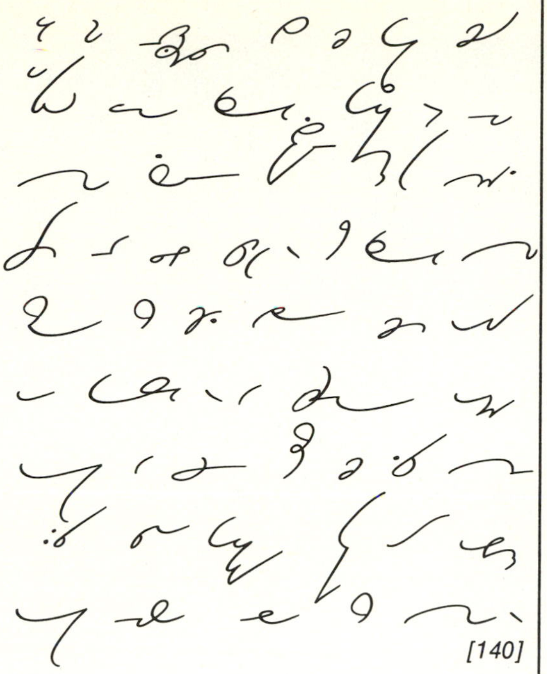

[140]

25

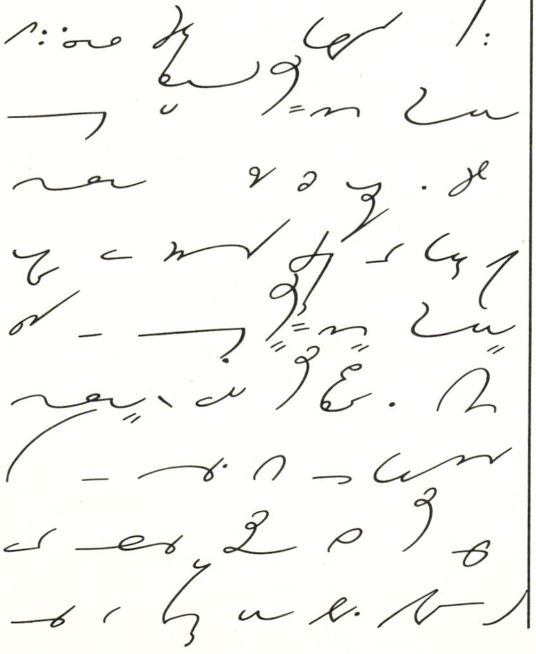

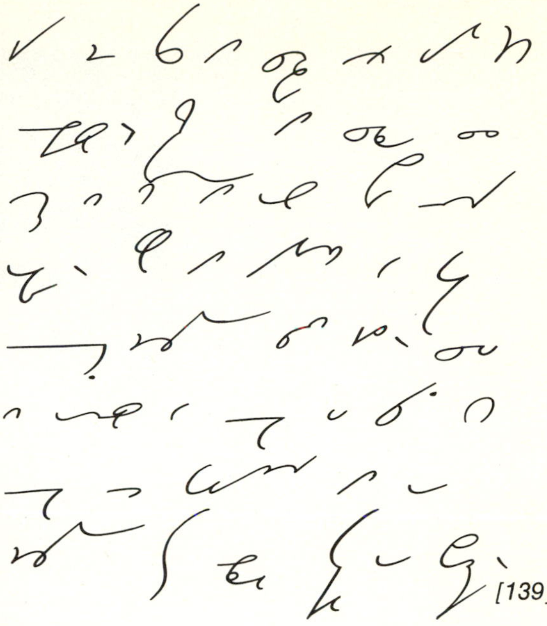

[139]

26

[83]

Unit 2
PRINCIPLES REVIEW

In Unit 2 you will have the opportunity to practice reading and writing words that illustrate Gregg Shorthand theory. A review of Gregg Shorthand theory is also included in the introductions to the lessons of the units that follow. As you already have learned, it is not necessary to memorize the rules for writing Gregg Shorthand, but the ability to apply the rules is important in order to construct quickly and accurately outlines for words you may never have encountered previously.

Shorthand Theory Review

When you practice lists of words such as those that follow, use this procedure:

1 Read the words that illustrate the principle. When you cannot immediately read a word, spell the shorthand symbols in it. If the spelling does not give you the meaning, refer to the key.

2 Make a shorthand copy of the words in your notebook.

27 PRINCIPLES

Past Tenses

Circle Joinings With Curves

Circle Joinings With Straight Lines

Joinings of O and OO Hooks

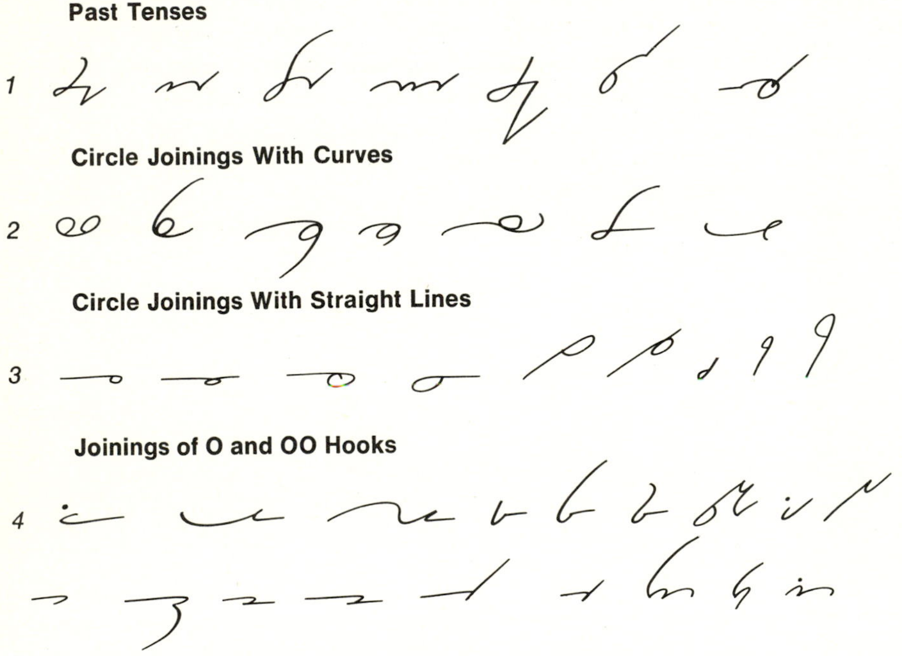

1 Finished, worked, baked, cooked, changed, attend, inquired.

2 Array, bear, gave, case, guard, beam, lease.

3 Me, mean, my, aim, day, date, she, each, age.

4 Home, loan, grown, shown, bone, phone, adopt, hot, dot.
New, move, noon, moon, mood, nut, book, push, hook.

Reading and Writing Practice

28

[194]

29

[147]

30

[154]

31

[173]

32

[107]

Model Letters

1 Short letter — double spaced, semiblocked style, standard punctuation.

2 Short letter — single spaced, blocked style, standard punctuation.

3 Average-length letter, semiblocked style with attention line, standard punctuation.

4 Long letter, indented style, standard punctuation.

5 Interoffice memorandum.

6 Two-page letter, blocked style with subject line and postscript, standard punctuation.

Pruitt Sitz Company

822 Carroun Street • Seattle, Washington 98155

Personnel Department

June 24, 19--

Ms. Maria C. Lopez
Wilson and Company
146 West Street
Wilmington, Delaware 19804

Dear Ms. Lopez:

It was kind of you to send me the clipping from the June 18 issue of the Daily Times reporting on my participation in your conference. I am pasting it in my scrapbook.

I thoroughly enjoyed my visit to Seattle.

Sincerely yours,

Harry C. Green
Personnel Manager

HCG:BB

1

SABIN SALES SPECIALTY CORP.

216 Williams Avenue • Jackson, Mississippi 39219

June 20, 197-

Mrs. Carole Thomas
730 Clark Street
Philadelphia, Pennsylvania 19150

Dear Mrs. Thomas:

It was indeed a pleasure to receive your letter of February 12. We were concerned about your not having paid your bills for the months of November, December, and January, but we knew that there must have been a good reason.

Won't you come in to our office on Friday, March 3, at 2 p.m., at which time we can work out a special plan that will enable you to pay your bills over an extended period of time.

We value you as a customer and want to continue our business relationship for many years to come.

Cordially yours,

Donald H. Wright
Customer Relations Manager

DHW:KD

2

NEW ENGLAND PRODUCTS

44 TREMONT STREET
BOSTON, MA 02112

August 17, 197-

Union Manufacturing Company
130 Randolph Street
Springfield, MA 01126

ATTENTION: Mr. Martin

Gentlemen:

In many business organizations, sending out a big mailing creates difficult problems. High-paid workers are diverted from their regular jobs to fold and stuff circulars and other advertising material into envelopes in order to meet a mailing deadline. The operation of the office is disrupted, and important work must be neglected.

This will not happen, however, in an organization that has installed a Harper Mailer 161. This unit folds mailing pieces, inserts them in envelopes, and seals the envelopes at the rate of 5,000 an hour. Thus in one ordinary working day you can process as many as 40,000 pieces while your regular staff goes about its regular duties.

Wouldn't you like to have us install a Harper 161 in your office on a ten-day trial basis? To arrange this, simply return the enclosed card.

Very truly yours,

Howard C. West
Product Manager

HCW:DS

3

HALL-ODEE INCORPORATED
36 EAST PARK DRIVE · GARY, INDIANA 46505

April 14, 19--

Mrs. Charles E. Morton
511 Spring Avenue
Gary, Indiana 46505

Dear Mrs. Morton:

I must make a confession. When I came here last fall to take over the Gary branch of Hall-Odee Incorporated, I was sure that it would be easy to sell a great deal of furniture in a short time. The sight of the homes here in Gary must have caused me to be overoptimistic.

In anticipation of the sales that I expected, I bought large quantities of fine furniture. In spite of the quality of the furniture and the appeal of our low prices, however, sales fell far below my expectations. Now I have a warehouse full of merchandise that must be moved. What's more, there are new shipments on the way from several manufacturers.

The time for action has come. On Saturday, May 6, you will see in the Gary newspapers an announcement of stock-disposal sales. Prices will be low. In many cases, our furniture will be offered at cost and even less. Of course, we expect a great response. Because of this, I feel that you and a few other preferred customers should have the opportunity to shop in comfort before public announcement is made of the sale.

Therefore, please consider this a personal invitation for you to shop at our convenience on May 3, 4, or 5. When you come, please give the enclosed card to one of our salesmen. He will then take you to the floor on which the sale will be held.

Very truly yours,

August C. Mann

August C. Mann
Manager

ACM:RE
Enc.

4

interoffice memorandum

To	Carla Perez	From	L. C. James
Dept.	Inventory Control	Dept.	Personnel Department
Floor	33	Floor	29
Subject	Meeting for New Employees	Date	June 2, 19--

This memorandum is your invitation to attend a meeting for new employees on June 15 in Room 417. The meeting will start promptly at 10 o'clock.

At this meeting you will learn about the various departments of the company and their contributions to our business as a whole. You will also meet a number of the executives of the company.

If you have any questions about our organization and its policies, you will have an opportunity to ask them at this meeting.

After this meeting you will have a better picture of our organization and the products it makes.

L.C.S

LCS:HH

5

McGRAW LITERARY AGENCY
738 University Park, Jacksonville, FL 32204 / 248-9773

ESTHER McGRAW, PRESIDENT
WILLIAM H. McGRAW, VICE-PRESIDENT AND GENERAL SALES MANAGER

February 22, 19--

Mrs. Kevin L. Murphy
The Edison Manufacturing Company
165 Lee Avenue
Atlanta, Georgia 30304

Dear Mrs. Murphy:

Subject: Employees' Handbook

I am sending you today by express all the material that we have available on how to prepare an employees' handbook.

You will be interested, I am sure, in our experience in helping the Martin Miller Company prepare its latest handbook. When we were called in, that company already had a handbook but it was out of date. The organization had grown considerably since that handbook was prepared; consequently, the handbook had to be completely rewritten. The new handbook was ready at the end of last year. It benefited by many lessons that had been learned during the work on the first handbook.

While working with the Martin Miller Company, we learned that the following three points are important in preparing a handbook:

1. It should not be a rule book listing things that should and should not be done by employees.

2. It should take advantage of the pleasant feeling of satisfaction with which an employee starts a new job. The handbook should play a definite part in maintaining that feeling of satisfaction.

3. It should set down facts that will make employees feel that they are important parts of the company. It should give them information on every phase of the company's organization and activities.

In the first edition of the handbook we tried to put in a section that was devoted to the history of the company. We had often felt a need for this. We also felt that this objective was not covered fully enough in the first handbook. This handbook was prepared with the employee exclusively in mind.

These are just a few thoughts that come to me at this time. I am sure that the Martin Miller Company would be glad to send you a copy of their new handbook. I believe that you may find many suggestions in it that you would be able to use when you prepare your handbook.

6

Mrs. Kevin L. Murphy 2 February 22, 19--

Needless to say, we are at your service. If you think that a visit with one of our representatives would be helpful, please call us. We will be glad to arrange an appointment.

Cordially yours,

William H. McGraw

William H. McGraw
Vice President and
General Sales Manager

WHM:IRT

P.S. I have just learned that Fred Hopkins, the member of our staff who worked with Martin Miller Company, will be in Jacksonville all next week. Would you like to meet him and talk with him?

6

Lesson 7

Shorthand Theory Review

33 PRINCIPLES

Under Th

1

Over Th

2

Comma S

3

Left S

4

OO-s Without an Angle

5

OO-s With an Angle

6

1 Though, throw, thrown, health, threads, thrilling, both.

2 Path, bath, smooth, thin, thick, teeth, these, method, tooth.

3 Safes, saves, seeks, sags, stay, sun, sum, so, sashes, sages, satchels, marches, rages, missions, these, say, as, easy, fast, gas, kiss.

4 Space, sabers, series, slip, eats, needs, sense, seems, knows.

5 Us, just, discuss, disgust, boost, strenuous, conspicuous, continuous.

6 Studious, injurious, victorious, curious, erroneous, courteous.

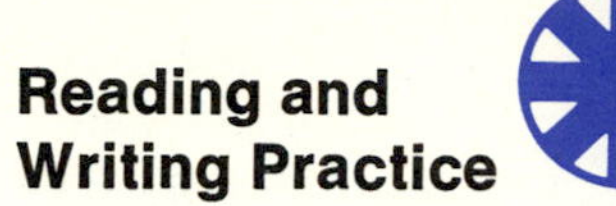

Reading and Writing Practice

34

[174]

35

[110]

36

[207]

Shorthand Theory Review

37 PRINCIPLES OF JOINING

1 The word beginning *re-* is represented by *r* before a downstroke or a vowel.

Reflect, revert, region, resort, repeat, refer, react, reorganize, readjust.

2 The word beginning *de-* is represented by *d* except before *k, gay.*

Delight, deposit, depend, delay, decide, decay, degrade.

3 The word endings *-ure* and *-ual* are represented by *r* and *l* except after downstrokes.

Failure, feature, nature, moisture, leisure, insure, fissure.
Actual, equal, schedule, mutual, visual, casual, usual.

4 *Ul* is represented by *oo* when it precedes a forward or upward stroke.

Culminate, ultimate, results, culture, adults, multitude, insult.

5 *Con-* and *com-* are written with the *n* or *m* when followed by a vowel.

Connive, connotation, connect; commerce, comedy, comma, commit.

6 *In-, un-, en-* and *im-, em-* are represented by *n* or *m* before a consonant. When a vowel follows, these word beginnings are written with the initial vowel.

but

but

Inspiration, insist; unless, unfair; enjoy, engine *but* innovation, unknown.
Impress, impression; embarrass, emphasis *but* immaculate; emotional.

Reading and Writing Practice

38

15 20

[227]

[113]

39

40

[130]

41

[100]

42

[100]

Shorthand Theory Review

43 RULES FOR WRITING

1 Omit the circle vowel in *-dition, -dation, -tition, -tation, -mition, -mation, -nition,* and *-nation.*

Addition, accommodation, repetition, confrontation, transmission, inflammation, recognition, donation.

2 A minor vowel may often be omitted when two vowels occur together. *Oo* is often used to represent the diphthong *u.*

Tune, tulip, reduce, amuse, news, due, avenue, revenue.

3 An unaccented medial *oo* is omitted for speed and legibility.

Accuracy, formula, saturate, popular, occupy, soluble.

4 The vowel usually inserted in a monosyllable is frequently omitted in longer words using the same phonetic combination.

Bit, arbitration; pet, petition; car, carbon, carpet; cape, landscape.

5 Generally, minor vowels are omitted, but they are written when the unaccented endings *-ar, -er,* and *-al* follow the downstrokes *ish, chay,* and *j. Exception:* the word endings *-tional* or *-sional.*

Dictionary, stationer, rancher, ranger, cordial, optional, professional.

Reading and Writing Practice

44

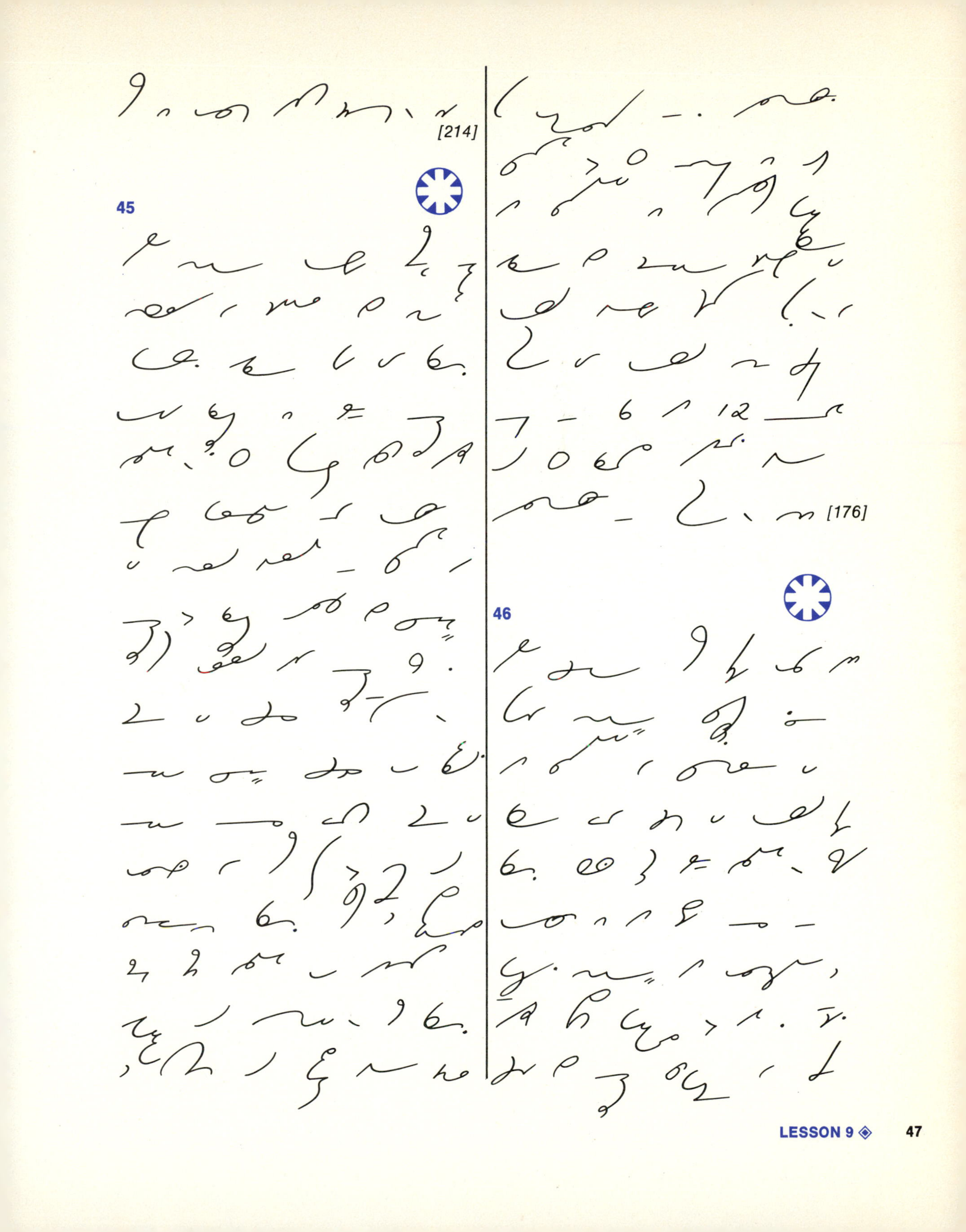

[214]

45

[176]

46

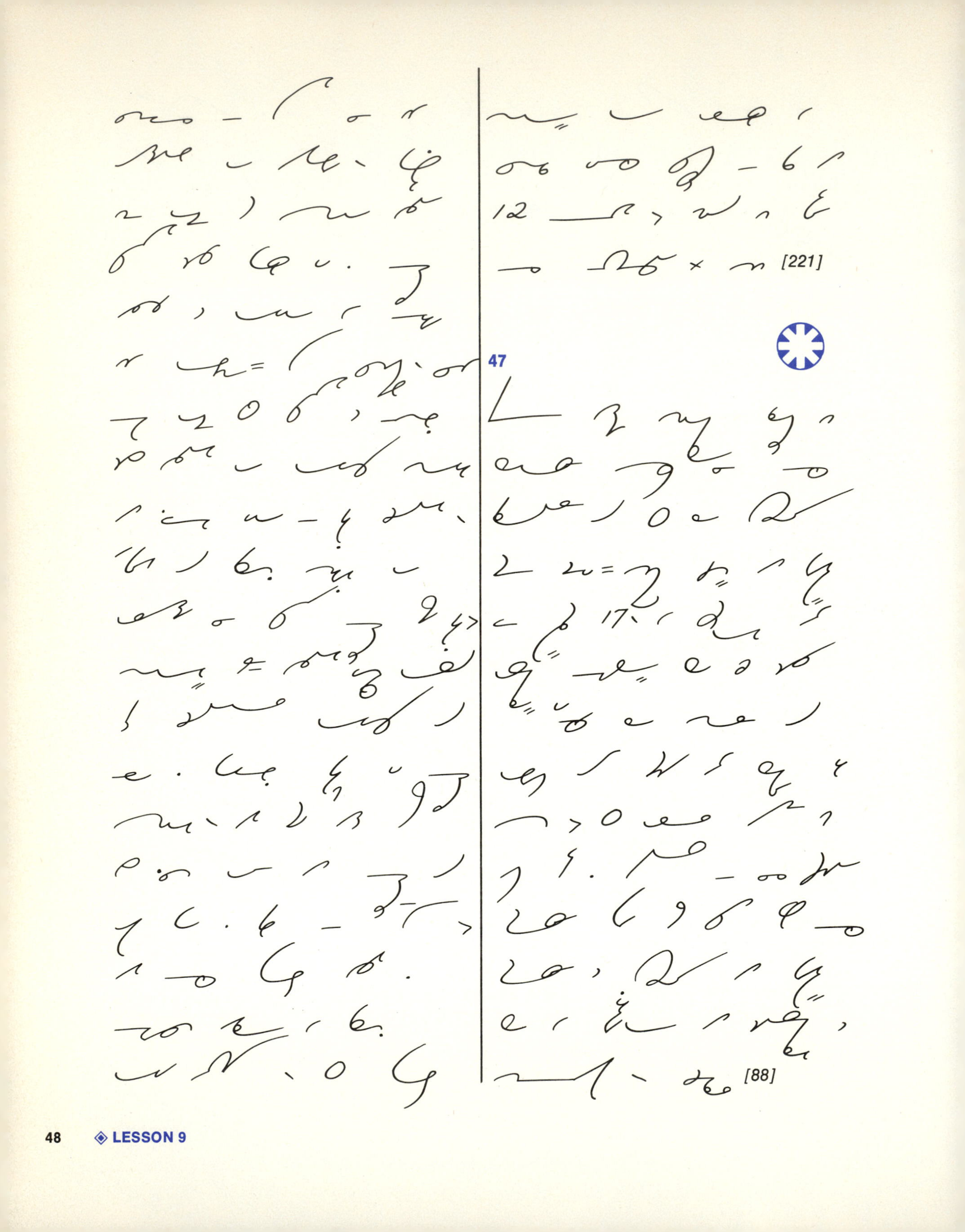

12

[221]

47

17

[88]

LESSON 10

Shorthand Theory Review

48 RULES FOR WRITING

1 When a word ending in *n* or *m* is followed by *-ness,* a jog is used to join the characters.

Meanness, cleanness, openness, plainness, thinness, dimness.

2 An unaccented circle vowel is omitted for speed and legibility.

Similar, tolerate, federal, generation, generous, utilize.

3 In compound words, it is unnecessary to repeat the double consonant sound as in *bookkeeper.*

Bookkeeper, roommate, earring, penknife, storeroom, newsstand, nighttime.

4 For many compound words, the form for each separate word may be joined.

Baseball, background, hillside, carload, widespread.

Reading and Writing Practice

49

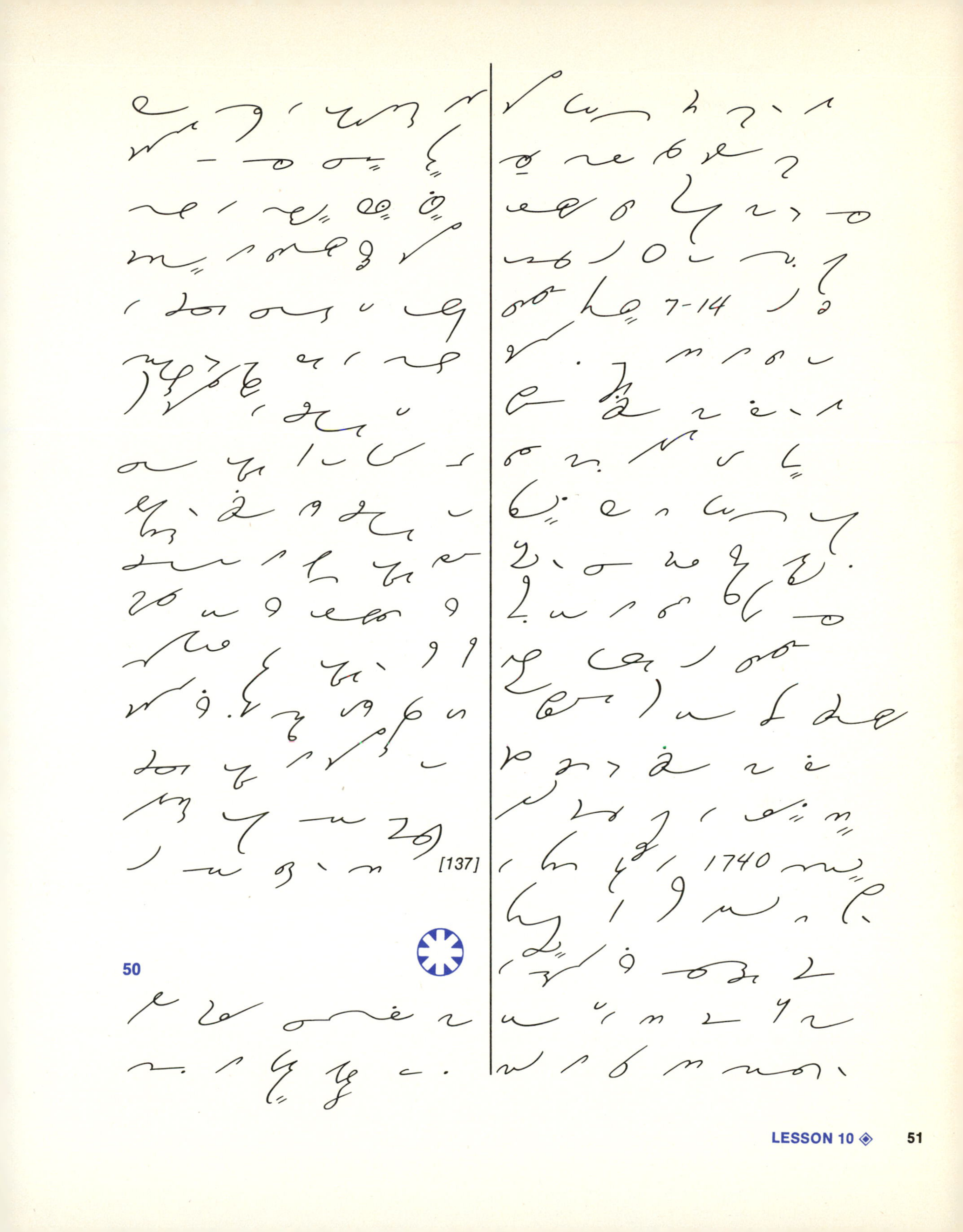

7-14

[137]

1740

50

[228]

51

[153]

2

DICTATION AND TRANSCRIPTION SPEED BUILDING

Carte Blanche
WELCOME
master charge
THE INTERBANK CARD
Your
BANKAMERICARD
welcome here
DINERS CLUB
INTERNATIONAL CREDIT

Unit 3

CREDIT DEPARTMENT

In Unit 3 you are secretary to Harold Profetta, manager of Credit and Collections. All letters are signed by him over his title, Credit Manager. All memorandums are initialed by him.

The credit manager investigates the references given by customers applying for credit, establishes the limits of credit to be allowed each credit customer, and advises customers on ways to establish and maintain a good credit standing.

He develops collection letters suitable to most occasions and uses his judgment in choosing those appropriate to each situation. When it becomes apparent that his department cannot collect a delinquent account, he turns the matter over to the company attorney.

He keeps in close touch with the Sales Department about customers whose credit ratings are precarious so that additional sales will not be made to them. He reports to management regularly about the state of current accounts.

LESSON 11

Shorthand Vocabulary Builder

52 WORD FAMILIES

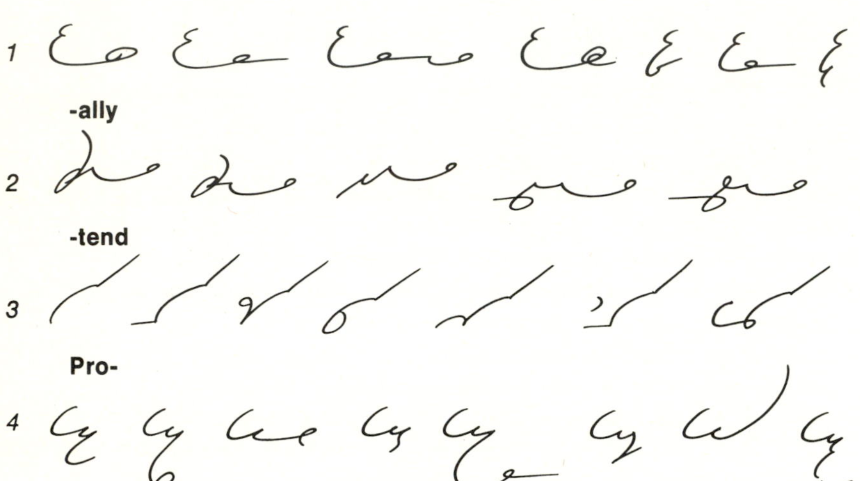

1 Supply, supplement, supplementary, supplier, support, supreme, suppose.

2 Vitally, finally, totally, naturally, materially.

3 Tend, intend, extend, attend, contend, superintend, pretend.

4 Proper, probation, promise, process, problem, profit, prompt, prosperity.

Building Transcription Skills

You should strive to improve your punctuation and spelling skills while striving to increase your shorthand and transcription speed.

PRACTICE SUGGESTIONS

To sharpen your transcription skills, pay special attention to the punctuation and spelling tips presented in the first and third lessons of each chapter. If you follow these simple suggestions, your skills should improve noticeably:

1 Read each punctuation or spelling tip carefully to be sure that you understand it. Then study the illustrative examples.

2 Read the Reading and Writing Practice. Each time you see an encircled punctuation mark, note the reason for its use, which is indicated directly above the encircled mark.
3 Make a shorthand copy of the Reading and Writing Practice. As you copy, insert the punctuation marks in your notes.
4 When a spelling word appears in the Reading and Writing Practice, spell the word aloud, if possible. Spelling aloud will help to impress the correct spelling on your mind. Spelling words will be highlighted in the shorthand and margins in a second color.

The Transcription Typing and Transcription Speed Building materials in the second, fourth, and fifth lessons of each chapter are designed to help you evaluate your transcription skills. In addition to featuring the application of punctuation and spelling tips presented in previous lessons, these materials contain a typing word count so that they can be used to measure your transcription speed.

53 PUNCTUATION PRACTICE ■ , introductory clauses

When a sentence consists of an introductory dependent clause and an independent clause, use a comma to separate the introductory dependent clause from the rest of the sentence. The words *after, although, as, before, if, since, unless, when,* and *while* are frequently used to begin dependent clauses.

Introductory commas will be treated under the four headings listed below. Next to each of these headings is the indication that will appear in the Reading and Writing Practice exercises for that use of the comma.

, when clause	when (,)	**, if clause**	if (,)
, as clause	as (,)	**, introductory**	intro (,)

All introductory dependent clauses beginning with words other than *when, as,* and *if* will be classified as ", introductory."

When the original shipment is located, we will make the necessary adjustments.

As you know, we guarantee our cameras for a year.

If you are in urgent need of the notebooks, wire us.

Unless we receive our supplies soon, we shall be in difficulty.

■ , conjunction

When a sentence consists of two independent clauses joined by the conjunction *and, but, or,* or *nor,* use a comma *before* the conjunction to separate the clauses.

He was graduated in May, and he began to work for the credit department in June.

I would like to see him, but I will be out of town on Wednesday.

The credit manager and his staff discussed and selected a new series of form letters. (Do *not* use a comma between the parts of a compound subject or a compound predicate.)

◈ Exception: When a sentence starts with a dependent clause that applies to both independent clauses that follow, do not use a comma to separate the independent clauses.

Before we make a decision, we must have all the facts and we must discuss them thoroughly. (The *before* clause applies equally to the two independent clauses; therefore, no comma is used before *and*.)

but

Before she was graduated, she wanted to be a receptionist, but now she wants to be a secretary.

Each time this use of the comma occurs in the Reading and Writing Practice, it will be indicated thus in the shorthand: conj (,)

54 Business Vocabulary Builder

promissory note A written promise to pay on demand or at a specified future time a certain sum of money to a specified person or firm.

inventories Goods that a firm has on hand to meet customers' needs.

Progressive Dictation [50–80]

55 PREVIEW

[56]

[57]

[58]

[59]

56 Months ago, extended, expected, explanation, legal.

57 Deducted, 10 percent, payment, within, invoice, dated, difference.

58 Promptly, discounts, naturally, lose, overdue, to continue.

59 Problem, promised, totally, understand, process, proceedings.

LETTERS

[1 Minute at 50]

56 Gentlemen: Six months ago we extended credit to you for/purchases amounting to $560. Although we expected//prompt payment, we have received neither your check nor an explanation.///

Unless we receive your check by August 1, we intend to take legal action through proper channels. Yours truly, [1]

[1 Minute at 60]

57 Dear Miss Smith: On your check for $67.78, which we received/today, you deducted 10 percent for payment within ten days.

Your invoice was//dated January 6, and your check was issued on January 24./// Therefore, please send us your check for $7.53 for the difference. Yours truly, [2]

[1 Minute at 70]

58 Gentlemen: When our customers pay their bills promptly, we can in turn take our discounts and thus keep/our prices low. When they do not pay promptly, naturally we lose our discounts.

You have owed us//$511 for five months. When do you intend to pay this overdue account? We must///have an answer if we are to continue to supply you with merchandise. Yours very truly, [3]

[1 Minute at 80]

59 Gentlemen: You present us with a problem. You have owed us $75 since July 1 and promised/us on September 12 that you would pay by the end of that month.

Still we have not received the $75.//We are totally at a loss to understand why. If we do not receive your check by November 1, we///shall start to process collection papers and thus get our money through legal proceedings. Very truly yours, [4] [260]

60

as

over·due

vi·tal·ly

intro

prom·is·so·ry

conj

cus·tom·ers'

ap·prov·al

[177]

61

sup·ple·men·ta·ry

as

pros·per·i·ty

when

da·ta

intro

intro

up·swing

ma·te·ri·al·ly

intro

[187]

62

Ad·min·is·tra·tive

conj

adopt·ed

to·tal·ly

intro

conj

pro·ces·sors

re·spon·si·bil·i·ty

if

rec·om·men·da·tion

[204]

63

Rite·way Gro·cery

intro

intro

co·op·er·ate

[111]

LESSON 12

Shorthand Vocabulary Builder

64 WORD BEGINNINGS

De-, Di-

Ul-

Con-

Over-

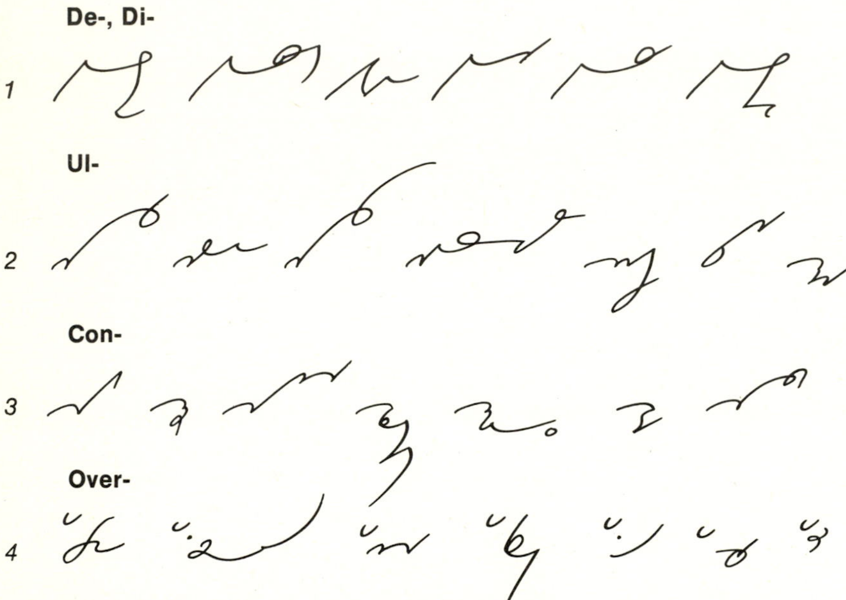

1 Deliver, delightful, departure, dilute, dilate, diligence.

2 Ultimate, ulterior, ultimatum, ultramodern, cultivate, adult, consult.

3 Condition, concession, conduct, conservative, consolingly, consist, continuation.

4 Overpower, overwhelmed, overworked, overcharge, overhand, overnight, overseas.

Building Transcription Skills

65 TRANSCRIPTION TYPING

14

25

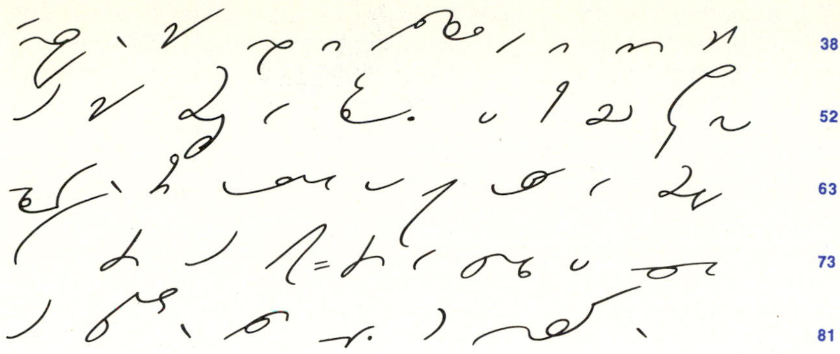

38

52

63

73

81

66 **Business Vocabulary Builder**

conservative Moderate; believed to involve little risk.

credit memorandum A record issued to reduce a debt by the amount specified on it.

ultimatum A final proposition or the final terms offered.

Stair-Step Dictation

67 PREVIEW

[68]

[69]

[70]

68 Error, conditions, recent, entitled, terms, merchandise, oversight.

69 Ultramodern, pillowcases, concession, departure, practice, you have not.

70 Valuable, we cannot, understand, damage, ignore, ultimately.

LETTERS

68 Gentlemen: You are right. We made an error when you paid Invoice 654. We have reviewed the conditions of[1] the recent sale and find that you were entitled to the 10 percent discount for payment within ten days of the[2] date of delivery.

We usually allow this discount for payment within ten days of the date of the invoice,[3] but you requested and received a change in terms because there was such a long delay in shipping the merchandise.[4]

We are sorry for this oversight. A credit memorandum for $18.24 is enclosed. Yours truly,[5]

69 Gentlemen: On September 10 you purchased 48 dozen Ultramodern sheets and 48 dozen[6] Ultramodern pillowcases for use in your new motel. You were given our wholesale price although making this[7] concession was a departure from our usual practice.

You have not paid our Invoice 167 for these goods, although[8] the condition of the sale was that payment be made within ten days.

Twenty-five days have now passed without receiving[9] your check. We must ask that you send us full payment for this order by October 30. Yours truly,[10]

70 Gentlemen: Credit is one of a person's most valuable assets. It should be protected totally by paying[11] bills when due or by explaining why payment is delayed.

We cannot understand why you would damage your credit[12] and your good name in the business world by continuing to ignore our efforts to establish communication[13] with you.

You will ultimately have to pay not only the amount you owe us ($159)[14] but also all court costs if you continue to overlook our efforts to collect this balance. Yours truly,[15]

[300]

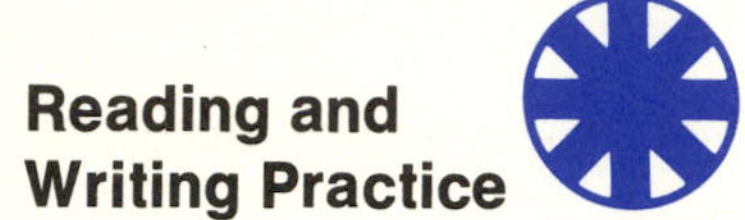

Reading and Writing Practice

71

ini·tial

as

in·ves·ti·ga·tion

intro

con·ser·va·tive

[136]

over·land

72

Smith·son

12387

air·freight

un·for·tu·nate·ly

intro

apol·o·gies

cus·tom·ers'

[127]

73

con·sis·tent·ly

ob·li·ga·tions

due

dil·i·gent·ly

intro

intro

ul·ti·mate·ly

conj

ul·ti·ma·tum

intro

at·tor·ney

[200]

LESSON 13

Shorthand Vocabulary Builder

74 BRIEF-FORM POWER

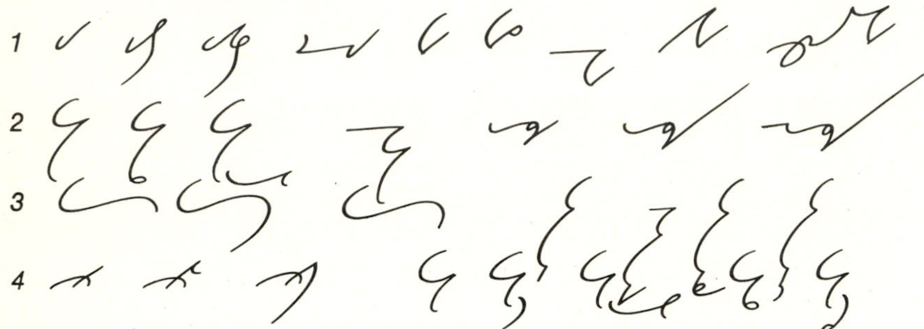

1 What, whatever, whatsoever, somewhat; part, partly, impart, depart, counterpart.
2 Probable, probably, probabilities, improbable; request, requested, unrequested.
3 Progress, progressive, progression; publish-publication, unpublished, publisher, publications.
4 Quantity, quantities, quantitative; purpose, purposeful, purposeless, purposely, purposefully.

75 CITIES

New-

New Wilmington, New Stanton, New Castle, New London.

Building Transcription Skills

76 PUNCTUATION PRACTICE ■ , parenthetical

Use commas to set off parenthetical expressions that are not necessary to the completeness of the structure or the thought of a sentence. Such expressions may be used to provide transition from one thought to the next or to reflect the writer's attitude toward the information presented. Some of the expressions frequently used parenthetically are listed below. Also use commas to set off names or titles in direct address.

accordingly	furthermore	in my opinion	of course
consequently	however	moreover	therefore
for example	in addition	needless to say	too

There will be no need, however, to hurry.

You, too, will be glad to hear the results of our latest survey.

She is a young woman who, in my opinion, will make a fine addition to our staff.

Yes, Mr. Edmunds, we do provide free delivery.

Each time a parenthetical expression occurs in the Reading and Writing Practice, it will be indicated thus in the shorthand: par (,)

■ **, apposition**

Use commas to set off words, phrases, and clauses that identify or explain a preceding reference.

Her decision to take the job was based on two factors, the starting salary and the opportunities for promotion.

Mr. Collins, the chairman of the board, is retiring on Friday, July 8.

He was born in Chicago, Illinois, on December 21, 1947.

Her latest book, Effective Writing, *was published last month.*

Each time an expression in apposition appears in the Reading and Writing Practice, it will be indicated thus in the shorthand: ap (,)

◈ Exception: No commas should be used when a noun and its appositive are so closely related that they are read as a unit without a pause in between.

The book Effective Writing *contains some examples of excellent collection letters.*

My brother John was an accountant for their firm.

77 Business Vocabulary Builder

on consignment Under an agreement that goods sent to an agent will be sold by him. Goods are paid for by the retailer only after they are sold.

admonitions Warnings.

Progressive Dictation [50–80]

78 **PREVIEW**

[79]

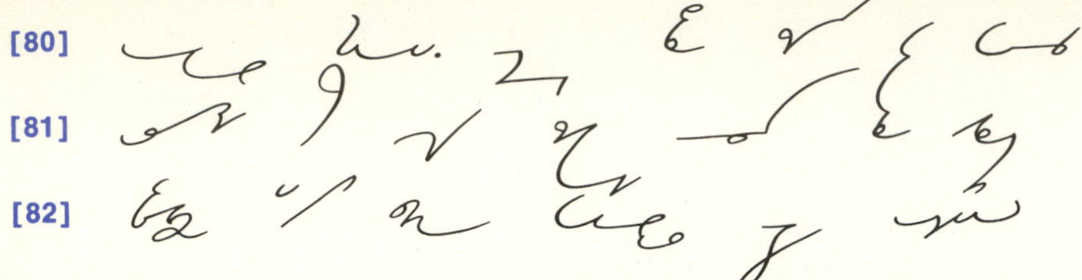

79 Grocery, excellent, management, progressive, counterparts, reliable.

80 Will you please, following, information, experience, extending, publisher, permit.

81 Reduced, advantage, questioned, established, meantime, to serve you.

82 Sportswear, overdue, usual, promissory, unpaid, restored.

LETTERS

[1 Minute at 50]

79 Gentlemen: The New London Grocery Company is an excellent/credit risk. The management is progressive, and the store is growing//much faster than its counterparts in New London. It has met all///commitments on time, and is our most reliable customer. Yours truly, [1]

[1 Minute at 60]

80 Gentlemen: Will you please give us the following information about the New Stanton/Publishing Company, which has requested credit from our firm:

What has been your//experience in extending credit to this publisher?

Will this company///probably pay its bills on time?

How much should we permit this company to charge? Yours truly, [2]

[1 Minute at 70]

81 Gentlemen: We suggest that your Order 814 be reduced one-half and that you take advantage/of the 15 percent discount by paying cash.

We have questioned your credit references and//feel that you should not become involved in large credit purchases until you are better established.///In the meantime, we shall be delighted to serve you on a cash basis. Yours cordially, [3]

[1 Minute at 80]

82 Dear Madam: We have approved your order for sportswear although your Invoice 234 is somewhat overdue. At/your request, we have departed from our usual practice, and we have issued the enclosed promissory note//for $451.92, the amount of the unpaid invoice. You will now have a large///enough quantity of merchandise for your sale.

When you have paid this note, we will restore your credit limit. Yours truly, [4]

[260]

Reading and Writing Practice

83

20

ap

con·sign·ment

intro

re·luc·tant

re·frained

par

pub·li·ca·tion

if

if

[164]

84

Phar·ma·cy

as

over·due

Dun

bank·rupt·cy

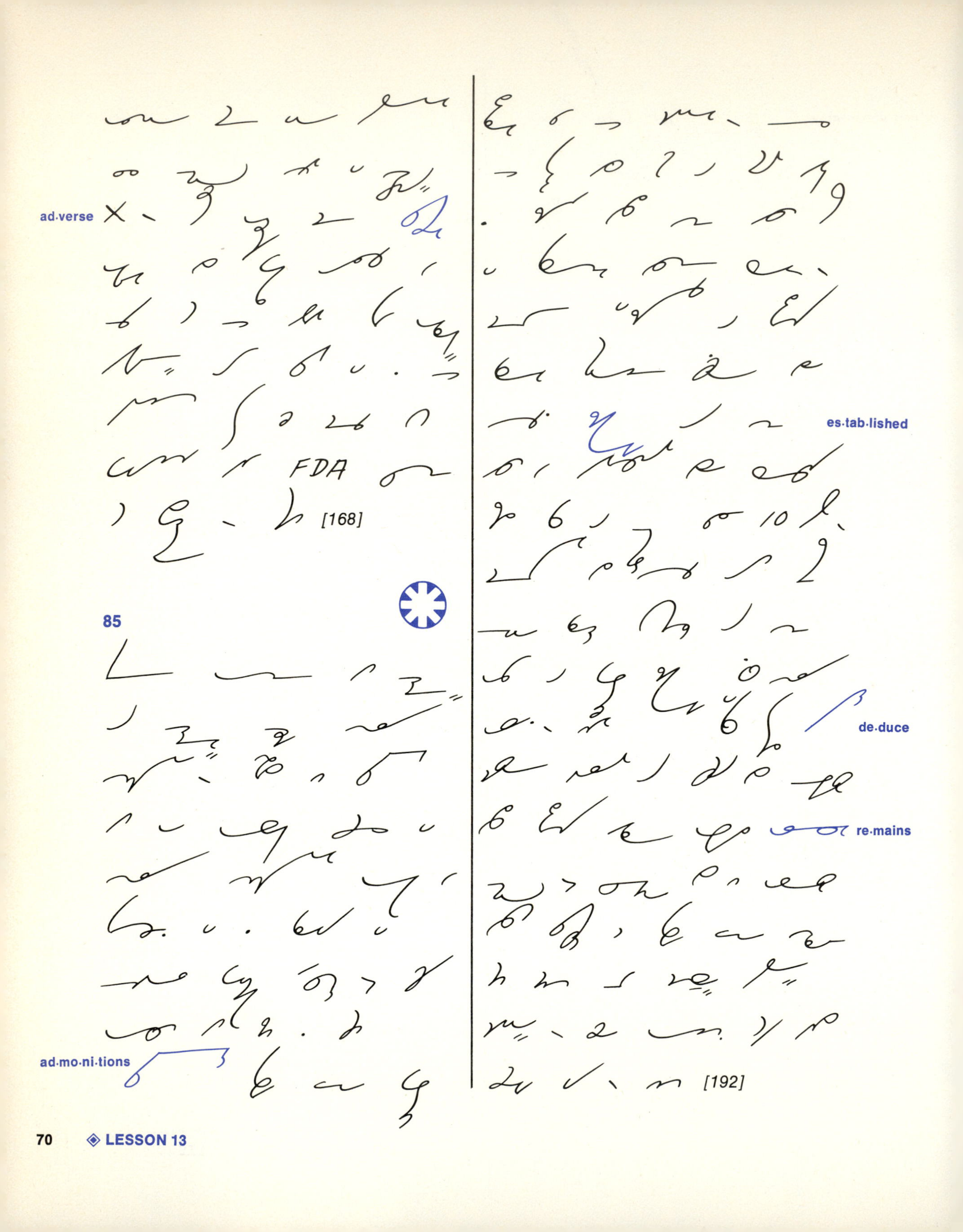

ad·verse

FDA [168]

85

ad·mo·ni·tions

es·tab·lished

de·duce

re·mains

[192]

LESSON 

Shorthand Vocabulary Builder

86 WORD-BUILDING PRINCIPLES

Omission of Short U

1

Omission of E From U

2

Omission of Minor Vowel

3

Omission of Vowel in -ition, -ation, Etc.

4

1 Run, runner, lunch, bunch, fund, fundamental, fun.

2 Due, continue, issue, induce, inducement, produce, suitable, new, renew.

3 Previous, period, union, valuation, seriously, companion, studious, erroneous.

4 Omission, admission, donation, recommendation, permission, stationery, hesitation.

Building Transcription Skills

87 TRANSCRIPTION TYPING

10

19

30

37

49

58

68

72

88 **Business Vocabulary Builder**

valuation Value set upon an item; appraised price.

reciprocate To give or take in response or return.

induced Persuaded.

Stair-Step Dictation

89 **PREVIEW**

[90]

[91]

[92]

90 Yearly, decreased, better, formerly, overambitious, solicit, report.

91 Obtained, application, fundamentals, companion, fashions, telephone.

92 Hesitation, request, upward, valuation, previous, published, outstanding.

LETTERS

90 To: Mr. Newsome, President Subject: Annual Report of Credit Department The Credit Department has[1] just issued its yearly summary, which is enclosed. You will see that loss from bad debts has decreased 13 percent[2] over the previous period. Part of this improvement was produced by better cooperation between[3] the Credit Department and Sales. Under our new arrangement the Credit Department must give its permission before[4] any order is shipped. Formerly, an overambitious sales representative would solicit orders from[5] bad credit risks, who could not pay their bills.

I would welcome a conference after you have read the report. Yours truly,[6]

91 Dear Ms. Byers: We have obtained recommendations that enable us to approve your application for credit[7] up to $500. We are, therefore, happy to welcome you as a credit customer.

We are[8] enclosing a booklet which we have just issued entitled *Fundamentals for Building a Good Credit Rating* and[9] a companion piece setting forth the terms under which your account will be operated.

Our sales representative,[10] Jack Newton, will be in New Bedford on Wednesday, February 12, to show our spring fashions. He has asked me to[11] say that he will telephone you that morning to invite you to have lunch with him. Very sincerely yours,[12]

92 Gentlemen: We feel some hesitation in granting your request for an upward valuation of your credit[13] limit from $1,000 to $2,000.

In two previous periods, May and November of[14] last year, we had to wait two months for payment. Although your published financial statement shows that your business is growing[15] rapidly, we think that for the time being we should continue to limit your credit so that there is never[16] more than $1,000 outstanding.

We hope to raise your credit line within the next six months. Very truly yours[17] [340]

Reading and Writing Practice

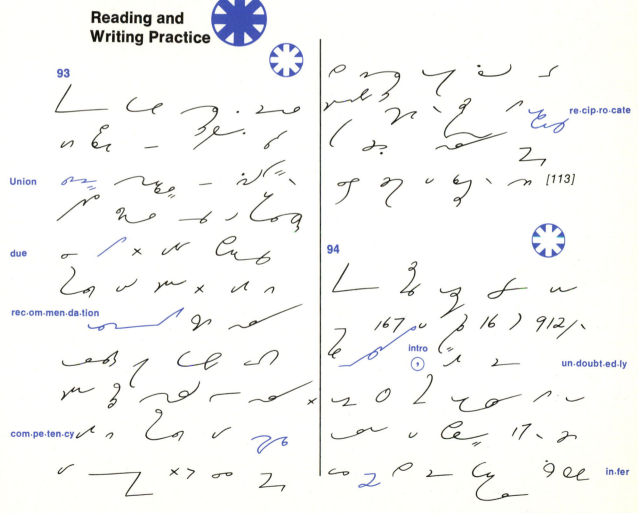

93

Union

due

rec·om·men·da·tion

com·pe·ten·cy

re·cip·ro·cate

[113]

94

167 16 912

intro ,

un·doubt·ed·ly

17

in·fer

nev·er·the·less

intro

se·ri·ous

intro

intro

cor·dial

[132]

95

lib·er·al·ly

when

fun·da·men·tal·ly

par

sta·tion·ary

di·sas·trous

prom·is·so·ry

15

intro

un·for·tu·nate·ly

fore·run·ner

[187]

LESSON 

Shorthand Vocabulary Builder

96 PHRASING FOR SPEED

To

1 

In

2

Of

3

Time

4 

As

5

1 To pay, to buy, to say, to plan, to spend, to speak, to supply, to ship, to judge.

2 In the, in that, in this, in it, in our, in which, in fact, in order, in addition.

3 Of our, of these, of which, of this, of those, of them, of my, of such, of the.

4 Same time, next time, few times, several times, any time, from that time, this time, some time ago, one time, about this time, at that time, at which time.

5 As you know, as you see, as low, as little, as good, as well, as much.

Building Transcription Skills

97 Business Vocabulary Builder

forbearance Patience.

apparel Clothing or garments.

collection procedure Classification of credit risks and development of a series of letters to be used usually in each situation.

Reading and Writing Practice

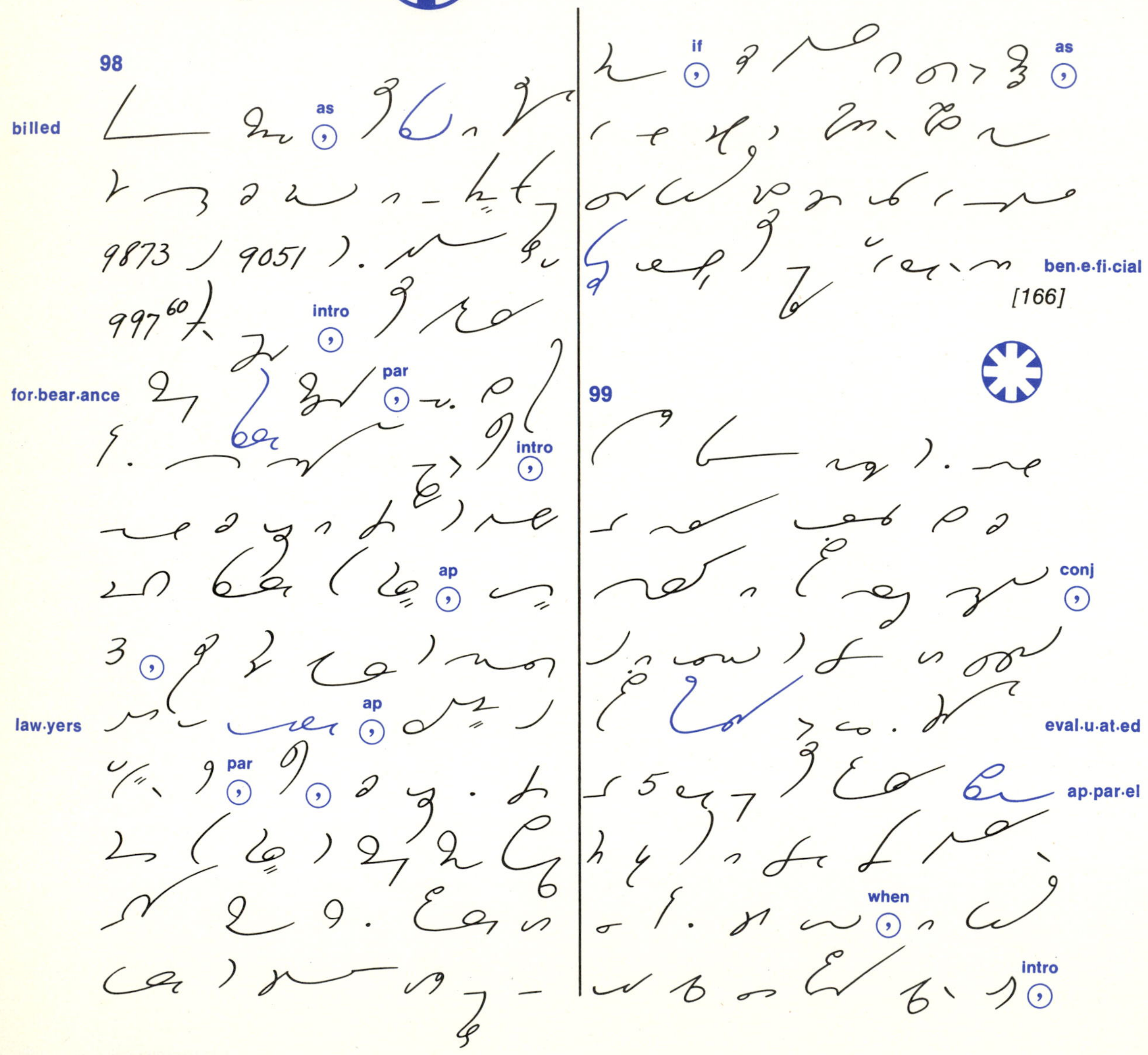

[87]

100

procedure

as

par

classify

fewer

par

decisive

par

communication

delinquent

as

standardized

if

[241]

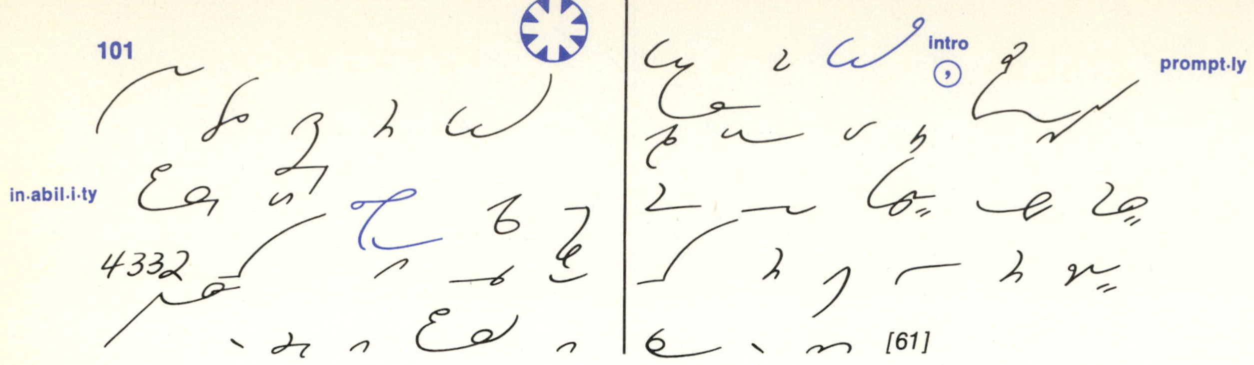

Transcription Speed Building

102 Credit

12
24
35
45
59
70
81
93
102
113
124
137

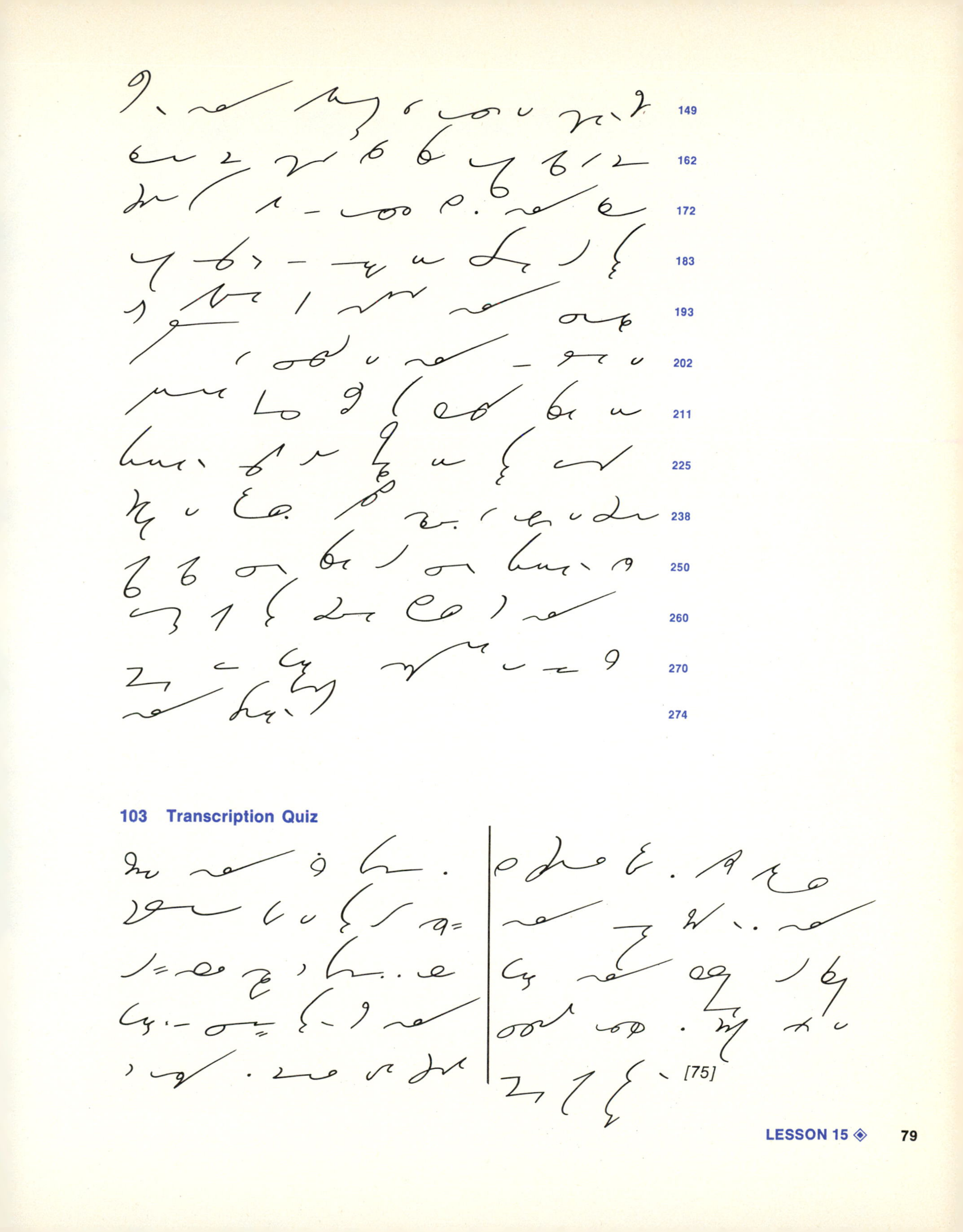

149

162

172

183

193

202

211

225

238

250

260

270

274

103 Transcription Quiz

[75]

Unit 4
SALES DEPARTMENT

In Unit 4 you are secretary to several sales managers in a large company selling many products. One is in charge of selling clothing, another is in the office machines division, and so on.

Follow your instructor's directions as to signatures.

The sales managers are responsible for assigning and supervising the sales representatives in the field. They send them sales promotion ideas, arrange training conferences for them, and stimulate the sales efforts of the sales representatives by fostering competition among them. When there are problems, the sales managers write directly to the customers.

Their relations with other departments are crucial to the success of the sales operation. They must work closely with the advertising department, the credit department, the manufacturing arm, and the purchasing department.

LESSON 16

Shorthand Vocabulary Builder

104 WORD FAMILIES

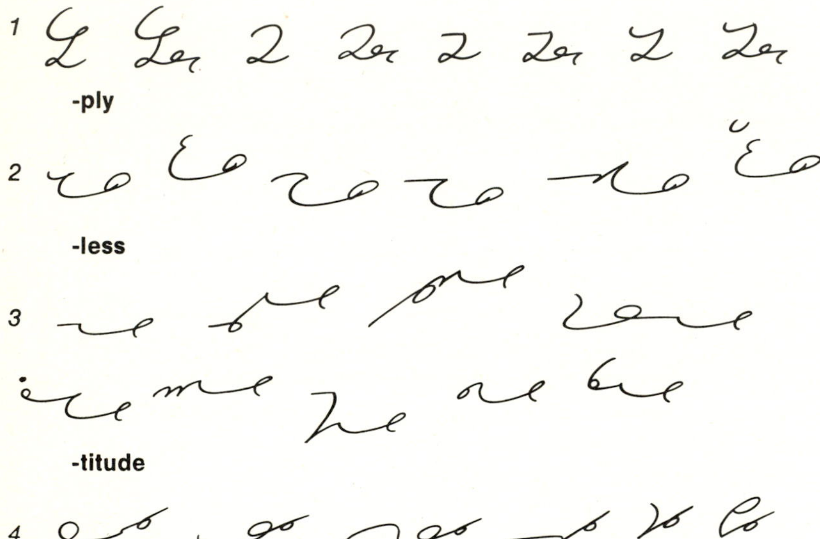

1 Prefer, preference; confer, conference; infer, inference; refer, reference.
2 Reply, supply, comply, imply, multiply, oversupply.
3 Unless, needless, doubtless, flameless, helpless, worthless, nevertheless, useless, peerless.
4 Altitude, latitude, gratitude, multitude, fortitude, aptitude.

Building Transcription Skills

105 PUNCTUATION PRACTICE ■ , nonrestrictive

Nonrestrictive, or nonessential, phrases and clauses are descriptive or explanatory and can be omitted from a sentence without changing the meaning of the sentence.

Use commas to set off a nonrestrictive phrase or clause from the main part of the sentence.

Page 3, which contains the names of our sales representatives, is missing from my copy of the annual sales report. (*Which contains the names of our sales representatives* is merely explanatory and not essential.)

The notebook with the red cover contains my notes on the conference in Florida. (*With the red cover* is essential in describing which notebook is meant.)

Mr. Jones, whom you met yesterday, placed an order for 36 suits. (The *whom* clause is merely descriptive and not essential in describing which man is meant.)

The man who works hardest will earn the highest pay. (The *who* clause is essential in describing which man will earn the highest pay.)

I telephoned him at three, after I rechecked our prices. (*At three* clearly tells when; therefore, the final clause is merely explanatory and not essential.)

I'll call you after I draft a copy of the report. (Here, the *after* clause is essential in describing when the call will be made.)

Each time the nonrestrictive use of the comma occurs in the Reading and Writing Practice, it will be indicated thus in the shorthand: nonr (,)

106 Business Vocabulary Builder

advertising promotion Advertising concentrated on the sale of a specific item.

latitude Freedom from narrow limits.

multitude A great number of persons or things.

complied Consented; acted in accordance.

Progressive Dictation [60–90]

107 PREVIEW

[108]

[109]

[110]

[111]

108 Oversupply, bathing, useless, dispose, markdown, reverse.

109 Aptitude, infer, develop, excellent, representative, conference, preference.

110 Although, latitude, choosing, territory, transfer, replacement, at least.

111 Announce, southern, highest, runner-up, top-notch, gratitude.

LETTERS

[1 Minute at 60]

108 Gentlemen: We have an oversupply of bathing suits. Needless to say, they will be/ useless unless we can dispose of them this month. We are, therefore, offering them at//a markdown of 30 percent.

In order to take advantage of this unusual///offering, please telephone your order and reverse the charges. Yours cordially, [1]

[1 Minute at 70]

109 Dear Mr. Jones: From your score on the sales aptitude test, we can infer that you would develop/into an excellent sales representative for our products.

We are happy to invite you to//come to Mobile at our expense for a conference on June 10 so that we can discuss your joining///our staff. Please decide your preference as to territory before your visit. Cordially yours, [2]

[1 Minute at 80]

110 Dear John: Although we like to allow our sales representatives as much latitude as possible in choosing/their territory, nevertheless we cannot comply with your request for a transfer at this time.

We have just//hired a new man who may become your replacement, but he will not start training until June. Needless to say, he cannot///handle your territory until he has worked for at least two months.

Will you be willing to wait? Yours cordially, [2]

[1 Minute at 90]

111 To All Sales Representatives: I am happy to announce that the southern region had the highest total sales for June. Fay/ Harvey led in volume, and Bill Overton was runner-up. Reference should also be made to Sam Miller, who had the highest//increase in sales for the month.

All of us in the home office realize that unless we have top-notch sales personnel, our///efforts are worthless. Each of you has my personal gratitude for making June one of the best months in our history. Yours truly, [3] [300]

Reading and Writing Practice

112

flame·less

prac·ti·cal·ly

nonr

worth·less

intro

re·tail·ers

intro

intro

vary·ing

intro

lat·i·tude

mul·ti·ply

if

grate·ful

[208]

113

doubt·less

nonr

Mid·west

iden·ti·fied

mul·ti·tude

el·i·gi·ble

intro

intro

intro

pub·li·ca·tions

par

conj

pres·sure

intro

[196]

114

in·fer

when

posted

when

intro

in·stances

grat·i·tude

priv·i·lege

South·west

[182]

Shorthand Vocabulary Builder

115 WORD ENDINGS

-ulate

1 Formulate, tabulation, regulator, congratulated, stipulate, simulate.
2 Onward, forward, afterward, rewarded, awkwardly, straightforward, backward.
3 Commercial, social, confidential, credentials, initially, potential, especial, essential.
4 Capture, lecture, premature, rapturous, curvature, disfigure.

Building Transcription Skills

116 TRANSCRIPTION TYPING

11
21
30

117 Business Vocabulary Builder

market research Scientific analysis of expected sales from a product.

stipulate Arrange definitely; specify.

mailgram A combination of telegram and mail. The message is sent electronically to the post office from which it is mailed for next-day delivery.

Stair-Step Dictation

118 PREVIEW

[119]

[120]

[121]

119 Confidential, tabulation, electronic, calculators, outstanding, simulated.

120 Premature, outcomes, rewarding, regional, stipulation, simulations.

121 Lecture, keynote, profitable, straightforward, afterward, participation, social.

LETTERS

119 To All Sales Representatives: I am enclosing a confidential tabulation of sales figures for[1] electronic calculators of all manufacturers. You will see that Smith-Wilson is fourth on the list.

Initially[2] we were tenth, so you can see that your sales efforts have been rewarded. You are to be congratulated[3] for moving forward so rapidly in this difficult market.

At our sales conference in December, I plan[4] to discuss new techniques for demonstrating the outstanding features of our machine. I plan also to arrange[5] for simulated sales presentations which will be evaluated afterwards. You will receive more information[6] about this later. In the meantime, please send me any suggestions you may have for this sales conference.[7]

120 To All Sales Representatives: Our sales conference will be held at the Kansas City Hilton on December[8] 3-7. I have made arrangements for rooms from December 2 through 6. It may be premature to forecast[9] outcomes, but I am looking forward to a rewarding meeting.

I am following Sam Miller's suggestion. Each[10] regional sales manager is to arrange for a simulated sales presentation of our electronic[11] calculator. The sales managers may make the presentations themselves, or they may designate one or several[12] of their sales representatives to work them up. The only stipulation is that the actual simulations[13] be limited to 20 minutes each.

The complete sales conference program will be sent to you next week.[14]

121 Dear Dr. Green: Would it be possible for you to give the same lecture that you gave at the Sales Executives[15] Club convention at Smith-Wilson's sales conference in Kansas City at 9 a.m. on December 3?

This keynote[16] speech would set the stage for a very profitable conference, for your straightforward presentation strikes just[17] the right note. A question-and-answer session afterward would be helpful too. We hope that you will plan to arrive[18] early on December 2 to attend the social hour and dinner.

We would be able to pay you $500[19] and expenses for your participation. I look forward to a favorable reply. Cordially yours,[20]

[400]

Reading and Writing Practice

122

Des·serts
apol·o·gize

intro

intro

proj·ect

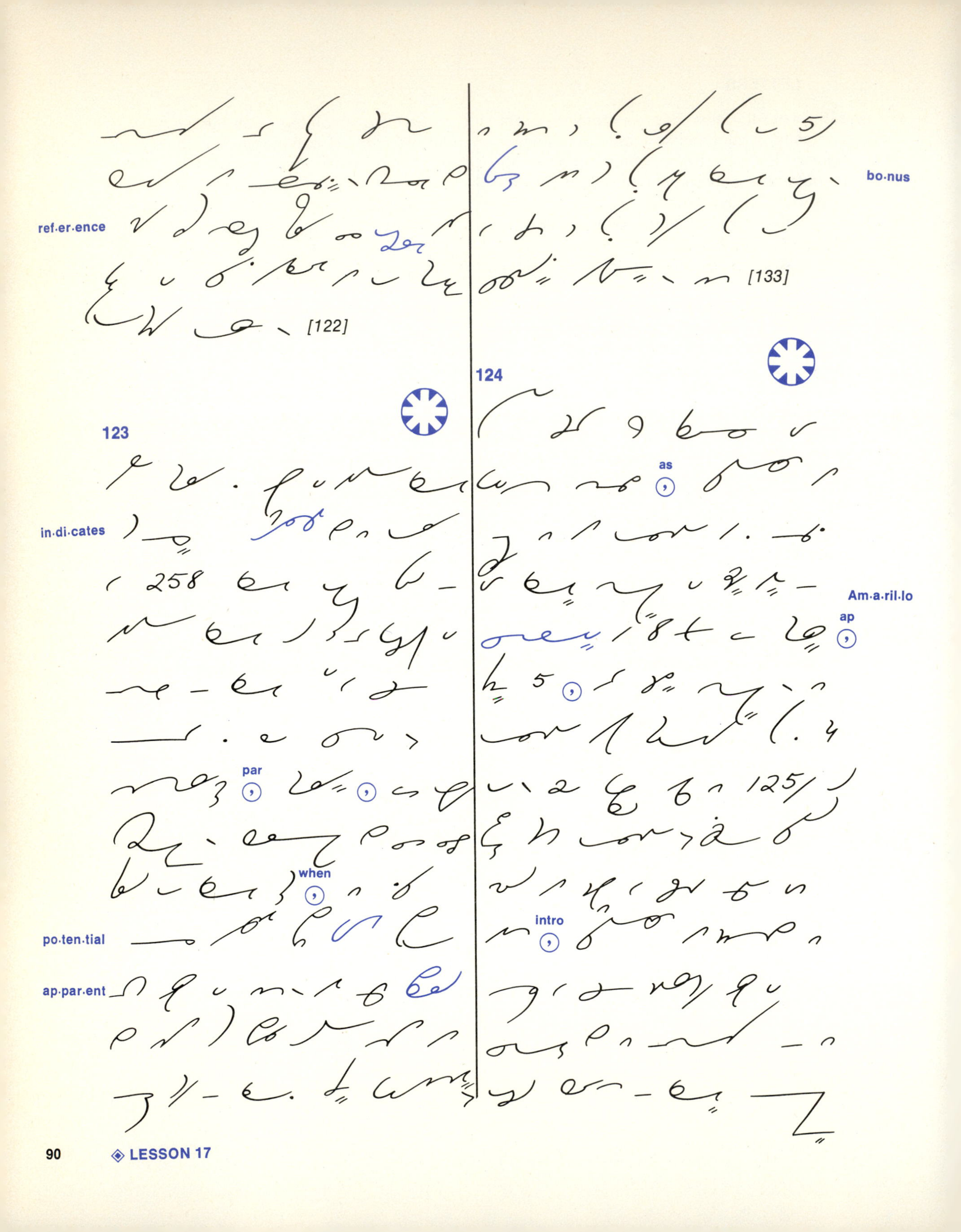

ref·er·ence

[122]

bo·nus

[133]

123

in·di·cates

par

when

po·ten·tial

ap·par·ent

124

as

Am·a·ril·lo

ap

intro

Con·fi·den·tial·ly

intro

au·di·ence

intro

par

intro

in·vi·ta·tion

conj

[219]

125

spot

XYZ

5

com·mer·cials

intro

in·qui·ries

pro·spec·tive

if

[104]

126

Mail·gram

intro

35

ini·tial

15

[65]

LESSON 18

Shorthand Vocabulary Builder

127 BRIEF-FORM POWER

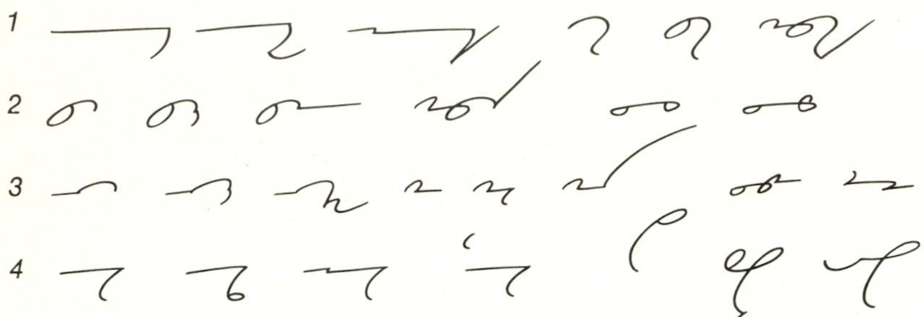

1 Manufacture, manufacturer, unmanufactured; company, accompany, unaccompanied.
2 Acknowledge, acknowledges, acknowledgment, unacknowledged; immediate, immediately.
3 Enclose, encloses, enclosure; one-won, once-oneself, onetime, anyone, someone.
4 Important, importantly, unimportant, self-important; about, whereabouts, runabout.

128 CITIES

St.-

St. Louis, St. Joseph, St. Augustine, St. Paul, St. John, St. Charles.

Building Transcription Skills

129 PUNCTUATION PRACTICE ■ , questions within sentences

Direct questions may appear at the beginning, middle, or end of a sentence. Use commas to set off such questions.

You know the procedure for preparing this report, don't you?
I told you, didn't I, that I'd be in Chicago on Friday?

When questions within sentences occur in the Reading and Writing Practice, they will be indicated thus in the shorthand: qws (,)

130 **Business Vocabulary Builder**

subcontract A contract that is under, or subordinate to, a previous contract.

Telex An electronic intercommunications system.

sight draft A bill or draft that requires payment on sight or when it is presented.

Progressive Dictation [60–90]

131 PREVIEW

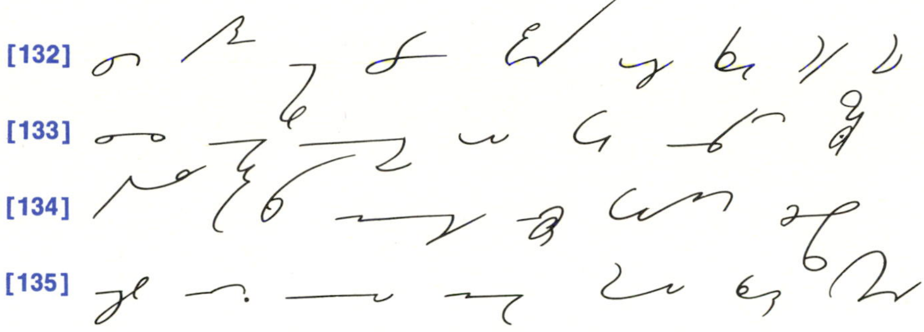

132 Acknowledge, dozen, invoice, payment, expected, receipt, chairs, forward, further.

133 Immediate, impossible, manufacturer, raw, presentation, medical, association.

134 Delete, item, unmanufactured, unwise, production, we may be able.

135 Unsatisfactory, enclosing, memorandum, unimportant, flaw, serious, defect.

LETTERS

[1 Minute at 60]

132 Gentlemen: We acknowledge your order of July 5 for 2 dozen chairs. The chairs/will be shipped immediately by freight. The invoice is enclosed. Please note that payment//is expected within ten days of receipt of the invoice, not within ten days of///receipt of the chairs.

We look forward to further orders from your company. Yours truly, [1]

[1 Minute at 70]

133 Dear John: Immediate shipment of No. 431 will be impossible because the/ manufacturer cannot get raw materials. The situation should delay delivery//about 30 days.

The accompanying enclosure may help you, John, in working up that important/// one-time presentation to the County Medical Association next week. Good luck. Yours truly, [2]

[1 Minute at 80]

134 To All Sales Representatives: Please delete No. 452 from your list. The item is still unmanufactured,/and I doubt that it will be in the near future. The manufacturer has had such difficulty in starting// up his plant that we would be unwise to promise delivery until manufacturing actually///begins.

Once the company gets into production, we may be able to offer this item again. [3]

[1 Minute at 90]

135 Gentlemen: Thank you for telling us about the unsatisfactory condition of one of the chairs you ordered from us./We are enclosing a credit memorandum for $72.11, the cost of the chair.

Please do not//return the chair, as our seeing it is unimportant. We know that you would not have told us about the flaw if it were not///a serious defect.

Our salesman, Floyd Keith, plans to visit you soon to discuss your needs for fall merchandise. Cordially yours, [4] [300]

Reading and Writing Practice

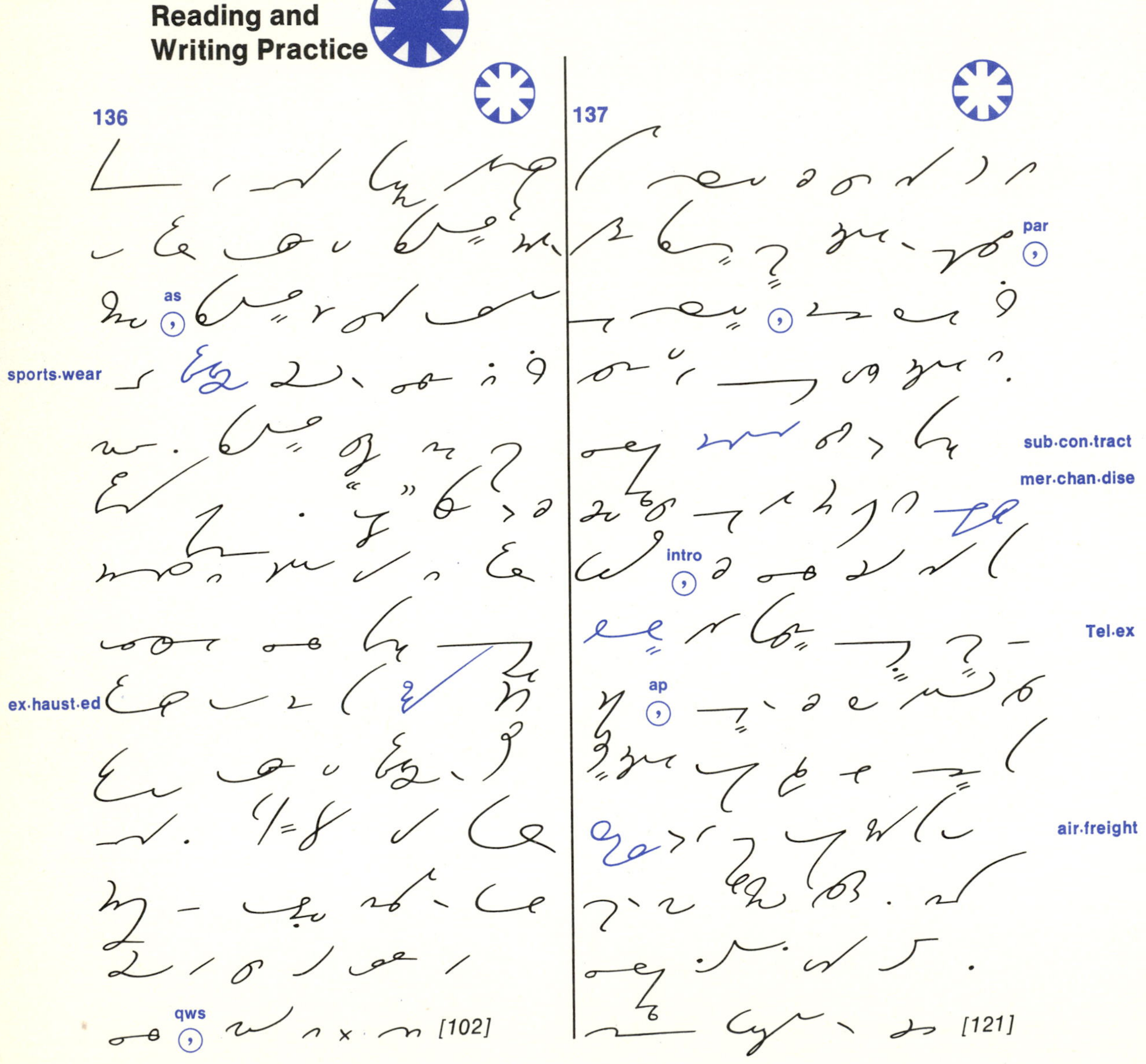

138

324

no·ti·fied

ap

doc·u·ment

intro

re·frig·er·a·tors

intro

in·con·ve·nience

[110]

dis·abled

par

ac·knowl·edged

when

em·ploy·ees

[169]

139

ap

intro

LESSON 19

Shorthand Vocabulary Builder

140 WORD-BUILDING PRINCIPLES

-md

1

-nd

2

-ld

3

-rd

4

1 Seemed, famed, claimed, fumed, jammed, confirmed, trimmed.

2 Assigned, bonded, cylinder, mind, island, surrender.

3 Canceled, field, old, folder, handled, mailed.

4 Hired, fired, ignored, board, pardon, hardly, appeared, assured.

Building Transcription Skills

141 TRANSCRIPTION TYPING

11

23

34

45

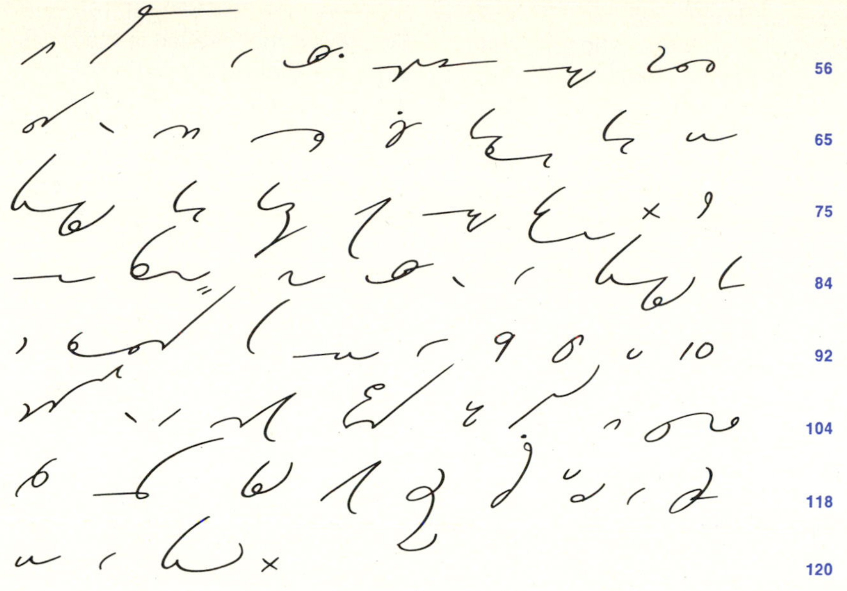

142 Business Vocabulary Builder

tie-in The advertising of two related goods or services simultaneously.

priority Order of preference based on urgency or importance.

Stair-Step Dictation

143 PREVIEW

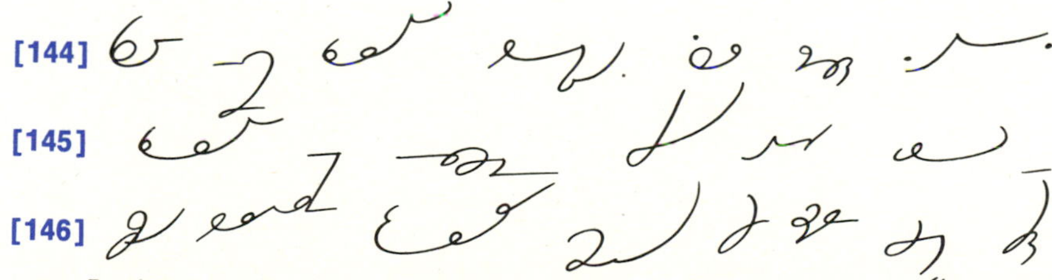

144 Pardon, inconvenience, surrendered, telephoned, hardly, excuse, handling.

145 Cylinder, engine, mechanism, jammed, throughout, oiled.

146 Assigned, territory, splendid, confirmed, faith, western, San Francisco, interviews.

LETTERS

144 Gentlemen: We beg your pardon for the inconvenience in getting your shipment. We sent a sight draft and order[1] bill of lading to the bank in Old Lyme, Connecticut, and expected you to get your order when you paid the[2] sight draft and the bank surrendered the bill of lading.

When you telephoned to say that the

bank had not received the[3] documents, we checked with the newly hired clerk who prepared the papers. She mailed them to our bank in Lynn, Massachusetts.[4] This morning's telephone call assured us that you now have your shipment. We can, however, hardly excuse ourselves[5] for the way your order was handled. Needless to say, your next order will receive better handling. Yours truly,[6]

145 Gentlemen: Repair parts for the cylinder of your Engine 665 were mailed today along with a folder[7] describing the steps to be followed in installing it.

Apparently, the mechanism in this particular[8] model can easily be jammed if the cylinder is not properly installed, so please be very careful[9] to keep the folder before you throughout the operation. After your engine has been repaired, be sure to keep[10] it well oiled at all times.

Please be assured that we are always able to supply parts for any of our engines.[11] We believe that service is the basis for a satisfactory relationship with our customers. Yours truly,[12]

146 Dear Al: Six months after you were hired, you were assigned to a territory that presented splendid opportunities.[13] The way you handled your problems during the past two years has confirmed our faith in you.

Norbert Anderson[14] is retiring in June, and we are looking for a new regional manager for our western division. Would[15] you like to be considered along with two other field sales representatives? The western regional manager[16] is expected to live in or near San Francisco.

After you have discussed this matter with your family,[17] please telephone me as to whether you want to come to the home office for interviews. Very sincerely yours,[18] [360]

Reading and Writing Practice

147

par

en·thu·si·as·tic

Su·preme

par

intro

vig·or·ous

can·celed

intro

sup·port

intro

rec·om·mend

ap

1973

pri·or·ity

[177]

148

nu·cle·ar

40

intro

ap·point·ments

par

ground·work

pre·lim·i·nary

par

com·pet·i·tors

sim·i·lar

4

if

112

par

qws

[271]

149

ap

reg·u·lar·ly

Ac·me

ter·ri·to·ry

new·com·er

plums

[95]

150

intro

poly·es·ter

strike

guar·an·tee

intro

[110]

source

Shorthand Vocabulary Builder

151 PHRASING FOR SPEED

That

1

About

2

Does

3

If

4

One

5

1 That is, that is not, that are, that will be, that would be, that it will be, that may be, that must be.

2 About it, about its, about the, about that, about this, about these, about those, about them, about my.

3 Does this, does not, does not have, he does, he does not, who does not have, that does not, this does not.

4 If you, if you will, if you can, if you would, if you know, if you have, if it is, if you need, if so.

5 One of the, one of those, one of them, one of our, any one, each one, for one, one thing, one half, one way, one time, one year, only one, this one, every one of the.

Building Transcription Skills

152 Business Vocabulary Builder

expires Runs out.

agenda List of things to be done or items to be discussed at a meeting.

Reading and Writing Practice

153

guar·an·tee

ex·pires

wor·ry

one-half

ad·di·tion

thor·ough

sub·ject·ed

intro

[190]

154

intro

con·tin·ue

out·stand·ing

qws

[94]

dem·on·strate

agen·da

if

[107]

155

17–20

156

week

pros·pects

if

if

com·ments

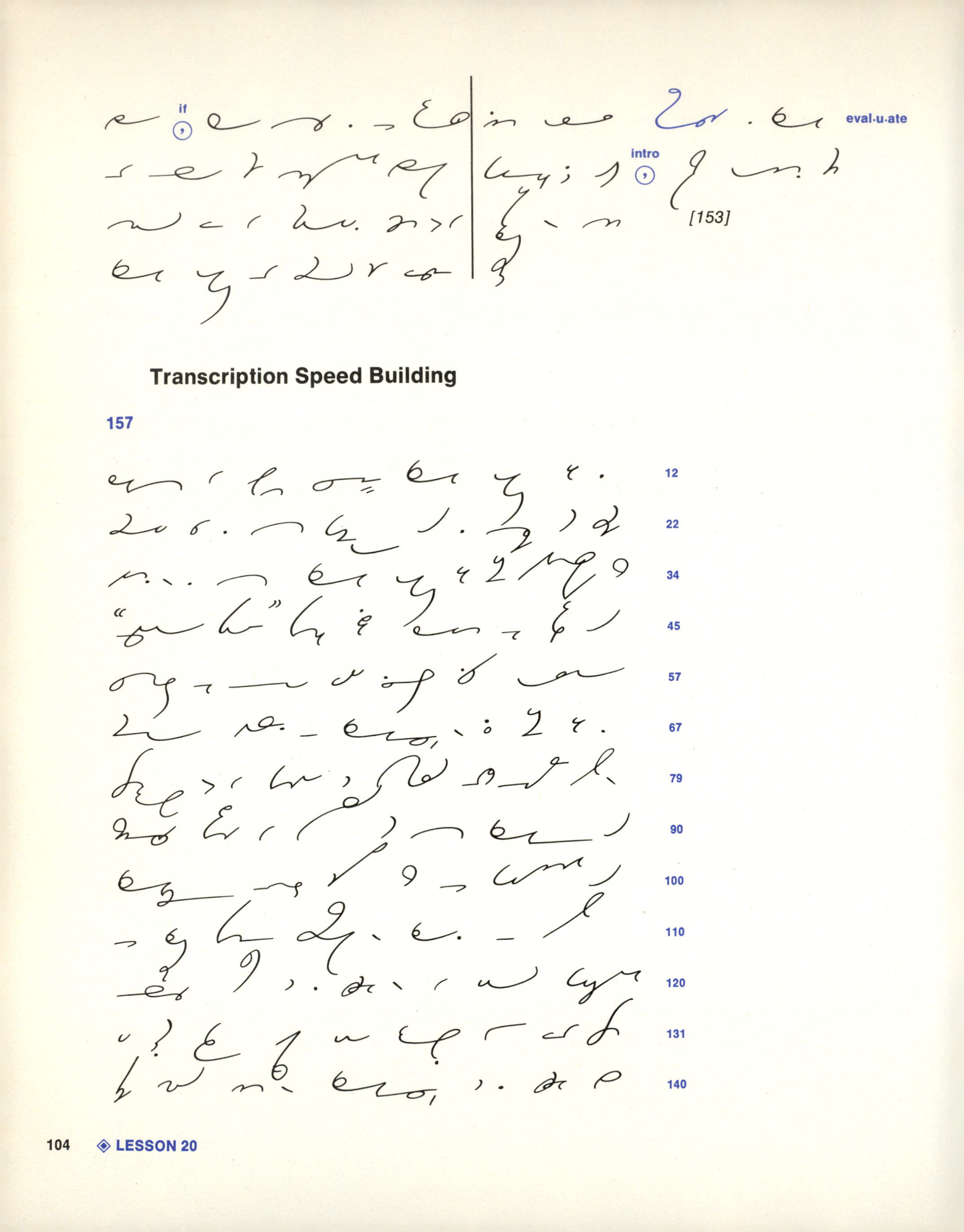

if eval·u·ate

intro

[153]

Transcription Speed Building

157

12

22

34

45

57

67

79

90

100

110

120

131

140

150

162

176

188

200

210

224

238

246

158 Transcription Quiz

[107]

Edwards Personal Preference Schedule

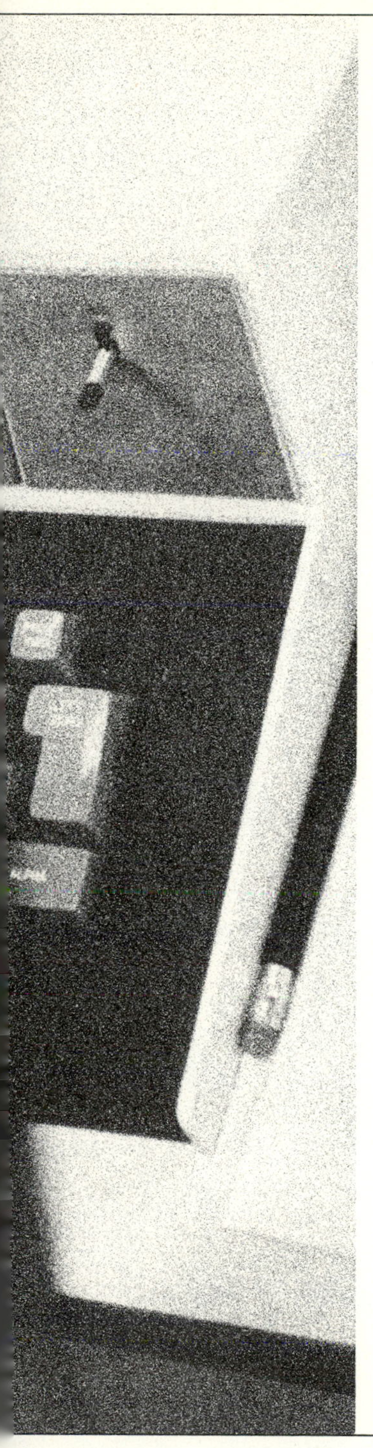

Unit 5

PERSONNEL SERVICES

Congratulations. You have been selected as secretary to Ms. Helene Redfield, director of personnel at Foremost Company. After Ms. Redfield and her staff receive requests for new personnel from various departments and then their administrative approval, they screen applicants. After candidates have been approved by the Personnel Department, they are interviewed by the departments seeking new employees. The personnel staff is also in charge of in-service training of employees and, in consultation with their supervisors, of their transfers and promotons. Sometimes the unpleasant responsibility for firing a worker also becomes theirs. The Personnel Department is responsible for policies inaugurated to improve the quality of employee performance.

Naturally, Ms. Redfield and her staff must constantly demonstrate skill in cooperating with key administrators and supervisors. You have a chance here not only to watch a professional personnel officer but also to familiarize yourself with the techniques used in business in administering forward-looking policies.

LESSON 21

Shorthand Vocabulary Builder

159 WORD FAMILIES

-iate

-ction

-rating

-titute

1. Appreciate, associate, negotiate, substantiate, officiate, depreciate, initiate.
2. Selection, inspection, protection, production, election, action.
3. Cooperating, generating, separating, operating, decorating, redecorating.
4. Substitute, institute, constitute, destitute, institution, restitution, constitution.

Building Transcription Skills

160 PUNCTUATION PRACTICE ■ , series

Use commas to separate items in a series of three or more words, phrases, or clauses. Do not use a comma after the last item unless it is the word *etc.*

Bob, Tom, and Paul all joined the department last March.

John wrote the report, Sandy typed it, and Al proofread it.

Type the words January, February, March, *etc., across the top of the report.*

Each time a series occurs in the Reading and Writing Practice, it will be indicated thus in the shorthand: ser (,)

■ **, and omitted**

If two adjectives precede a noun and each modifies the noun separately, separate the adjectives with a comma. However, do not use a comma if the second adjective and the noun form a unit that is modified by the first adjective.

We developed our personnel policies after we made a careful, detailed study of the policies followed in other firms.

She is certainly a loyal, discreet employee.

He prepared an imaginative business report.

Each time this use of the comma occurs in the Reading and Writing Practice, it will be indicated thus in the shorthand: and o

161 Business Vocabulary Builder

constitute Set up; establish.

substantiated Established the truth of by proof or competent evidence; verified.

Progressive Dictation [60–90]

162 PREVIEW

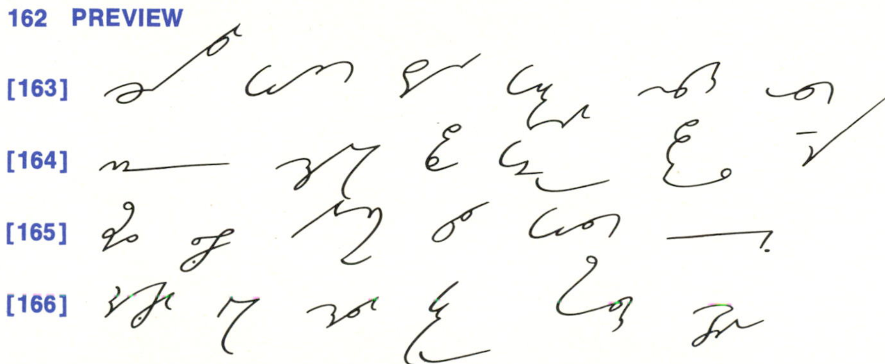

163 Candidates, production, assistant, prospects, credentials, reaction.

164 Woman, considerable, experience, personality, exceptionally, interested.

165 Efficiently, initiate, discover, attitude, protection, mentioning.

166 Substantiates, trouble, constitutes, possibility, evaluations, computer.

LETTERS

[1 Minute at 60]

163 To: Sheila King Subject: Production Assistant After interviewing 20/candidates for production assistant in our publishing division, I have made a//selection of two women and one man who seem to be likely prospects.

I am///enclosing their credentials for your reaction. I would appreciate hearing from you. [1]

[1 Minute at 70]

164 To: Harry Miller Subject: Telephone Training A young woman who has had considerable/experience in operating a telephone answering service applied for a position//today. My reaction to her personality was exceptionally favorable, so I told///her that we may have a vacancy for her. Would you be interested in hiring her? [2]

[1 Minute at 80]

165 Dear Joe: I appreciate your telling me that Bobby Simms is not operating as efficiently as he/did when he was first employed. I will initiate an interview with him this week and attempt to discover//the reasons for the change in his attitude toward his job. For your protection, I shall avoid mentioning your///reaction to his work.

After talking with him, I will recommend a course of action we should follow. Cordially yours, [3]

[1 Minute at 90]

166 Confidential. Dear Joe: My interview with Bobby Simms substantiates your report that he has lost interest in his job. Trouble/at home constitutes the basic problem for Bobby.

I discussed the possibility of his receiving such good evaluations//that he would qualify for computer science training. He left my office in a much better state of mind.

I///could negotiate a transfer, but instead I suggest that he stay where you can keep a close eye on him. Cordially yours, [4] [300]

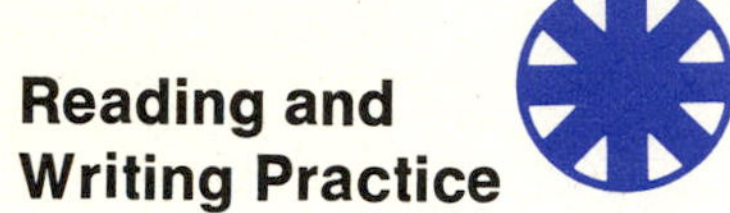

Reading and Writing Practice

167

gen·er·at·ed

ap·pli·ca·tion

par

head·quar·ters

bat·tery

par

can·di·dates

intro

ac·a·dem·ic

intro

ser

con·sti·tute

if

[244]

168

re·ac·tion

par

re·mark·able

and o

com·pe·tent

ag·gres·sive

[119]

169

As·so·ciate

ser

[82]

LESSON 22

Shorthand Vocabulary Builder

170 WORD BEGINNINGS

Dis-, Des-

1

Com-

2

Trans-

3

Under-

4

1 Disappear, disappointment, disclose, describe, desolation, destitute.

2 Comfort, companion, combative, complainingly, compensate, compute, compose, compete.

3 Transmit, transported, transfusions, transistorize, untranslatable, translucent.

4 Underbid, underbrush, undercharge, undernourished, underline, underhanded, undertow.

Building Transcription Skills

171 TRANSCRIPTION TYPING

11

20

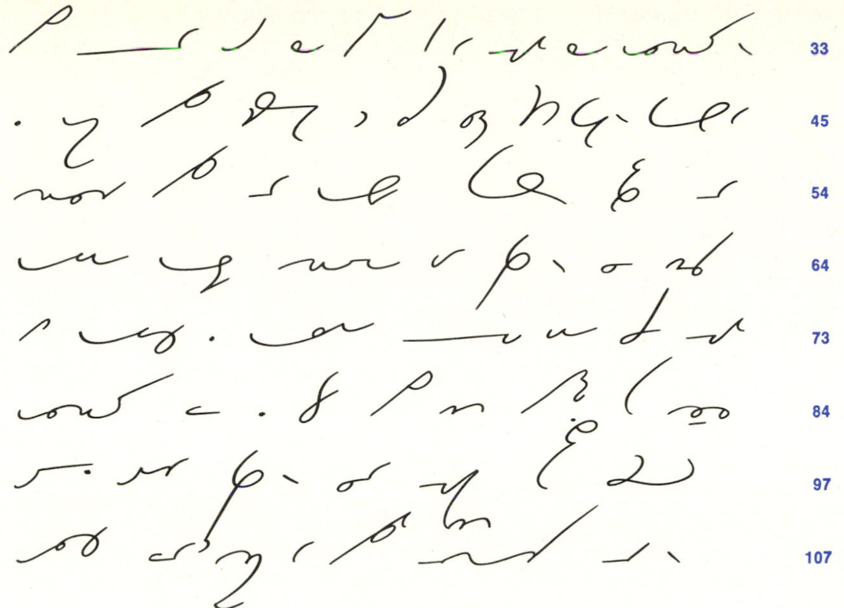

172 Business Vocabulary Builder

combative Disposed to fight; argumentative.

compressed Pressed together.

seminar A meeting for an exchange of ideas and information on a topic of mutual concern.

Stair-Step Dictation

173 PREVIEW

[174]

[175]

[176]

174 Describe, computing, compensation, alphabetize, multiplication.

175 Recommendation, inexperienced, disturbed, supervisor, negative.

176 Typist, whiz, undertake, uncomplainingly, confidante, Portland.

LETTERS

174 To the Accounting Department: Subject: Job Breakdown Prepared From Your Outline The following steps describe the routines[1] to be followed in computing the

weekly compensation of clerical employees:
1. Collect and[2] alphabetize the time cards.
2. Refer to each employee's master card, which discloses his hourly rate of[3] compensation, his exemptions, and the amount of tax to be withheld.
3. Refer to the chart for multiplication[4] of rate times hours worked. Do NOT undertake the computation yourself, for the work has already been done.
4.[5] Compute the deductions and subtract on the calculator.
5. Send your finished computations to your supervisor.[6]

175 Dear Miss Willins: I have received your request for a recommendation based on your work in this company.

Perhaps[7] you should ask other employers for whom you have worked more recently to describe your work. Our reports indicate[8] that you were inexperienced when you were here, that you often disturbed your working companions, and that you[9] became combative whenever criticized by a supervisor.

Because I assume that you have matured a[10] lot in the five years since you were here, I would not want to damage your chances for employment by transmitting such[11] negative evaluations. Please refrain from referring prospective employers to this office. Yours truly,[12]

176 Dear Ms. Rich: I am happy to describe the work of Betty Disney, who was secretary for five years to our[13] vice president in charge of marketing.

Mrs. Disney is an excellent typist, an expert in English grammar[14] and usage, and a whiz in transcribing letters. More important, she is always willing to undertake[15] uncomplainingly any assignment for her employer. She understands the problems of our younger workers and[16] often becomes their confidante. She deals effectively with executives and administrators.

In other words, her decision to accompany[17] her husband to Portland, where he has been transferred, is a great loss to our company. Yours very truly,[18] [360]

Reading and Writing Practice

177

nonr

ter·mi·nat·ed

ap

some·times

un·yield·ing

and o

fre·quent·ly

dis·rupt·ed

par

[174]

178

per·ma·nent

un·der·com·pen·sat·ed

conj

intro

140

36

sched·ule

conj

12

intro

es·tab·lished

24

intro

ac·cus·tomed

[194]

179

af·fir·ma·tive

intro

intro

guide·lines

as

cler·i·cal

sem·i·nar

[237]

Shorthand Vocabulary Builder

180 BRIEF-FORM POWER

1 Great, greatly, greatness, greatest; thing, anything.
2 When, whenever; send, sender, sends, sending; think, thinks, unthinkable.
3 Be, being; with, withdraw, withhold, withstand, notwithstanding.
4 Hour, hourly; will, willed, willfully, willingly, unwillingly.

181 CITIES

Fort-

Fort Worth, Fort Madison, Fort Wayne, Fort Myers, Fort Dodge, Fort Knox.

Building Transcription Skills

182 PUNCTUATION PRACTICE ■ additional expressions in apposition

Use commas to set off additions to personal names (such as *Jr., Sr.,* and *M.D.*) or to names of firms (such as *Inc.* or *Ltd.*).

Thomas Payne, Sr.
Richard D. Meyer, M.D., addressed the employees' Health and Physical Fitness Club.
He was formerly employed by Top-Line, Inc., a clothing manufacturer.

These expressions in apposition will be occasionally called to your attention in the Reading and Writing Practice and will be indicated in the shorthand thus: ap (,)

■ **commas in numbers**

1 Commas are usually used to divide numbers into groups of three figures, starting from the right.

$1,276,973	7,621 accidents	37,269,432 people

2 No commas, however, should be used in telephone numbers, large serial numbers, house or street numbers, room numbers, and page numbers.

412-799-3660	Model 6664	Room 3722
No. 37898	1809 Harrison Street	page 1492

These uses of the comma in numbers will occasionally be called to your attention in the margin of the Reading and Writing Practice thus: *Transcribe:* $1,250,000 *Transcribe:* 4336

183 Business Vocabulary Builder

verification Proof of truth or accuracy.

credentials That which give credit or confidence.

fringe benefit An employment benefit paid for by the employer in addition to one's wages or salary.

Progressive Dictation [70–100]

184 PREVIEW

[185]
[186]
[187]
[188]

185 Employees, appreciate, opportunities, outstanding, statistical, scarce, Florida.
186 Results, interviews, successful, junior, accountant, available.
187 Executive, sessions, participating, administrators, congratulations.
188 Computer, qualified, vacancy, notwithstanding, temporary, acceptance.

LETTERS

[1 Minute at 70]

Dear Mr. Hennings: One of our employees, Mildred Miller, is moving to Fort Myers and is/seeking office employment there. I would greatly appreciate any leads you can give her about//opportunities there.

Miss Miller is an outstanding statistical

typist. If statistical///typists are as scarce in Florida as they are here, Miss Miller won't have any problems. Yours truly, [1]

[1 Minute at 80]

186 Dear Mr. Winton: I am glad to be able to tell you that the results of your employment tests and your two/interviews with the staff of the Personnel Department were successful.

At the time of your interview there were// no openings. However, one has just become available. We can now definitely offer you a job in///the Accounting Department as a junior accountant beginning on February 15. Yours cordially, [2]

[1 Minute at 90]

187 Dear Miss Smithson: I am greatly pleased to be able to tell you that you have been selected for our junior executive/ training course.

Hour-long sessions will be held every week for ten weeks with our top executives participating. Our training//director, Vivian Stover, will also conduct discussions of case problems involving actual situations faced///by administrators in this company.

Congratulations on being chosen for this honor. Very cordially yours, [3]

[1 Minute at 100]

188 Dear Miss Knight: The head of our computer unit thinks that you are qualified for a vacancy that will be available for a part-time/night worker at an hourly rate of $5.60 starting on September 7.

Would you be interested in such a//position notwithstanding its temporary nature and night hours? If so, please send me your acceptance at once as I am considering/// interviewing other applicants. This position would probably lead to full-time employment if your performance meets our standards. Yours truly, [4] [340]

Reading and Writing Practice

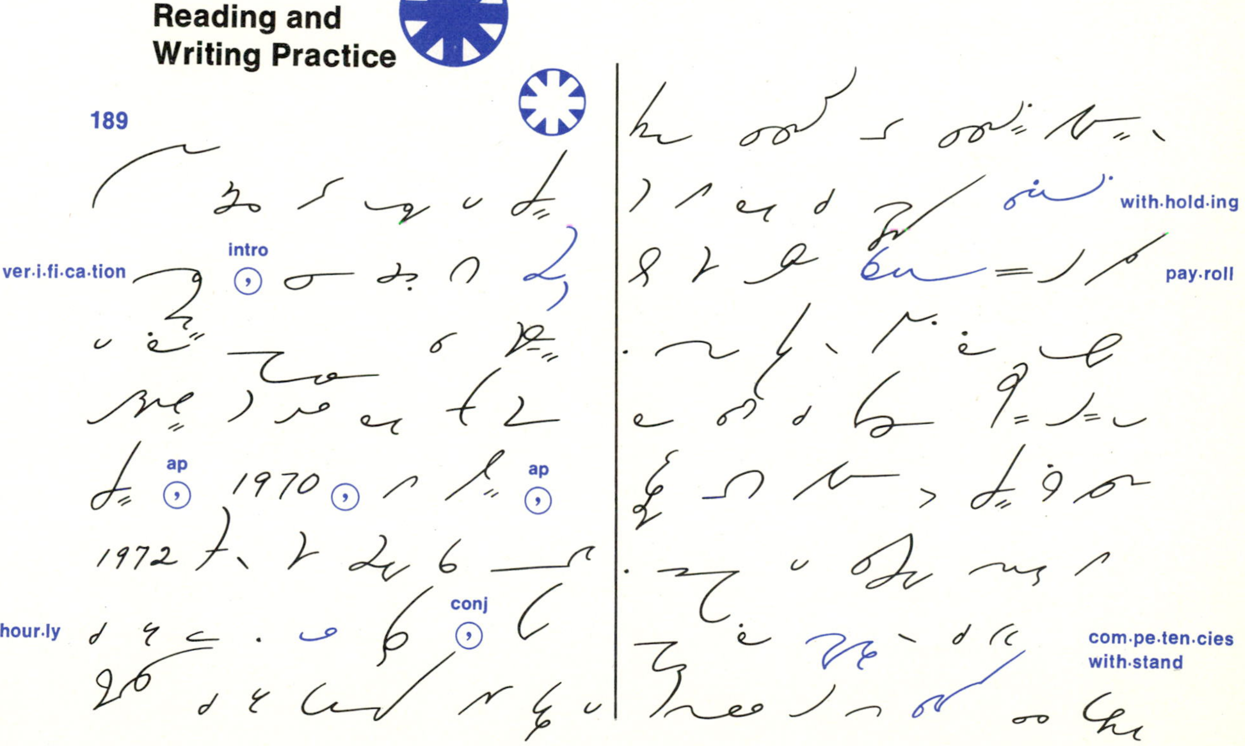

intro

re·main

if

en·vy

conj

en·thu·si·as·ti·cal·ly

com·ple·tion [217]

190

op·tion

Transcribe $20,000

par

pre·mi·ums

fringe

conj

[133]

191

ap

Transcribe Sr.

sem·i·nars

conj

im·ple·ment

dis·cus·sions

ser

pro·duc·tive

if

[140]

192

cre·den·tials

Per·son·nel

im·me·di·ate·ly

intro

par

[135]

LESSON 24

Shorthand Vocabulary Builder

193 WORD-BUILDING PRINCIPLES

Amounts

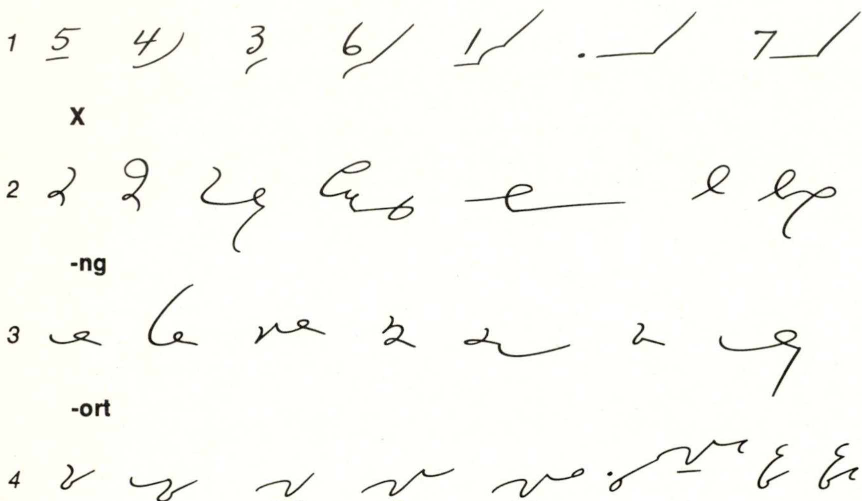

1 500; $400; 3,000; $6,000; $100,000; a million dollars; $7,000,000.

2 Fix, affix, flexible, approximate, maximum, tax, taxicab.

3 Ring, bring, string, swing, single, song, language.

4 Sort, resort, quart, quarter, quarterly, headquarters, sport, supports.

Building Transcription Skills

194 TRANSCRIPTION TYPING

10

3,265 18

32

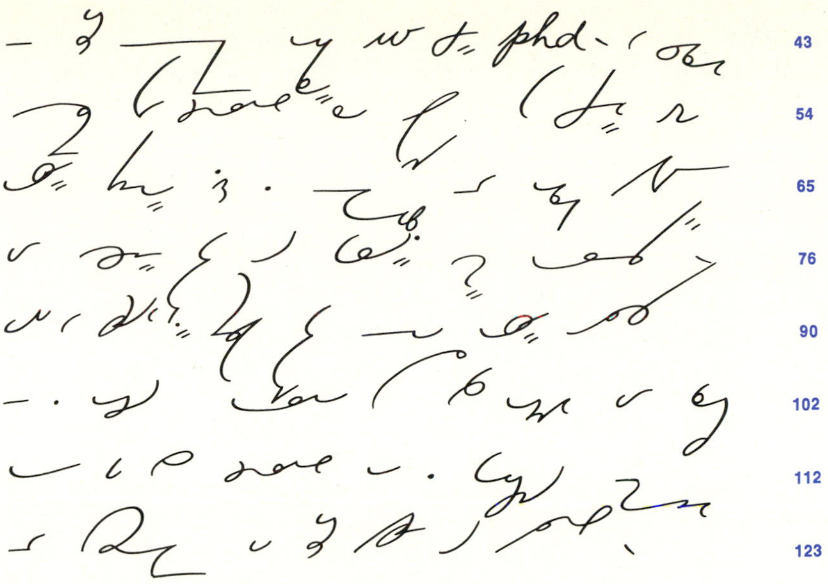

195 Business Vocabulary Builder

sector Subdivision.

in-service course Program of studies and activities sponsored by a company or institution specifically tailored for employees.

motivation training A special program of studies and activities designed to help employees.

Stair-Step Dictation

196 PREVIEW

[197]

[198]

[199]

197 Specialist, approximate, maximum, support, maintaining, competitors.

198 Quarterly, headquarters, resignations, severances, warn, budget.

199 Unfortunately, classification, customary, influence, decision, eligible.

LETTERS

197 To: Mr. Norman Porter, President Subject: Competitive Salaries Ann Stockton, our wage-and-hour specialist,[1] has just compared the salaries paid our office workers with those reported in the annual salary survey[2] published by the Administrative Management Association. Although the language used in job titles differs[3] slightly from ours, she sorted out from the titles used by AMA those that approximate ours.

No data is[4] given on maximum and minimum levels, but the average salaries we pay are approximately[5] $100 a year higher than those paid by other national firms. This fact lends support to our[6] company policy of maintaining strength over our competitors by attracting superior personnel.[7]

198 To All Department Heads: Subject: Personnel Needs It is time for our quarterly listing of the personnel needs[8] of each department in the headquarters complex.

I am enclosing the list of resignations, transfers, and[9] severances for each department so that you can see the approximate number of employees needed to maintain[10] your present strength.

At the beginning of the fourth quarter, though, I should warn you that we have only $6,000[11] remaining in our budget for new personnel. This does not mean replacements.

Our needs must be kept flexible[12] in terms of new products, completed projects, and so on, so please bring your request down to the lowest possible figure.[13]

199 Dear Mr. Allen: I have discussed your salary request with the manager of our Sales Department.[14] Unfortunately, the maximum beginning salary that we can offer for this classification is fixed at[15] $10,000. I should point out, however, that it is customary to raise the salaries of outstanding[16] employees by as much as $4,000 a year, bringing your salary within the range of the other[17] company you mentioned within a year.

While I hesitate to influence the decision of an applicant in[18] terms of salary only, I should point out that you should consider the future as well as the present. You[19] would be eligible to join our bonus plan after one year. In three years you can earn more here than elsewhere. Yours truly,[20] [400]

Reading and Writing Practice

200

head·quar·ters

el·i·gi·ble

conj

eval·u·at·ed

max·i·mum

Transcribe: $4,000

ef·fect·ed

conj

sec·tor

intro

[237]

201

mo·ti·va·tion

pro·duc·tiv·i·ty

work·ers'

par

ap

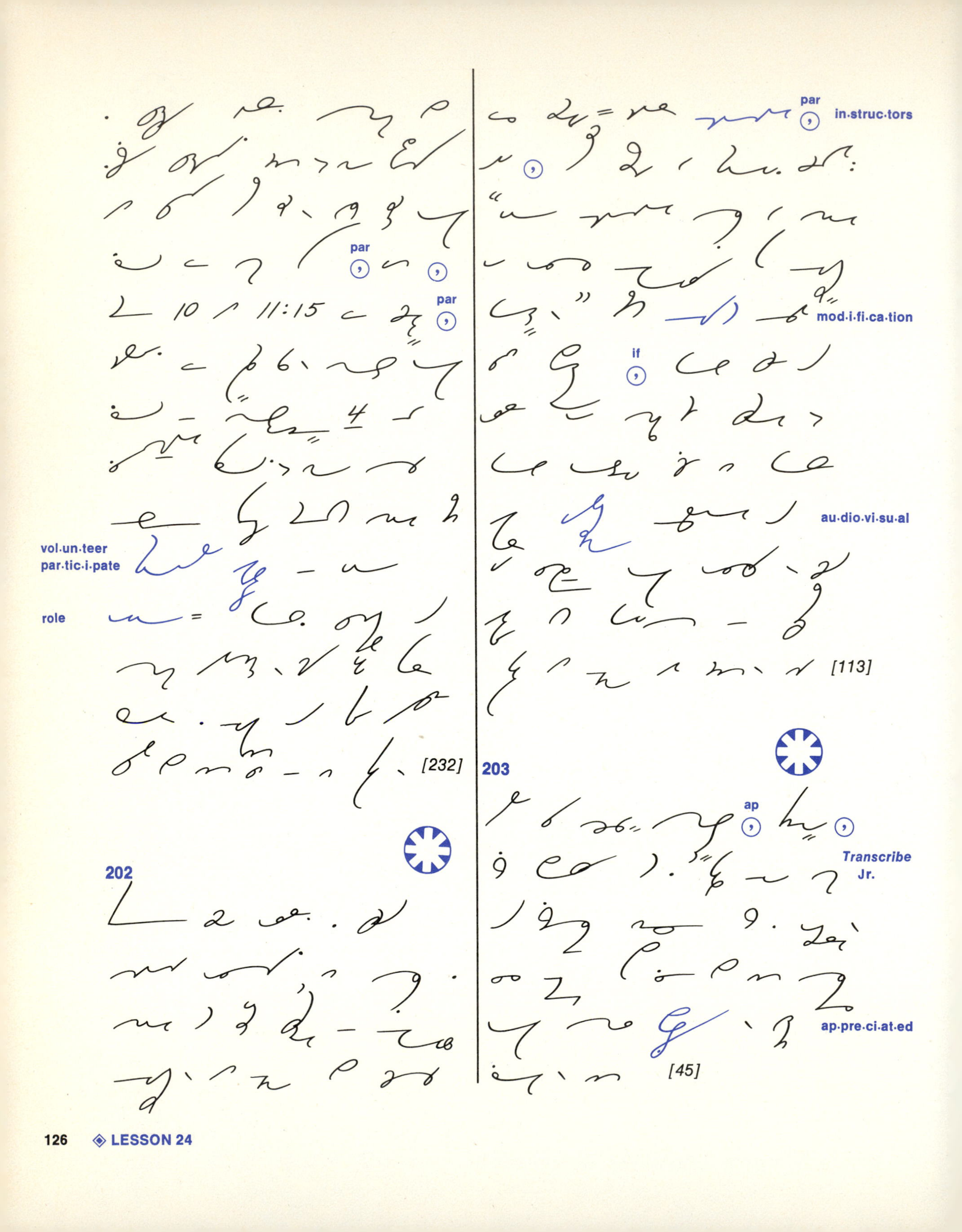

par

10 11:15

par

4

vol·un·teer
par·tic·i·pate

role

[232]

202

par in·struc·tors

mod·i·fi·ca·tion

if

au·dio·vi·su·al

[113]

203

ap

Transcribe Jr.

ap·pre·ci·at·ed

[45]

Shorthand Vocabulary Builder

204 PHRASING FOR SPEED

Omission of A in Phrases

1

Long, Along

2

Next

3

After

4

Must

5

1 As a result, at a loss, in such a way, for a moment, at such a time, in a position, in such a manner.

2 Long time, for a long time, as long, so long, along the, along these lines, along those, long ago.

3 Next time, next year, next meeting, next month, next morning.

4 After the, after that, after that time, after them, after which, after this, after those.

5 I must, he must, he must have, she must, she must be, we must, we must be able, I must be able, I must say, that must be, I must have.

Building Transcription Skills

205 Business Vocabulary Builder

appraising Setting a value on.

directive A general instruction as to procedure.

performance evaluation A formal plan for measuring the effectiveness and efficiency with which an employee executes the duties required in his job.

Reading and Writing Practice

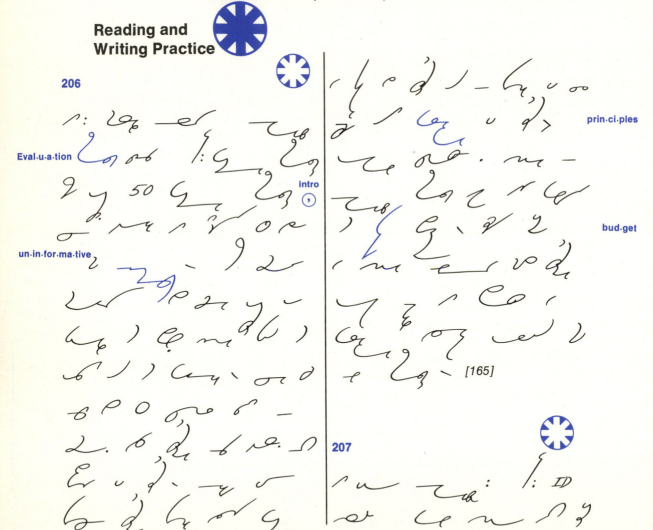

206

Eval·u·a·tion

intro

un·in·for·ma·tive

prin·ci·ples

bud·get

[165]

207

ID

conj

dis·miss·al

di·rec·tive

intro

com·pa·ny's

[63]

208

ap

Por·ta·bil·i·ty

intro

as

unions

par

intro

ac·cu·mu·lat·ed

par

siz·able

de·vise

AMA

[233]

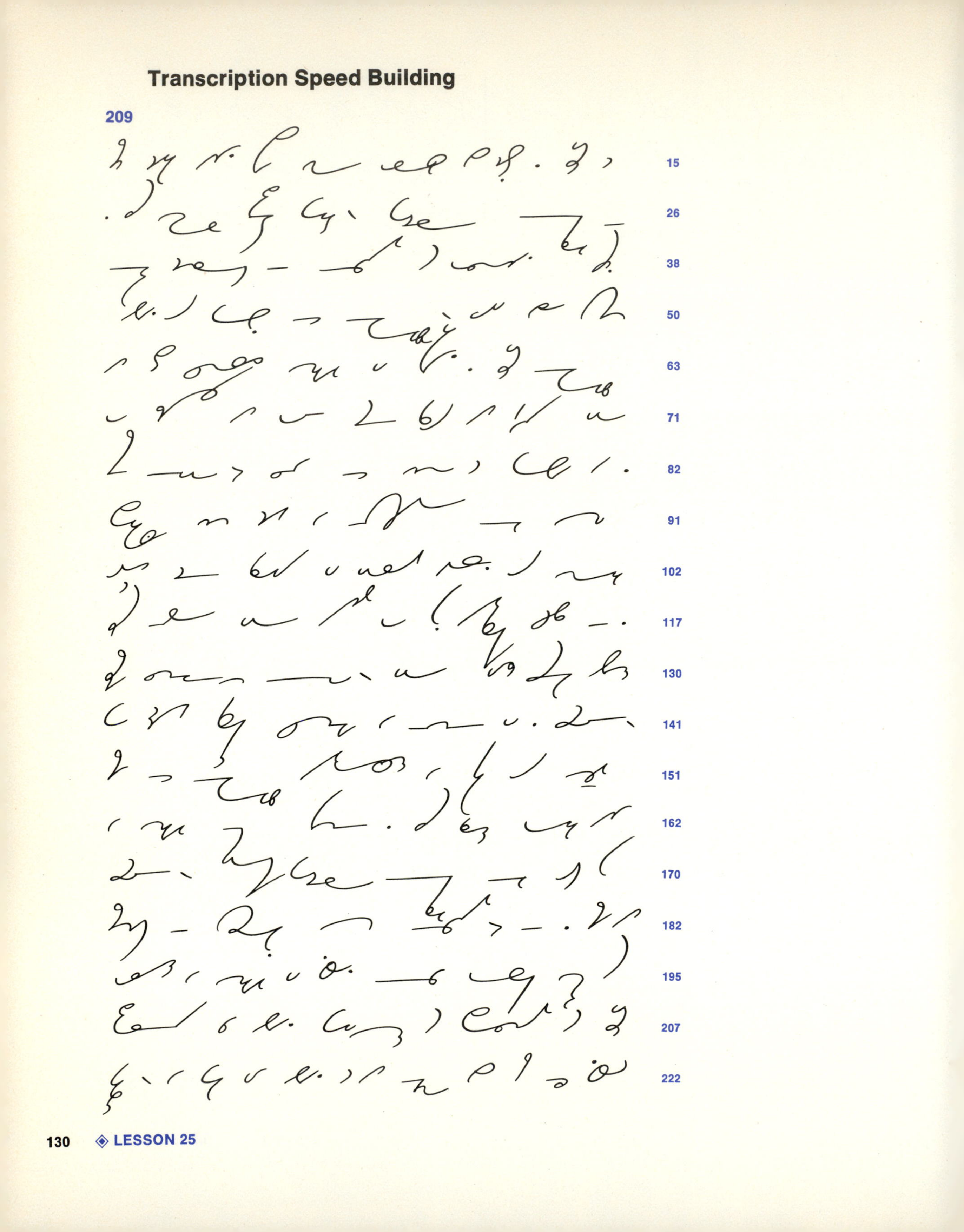

Transcription Speed Building

209

15

26

38

50

63

71

82

91

102

117

130

141

151

162

170

182

195

207

222

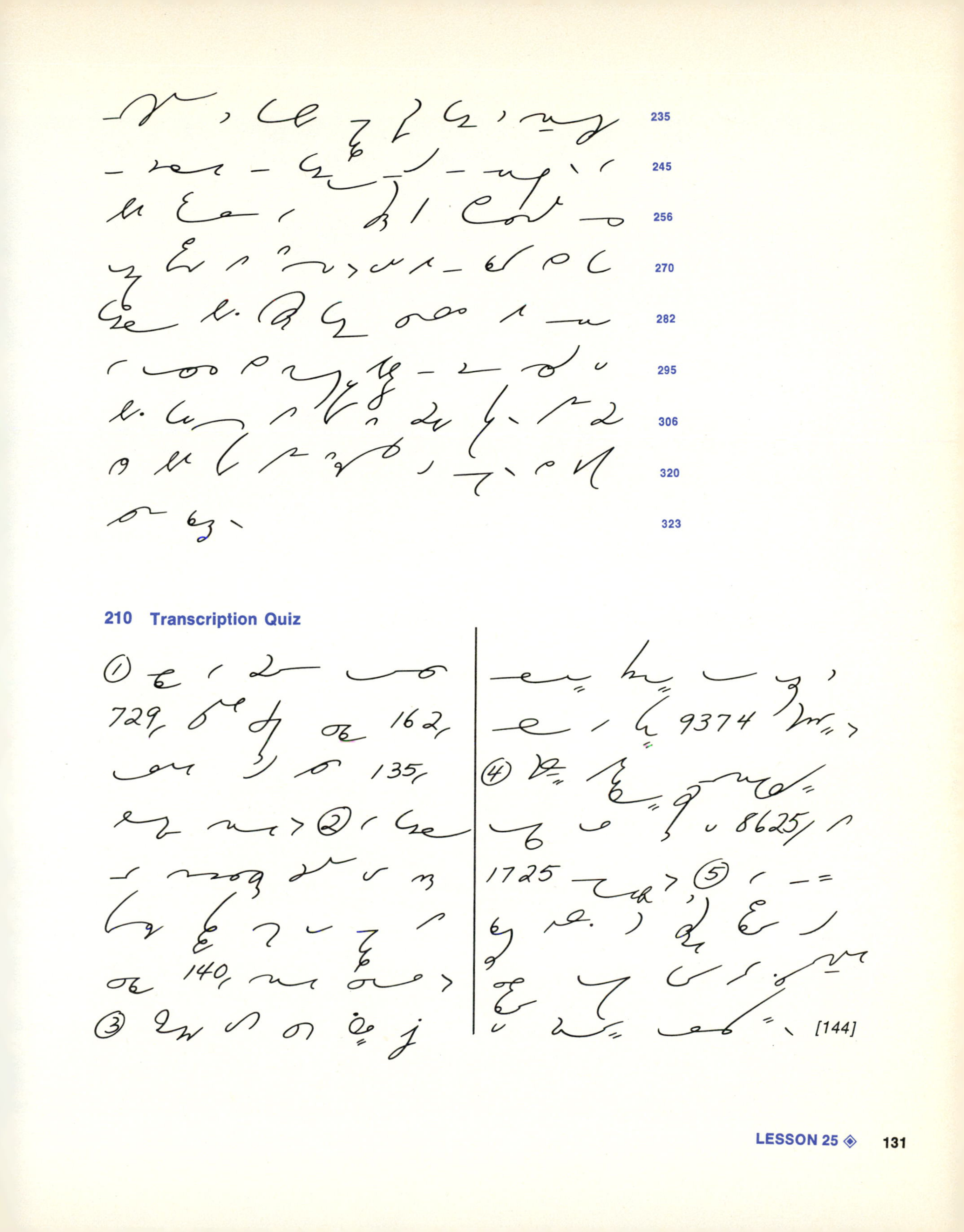

235

245

256

270

282

295

306

320

323

210 Transcription Quiz

[144]

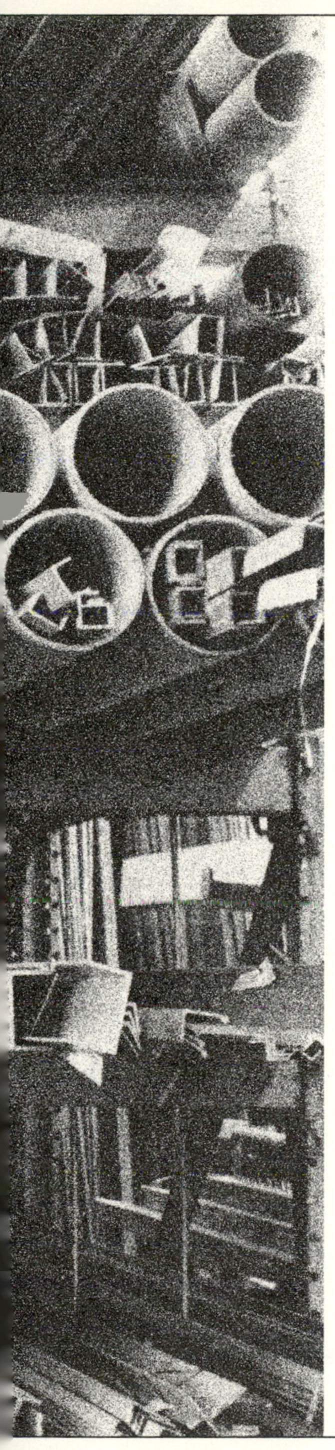

Unit 6
PURCHASING

In the Purchasing Department of Foremost Company, you are assigned as secretary to Fred Bowles, director. Mr. Bowles is responsible for procuring raw materials (1) of acceptable quality, (2) at the right time to meet manufacturing schedules, and (3) at the best possible prices. He also approves departmental budgets for supplies and equipment and orders them. He is troubleshooter when the wrong merchandise arrives, when it does not meet specifications, or when emergency requirements arise.

The purchasing director must be thoroughly conversant with business conditions and sensitive to changes that may affect supplies, prices, and deliveries. In fact, by working in this department you will become aware of some of the calculated risks business takes in trying to meet its needs.

LESSON 26

Shorthand Vocabulary Builder

211 WORD FAMILIES

-tional

1 

-est

2 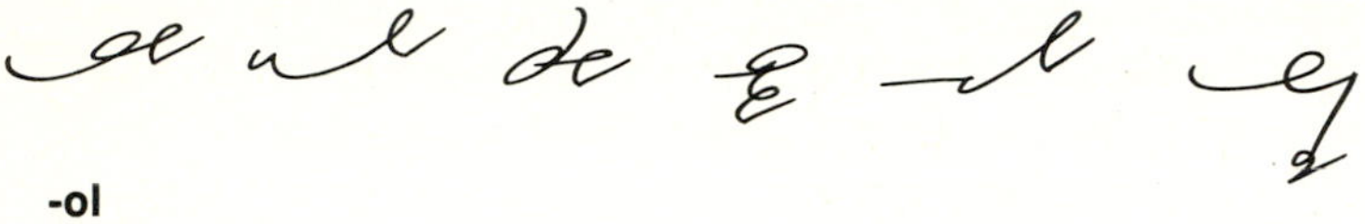

-ol

3 

-quire

4 

1 National, additional, exceptional, traditional, educational.
2 Latest, oldest, finest, nicest, modest, largest.
3 All, call, stall, dollar, ball, solve.
4 Acquire, inquire, inquiry, require, requirement, esquire.

Building Transcription Skills

212 PUNCTUATION PRACTICE ■ hyphens

Most questions concerning the use of a hyphen are answered by the dictionary. Check the dictionary to help determine the correct use of a hyphen.

■ **hyphenated before noun**

Use a hyphen between two words that express one thought and that precede the noun which they describe.

A well-organized person (noun) *is an asset to a company.*
We are concerned about your past-due account (noun).

When a hyphenated expression occurs in the Reading and Writing Practice, it will occasionally be called to your attention in the margin thus: **full-page** ***hyphenated before noun***

■ **no noun, no hyphen**

If no noun follows the compound expression, do not use a hyphen.

Please stop in and let us bring your passbook up to date.

Occasionally, these expressions in which a hyphen is not used will be called to your attention in the Reading and Writing Practice thus: **out of stock** ***no noun, no hyphen***

■ **hyphen after self**

Use a hyphen after *self* when *self* is joined with another word to form a compound.

A self-critical *person examines his own work habits continually.*
The selfsame *music will accompany the dance routines in the stage production of the show.* (*Self* is part of the root word; it is not forming a compound.)

■ **hyphen in compound numbers**

When a number is written as a word, use a hyphen for numerals between 21 and 99, but do not use a hyphen after the words *hundred* and *thousand* in higher numbers.

Twenty-one *architects attended the meeting.*
The wedding invitation was for the year nineteen hundred and thirty-seven.

213 **Business Vocabulary Builder**

recycled Restored to a previous condition.

pilfering Stealing.

confirmation Verification; an act of assuring the certainty.

Progressive Dictation [70—100]

214 PREVIEW

[215]

[216]

[217]

[218]

215 Locks, exit, closers, complex, equipment, cylinder.
216 Eastern, security, inquiring, hardware, warehouse, supervisor.
217 Reputation, engineering, influenced, higher, density, population.
218 Thoughtful, satisfied, architects, innovative, pick-resistant, ridges.

LETTERS

[1 Minute at 70]

215 Dear Mr. Call: Please send us information concerning your product line of door locks, exit/devices, and door closers. We are building a new office complex and wish to install the latest safety//equipment available. One of our purchasing agents has had some good comments from a/// supplier about your new cylinder lock. We are anxious to learn your ideas for safety. Sincerely, [1]

[1 Minute at 80]

216 Gentlemen: Today I wrote to the Eastern Security Company inquiring about their latest product/line of door locks, exit devices, and door closers. This is the firm that supplied the safety hardware for our// warehouse in Martinsburg. Sam Part, the warehouse supervisor, has always been satisfied with the locks and door closers/// installed in that facility. Perhaps we can do business with this firm after your study. Yours very truly, [2]

[1 Minute at 90]

217 Dear Sir: Thank you for inquiring about the latest door hardware that our company produces. Eastern Security/Company has built a reputation for its products through excellent engineering, research, and development. Today//development of security hardware is being influenced by new building codes and the trend to higher-density population.///I have directed Mr. Alan Banker, our representative, to send you data and call on you soon. Yours truly, [3]

[1 Minute at 100]

218 Dear Mr. Banker: We are well satisfied with the thoughtful security plan you presented for our new office complex. Eastern Security/Company has again satisfied our architects with innovative products. The pick-resistant cylinder lock is an excellent//security device for the storage areas and the computer rooms. Since this lock uses a key with milled holes rather than the///traditional ridges and cuts and since the key must be made by your plant, how much will additional keys cost? We rely on Eastern. Yours truly [4] [340]

219

ball bear·ings

man·u·fac·ture

intro

tons

ball-bear·ing *hyphenated before noun*

30 [124]

220

req·ui·si·tions

intro

par

ex·cep·tion·al·ly

conj

pil·fer

ex·cess

par

par

par

[220]

dol·lar-for-dol·lar *hyphenated before noun*

re·cy·cled

up to date *no noun, no hyphen*

[139]

221

en·vi·ron·men·tal

pol·lu·tion

self-eval·u·at·ing

as

prac·ti·ca·bil·i·ty

222

Transcribe: 19823

19823

mar·ga·rine

[64]

LESSON 27

Shorthand Vocabulary Builder

223 WORD ENDINGS

-ment

1

-ful

2

-lty

3

-ings

4

1 Treatment, moment, payment, fundamentally, supplementary.

2 Thoughtful, carefully, useful, mindful, helpfulness, delightfully, willfully.

3 Loyalty, faculty, casualty, penalty, frailty.

4 Proceedings, sidings, drawings, savings, holdings, sightings, sayings.

Building Transcription Skills

224 TRANSCRIPTION TYPING

7

20

30

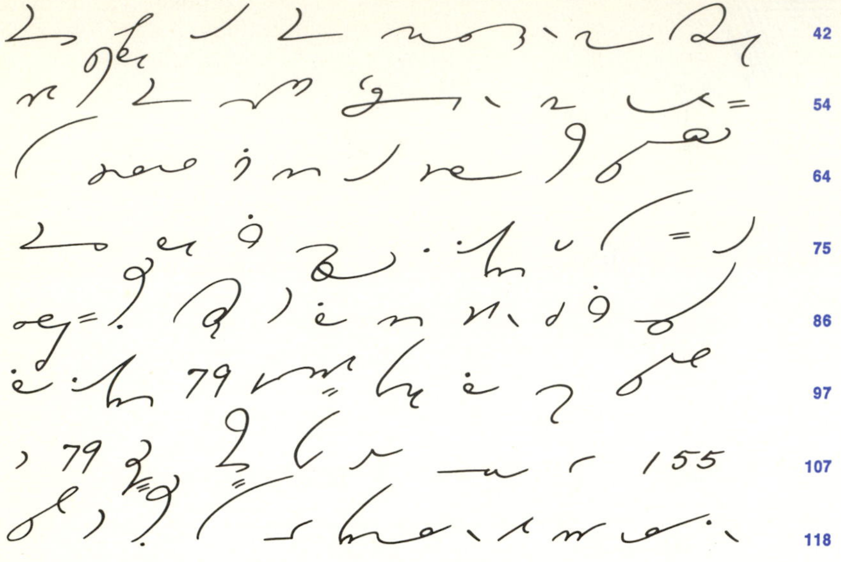

225 **Business Vocabulary Builder**

disposition The act or manner of getting rid of.

weighed Balanced in one's mind; evaluated; pondered.

discount A reduction from the full price.

Stair-Step Dictation

226 PREVIEW

[227]

[228]

[229]

227 Pace, stationery, desirable, individualize, reclaimed, pulp.

228 Associates, elated, attractively, dissatisfied, superior, greetings.

229 Gold-monogrammed, initials, aqua, beige, anniversary.

LETTERS

227 Dear Mr. Crane: As a change of pace in our end-of-year gift giving, we are presenting to each secretary[1] on our staff a box of stationery this year. We realize that it would be desirable to personalize[2] the stationery, but we are ordering too many packages to individualize the gift to each[3] staff member. Please help us choose an attractive box that they will use, knowing that their letters do not just carry words[4] but also a pleasant "picture" of themselves. At present we are considering the paper made from reclaimed cotton[5] fibers rather than wood pulp. If the price of this paper is too high, we will change this requirement. Yours truly,[6]

228 Dear David: Again this year our company has chosen Riva Pears as a gift for our business associates.[7] In the past when our friends have received this rare fruit from us, they have been elated. We have spot-checked good friends on the[8] gift list to see if the fruit has arrived safely and has been attractively boxed. Not one dissatisfied person[9] have we located. Thank you for helping us send our good wishes with your superior product. On the enclosed[10] sheet we have listed names and addresses of those to whom you will ship the fruit. Also we have enclosed our business[11] cards with our personal greetings; a card is to be put in each package before shipment. Very cordially yours,[12]

229 Gentlemen: Please send us 100 sets of gold-monogrammed playing cards with the initials *PPG*. From the[13] available color combinations we have chosen 50 sets to be colored aqua and green and 50[14] sets to be colored brown and beige. These playing cards will be gifts to friends of the company, so we hope each set will[15] be attractively boxed. They will be presented on April 15, the anniversary date of the founding[16] of our firm. Please send the cards on March 30 at the latest so that we will be sure these gifts will be part of[17] the celebration. Before packaging, please remove any tag which indicates the price of the item. Yours truly,[18] [360]

Reading and Writing Practice

230

lab·o·ra·to·ry

mind·ful

par

par

ar·ea

[117]

231

Pi·cas·so

par

intro

par

Transcribe: 76811

76811

conj

[133]

232

ap

con·fi·den·tial

ap

sur·vived

pre·lim·i·nary

weighed

fun·da·men·tal·ly

out of date
no noun, no hyphen

conj

mis·giv·ings

intro

ap

suit·abil·i·ty

mem·o·ran·dum

ev·ery day

if

[272]

233

men's

sup·ple·men·ta·ry

week's

nonr

ob·vi·ous·ly

shab·by

if

[135]

Shorthand Vocabulary Builder

234 BRIEF-FORM POWER

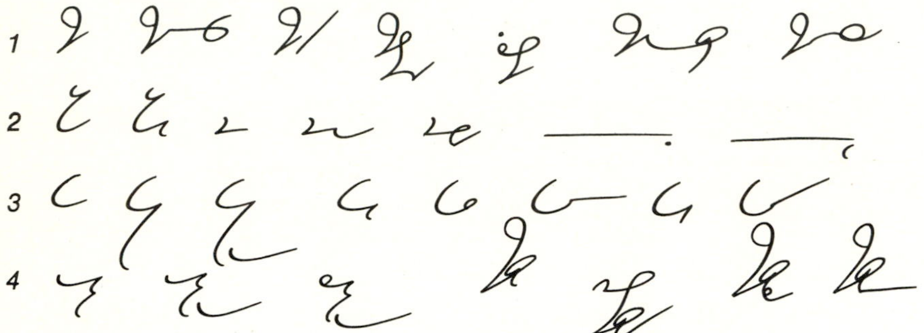

1 After, aftermath, afterward, aftereffect, hereafter, afterlife, aftercare.

2 Opportunity, opportunities; soon, sooner, soonest; morning, mornings.

3 Present, presentable, presentability, presents, presently, presentment, presentation, presented.

4 Responsible, responsibility, irresponsibility; advertise, unadvertised, advertiser, advertisement.

235 CITIES

-burg, -burgh

Pittsburgh, Harrisburg, Ebonsburg, Newburg, Martinsburg, Plattsburg, Shippensburg.

Building Transcription Skills

236 PUNCTUATION PRACTICE ■ additional hyphen usage

Compound words are listed in the columns of an unabridged dictionary. Check the dictionary to help determine the correct use of a hyphen.

■ **hyphen after prefix before a capitalized word**

Use a hyphen after a prefix which is used before a capitalized word.

In mid-October *the* trans-Alaskan *pipeline will be completed.*

■ **hyphen after prefix before a word beginning with an identical letter**

To prevent misreading, use a hyphen after a prefix ending with *a* or *i* when the base word starts with the same letter.

The anti-intellectual *atmosphere of the conference disappointed the teachers.*

When the prefix ends in *o* or *e,* the hyphen may usually be omitted.

The author will cooperate *with the committee and* reenter *his novel in the competition.*

237 Business Vocabulary Builder

prototype An original model upon which later forms are based.

stockpile A supply of material stored and maintained for future use.

Progressive Dictation [70–100]

238 PREVIEW

[239]

[240]

[241]

[242]

239 Royal, extinguishers, suggest, advantageous, regularly, code.

240 Underwriters, laboratories, industry, inspectors, occupants.

241 Opinion, locking, pin, powder, occupied, site, Shippensburg.

242 Technician, demonstrate, precautions, accidentally, sprayed, eyes.

LETTERS

[1 Minute at 70]

239 Dear Mr. Royal: We wish to obtain fire extinguishers for our new office building which/will be completed September 1 of this year. Would you suggest that we purchase these extinguishers,//or would it be more advantageous to rent the equipment from your company? In either case,///will you check the system regularly? This is a requirement of the building code. Sincerely yours, [1]

[1 Minute at 80]

240 Gentlemen: The fire extinguishers that we are purchasing for the new office building have the highest/Underwriters' Laboratories ratings in the industry. They will be delivered to the new building on September//1, which is seven days before the building is occupied. This will give the inspectors seven days to check the///installation of each extinguisher and request replacements before any occupants move in. Yours truly, [2]

[1 Minute at 90]

241 Dear Mr. Royal: Six months ago we ordered 40 fire extinguishers, Model R702. After the installation/our inspectors examined each one, and in their opinion, nine should be replaced. In most cases the locking pin cannot//be removed quickly. In one instance there is evidence that the dry powder is leaking. These units must be replaced///immediately so that the building can be safely occupied. Your plant in Shippensburg is close to the building site. Yours truly, [3]

[1 Minute at 100]

242 Dear Mr. Royal: All of the occupants are moved into the new office building where we installed 40 of your fire extinguishers,/Model R702. Each has been informed that your technician will come to demonstrate the safe operation of the R702.//Please have your demonstrator prepared to inform us what precautions should be taken in case the dry powder chemical is accidentally///sprayed on the skin or in the eyes. Is the date October 3 all right for the demonstration? Our maintenance crew will be present. Cordially, [4] [340]

Reading and Writing Practice

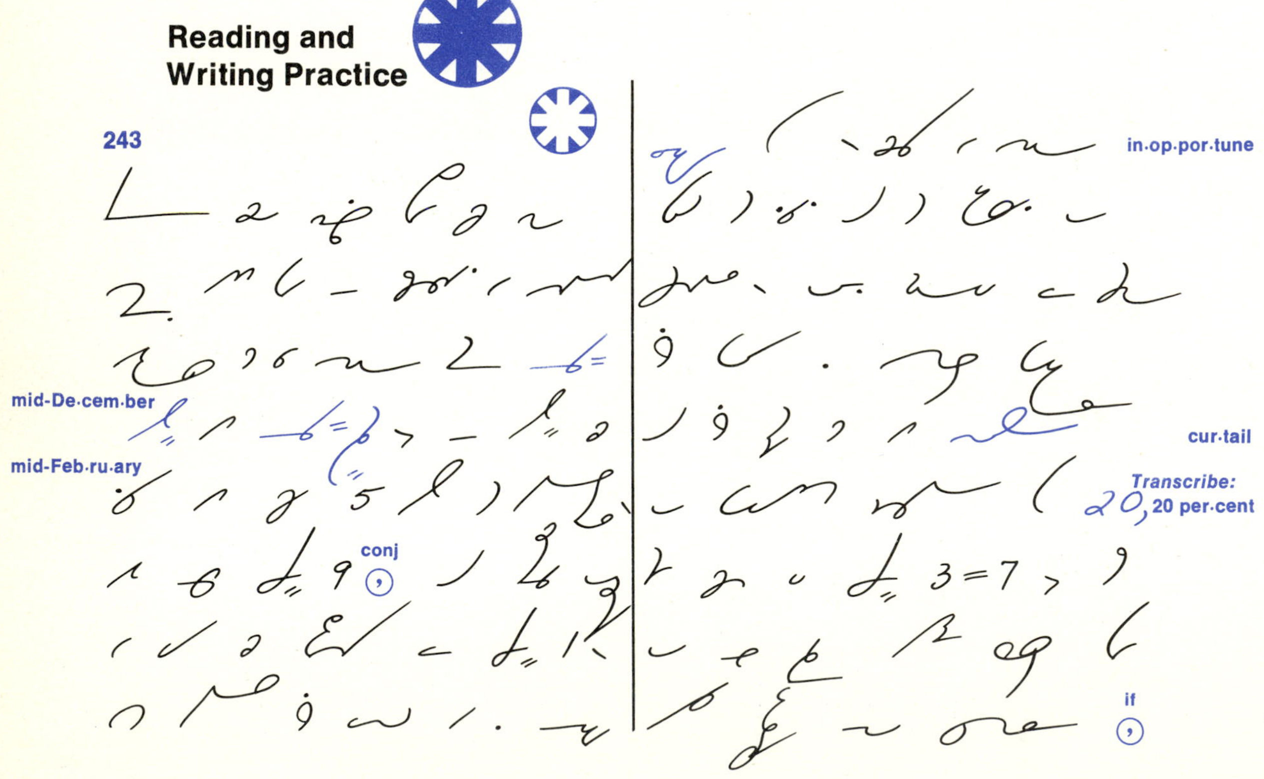

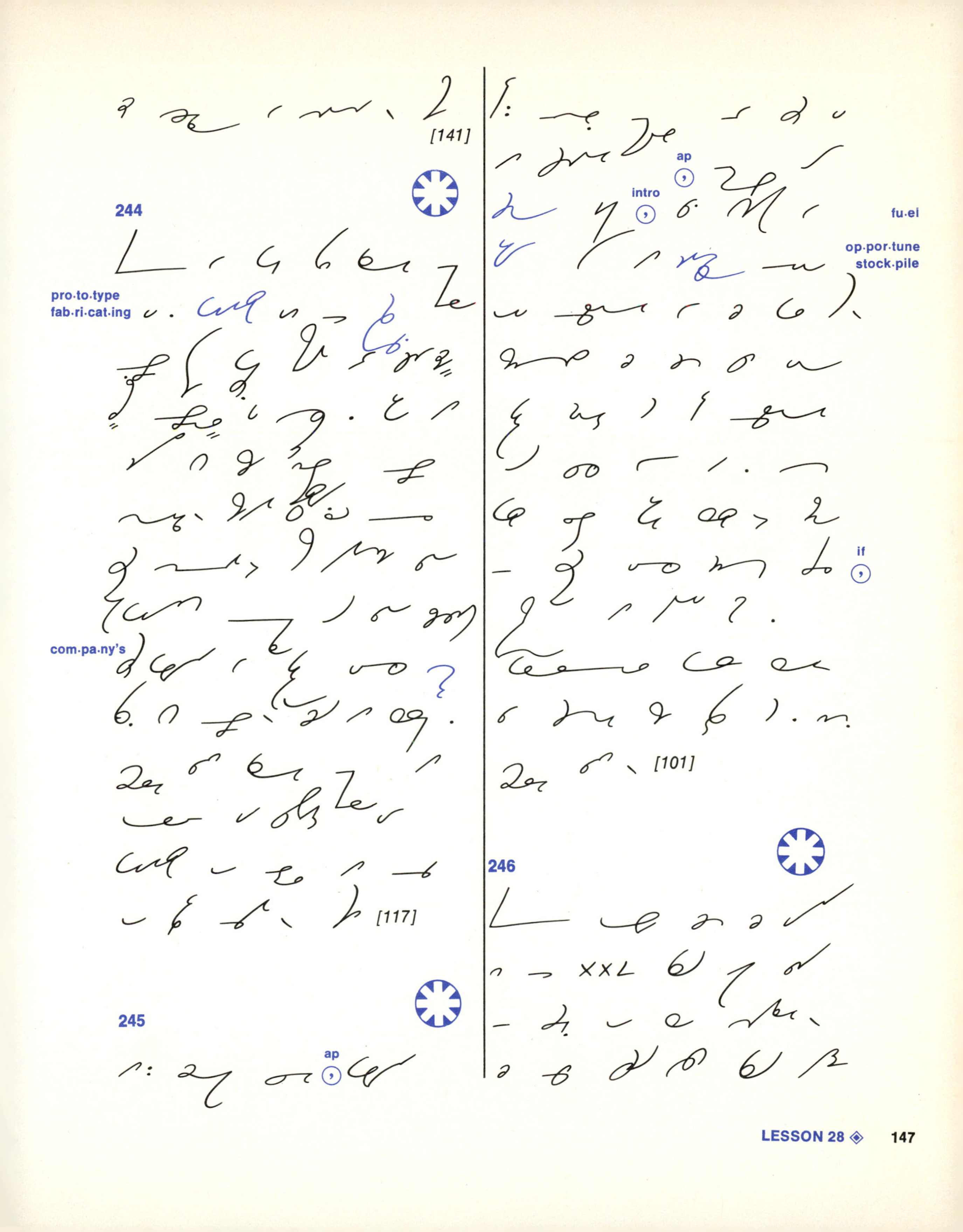

[141]

244

pro·to·type
fab·ri·cat·ing

com·pa·ny's

[117]

245

ap

ap

intro

fu·ei

op·por·tune
stock·pile

if

[101]

246

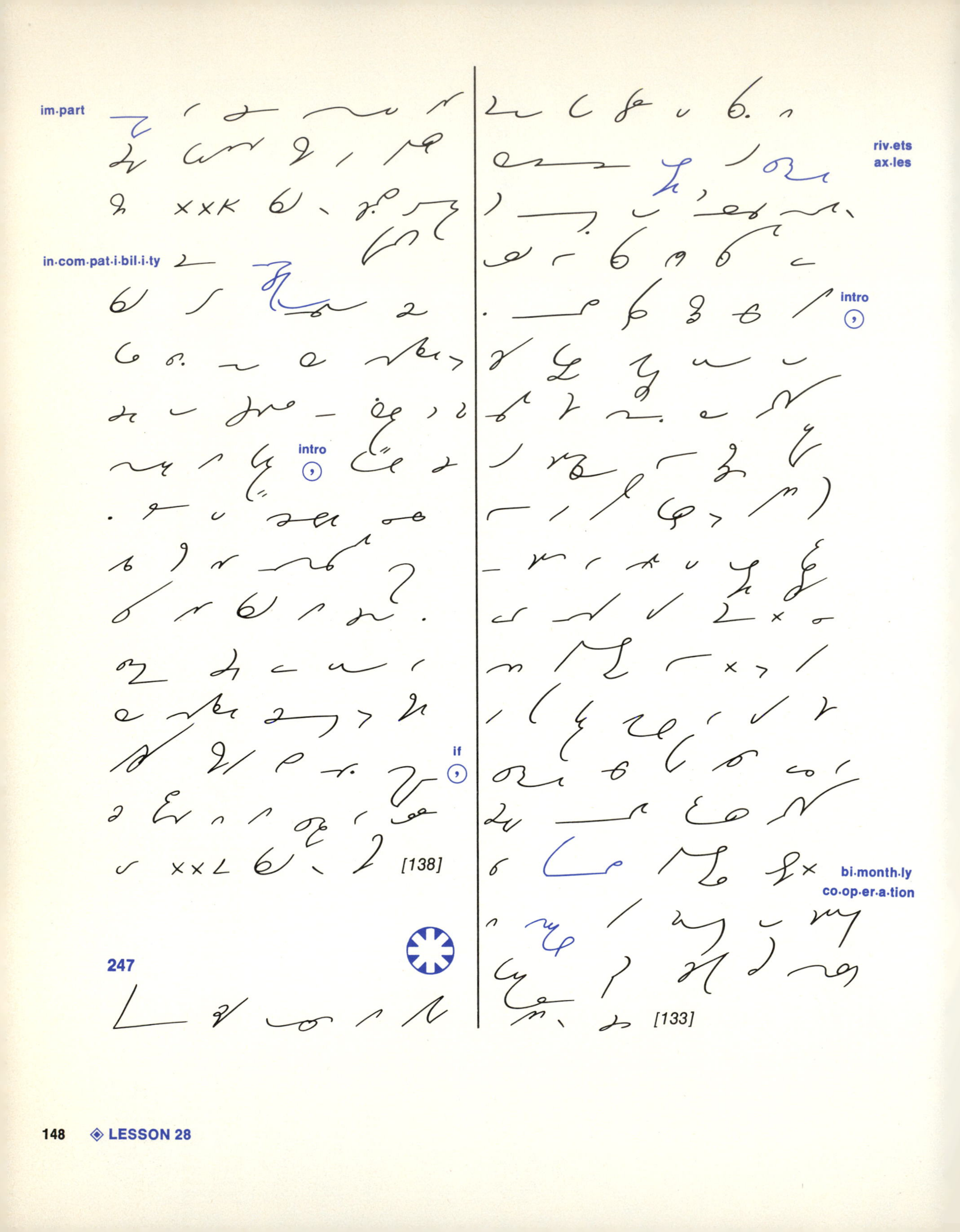

im·part

in·com·pat·i·bil·i·ty

intro

if

[138]

247

riv·ets
ax·les

intro

bi·month·ly
co·op·er·a·tion

[133]

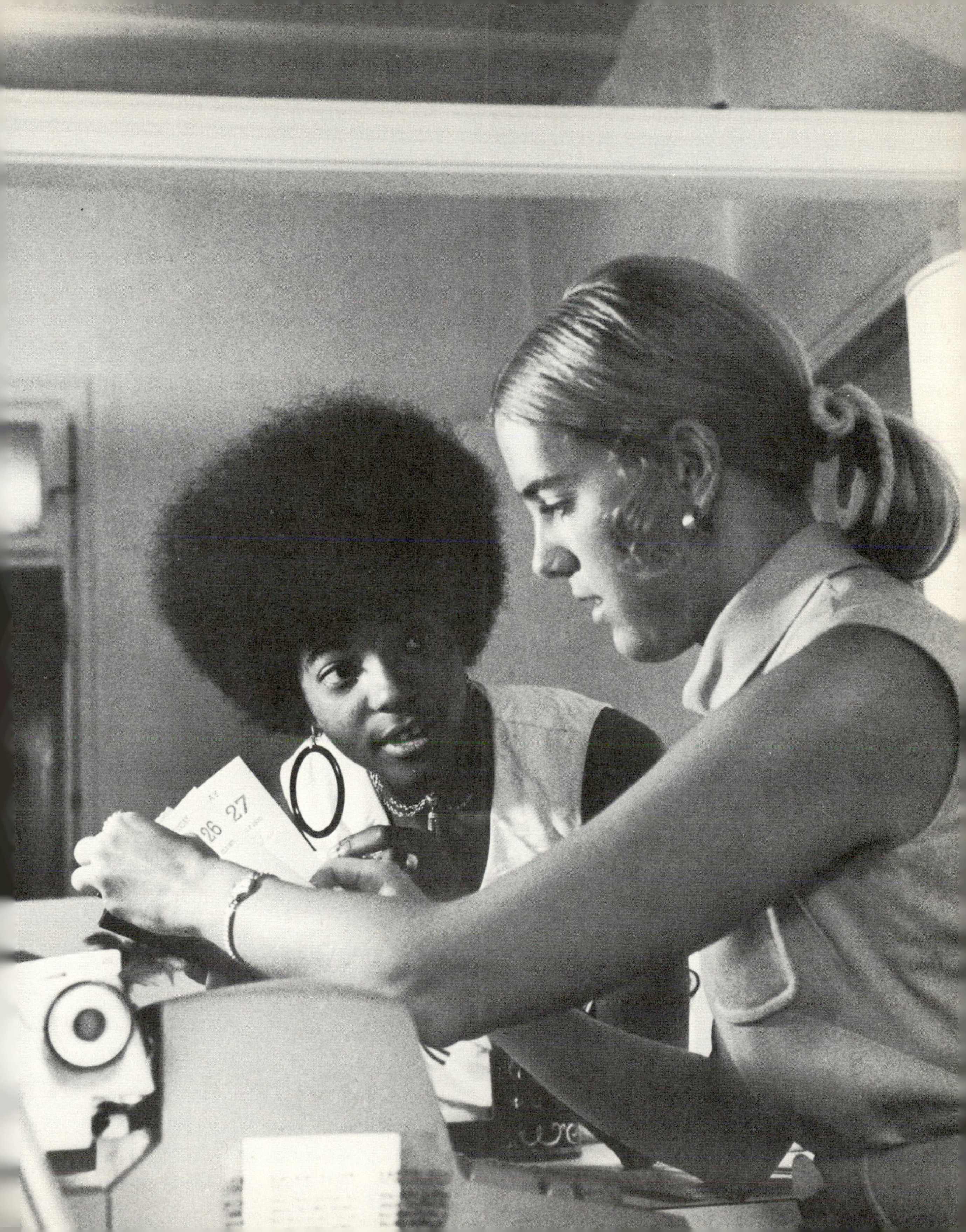
26 27

LESSON 29

Shorthand Vocabulary Builder

248 WORD-BUILDING PRINCIPLES

Ses

1

W Dash

2

-ngk

3

Tern, Etc.

4

1 Addresses, system, bases, criticism, scissors, lenses, releases.

2 Always, hardware, twice, quickly, liquid, inadequate, requisition.

3 Ankle, banker, frankly, sanction, shrink, anxious.

4 Turn, term, terminal, eastern, northern, external.

Building Transcription Skills

249 TRANSCRIPTION TYPING

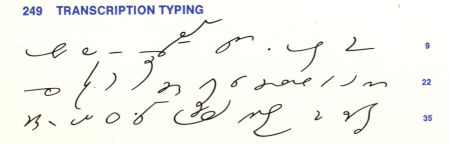

9

22

35

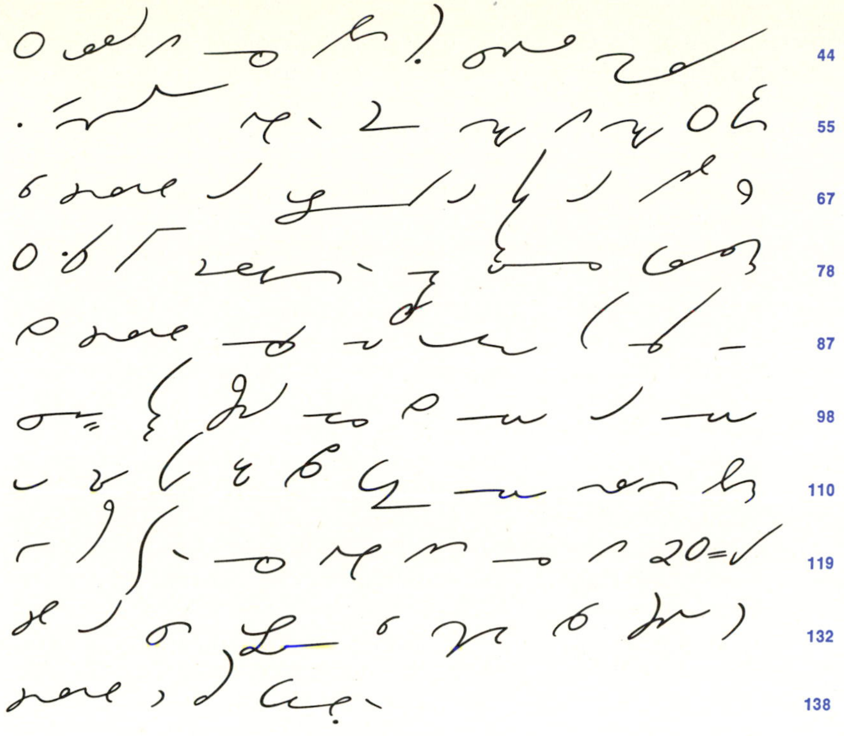

250 Business Vocabulary Builder

requisitions Written requests for something needed.

stoppages Obstructions.

memorandum A written communication within a business office.

Stair-Step Dictation

251 PREVIEW

[252]

[253]

[254]

252 Crystal, companion, china, artisans, pottery, introductory.

253 Fashion, fabric, interfacing, successfully, collar, nonwoven, experiments.

254 Cowhide, tannery, buckle, alligator, metal, sport.

LETTERS

252 Gentlemen: Your crystal design, Frost, has been chosen as the companion piece for our latest china pattern. The[1] sparkle created by the deep facets in the lead crystal complements our china. I congratulate your[2] artisans. We will order the crystal in lots of 50 as each new lot of china is ordered from the pottery.[3] Our present target is to introduce the latest china and crystal pattern on August 25. Can[4] you have the first lot shipped to our warehouse by July 1? We will then send complete settings to our dealers in time[5] for the introductory show. You can be sure that your crystal will be displayed prominently. Cordially yours,[6]

253 Gentlemen: I am enclosing a piece of fashion fabric and a picture of one of our new outfits. We have[7] not yet located an interfacing which can be used successfully with this fabric to create a soft collar[8] on the jacket. The woven interfacings we have used up to this time have been too heavy and have shown through[9] the fabric. May we order a small quantity of your nonwoven interfacing with which we can experiment?[10] If we find that your product works well with our fabric, we will place a large order for the spring showing. Yours truly,[11]

254 Dear Mrs. West: We will purchase cowhide from your tannery to make two styles in our top line of men's belts. At[12] the present time we need rugged suede cowhide for a belt 1¾ inches wide. A brass buckle will be[13] used on this sport model. For a dress belt we need alligator-grained cowhide to make a 1½-inch belt.[14] On the dress belt we frequently cover the buckle with the same leather used for the rest of the belt. Can you[15] recommend a glue that will make the leather adhere to the metal buckle? The leather for the sport model will be[16] tan; for the dress belt we want two colors, black and brown. The dye used must not fade or rub off. Yours very truly,[17]
[340]

Reading and Writing Practice

255

ther·mom·e·ters

intro

in·ad·e·quate

ZIP Code

intro

if

[143]

256

con·struc·tive

intro

typ·ists

ex·er·cise

nonr

Buy·ers'

intro

if

if

scis·sors

if

econ·o·my

intro

dan·ger·ous

cir·cum·vent

req·ui·si·tions

par

year's

[318]

257

sup·port·ed

[167]

LESSON 30

Shorthand Vocabulary Builder

258 PHRASING FOR SPEED

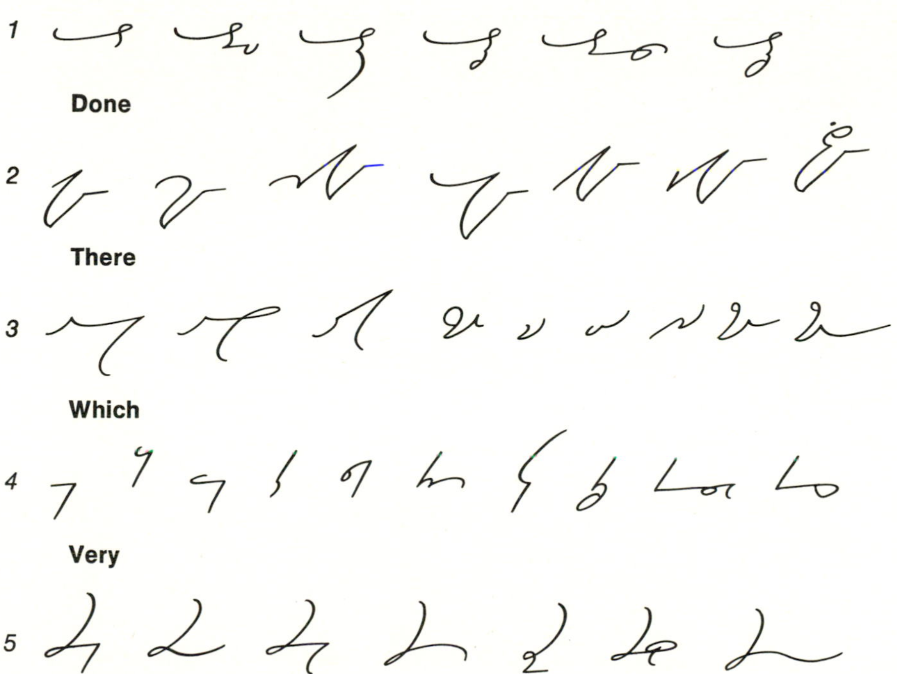

1 Let us, let us know, let us have, let us see, let us make, let us say.

2 To be done, can be done, could be done, will be done, would be done, should be done, has been done.

3 There will be, there may be, there would be, as there is, is there, of their, to their, if there are, if there will.

4 In which, of which, on which, which is, with which, which you can, by which, which way, which means, which may.

5 Very much, very well, very important, very good, very soon, very nice, very glad.

259

Business Vocabulary Builder

adjustment A settlement of a claim or debt.

custom-made Made according to the specifications of one purchaser.

specifications A statement prescribing materials and workmanship for something to be built.

Reading and Writing Practice

260

sec·re·tar·i·al

ap

intro

hinges

conj

intro

conj

[138]

261

ther·mal

par

if

intro

[123]

262

pre·shrunk

den·im

cus·tom-made hyphenated before noun.

intro

wheth·er

pre·clude

[126]

263

Ship·pens·burg

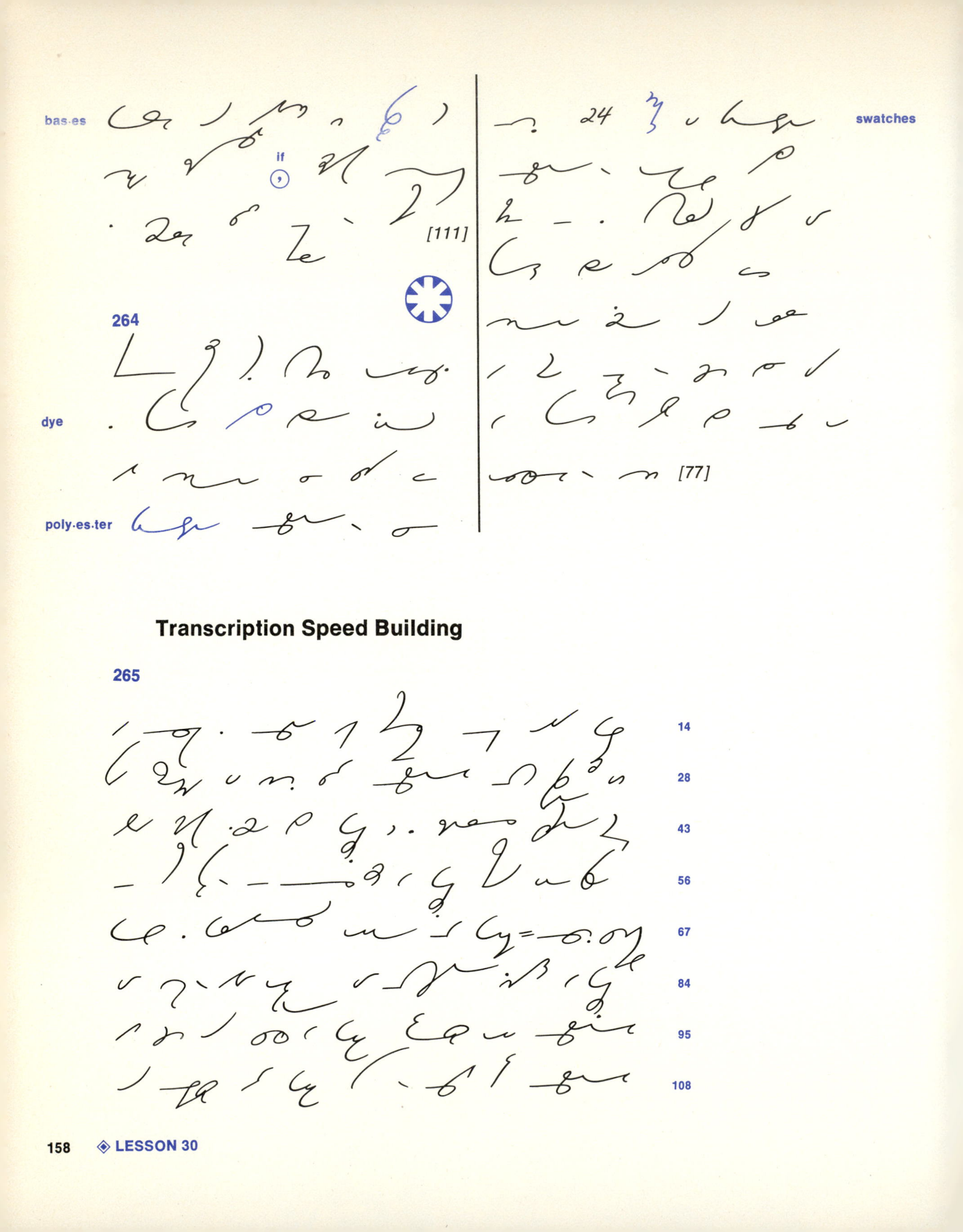

bas·es

if

[111]

264

dye

poly·es·ter

24

swatches

[77]

Transcription Speed Building

265

14

28

43

56

67

84

95

108

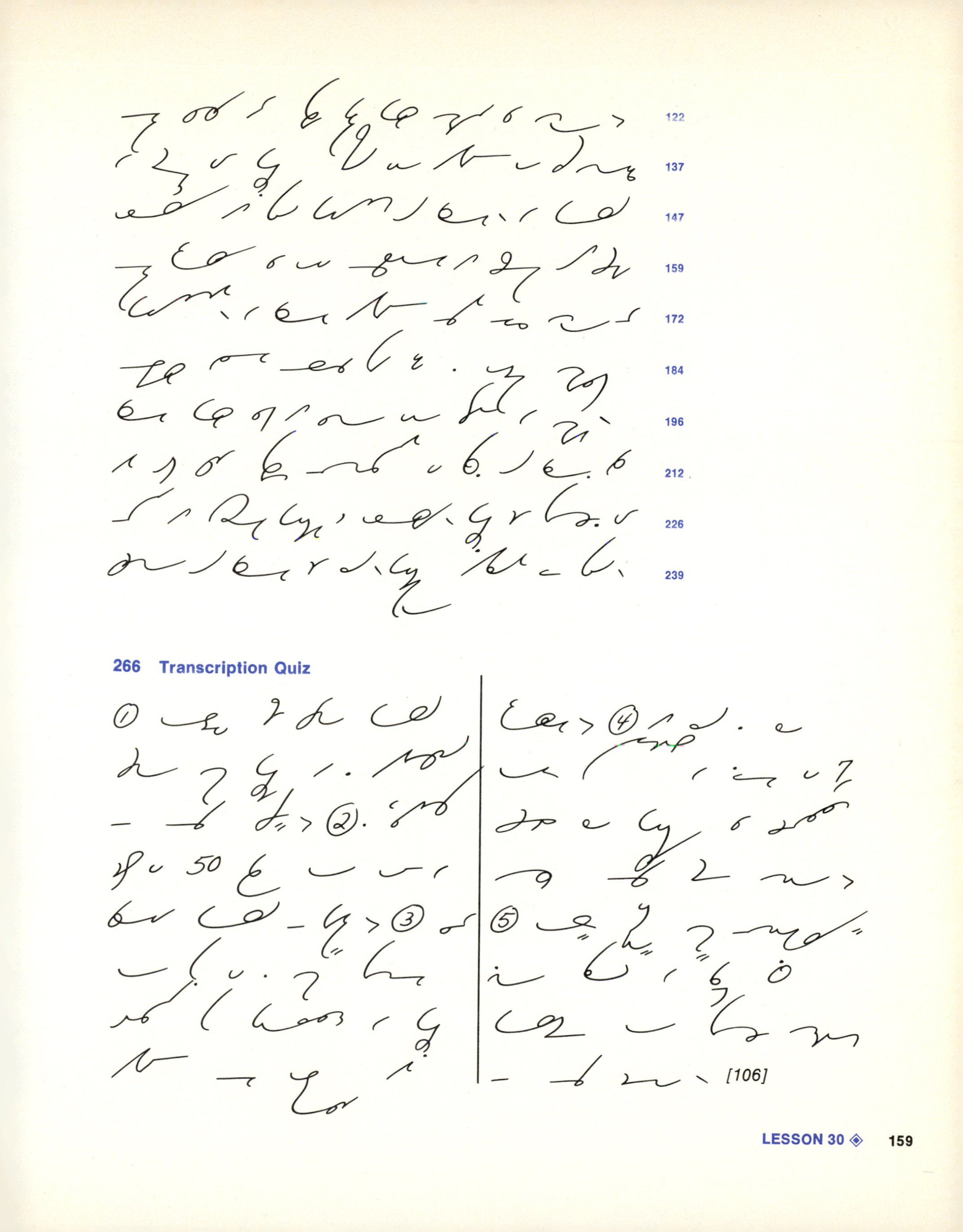

122

137

147

159

172

184

196

212

226

239

266 Transcription Quiz

(1)

(2)

50

(3)

(4)

(5)

[106]

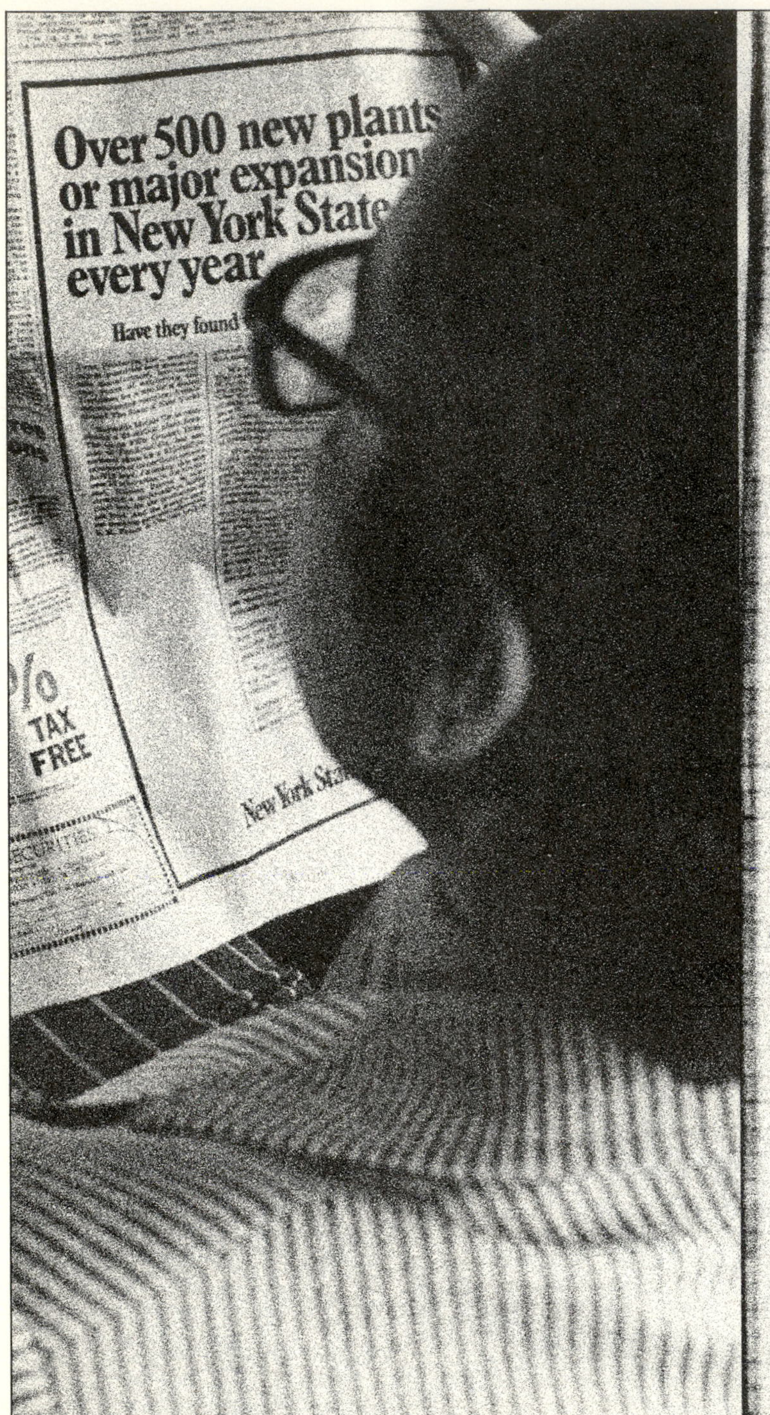

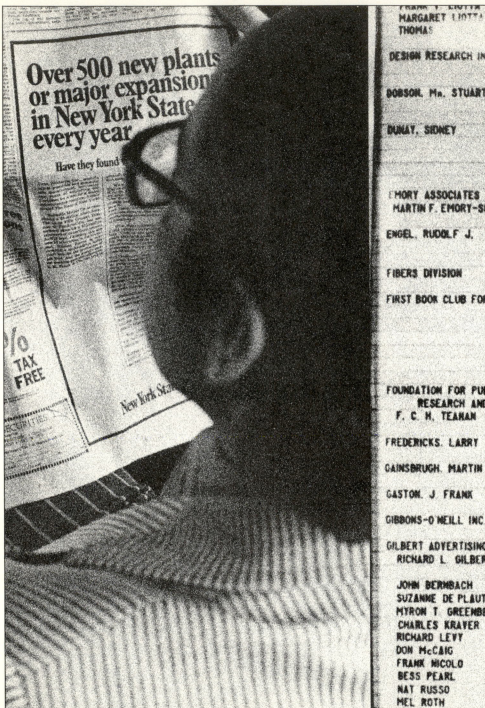

Over 500 new plants
or major expansion
in New York State
every year
Have they found
TAX
FREE
MARGARET LIOTTA
THOMAS
DESIGN RESEARCH INSTITUTE
DOBSON, Mr. STUART C. 5TH
DUNAY, SIDNEY
EMORY ASSOCIATES 12TH
MARTIN F. EMORY-SUCCESSOR TRUSTEE
ENGEL, RUDOLF J. 21ST FL.
FIBERS DIVISION 6TH
FIRST BOOK CLUB FOR BOYS & GIRLS 8TH
FOUNDATION FOR PUBLIC RELATIONS
RESEARCH AND EDUCATION
F. C. H. TEAHAN 12TH
FREDERICKS, LARRY 15TH
GAINSBRUGH, MARTIN R. 5TH
GASTON, J. FRANK 5TH
GIBBONS-O'NEILL INC. 7TH
GILBERT ADVERTISING AGENCY, INC. 15TH
RICHARD L. GILBERT
JOHN BERNBACH
SUZANNE DE PLAUTT
MYRON T. GREENBERGER
CHARLES KRAVER
RICHARD LEVY
DON McCAIG
FRANK NICOLO
BESS PEARL
NAT RUSSO
MEL ROTH

Unit 7
PUBLIC INFORMATION

On this job you will act as secretary to Newton Busche, director of Public Information at Universal Industries — a pleasant assignment, especially if you have a secret yen to become a writer yourself, for while working with Mr. Busche you will be able to analyze how such work is handled.

For a company to be successful, it must create a favorable image. That is why large corporations usually have a public information unit, whose responsibility it is to present their company and its policies as well as its executives and their activities in the news media in a way that builds public confidence. Often this may require sending out a press release; sometimes it involves asking that unfavorable publicity be withheld or rectified. It also means arranging company tours, scheduling photography sessions, or setting up interviews.

LESSON 31

Shorthand Vocabulary Builder

267 WORD FAMILIES

-cate

-bute

-tain

-or

1 Locate, indicate, duplicate, communicate, educate, reciprocate.

2 Tribute, attribute, contribute, distribute, distribution, undistributed, redistribute.

3 Maintain, certain, ascertain, contain, captain, detain, pertain, container.

4 Or, nor, more, store, ignore, floor, core.

Building Transcription Skills

268 TYPING STYLE STUDY ■ numbers

In correspondence and in manuscripts, words or figures are used to express numbers. Numbers written as words are formal and less obtrusive. Numbers written as figures are emphatic and quickly comprehended.

■ numbers written as words

Use words to express numbers (1) under 11 where special emphasis is not essential, (2) at the beginning of sentences, and (3) designating ages.

I remember seeing two lamps and four trays on the tables.
Seventeen volleyball players will arrive later.
Jane is twenty-three years old.

■ numbers written as figures

Use figures to express numbers (1) above 10 except in nontechnical and formal correspondence, (2) when special emphasis is desired, as in business, journalistic, and technical writing, (3) in dates and times, (4) in percentages and measurements, and (5) in amounts of money and market quotations.

The parade consisted of 13 bands and 150 marchers.
Please send me 2 dresses, 3 blouses, and 1 skirt immediately.
Dinner will be served to the Prime Minister at 8 o'clock on September 23.
When 75 percent of the floor is completed, the 4- by 9-foot door will be hung.
The stock will be sold at 70⅜, and his profit will be $10.30 a share.

For consistency, related numbers are expressed in the same style.

There were 22 men, 25 women, and 7 children present.

269 Business Vocabulary Builder

first quarter First of four equal parts of a year; that is, January, February, March.

keynote speaker The person who presents the major speech at an assembly.

house organ A publication of a company for its employees and clients.

Progressive Dictation [70–100]

270 PREVIEW

[271]

[272]

[273]

[274]

271 Lennox, wide, international, adviser, Pittsburgh, officer, American.
272 President, professional, Baxter, director, responsibility, conference.
273 Federal, appointed, transmission, government, division, distributors, importers.
274 Tower, terminal, industrial, interstate, regulations, traffic.

LETTERS

[1 Minute at 70]

271 Dear Mrs. Tanner: Richard L. Groomes has been appointed vice president of the trust department/of Lennox Bank. Mr. Groomes has had wide experience in commercial and international banking.//For the past eight years, he has been an adviser for the trust accounts here in Pittsburgh. Before joining///Lennox, Mr. Groomes was an officer for American Bank. Very cordially yours, [1]

[1 Minute at 80]

272 Dear Mr. Gregg: The new president of the Business and Professional Advertising Association is/Ruth M. Williams. Mrs. Williams is the advertising director for the Store Display Company and has been//a member of the Association for thirteen years. The new president has appointed Paul Baxter to be///the program director for the next year. Baxter's first responsibility will be planning the conference. Cordially, [2]

[1 Minute at 90]

273 Gentlemen: The Federal Energy Administration appointed C. W. Hunter chairman of a natural gas/transmission and distribution committee. This committee was formed to advise the government on all programs which affect the//natural gas supply. Hunter, who is a division head for West Natural Gas Company, heads the 32-member panel,///which is made up of government officials, natural gas distributors and importers, and customers. Sincerely, [3]

[1 Minute at 100]

274 Gentlemen: The Tower Trucking Company will move to a new and larger terminal in the Plum Industrial Park on February/1. The Interstate Commerce Commission has advised us that the loading and unloading regulations for truckers will be the same as those//at our present terminal. This new terminal is easy to locate and eliminates city traffic for truckers arriving from all///parts of the state. Six new loaders will be employed at the new terminal. Mr. Lee White will continue as our terminal manager. Yours truly, [4] [340]

275

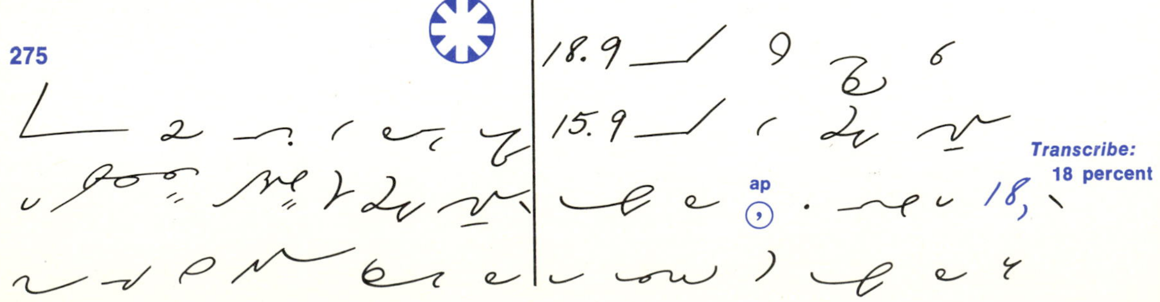

Transcribe: 96 cents

ap

ap

strat·e·gies

intro

intro

back·ground

[184]

276

ap

key·note

ap

ap

Transcribe: 10 a.m.

ser

da·is

Transcribe: 1 p.m.

[160]

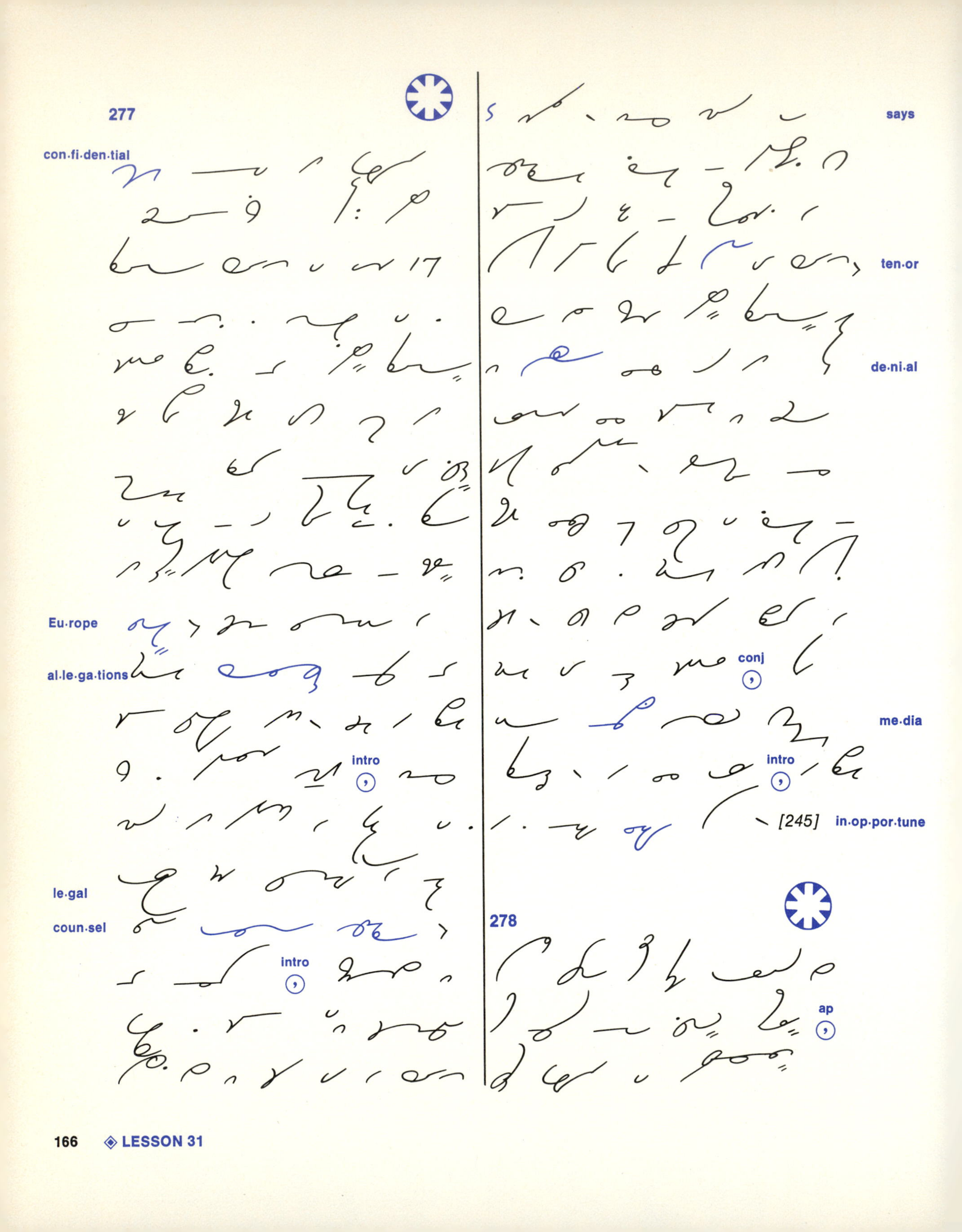

277

con·fi·den·tial

Eu·rope

al·le·ga·tions

intro

le·gal

coun·sel

intro

says

ten·or

de·ni·al

conj

me·dia

intro

[245]

in·op·por·tune

278

ap

NSA

ap

ef·fec·tive·ly

ad·min·is·tra·tors

its

conj

intro

intro

[190]

279

ap

Dem·o·crat·ic
fund-rais·ing
hyphenated before noun

near·by

ap

intro

[109]

LESSON 32

Shorthand Vocabulary Builder

280 WORD BEGINNINGS

Tern-, Etc.

1 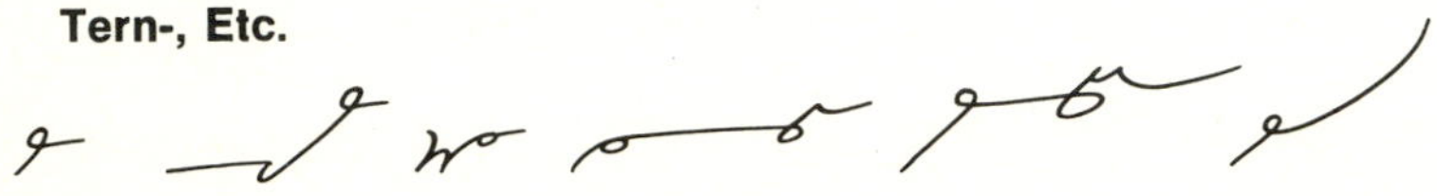

Ex-

2 

Sub-

3 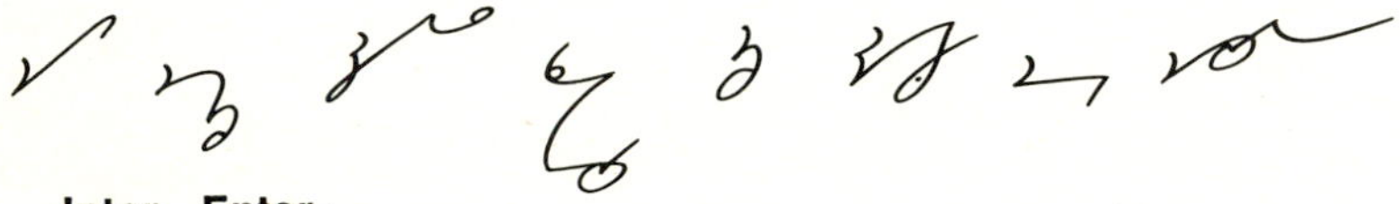

Inter-, Enter-

4 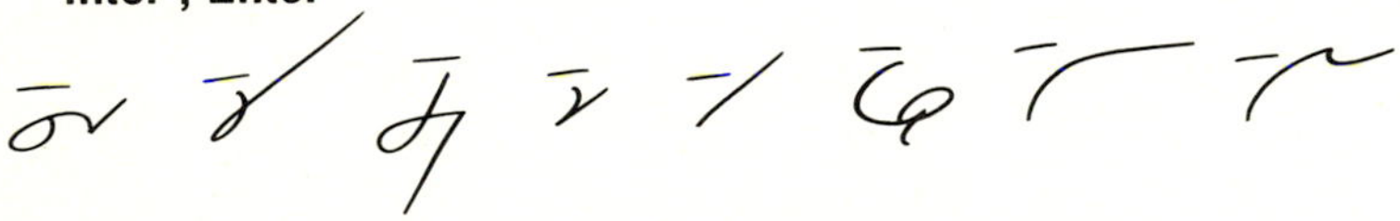

1 Turn, modern, southern, thermometer, dermatology, termed.

2 Explain, excuse, expel, expressly, exterminator, extricate, exit.

3 Subdue, subconsciously, subsidiary, suburbanite, subway, substantiate, submission, subtitle.

4 Interact, interceded, interchange, interstate, entered, enterprise, entertainment, entertainer.

Building Transcription Skills

281 TRANSCRIPTION TYPING

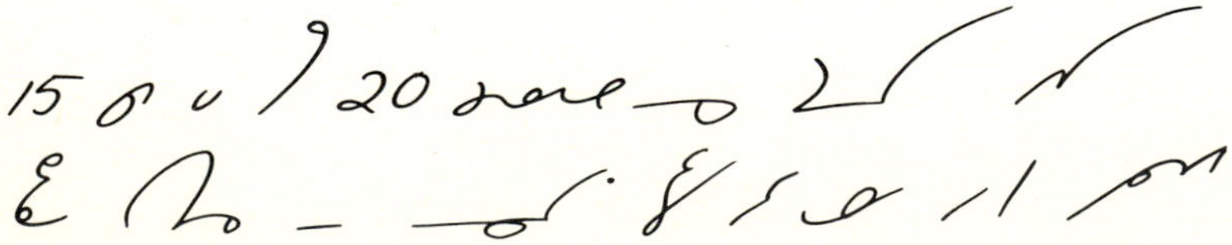

12

28

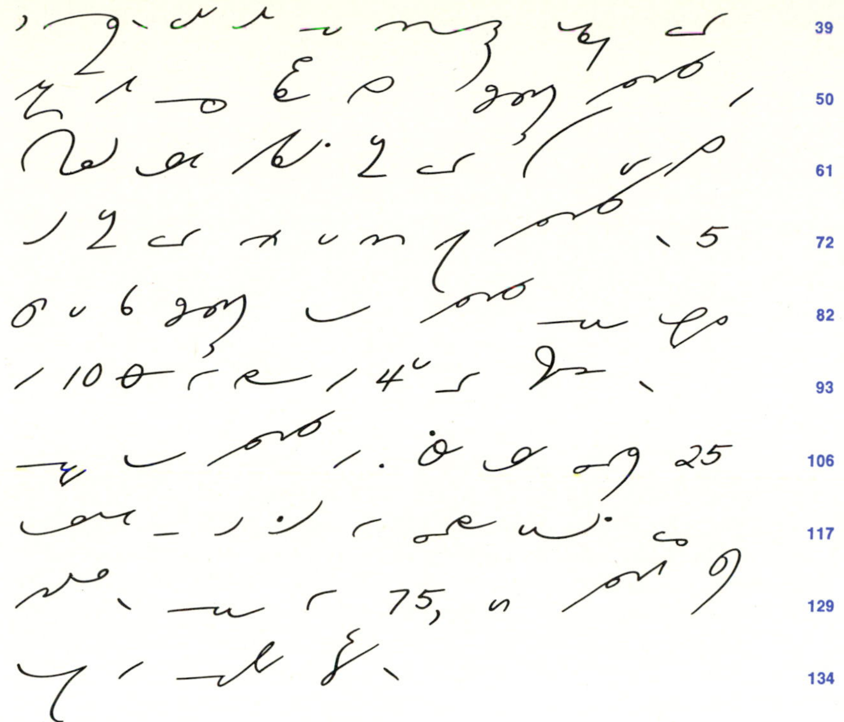

282 **Business Vocabulary Builder**

M.B.A. degree Master of business administration degree.

glossy print A photograph on smooth, shiny paper.

firm date A date fixed formally; definite date.

Stair-Step Dictation

283 PREVIEW

[284]

[285]

[286]

284 Stockholders, overwhelmingly, proposals, aliens, outstanding.

285 Vocational, large-scale, outset, graduates, facility.

286 Newest, engine, conventional, combustion, pollutants, machinists', assembly.

LETTERS

284 To: The Stockholders of the *News:* At the Board of Directors meeting on June 12, the stockholders voted[1] overwhelmingly to approve the proposals which would protect this paper from take-over attempts by foreign interests. The[2] changes include the provision that aliens cannot own or control more than 12 percent of the outstanding[3] stock. No single alien can own or control more than 6 percent. The *News,* which operates 17 daily[4] papers, has a circulation ranging from 15,000 to 55,000 in seven states. The stockholders[5] also reelected the Board of Directors of the *News* for another term of office. Sincerely yours,[6]

285 Dear Alumni: City College is concerned about careers at all levels. Within the month, City College[7] will begin the first nationwide vocational guidance counseling program. This large-scale counseling is possible[8] because of the farsighted ideas of the members of the Vocational Department at City College and[9] the large computer now in use at the College. Through this program, millions of people can match their training with the[10] jobs available across the country. At the outset only graduates and students of the College can use[11] the services provided in this guidance program. The facility may be open to others soon. Cordially,[12]

286 Dear Mr. Walsh: Rhode Island Motors wishes to introduce the newest in engine design. The Pre-Charge Engine[13] (PCE) closely resembles the conventional internal combustion engine, but the new PCE saves[14] fuel and produces fewer pollutants. Experiments have been run with the engine installed in Rhode Island Motors[15] compact cars and pickup trucks. The results of these tests have proved that the engine does perform well in actual[16] road testing. From the designers' plans and the machinists' model, the engineers feel confident that the PCE[17] can be mass-produced in one year's time. No assembly-line adjustments will be necessary. Sincerely,[18] [360]

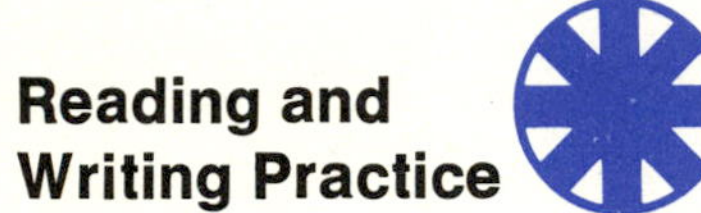

Reading and Writing Practice

287

ap

per·son·nel

intro

sought

20, 14, 1964

B.A. BA

M.B.A. MBA

intro

ser

nonr

ap

dem·on·strat·ed

in·valu·able

[284]

288

stock·hold·ers

ap

intro

dis·grun·tled

intro

dis·sem·i·na·tion

re·read

nonr

if

[150]

289

ap

TV

18

ap

KJK

8 ser

15

5

if

pre·re·cord·ed

par

for·mat

[177]

LESSON 33

Shorthand Vocabulary Builder

290 BRIEF-FORM POWER

1 Speak, speaker, speaks; big, bigger, biggest; great, greater.

2 Over, passover, turnover, oversize, overweight, oversleep, stopover, moreover.

3 How-out, anyhow, somehow, outlet, however; wish, wishing, wishes, wishful, wished.

4 Correspond-correspondence, correspondent, correspondingly; particular, particulars, particularize, particularly; time, times.

291 CITIES

-mont

Claremont, Oakmont, Piedmont, Larchmont.

Building Transcription Skills

292 SIMILAR WORDS ■ affect, effect; council, counsel

Study the following words which sound similar and which are sometimes confused.

affect To influence; to change.

effect (*noun*) Result; outcome.
(*verb*) To bring about.

council An assembly of persons.

counsel A lawyer; advice.

293 **Business Vocabulary Builder**

drive An organized effort to accomplish a purpose, such as raising money.

press release News or publicity released for publication.

kickoff A beginning, such as a kickoff dinner.

Progressive Dictation [80—110]

294 PREVIEW

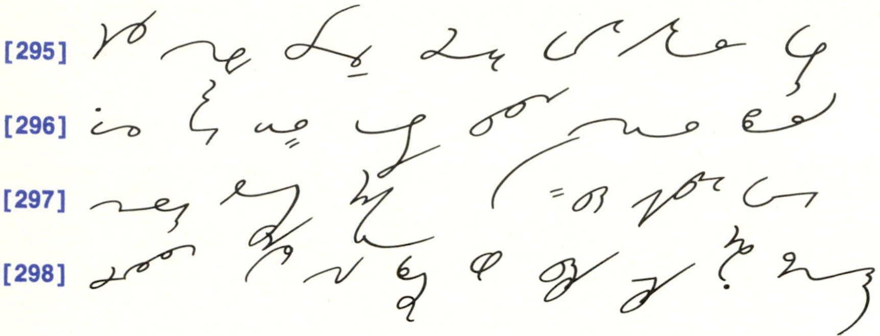

295 Fortunate, greatest, banquet, philosophy, pertains, discipline, preaches.

296 Hockey, suspension, Oregon, levied, attacked, goalie, excellent.

297 Commercials, televised, football, time-outs, touchdowns, permission.

298 Synthetic, tennis, court, surfaces, ice, outside, inside, sweeping, exclusive.

LETTERS

[1 Minute at 80]

295 Gentlemen: We are indeed fortunate to have one of the greatest coaches in the world as our banquet speaker./Coach Blair Prose, who has led his college team to three national championships, eight Big Ten titles, and four Bowl//victories, has accepted our invitation. Prose believes his coaching philosophy pertains to all people who/// wish to win in business. Hard work, discipline, and dedication are the virtues that he preaches. Yours truly, [1]

[1 Minute at 90]

296 Dear Mr. Larson: Tom Fields of the West Hockey Team has called a press conference to announce the purchase of Sam Howe, a top/goalie. Howe has recently been removed from the suspension list after paying his $1,500 fine and sitting//out five games as a member of the Oregon Hockey Team. Despite this long suspension, which was levied because Howe attacked///a referee, he is in first-rate skating condition. His goalie record is excellent and fans like him. Cordially yours, [2]

[1 Minute at 100]

297 Gentlemen: Attorney Robert Jackson proposes the following program for television commercials to be shown during the nationally/televised football games. There will be three 1-minute TV time-outs to be taken during the first and third quarters of the game//and four during the second and fourth quarters. If there are enough game time-outs, touchdowns, or injuries, no TV time-outs will be called. The///TV manager must obtain permission from the field official before a television time-out can be called. Very sincerely yours, [3]

[1 Minute at 110]

298 Dear Tennis Pro: Oakmont Surfacing Company announces Sureturf, the synthetic for tennis court surfaces. In five years Sureturf has proven itself/to be the best synthetic by a wide margin. It makes a long-wearing base that withstands the snow and ice of Maine winters on outside courts and the dry air of//the inside courts. The colors added to Sureturf do not fade quickly. Conventional sweeping methods can be used to dry the surface after a rain and///return the courts to playing condition quickly. Oakmont Surfacing Company is the exclusive contractor for Sureturf. Very truly yours, [4] [380]

Reading and Writing Practice

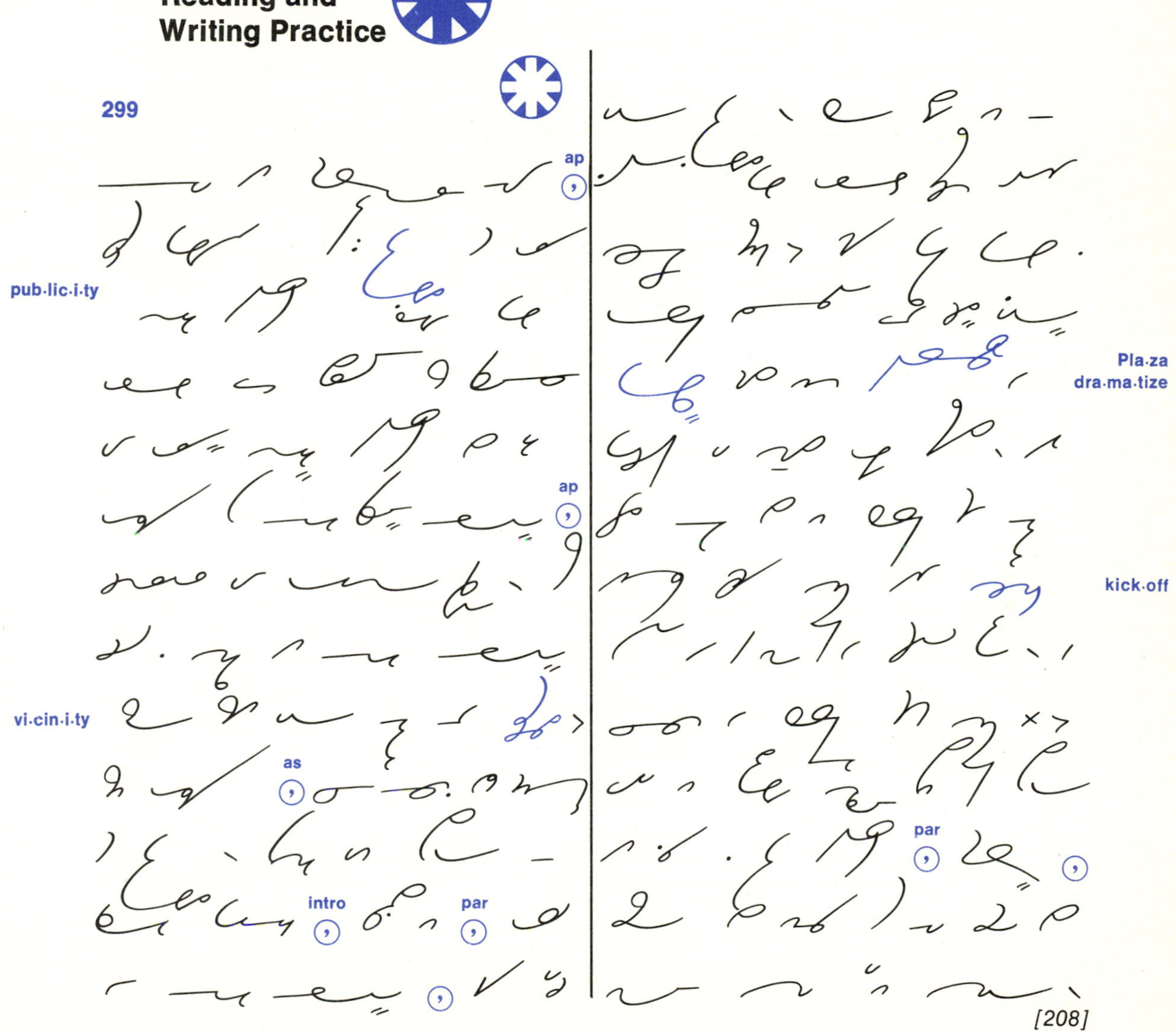

300

ap

par

ap

ap

par

ser

intro

conj

civ·ic-mind·ed *hyphenated before noun*

lun·cheon

par·tic·i·pates

Ro·ta·ry

75

345-6329

[252]

301

intro

one-fourth

ap

sought

intro

intro

per·ti·nent

ser

pho·to·graph

ap

[197]

302

ap

intro

par

ap

tech·ni·cal

if

Transcribe:
9 o'clock

[138]

Shorthand Vocabulary Builder

303 WORD-BUILDING PRINCIPLES

Div-, Dev-, Dif-, Def-

Ind-, Ent-, Ant-

-ow

Abbreviated Words

1 Divide, division, devote, devised, differences, diffident, defective, definite.

2 Industry, industrial, indicate, entry, entire, anterior, anticipate, antique.

3 Account, amount, allowance, announcement, aloud, brown, flowers, house, tower, pound, council, count.

4 Algebra, alphabet, anniversary, arithmetic, atmosphere, convenient-convenience, equivalence-equivalent, memorandum, philosophy, privilege, reluctance-reluctant, inconvenienced, significance-significant, significantly.

Building Transcription Skills

304 TRANSCRIPTION TYPING

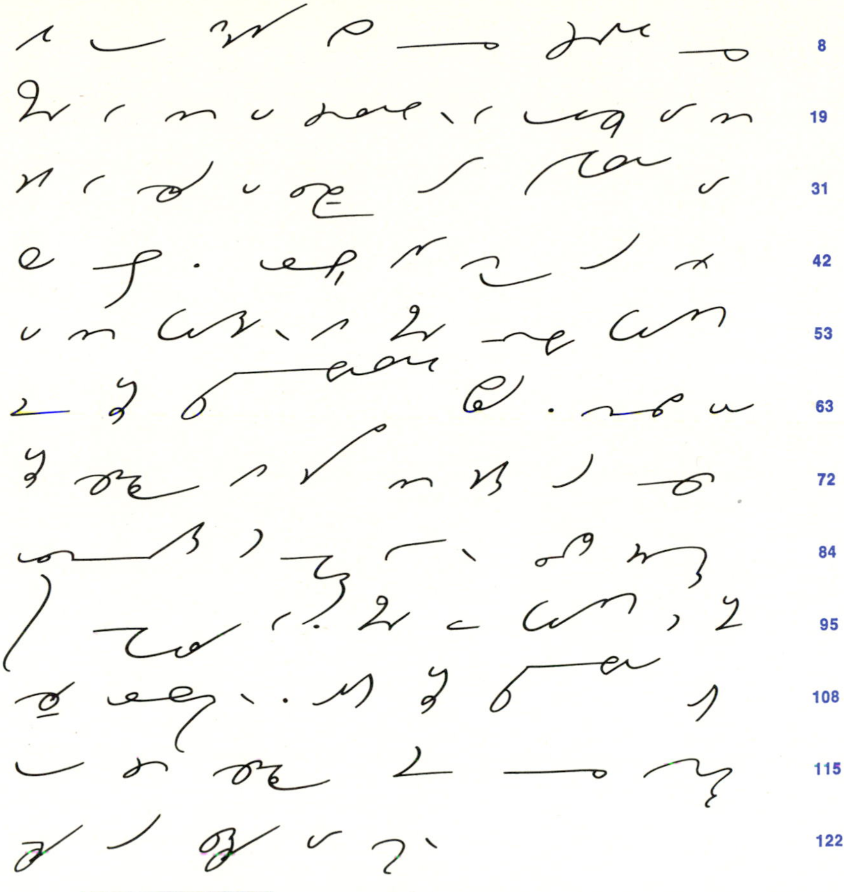

305

Business Vocabulary Builder

stockholders Those who own shares of a corporation and therefore are entitled to dividends and other rights of ownership.

interchange An exchange.

headquarters A center of operations.

Stair-Step Dictation

306 PREVIEW

[307]

[308]

[309]

307 Unusual, jewelry, delicate, link, spools, precious.
308 Premier, insignia, fantastic, shirts, anklets, washable.
309 Equestrian, society, jockeys, Briton, superiority, maximum, variety.

LETTERS

307 Dear Mr. Dana: Clarissa and Company has a new product which will be marketed in your area[1] next fall. Please alert your sales staff to be ready to display this new and unusual high-fashion jewelry.[2] Clarissa and Company will supply your jewelry shop with spools of delicate gold link chains like the spools of ribbon[3] stocked by the department store. Every 12 inches a precious gem is safely secured in a link. Each customer[4] can buy any length of chain with diamonds or emeralds to create short or long necklaces which can be worn[5] separately or all together. There are four delicate chain designs, each on a separate spool. Cordially yours,[6]

308 Dear Miss Graham: Woven-In Corporation proudly invites you to its premier showing of "Tennis Whites With a[7] Touch of Color." All the high qualities that our insignia has always stood for are designed into this fantastic[8] line. Shirts and shorts, dresses and briefs, and socks and anklets have the stamp of Woven-In which is THE guide to good[9] tailoring. All fabrics are machine washable and dryable. This is the first complete line of women's tennis[10] wear Woven-In has designed, and the name means what it says. Each outfit has a bright touch of color on tennis white.[11] This stylish tennis wear was designed for the world's number one woman player. Very cordially yours,[12]

309 Dear Mrs. Royal: The members of the American Equestrian Society will discuss at the[13] convention the difference between European and American thoroughbred racing. Tribute will be paid to[14] two top jockeys, a North American and a Briton. In the past European jockeys have maintained[15] superiority in top international races. They allow their mounts to start a race slowly and ask maximum[16] effort in the last stretch. American jockeys have always tried to use their horse's talents with more variety.[17] They often ask their horse for top speed early in the race and slow the horse when the pace of the race is controlled. Yours truly,[18] [360]

Reading and Writing Practice

310

stock·hold·ers

10 ap

Transcribe: 10 o'clock

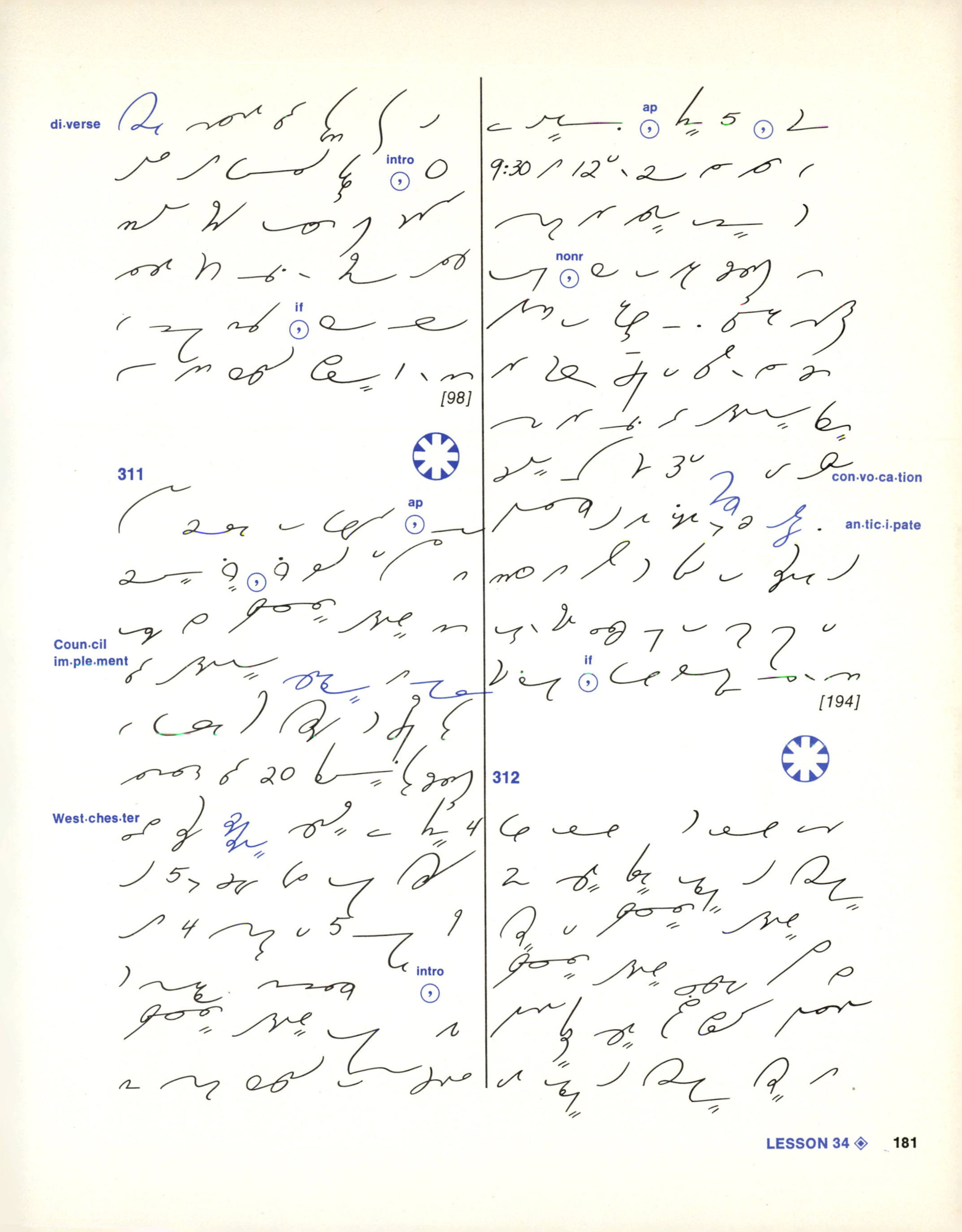

di·verse

intro

if

[98]

311

ap

Coun·cil

im·ple·ment

West·ches·ter

intro

ap

nonr

con·vo·ca·tion

an·tic·i·pate

if

[194]

312

nonr

doc·tor·ate

Tech·nol·o·gy

Ad·vi·so·ry

intro

Ful·bright

[130]

313

Rep·re·sen·ta·tives

intro

ac·tiv·i·ties

an·ni·ver·sa·ry

[117]

314

nonr

doc·tor·al

intro

sew·ing

[98]

Shorthand Vocabulary Builder

315 PHRASING FOR SPEED

This

1

Between

2

Hope

3

Shall

4

Some

5

1 In this, with this, on this, for this, this is, this is not, this time, from this, of this.

2 Between the, between us, between these, between those, between your, between them, between this.

3 I hope, I hope that, I hope that the, I hope you will, I hope you are, we hope, we hope you will be, we hope they will.

4 I shall, I shall have, I shall be, I shall not, I shall not be, I shall not have, we shall be glad, we shall make, we shall not, we shall need, we shall not be able.

5 Some of the, some of these, some of them, some of this, some of that, some of our, some of those.

Building Transcription Skills

316 **Business Vocabulary Builder**

graphics A written and pictorial representation of information on a two-dimensional surface; lines, strokes, and reproductions made from blocks, plates, and type are employed.

certified public accountants Accountants who have passed the appropriate tests and have received a license, or certificate, stating that the legal requirements of the state for serving the public have been met; abbreviated CPA.

Reading and Writing Practice

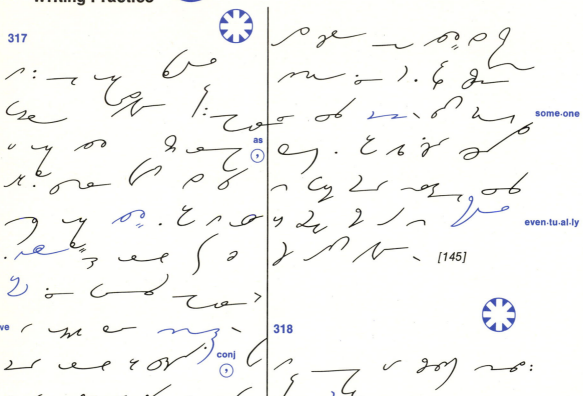

317

as ,

Ta·ki

tri·al

of·fered

con·clu·sive

conj ,

some·one

even·tu·al·ly

[145]

318

for·mat

year's

prep·a·ra·tion

nonr

par

conj

tra·di·tion·al

in·no·va·tions

conj

sum·ma·ry

intro

[183]

319

Com·mit·tee

intro

mod·ern

conj

ser

conj

ne·ces·si·ty

in·tact

high·lights

conj

sig·nif·i·cant

due

ap

if

con·sid·er

ser

cer·ti·fied

line

[247]

as·sem·ble

Transcription Speed Building

320

14

25

37

47

60

75

87

100
111
122
135
147
158
169
180
192
196

321 Transcription Quiz

[99]

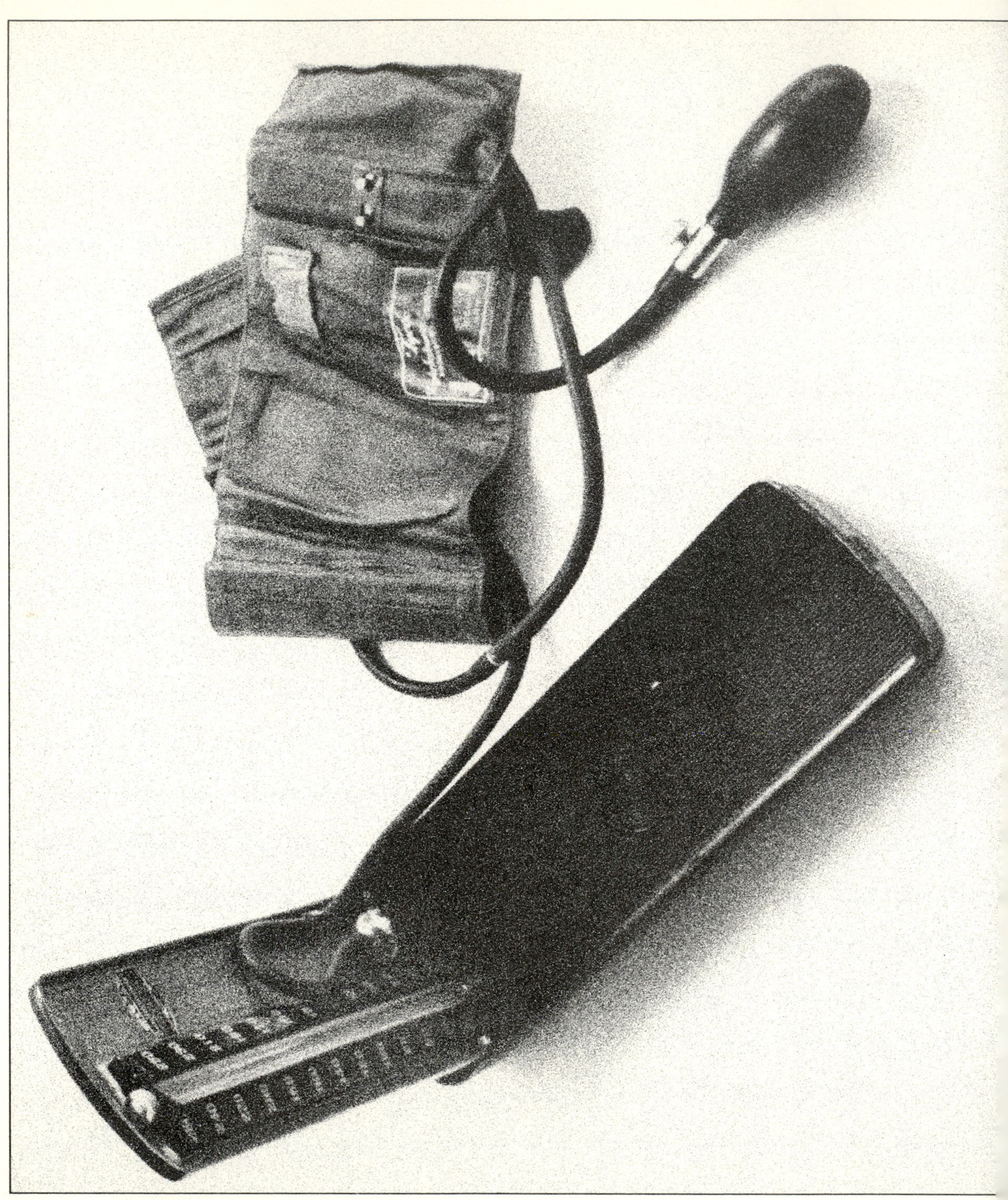

Unit 8

HEALTH SERVICES

In Unit 8 you are secretary to Dr. Lawrence Day, head of Health Services at RDS Corporation. Dr. Day has general responsibility for the health of all employees. He handles emergency treatment of injuries and minor illnesses incurred on the job, and he refers employees to physicians in private practice for serious illnesses. Dr. Day evaluates health claims of employees seeking indemnity from the company for job-related illnesses and provides the medical records required by government agencies.

You will probably be expected to assist Dr. Day in administering to his patients. To handle these assignments creditably, you will need a limited knowledge of medical terms and their correct spelling.

LESSON 36

Shorthand Vocabulary Builder

322 WORD FAMILIES

-itis

1

-count

2

-age

3

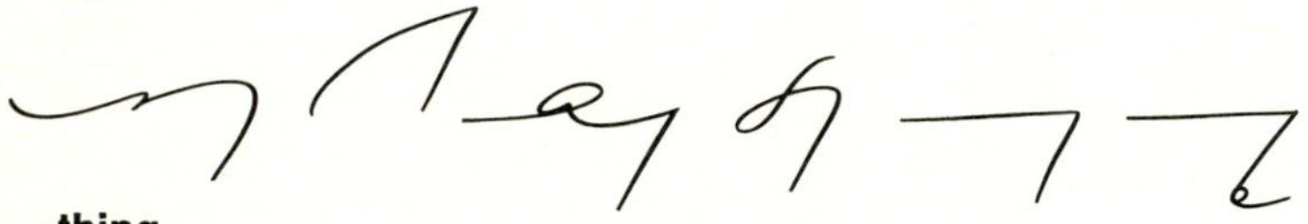

-thing

4

1 Neuritis, arthritis, tonsillitis, appendicitis, bronchitis, laryngitis.
2 Count, account, miscount, recount, accountant, discount.
3 Luggage, damage, mileage, package, manage, manager.
4 Thing, anything, nothing, plaything, everything, something, things.

Building Transcription Skills

323 SIMILAR WORDS ■ adverse, averse; advice, advise

Study the following words which sound something alike and which are sometimes confused.

adverse Opposing; unfavorable.

averse Unwilling; reluctant.

advice (*noun*) Counsel.

advise (*verb*) To recommend.

324 **Business Vocabulary Builder**

Ms. A title used preceding a woman's name.

retirement The act of withdrawing from a former occupation.

organically The adverb form of the adjective *organic,* which pertains to organs of the human body.

Progressive Dictation [80—110]

325 PREVIEW

[326]

[327]

[328]

[329]

326 Dear Ms., damage, medicines, react, slowdown, effects, cure.

327 Prescription, drug, discovered, adverse, chemical, medication.

328 Counter, customers', observing, badly, carefully, patient, ineffective, use.

329 Contacting, warn, neglect, counter, choose, properly, dangerous.

LETTERS

[1 Minute at 80]

326 Dear Ms. Miller: Damage can be done by mixing medicines. Whenever two or more medicines are taken at/the same time, they may react with one another so that the medicines do not do the jobs for which they were taken.//This mixing within the body may account for the slowdown in the cure of the ailments or may cause bad side///effects. Ask for advice before you take more than one medicine. Be sure the medicines will help, not harm you. Yours truly, [1]

[1 Minute at 90]

327 Dear Frank: When your last prescription was recorded in your drug file, it was discovered that you may be taking two/ medicines at this time which may cause an adverse chemical effect. In my opinion, you should call Dr. Huff, who prescribed this latest//medicine, and report to him that you are taking a medication prescribed by Dr. Bickley for your allergy. If he thinks/// the risk is small, he may recommend you continue both medicines; or he may find another effective medicine. Sincerely, [2]

[1 Minute at 100]

328 To the Staff: Careful management of medicines prescribed over the counter is becoming a problem. In my customers' drug files, I/have been observing that many people are taking drugs made up of chemicals which react badly with one another. Often these//prescriptions are written by more than one doctor. If each doctor is not carefully advised by the patient about each medicine being taken///the doctor cannot realize that his prescription will be ineffective. What can we do to help customers use our medicines for their good? [3]

[1 Minute at 110]

329 Dear Mr. Walbers: Thank you for contacting my patient, Frank Collins, to warn him about the two medications he was taking. I was able to change/his prescription so that he can continue taking his allergy medicine while taking this prescription. It is not an unusual thing for patients// to forget or neglect to tell their doctors about all the medicines they take. In most cases the over-the-counter medications which people choose///for themselves are the ones they most often forget to mention. If not used properly, over-the-counter drugs can be very dangerous. Sincerely yours, [4] [380]

Reading and Writing Practice

330

ep·i·dem·ic

nonr

ton·sil·li·tis

conj

re·spi·ra·to·ry

in·flam·ma·tion

if

dis·cour·age

[138]

331

ap

con·sul·tant

early

intro

neu·ri·tis

phy·si·cian

ar·thri·tis

nonr

intro

de·te·ri·o·ra·tion

ad·verse

[187]

332

ap

man·u·fac·tur·ers'

conj

as

ap·pen·di·ci·tis

ab·dom·i·nal

di·ag·no·sis

or·gan·i·cal·ly

intro

if

[146]

333

lar·yn·gi·tis

intro

when

bron·chi·tis

conj

ad·vice

intro

re·frain

[134]

334

nonr

X rays

draw·er

conj

intro

re·cu·per·at·ing

when

[131]

Shorthand Vocabulary Builder

335 WORD ENDINGS

-tition, -tation, Etc.

1

-ther

2

-cal, -cle

3

-gram

4

1 Station, condition, termination, institution, hesitation, permission, admission.
2 Gather, together, weather, either, bother, rather, neither, other.
3 Critical, chemical, political, typically, surgical, article, particle.
4 Diagram, monogram, programmed, telegram, cablegram.

Building Transcription Skills

336 TRANSCRIPTION TYPING

11

23

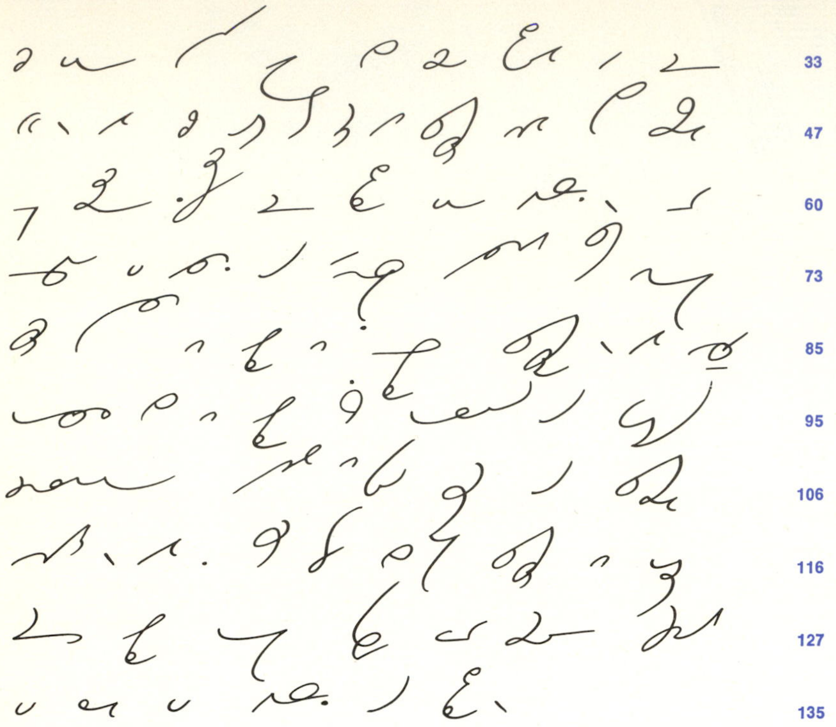

337 **Business Vocabulary Builder**

directive An order.

cardiogram The curve traced by a cardiograph, a machine which is used to record the movements of the heart.

rankles Embitters; irritates.

Stair-Step Dictation

338 **PREVIEW**

[339]

[340]

[341]

339 Diseases, arteries, prevented, diet, infants, discourage, obese, exercise.

340 Dangerous, cafeteria, choked, cage, lungs, windpipe, demonstrate.

341 Developing, blindness, glaucoma, eyeball, thicken, impaired.

LETTERS

339 To the Employees: Dr. Ann Stark has reported that many diseases of the heart and arteries can be[1] prevented if good foods are given to children when they are young. Good diet training should be started by parents.[2] Infants should be fed foods which contain less salt and less fat to discourage the development of high blood pressure.[3] Children must be taught to eat foods which have a low sugar content so that they will not become obese. Exercise[4] must be encouraged to control weight. The time to prevent heart diseases is when the body is young, not in middle[5] age. Follow these same good rules. Control your weight and diet, and your middle-aged body will fight heart attacks.[6]

340 Dear Mr. Holland: A dangerous accident happened last week in the company cafeteria; one of[7] our employees choked on a piece of meat. All the members of your food staff must be taught the following method to assist[8] any person who gets a piece of food caught in the throat. Stand behind the victim and put your arms around the[9] body under the rib cage. Brace your body and squeeze the victim sharply forcing air from the lungs. This sudden pressure[10] should force the food out of the windpipe. My staff in the medical department will demonstrate this simple but[11] effective method to all the members of your food staff. It is wise to have your members attend. Cordially yours,[12]

341 Dear Mr. Hunt: Our research station is developing new ways to prevent blindness. Glaucoma is the second[13] leading cause of blindness. This disease causes high pressure in the eye because small screenlike filters in the eyeball[14] thicken and the fluid in the eye cannot flow from the eyeball. If the pressure gets too high, the eye will be damaged[15] and vision impaired. This year our company has introduced a device which can be used by trained people, not[16] just doctors, to detect glaucoma in its early stages. When the disease is found early, the medication[17] can be started before it robs the victims of their sight. Drops can halt the development of glaucoma. Cordially yours,[18] [360]

Reading and Writing Practice

342

ap

In·sti·tu·tion

di·vi·sion

year·ly check·ups

nonr

intro

da·ta

intro

di·rec·tive

[214]

343

intro

ad·vised

di·ges·tive

intro

af·fect·ed

im·bal·ance

[95]

344

intro

ap

spe·cial·ist

car·dio·gram

days'

conj

pace·mak·er

intro

[130]

345

con·trib·ute

prac·ti·tion·ers

ran·kles

ap

di·ag·nos·ing

[132]

346

ter·mi·na·tion

hus·band

conj

com·pe·tent·ly

par

[143]

LESSON 38

Shorthand Vocabulary Builder

347 BRIEF-FORM POWER

1 Under, understate, undernourished, understood, misunderstood, underwriter, undertake.
2 Suggest, suggestion, suggestive, suggestively, suggests, suggested.
3 Worth, worthwhile, worthy, worthless, worthlessness, worthiness, noteworthy.
4 Upon, thereupon, whereupon; street, streets; envelope, envelopes, envelopment.

348 CITIES

-boro, -borough

Glassboro, Goldsboro, Hillsboro, Queensborough, Marlborough.

Building Transcription Skills

349 PUNCTUATION PRACTICE ■ ; no conjunction

Use a semicolon between two closely related independent clauses when the conjunction is omitted.

The new electronic watches contain an integrated circuit; this circuit regulates the flow of power with great precision.

To assist in reading, use a semicolon between two independent clauses when a transitional word *(however, yet, therefore, frequently)* separates the two clauses.

An integrated circuit for a watch is nearly invisible; however, it contains 1,300 miniature transistors.

Each time the semicolon occurs in the Reading and Writing Practice, it will be indicated thus in the shorthand: nc (;)

■ **; series**

When one or more items in a series already contain commas, use a semicolon to separate the items in the series.

All the advertising for the new product will be created by Harry Dunlop from Seattle, Washington; Lois Call from Chicago, Illinois; and Preston Fox from Baltimore, Maryland.

When the semicolon is used in this situation in the Reading and Writing Practice, it will be indicated this way in the shorthand: ser (;)

350 Business Vocabulary Builder

sick leave Time off from work with pay allowed because of illness.

DOA Dead on arrival.

Progressive Dictation [80–110]

351 PREVIEW

[352]

[353]

[354]

[355]

352 Inefficient, dejected, burdensome, fortunate, productive, pleasant.

353 Insomnia, locate, cycle, sleeplessness, removed, cured.

354 Burning, sensations, circulation, disorders, allergic, investigate, safety.

355 Supervisors, respiratory, packaging, conclusion, ink, gloves.

LETTERS

[1 Minute at 80]

352 Dear Mr. Fault: Some people in excellent health need eight hours of sleep each night. Less than eight hours of sleep for/a few nights can make some people inefficient and dejected. For them work becomes a burdensome chore even//though they usually consider their work pleasant. Other people are more fortunate and can be productive and///pleasant after only five hours of sleep each night. The latter are fortunate. Very sincerely yours, [1]

[1 Minute at 90]

353 Dear Ms. Sanders: Sometimes the causes of insomnia are difficult to locate. Under your doctor's direction, you may/ benefit from medication which will help you sleep. By using this medication, the cycle of sleeplessness may be removed;//then the insomnia will be cured. You must not try to prescribe a medication for yourself to cure insomnia. More///harm than good will be done. Talk with your family doctor about your insomnia. He will help you solve your problem. Cordially, [2]

[1 Minute at 100]

354 Dear Ralph: Thank you for calling my attention to Joseph Guilford. I do not believe the burning sensations in his feet are caused by the shoes/the company issued. Burning feet can be caused by circulation or nerve disorders or other illnesses. He may find that the burning//sensations are caused by an allergic reaction to the material in the stockings he wears. Please recommend that Mr. Guilford see///his family doctor, who will investigate the problem. We cannot permit a mill worker to enter the mill without safety shoes. Cordially, [3]

[1 Minute at 110]

355 To the Supervisors: It has been brought to our attention that respiratory ailments have increased in the printing and packaging sections within/the last six months. After working with Ellen Walters from printing and Thomas Cain from packaging, we have come to the conclusion that a new chemical in//the ink has caused the allergic reaction in some of the workers. Miss Walters successfully overcame her breathing difficulty by wearing a/// mask while she is on the job. The mask has a washable filter which Miss Walters replaces each day. Mr. Cain not only wears the mask but also wears gloves. [4] [380]

Reading and Writing Practice

356

ap

de·fi·cien·cy

intro

nc

ser

weight

un·der·nour·ished

doc·tor's

co·work·ers

conj

worth·while

[157]

coun·ter

cus·tom·ary

three-week *hyphenated before noun*

[147

357

three-month *hyphenated before noun*

ap·pen·di·ci·tis

358

Weiss's

ap

nc ; intro ,

DOA

conj ,

ac·cess

any·one

[145]

359

med·i·ca·tion

ap ,

ar·thri·tis

Transcribe:
1:30 p.m.

worth·while

[113]

360

Un·der·writ·ers

24-page
hyphenated before noun

ap ,

Re·spi·ra·to·ry

,

[58]

LESSON

Shorthand Vocabulary Builder

361 WORD-BUILDING PRINCIPLES

Days

1

Months

2

Dit, Det

3

Tem

4

1 Monday, Wednesday, Friday, Thursday, Tuesday, Sunday, Saturday.

2 January, March, May, July, September, November, February, April, June, August, October, December.

3 Audit, credit, credited, debt, detail, editor, editorial, ditto, detach, determine, deter, detect.

4 Item, itemized, system, temper, contemplate, tempest, temptation, temperature, temperament, temple, attempt.

Building Transcription Skills

362 TRANSCRIPTION TYPING

10
22
32
40
52
63
75
86
99
110
121
128

363 Business Vocabulary Builder

itemized Listed; set down unit by unit.

visible files Files designed or constructed to keep important parts or information in view.

criteria (*plural*) Standards or rules on which a decision can be based.

Stair-Step Dictation

364 PREVIEW

[365]

[366]

[367]

365 Insomnia, ailments, discomfort, obvious, asleep, soundly, stuffy, vanishes.

366 Ulcer, relaxed, painful, stressful, restrict, spicy, acid.

367 Fever, subsided, dosage, antibiotics, liquids, juice, broth, causative.

LETTERS

365 Dear Mrs. Glass: Insomnia is a serious problem. Many people suffer from it simply because they[1] have ailments which cause pain or discomfort. In this case the discomfort may waken them so often that their rest is[2] disturbed. Other forms of insomnia are caused by less obvious reasons. Some people fall asleep quickly only[3] to awaken early and find they cannot get back to sleep. Others cannot fall asleep for a long time after[4] retiring; then they sleep soundly. The reasons may be worry, a stuffy or noisy room, or bed clothing[5] which is too heavy. After careful investigation, if the cause is discovered, insomnia vanishes. Sincerely,[6]

366 Dear Ms. Stills: Since all your reports indicate that your ulcer is healing, let us review all the steps you can follow[7] to assure continued progress. First, there is no reason why you should not work each day, but stay relaxed. Your ulcer[8] will become painful again if you fall into stressful patterns of behavior. Constanty examine your[9] eating habits. A rigid diet is not necessary, but restrict your intake of spicy foods. Eat something[10] every two hours so that the acid secreted in the stomach will have something to work on other than the stomach[11] lining. Unfortunately, one attack will not give you immunity. Continue your good habits. Yours truly,[12]

367 Dear Mr. Wright: You must stay home and in bed for several days after the fever has subsided. The full dosage[13] of antibiotics must also be continued. If you do not continue these procedures, the disease is[14] likely to recur. The second time the disease strikes, the antibiotic may be less effective. Please do not[15] allow friends to visit in your room because the disease is contagious. Although your appetite will be small,[16] liquids are important for fast recovery. Drink as much fruit juice, beef broth, or water as possible. I am[17] delighted that we discovered the causative germ and quickly prescribed the correct antibiotic. Sincerely yours,[18] [360]

Reading and Writing Practice

368

tem·per·a·ture

intro

ad·verse·ly

Transcribe:
10 o'clock

if

yield

temp·ta·tion

[154]

369

ap

intro

ap

em·ploy·ees'

au·dit

if

form

vis·i·ble

cri·te·ria

conj

par

[184]

370

Per·son·nel

three-week
hyphenated before noun

ap

ap

intro

if

emer·gen·cy

conj

ex·press·ly

[155]

371

ap

intro

nonr

ap

sus·pect·ed

as

ap

ap

when

[107]

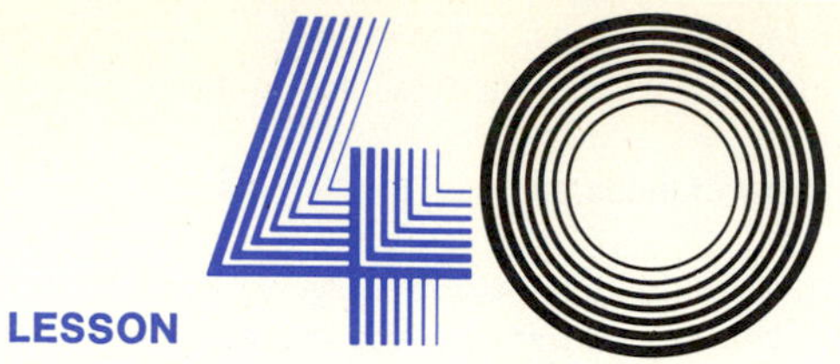

LESSON 40

Shorthand Vocabulary Builder

372 PHRASING FOR SPEED

Omission of Words

These

Glad

Many

You

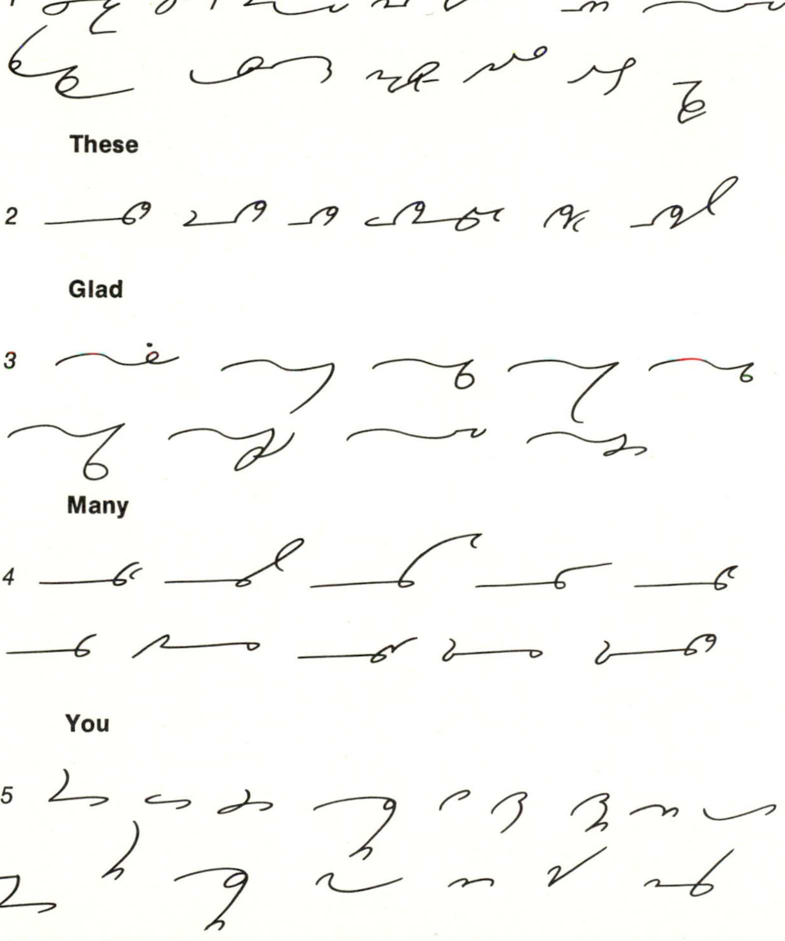

1 I am of the opinion, out of the question, son-in-law, one of the, up and down, in the world, glad to know, bill of sale, line of goods, once or twice, two or three, three or four, in the past.

2 Many of these, some of these, in these, on these matters, these things, in these days.

3 Glad to hear, glad to have, glad to say, glad to be, glad to see, glad to be able, glad to find, glad to know, glad to send you.

4 Many things, many days, many times, many of them, many of those, many of the, too many, many other, so many, so many of these.

5 From you, on you, send you, give you, thank you, thank you for, thank you for your, can you, will you, inform you, have you, gave you, you will, you can, you should, you made.

Building Transcription Skills

373 Business Vocabulary Builder

social security A measure by which the federal government provides economic aid to unemployed persons who are disabled or old. It is financed by assessment of employers and employees.

follow-up A system of pursuing an initial effort by supplementary action.

Reading and Writing Practice

374

ap·pli·ca·tion

rec·ords

ap ap

ac·ci·dent

ap

ap conj

[150]

ex·pect

if

375

ap

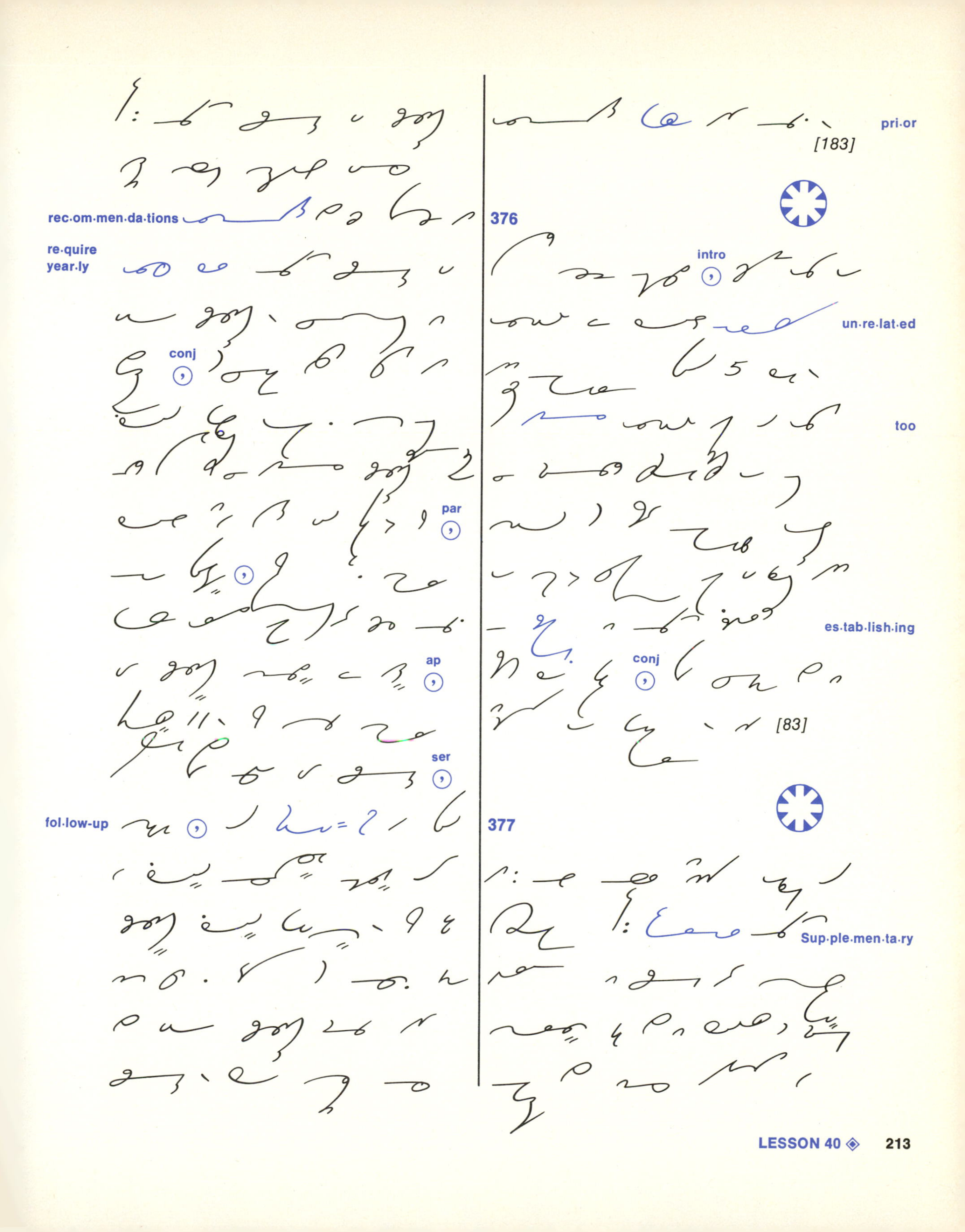

rec·om·men·da·tions

re·quire

year·ly

conj

par

ap

ser

fol·low-up

pri·or

[183]

376

intro

un·re·lat·ed

too

es·tab·lish·ing

conj

[83]

377

Sup·ple·men·ta·ry

med·i·ca·tion

par

[72]

Transcription Speed Building

378

9

19

30

43

55

66

77

90

102

114

125

137

149

158

169

180

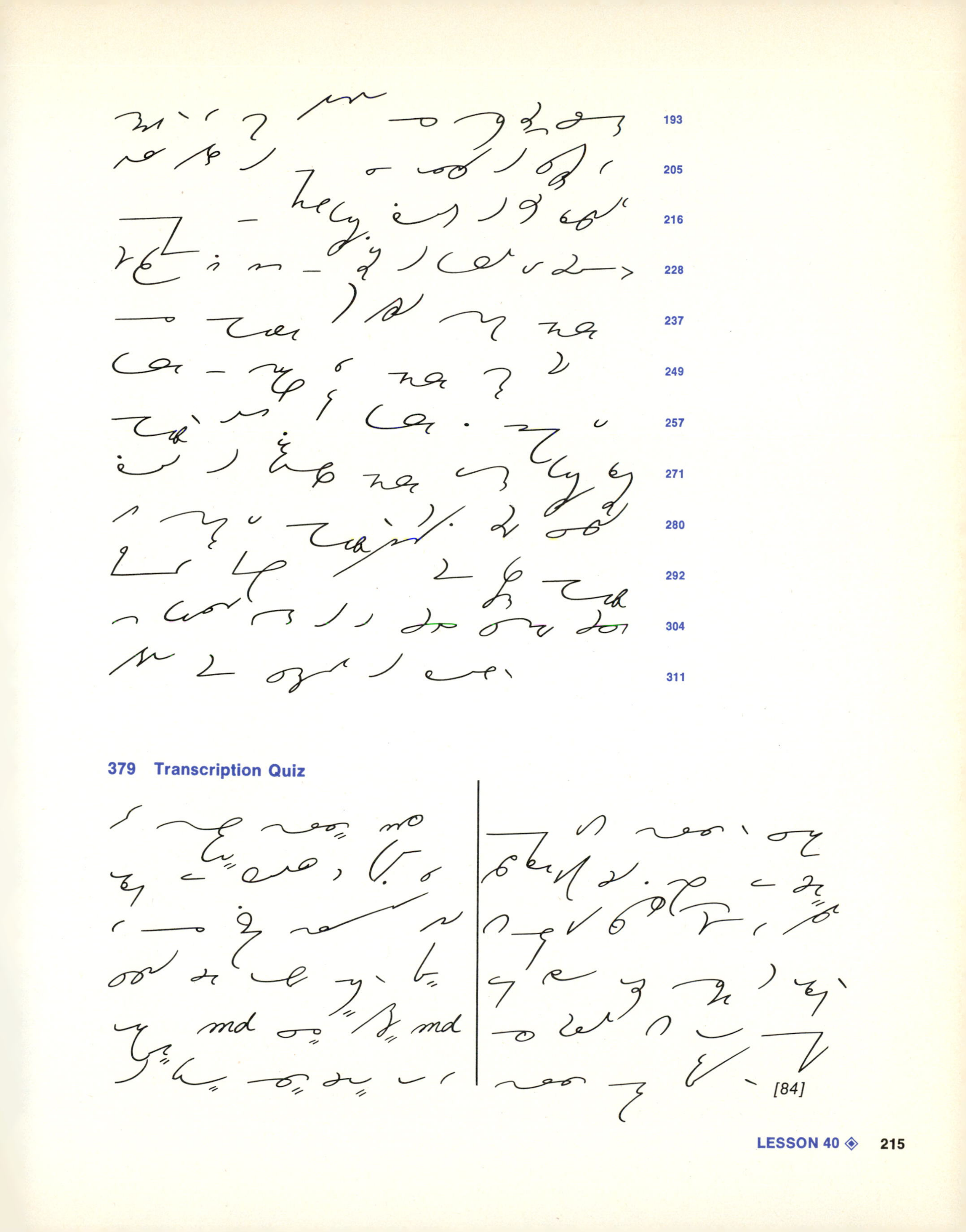

193
205
216
228
237
249
257
271
280
292
304
311

379 Transcription Quiz

[84]

Unit 9

ADVERTISING

If you are fashion-minded, you are going to enjoy your job as secretary to Myra Knox, head of the Advertising Department at Fashion World, a woman's specialty shop with branches in nearby college towns and shopping centers. The advertising staff either originates its own advertising materials or uses those supplied by its manufacturers. Fashion World advertises in high-fashion magazines, in newspapers, and even in college yearbooks. It publishes advertising brochures either to be mailed along with monthly bills or to be picked up in the shops. It advertises extensively on the radio and on television.

Most of the advertising for Fashion World creates an image of an exclusive shop having snob appeal. Miss Knox herself is rather a specialist in producing fashion shows and believes that they are very productive of sales. The Advertising Department is constantly being asked to donate newspaper space for advertisements sponsoring community projects (institutional advertising) at the expense of fashion advertising. It also receives many requests for prizes and individual gifts to be distributed at benefit parties.

LESSON 

Shorthand Vocabulary Builder

380 WORD FAMILIES

-ize

-ise

-book

-iety

1 Authorize, economize, summarize, criticize, apologize, sympathize.

2 Advise, comprise, enterprise, advertise, merchandise, supervised, surprise, surprisingly.

3 Book, textbook, handbook, bankbook, notebook, yearbook, passbook.

4 Anxiety, society, notoriety, variety, sobriety, propriety.

Building Transcription Skills

381 PUNCTUATION PRACTICE ■ " " direct quotation

Use quotation marks at the beginning and end of a direct quotation; that is, the exact words spoken or written by a person.

"Come to the party," Jane said, "and you will meet my cousin."

Jane said if we go to the party we will meet her cousin. (This is an example of an indirect quotation, which presents the thought of the speaker's comment, not the exact words.)

■ **, introducing short quote**

Short quotations are introduced by a comma.

A small handwritten sign said, "Be my guest."

Each time this use of the comma occurs in the Reading and Writing Practice, it will be indicated in the shorthand this way: isq (,)

■ **, inside quote**

■ **. inside quote**

■ **? inside quote**

Always place the comma and period inside the closing quotation mark.

"When the tide comes in," Harrison said, "the waves are rougher."

The question mark is placed inside the ending quotation mark if the direct quotation is a question. If the entire sentence is a question, the question mark is placed outside the ending quotation mark.

"Why can't I go to the races?" the little boy asked his dad.

but

Why did he say, "Where is the trapdoor"?

Semicolons and colons are always placed outside the ending quotation mark.

When punctuation is placed inside quotation marks in the Reading and Writing Practice, it will be indicated in the following ways: iq (,) iq (.) iq (?)

382 Business Vocabulary Builder

logotype A piece of type consisting of two or more elements cast in one piece.

dummy A layout of text and illustrations to guide the printer.

mats Sheets of paper material or wood fibers on which are recorded the impressions of type or drawing cuts for printing.

Progressive Dictation [80–110]

383 PREVIEW

[384]

[385]

[386]

[387]

384 Economizing, executive, criticized, fiercest, competition, weapon, sobriety, respectfully.

385 Handbags, requirements, sympathize, anxiety, after-Thanksgiving.

386 Variety, society, sketches, consider, November, limitations, reducing.

387 Publishers, yearbook, editor, representative, Glassboro, within, ideas, producing.

LETTERS

[1 Minute at 80]

384 To: Morris Brooks, President Subject: Economizing I can understand why the executive committee/criticized our expanded advertising budget. I am sure they realize, though, that it takes money to make//money. We are going to face the fiercest competition we have ever known, and our best weapon is expanded///advertising. With great sobriety I respectfully ask that the committee authorize the budget. [1]

[1 Minute at 90]

385 To: Henry Milstead, Sales Manager Subject: Special Promotion of Handbags Because of the need to economize under/our new budget requirements, I cannot authorize the advertising you requested in *Vogue* magazine. Although I//sympathize with you in your anxiety about moving this merchandise, you must realize my position. May I suggest that///you consider placing two after-Thanksgiving ads in *Women Today.* The sales from such ads last year were very successful. [2]

[1 Minute at 100]

386 To: Ann Crans, Art Department We have just received a variety of designer dresses suitable for the evenings when society/appears at gala holiday events. Will you please bring several sketches of these Third Floor dresses to my office at 11 o'clock//Thursday so that we can consider them for use in advertising this merchandise in the *Sunday///News* for November 29. Because of budget limitations, we are reducing these ads to a half page. [3]

[1 Minute at 110]

387 Dear Ms. Blanchard: We are publishers of textbooks, handbooks, and notebooks used widely in your college. We should also like to become the publisher of the/college yearbook for which you have recently been named editor. The enclosed booklet summarizes the information about yearbooks we have printed and//includes a list of colleges and high schools whose yearbooks we published last year. Our sales representative in your area will be in Glassboro within///the next two weeks. Would it be possible for you to meet with him to discuss the many ideas we have for producing your college yearbook? Yours truly, [4] [380]

Reading and Writing Practice

388

year·book

ac·cede

full-page hyphenated before noun

par

ex·pen·di·tures

logo·type

pre·ced·ed

ap

[160]

389

ap

isq

Transcribe: 23 percent

iq

col·le·giate

iq

so·ci·ety

eval·u·a·tion

ap

if

par

[167]

390

full-page hyphenated before noun

so·lic·it·ing

va·ri·ety

if

dum·my

co·op·er·ate
fund-rais·ing
hyphenated before noun

[147]

391

half-page
two-col·umn
hyphenated before noun

ap

ap ser ap

ap ap

ap ap

buy·er

cus·tom·ers

ser if

intro

[154]

Shorthand Vocabulary Builder

392 WORD BEGINNINGS

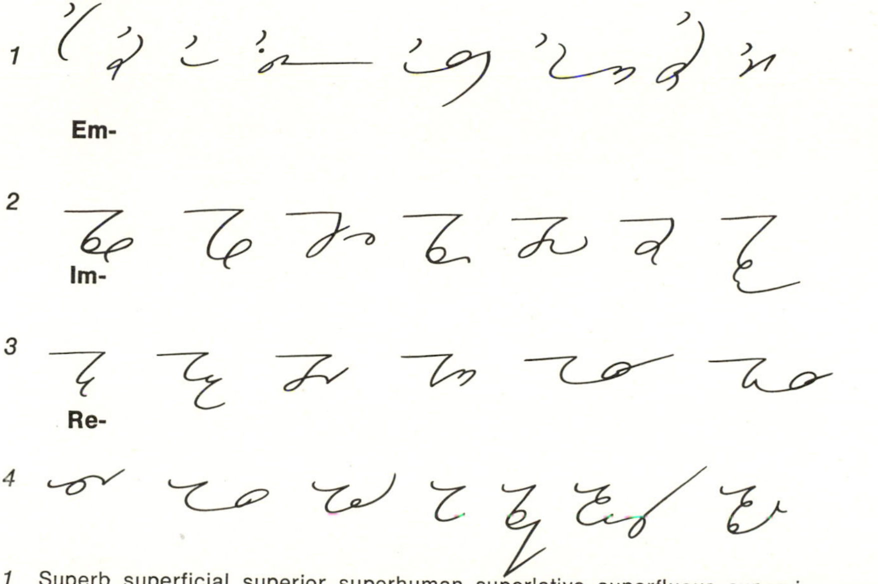

1 Superb, superficial, superior, superhuman, superlative, superfluous, supervise, superstition.
2 Embarrass, embrace, emphatically, embark, empowered, emphasis, embezzle.
3 Impose, improper, impact, impetuous, implied, impolite.
4 React, reply, reprint, represent, recharged, reciprocated, recipients.

Building Transcription Skills

393 TRANSCRIPTION TYPING

10

19

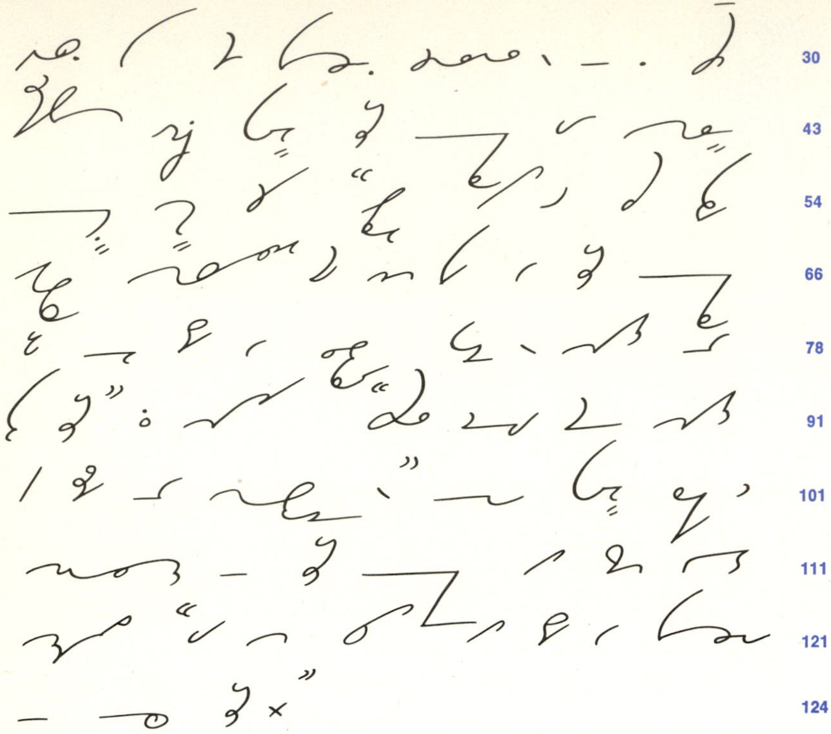

394 Business Vocabulary Builder

media (*plural*) Means of communication.

direct-mail advertising Fliers, catalogs, brochures, sales letters, and similar literature sent by mail to the address of potential buyers.

Stair-Step Dictation

395 PREVIEW

[396]

[397]

[398]

396 Disturbing, curtailed, reconsider, priorities, tastefully, suggested.

397 Superb, illustrate, distinctive, imposition, salon, mink, Persian.

398 Anchor, impolite, impetuously, justified, recoil, superhuman.

LETTERS

396 To the Staff: Subject: Revision of Plans for National Magazine Advertising After receiving the[1] disturbing word that our advertising budget for next year has been seriously curtailed, we must be more selective[2] in our advertising and reconsider our priorities. It is my impression that we should embark on[3] more advertising in popular women's magazines whose rates are much higher. Market surveys have proved that our[4] merchandise appeals to the young working woman who must dress tastefully on a limited budget rather than[5] to the so-called "trend setter." This idea is suggested so that you can react to it at our regular staff meeting.[6]

397 To: Ann Crans, Art Department Subject: Ad in the *Sunday News* on November 29 Your sketches were superb.[7] The models gave the impression that they were really at a society function, and at the same time you were[8] able to illustrate the distinctive imprint of the individual designer. I am sure that you will[9] receive this same reaction from many others. Would it be an imposition, Ann, to ask you to make the sketches[10] for a similar ad for fur coats to be run on Sunday, December 12? The fur salon has just received[11] a shipment of mink and Persian lamb coats and matching hats that merits our best promotional efforts.[12]

398 Dear Ken: I emphatically agree with you in criticizing our handling of the Anchor Society's[13] institutional advertising. Being impolite and acting impetuously are never justified[14] in a business relationship. I recoil just as you do when our corporate image is damaged by such[15] behavior. We would be superhuman if we did not make a mistake occasionally, but this one was[16] inexcusable. Thank you for telling us the circumstances. I have just telephoned Brother William to try to explain[17] what happened and to offer our sincere apologies. I have also taken steps within the Department[18] to see that such a situation does not recur. Please do your best to smooth things over. Cordially yours,[19] [380]

Reading and Writing Practice

399

re·cip·ro·cate

me·dia

par

conj

met·ro·pol·i·tan

ser

di·rect-mail hyphenated before noun

[286]

em·phat·i·cal·ly

fo·cus

par

intro

bro·chures

in·dis·pens·able
day-to-day
hyphenated before noun

par

400

if

tear

nonr

ven·ture

ap ser ap ser

ap intro

su·per·la·tives

[133]

401

su·pe·ri·or

line

conj

re·sponse

intro

par

ex·per·i·ment

re·cast

[149]

402

nonr

con·trib·ut·ed

re·cip·i·ents

par

[138]

Shorthand Vocabulary Builder

403 BRIEF-FORM POWER

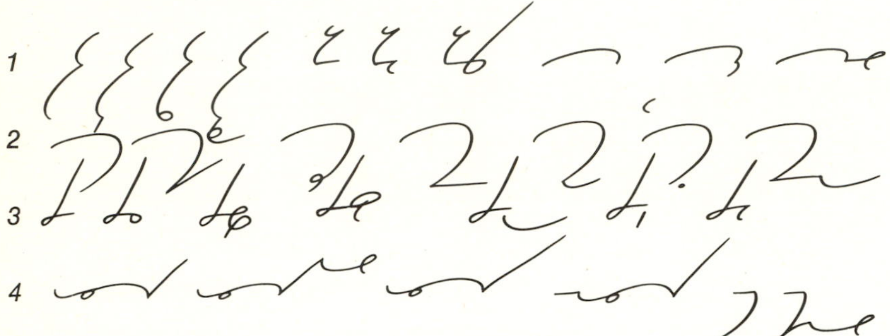

1 Public, publish-publication, publicly, publisher; opinion, opinions, opinionated; good, goods, goodness.

2 Govern, governed, governess, government, governor, self-governing, governmental.

3 General, generally, generalization, generalize, generality, generalship, generals.

4 Regard, regardless, regarded, unregarded; never, nevertheless.

404 CITIES

-wood

Farmwood, Oakwood, Elwood City, Plainswoods, Elmwood.

Building Transcription Skills

405 PUNCTUATION PRACTICE ■ the apostrophe

Singular Nouns To form a singular possessive, use an apostrophe and *s.*

my mother's package *Helen's job* *the committee's report* *the man's shirt*

Plural Nouns To form a plural possessive, form the plural of the noun first, then add an apostrophe or an apostrophe and *s*, depending on the plural form of the noun.

Singular	Plural	Plural Possessive
runner	*runners*	*runners' speeds*
boy	*boys*	*boys' dogs*
Jones	*Joneses*	*Joneses' house*
Walker	*Walkers*	*Walkers' yard*
woman	*women*	*women's shoes*
alumnus	*alumni*	*alumni's tickets*

Compound Nouns Use an apostrophe and *s* after the last unit of a compound noun to show possession.

brother-in-law's home *district attorney's car*

Inanimate Nouns In most cases the apostrophe and *s* should not be used with nouns referring to inanimate objects.

tire of the bicycle *color of the wall* *terms of the will* *hinges of the door*

Time and Measurement The apostrophe and *s* are used with some common phrases expressing time and measurement.

an hour's work *a dollar's worth* *two weeks' vacation* *New Year's resolutions*

406 **Business Vocabulary Builder**

fashion publicist A person or agent who specializes in bringing to the attention of the public news about fashions.

public relations Activities employed to promote a favorable relationship with the public.

Progressive Dictation [90–120]

407 **PREVIEW**

[408]

[409]

[410]

[411]

408 Accepted, invitation, portable, promenade, runway, angle.

409 Institutional, Oakwood, donation, semipublic, rotate, regardless.

410 Publicity, Paris, Kansas City, governed, remembered, Yours very cordially.

411 Board of governors, metropolitan, awards, opinionated, likelihood.

LETTERS

[1 Minute at 90]

408 Dear Mr. Elwood: We have accepted the invitation of Mrs. Harold Ames to hold a fashion show at your country club/next Thursday afternoon at 12:30. Mrs. Ames told us that you would set up a portable stage on which our models can//promenade. We generally also like to have a runway near the tables so that all luncheon guests can see the clothes being displayed///from every angle. Will it be possible to build this runway? If not, please let me know. Very cordially yours, [1]

[1 Minute at 100]

409 Gentlemen: We have received your request that we run an institutional advertisement preceding the annual drive of the Oakwood/Community Chest as our donation to the campaign. Although we feel that an organization such as ours has a semipublic//responsibility, we must rotate the space allotted for institutional advertising among the many organizations that///request it. Regardless of our great concern for the success of your drive, we must, however, say no this year. Very cordially yours, [2]

[1 Minute at 110]

410 Dear Mrs. Ames: Plans for the spring fashion show are falling into place as I indicated in our telephone conversation. I have asked Mr. Elwood/about building the runway. Your plans for publicity sound good. My only suggestion is that you stress that we shall be showing ten original//designer dresses from the Paris collections and that we are the only store in the Kansas City area where they are available. Just let me///know in what ways I can be helpful. I will be governed by your wishes in making this fashion show one to be remembered. Yours very cordially, [3]

[1 Minute at 120]

411 Dear George: I plan to attend the meeting of the Board of Governors of the Metropolitan Advertising Club next Thursday at 6 o'clock. Yes, I can also meet/with the awards committee at 5 o'clock to select the member who has done most for the club as its publicist during the past year. I am afraid that you may feel//that I was rather opinionated about this nomination last year because I objected to the choice of a government employee rather than a professional advertising person. Nevertheless, I would like///to stay on the committee this year, for there is no likelihood that the same problem will arise again. Maybe we can recommend a recipient. Cordially yours, [4] [420]

Reading and Writing Practice

412

su·perb

El·wood's

Puc·ci

semi·pub·lic

pub·lic·i·ty

qual·i·ty

[136]

413

bro·chure

di·rect-mail *hyphenated before noun*

conj

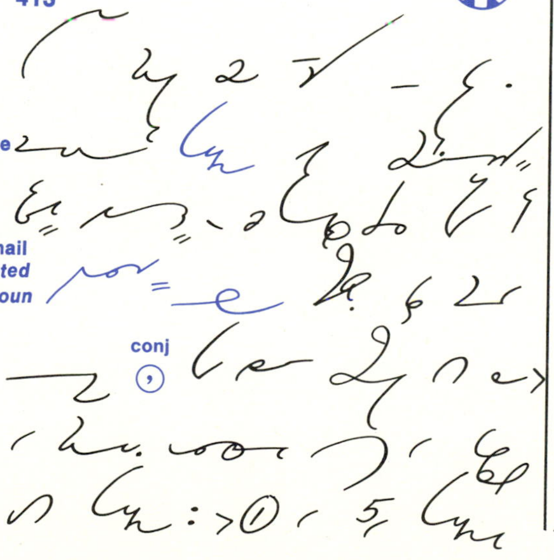

stuff·ers

mul·ti·ple

ser

piece

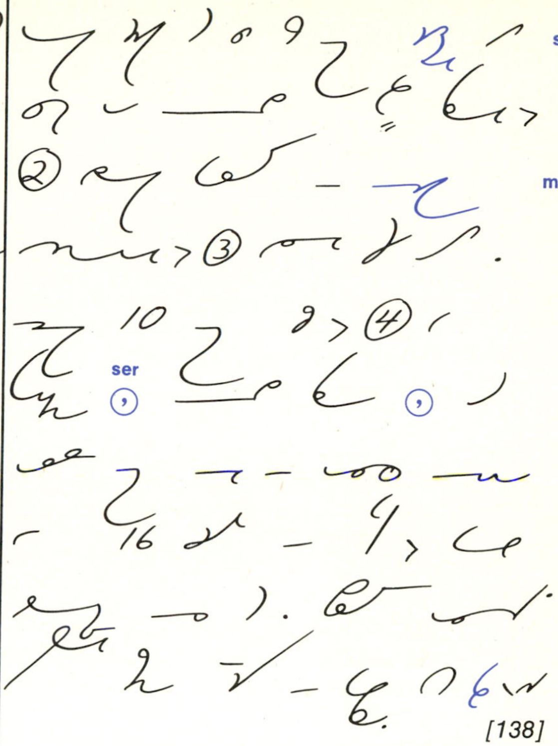

[138]

414

ap

en·tranced

Fleet·wood's

ap

ap

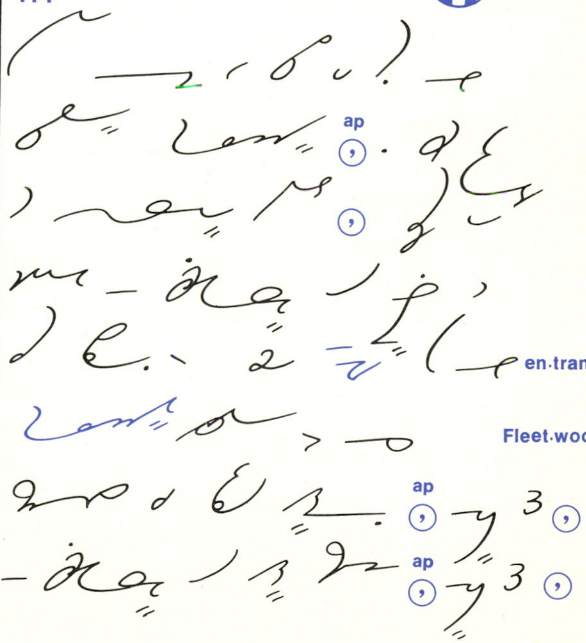

Transcribe:
11 o'clock
4 o'clock

conj

man·ne·quins

conj

pro·ceed

[167]

415

Clar·i·on
em·pow·ered

ser

nev·er·the·less
intro

nonr

intro

[110]

416

col·lege-bound
hyphenated
before noun

par

[74]

LESSON

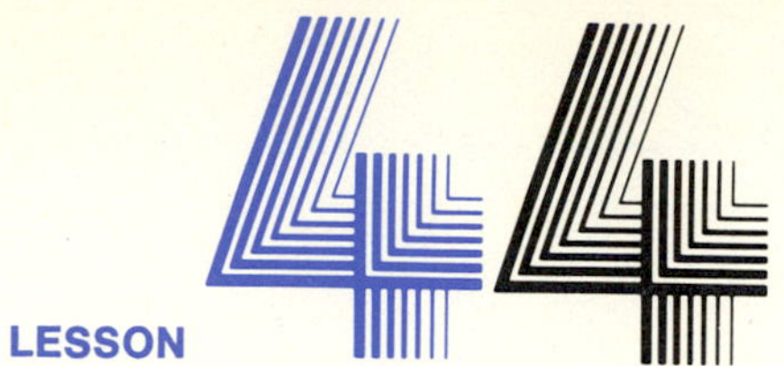

Shorthand Vocabulary Builder

417 WORD-BUILDING PRINCIPLES

I and a Following Vowel

Ĭa, Ēa

O on Its Side

Abbreviated Words

1 Flier, prior, diamond, quietly, science, diagnose.

2 Substantiate, depreciate, brilliant, comedian, area, create, creative.

3 Own, home, tone, stones, blown, moan, known, roam.

4 Delinquent, equivalent, memorandum, anniversary, reluctant-reluctance, convenient-convenience.

Building Transcription Skills

418 TRANSCRIPTION TYPING

14

26

39

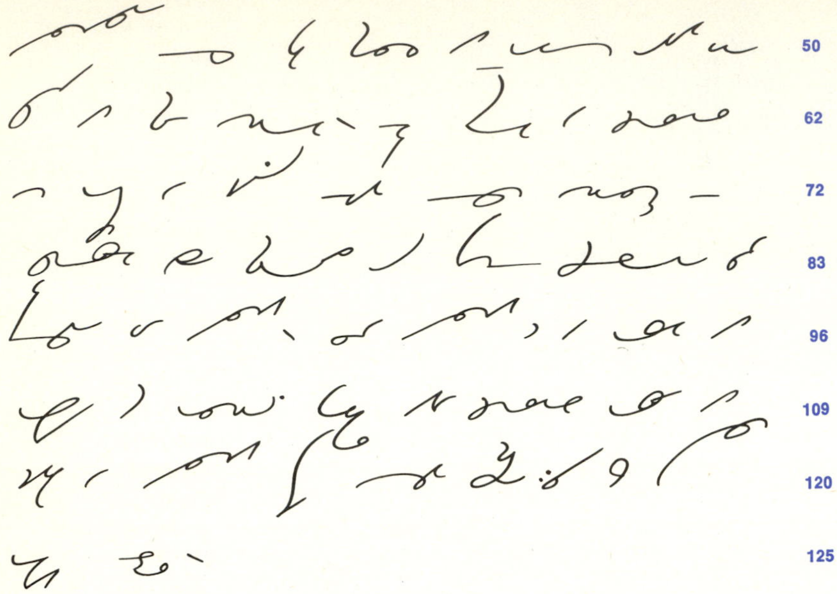

419 Business Vocabulary Builder

fliers Circulars, usually a single sheet, publicizing a product or an event and intended for mass distribution.

cassettes Cases containing ruled magnetic tape or photographic film.

Stair-Step Dictation

420 PREVIEW

[421]

[422]

[423]

421 Nomenclature, simulated, brilliance, classifying, diameter.

422 Magic, comedian, omelets, stuffers, incurring, handouts.

423 Violet, copywriters, onset, acquisition, swamped, resignation.

LETTERS

421 To: Mr. Tony Pryor Subject: Correct Nomenclature of Simulated Precious Stones I have received samples[1] of the new line and am impressed with the brilliance of the stones, especially the diamonds, and with their[2] radiation of light rays. Prior to planning the advertising campaign, though, I should like to verify the[3] information I have received. My own opinion is that a mistake has been made in nomenclature used in[4] classifying two of the six stones. Will you please verify the names of each one with a specialist before we proceed.[5] I should also like to have complete information about the diameter of the stones so that this detail[6] can be included in the advertising. I should appreciate your reply by next Thursday if possible.[7]

422 To: Phillip Holmes, Sales Manager Subject: Book Promotion Fliers I received a memorandum today from the[8] publishers saying that they have just produced a new one-page flier describing each of four new books which are now[9] available in our book department. The books are *Science Magic, My Life as a Comedian, How to Cook*[10] *Omelets,* and *Owning Your Own Home.* If you want to enclose them as envelope stuffers with bills this month, please send me a[11] memorandum specifying the number you need. If you think there is a possibility of incurring[12] additional postage if we do this, let me know how many fliers you would like for handouts in the book[13] department and we will forget the enclosures. When I have your reply, I will notify the publisher of our needs.[14]

423 To: William Hoenig, Personnel Department Subject: Replacement for Violet Johnson We lost one of our most[15] brilliant copywriters, Violet Johnson, just at the onset of our busy season. I know that we have been[16] told that we are to make no replacements before the first of the year. However, you will undoubtedly appreciate[17] the seriousness of our personnel problem just as we are getting the advertising underway[18] following the acquisition of Homelovers' Furniture Company. We are literally swamped with work. Will[19] it be possible for us quietly to replace Miss Johnson immediately without any fanfare? I[20] am enclosing a memorandum that Mary Otis, chief copywriter, sent me when she learned of Violet's[21] resignation. It will substantiate my assessment of the situation. I hope you can give us some relief.[22] [440]

Reading and Writing Practice

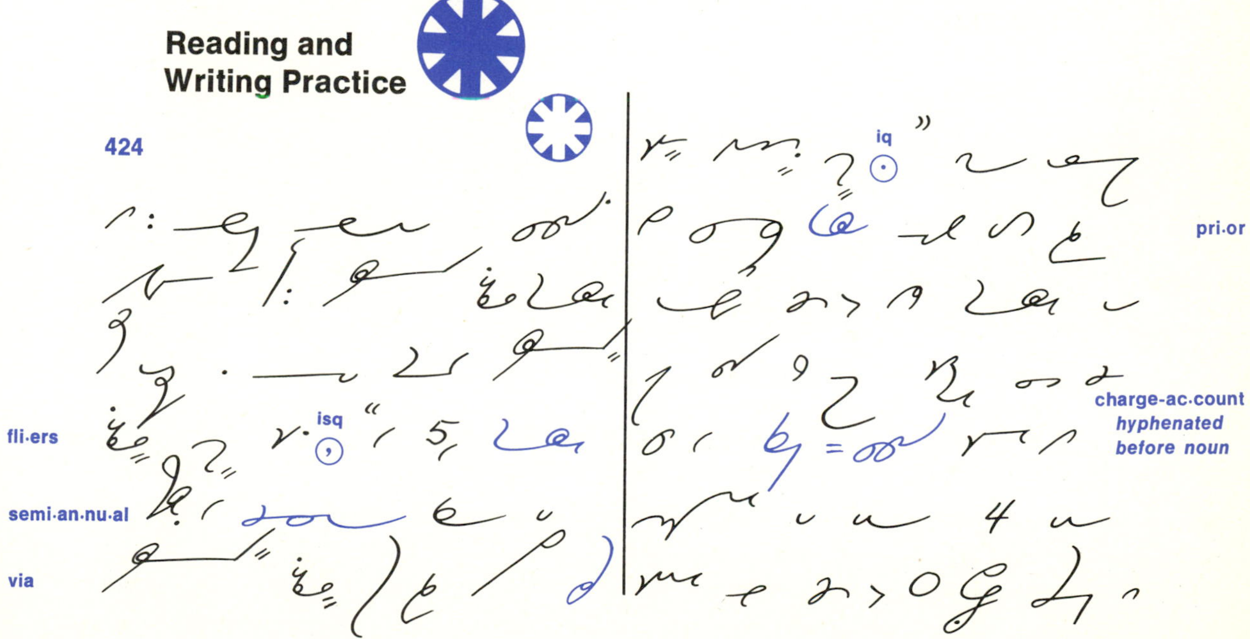

co·or·di·nate

on·go·ing

con·sol·i·dat·ing

[152]

425

ap

over·buy·ing

blaz·ers

ser

ap

conj

sur·plus

intro

al·ready

full-page *hyphenated before noun*

one-page *hyphenated before noun*

cas·settes

intro

po·ten·tial

de·pre·ci·ates

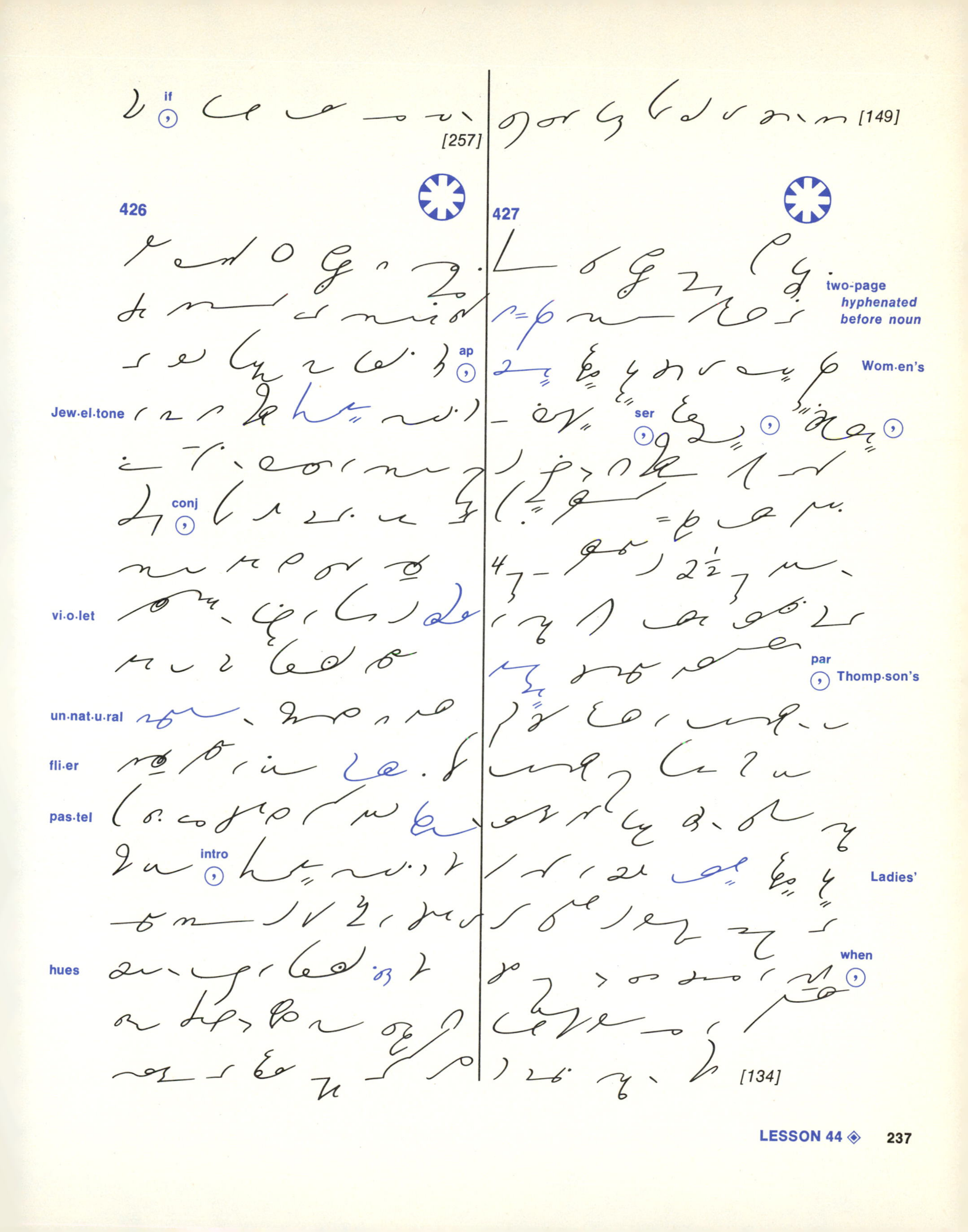

if

[257]

[149]

426

ap

Jew·el·tone

conj

vi·o·let

un·nat·u·ral

fli·er

pas·tel

intro

hues

427

two-page
hyphenated before noun

Wom·en's

ser

par

Thomp·son's

Ladies'

when

[134]

JAPAN AIR LINES
PARIS

Shorthand Vocabulary Builder

428 PHRASING FOR SPEED

Thing

-self, -selves

Out of

Not Yet

Every

1 Such a thing, the only thing, one thing, this thing, each thing, for one thing, that thing.

2 In itself, for itself, for yourself, for myself, for ourselves, for themselves, for yourselves, with themselves.

3 Out of this, out of town, out of date, out of the, out of that, out of the question, out of stock, out of state.

4 Has not yet, has not yet been, we have not yet, they have not yet, I have not yet, is not yet, have not yet been able.

5 Every time, every one, every one of those, every one of them, every one of these, every day, every month.

Building Transcription Skills

429 | Business Vocabulary Builder

newspaper mat A mold made from type metal that is used to reproduce copies of print and pictures, normally for long-run typed publications such as newspapers and magazines.

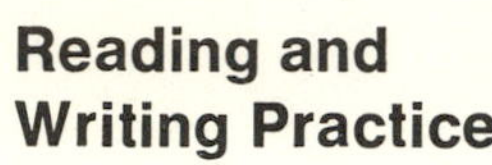

Reading and Writing Practice

430

ser

half-page hyphenated before noun

mats

if

econ·o·mize

intro

iden·ti·cal

par

gen·er·al·ize

if

oc·ca·sion·al·ly

nc

adapt

[147]

431

fli·ers

hinge

Transcribe: 10 o'clock

[72]

432

Jew·el·tone

ap

intro

full-page *hyphenated before noun*

il·lus·tra·tor

your·selves

[124]

433

in·quires

intro

de·ci·sions

pres·tige

par

out-of-town *hyphenated before noun*

out of stock *no noun, no hyphen*

too

out·weigh

conj

agen·da

[204]

Transcription Speed Building

434

12
22
33
45
55
68
81
91
102
114
128
140
151
164
175
187
199
210
219

230
240
251
260
270
282
295
305
316
331
337

435 Transcription Quiz

(1) Scaife

(2)

(3)

(4) 29 37

(5)

(6) 53

[97]

Unit 10
ADMINISTRATIVE SERVICES

As secretary to D. D. Williams, director of Administrative Services, your background in office administration will prove beneficial. Experience in her office will allow you to observe and evaluate some of the procedures discussed in your management courses.

Ms. Williams is in charge of all of the offices. She is concerned with reducing the amount of paper work wherever possible, and she strives to keep the workers' efficiency at a maximum. She is interested in systems development, work measurement, employee evaluation, motivational techniques, and improvements in office equipment.

Ms. Williams has more interest in professional organizations and the contribution they can make to personal improvement than probably anybody else you have worked for.

LESSON

Shorthand Vocabulary Builder

436 WORD FAMILIES

-ology

1

-cede

2

-let

3

-form

4

1 Biology, pathology, theology, apology, psychology, sociology.
2 Cede, accede, concede, intercede, precede, recede, receded, secede.
3 Let, booklet, pamphlet, leaflet, outlet, inlet.
4 Form, reform, perform, conform, deform, inform, informative, information.

Building Transcription Skills

437 SPELLING FAMILIES ■ double letters

1 Double the final consonant of a one-syllable word before a suffix beginning with a vowel when the root word ends in a single consonant and the ending consonant is preceded by a single vowel.

pin	pin*ned*	run	run*ning*	fit	fit*ted*
trip	trip*ping*	ship	ship*per*	blur	blur*red*

2 Double the final consonant of the root word before a suffix beginning with a vowel when the root word ends in a single consonant preceded by a single vowel and the accent falls on the last syllable of the root word.

oc•cur′	oc•cur′*ring*	trans•fer′	trans•fer*red*′
con•trol′	con•trol′*ler*	be•gin′	be•gin′*ning*

◈ Exception: Do not double the final consonant of a root word which ends in a single consonant preceded by a single vowel when:

1 The suffix begins with a consonant.

bad	bad*ly*	ship	ship*ment*	glad	glad*ness*

2 The accent of the root word is not on the last syllable.

can′cel	can′cel*ed*	ed′it	ed′it•*ing*	cred′it	cred′it•*ing*

3 The final consonant of the root word is preceded by more than one vowel.

look	look*ing*	conceit	conceit*ed*	eat	eat*en*

438 Business Vocabulary Builder

in-service courses Courses given to an employee during or after working hours.

seminar A meeting for the exchange of ideas on a predetermined topic.

Progressive Dictation [90–120]

439 PREVIEW

[440]

[441]

[442]

[443]

440 Reimbursable, supervisory, leaflet, adopted, distributed.

441 Owe, apology, congratulate, informative, textbook, biology, brilliant.

442 Urban, sociology, criterion, employee, engaged, consult.

443 Criteria, reform, tuition, theology, physiology, to make, reorder.

LETTERS

[1 Minute at 90]

440 To: Mary Wilson, John Adams, and Phillip Simon Subject: Reimbursable Programs for Employees Below the/Supervisory Level Will all of you members of the Training Policy Committee please meet with me in my office on Friday,//February 11, at 2 p.m. The purpose of the meeting is to plan an information leaflet which sets forth///the policy we have adopted. It is to be distributed to all employees below the supervisory level. [1]

[1 Minute at 100]

441 To: John Adams I owe you an apology, John, for not writing to you sooner to congratulate you on the informative textbook/in high school biology that was released recently. The book is so attractive in format, so clearly written, and so well illustrated//that it should attract many students into biology as a career even in the face of present receding enrollments.///I read it all—from the preface to the pamphlet describing its advantages over other textbooks. You have my best wishes for a brilliant future. [2]

[1 Minute at 110]

442 To: Ms. Ada Foreman Subject: Application for Reimbursement for a Course in Urban Sociology Unfortunately, Ms. Foremen, we cannot/grant your request for reimbursement for a course in urban sociology taken at City College. Although this course was taken at an excellent//college, it does not meet the criterion set forth on page 4 of our leaflet *Learning While Earning*. The leaflet states: "The course must be directly related///to the work in which the employee is engaged or for which he or she is preparing." Consult your supervisor about any future courses you plan to take. [3]

[1 Minute at 120]

443 To: Mary Wilson, John Adams, and Phillip Simon Subject: Revision of Policy Statement We have had to turn down so many requests for reimbursement for courses/that do not meet our criteria that I wonder if we should reform the general statement limiting reimbursement to job-related courses. We could list//the fields for which we will not pay tuition to employees below the supervisory level, such as biology, theology, psychology, sociology, ///and physiology. We have only 90 copies of the original leaflet on hand, so this is the time to make the change before we reorder. [4] [420]

Reading and Writing Practice

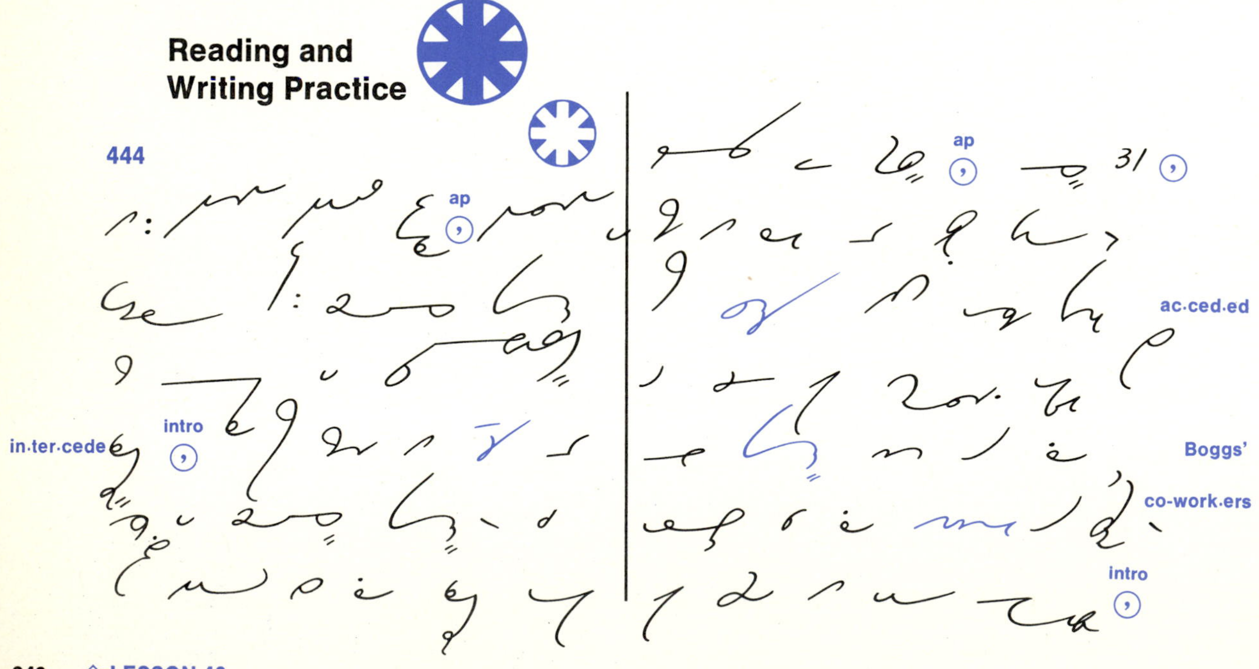

apol·o·gies

conj

con·tro·ver·sy

pre·ced·ed

[183]

445

ap

cler·i·cal

some·one

one-page

in-ser·vice

hyphenated before noun

intro

con·cede

intro

bi·ol·o·gy

par

psy·chol·o·gy

[227]

446

owe

conj

sem·i·nar

iq

par·tic·i·pat·ed

in·ci·den·tal·ly

intro

So·ci·ol·o·gy

intro

oc·cur·ring

if

[217]

dis·ap·point

LESSON

Shorthand Vocabulary Builder

447 WORD ENDINGS

-ification

1

-rity

2

-ly

3

-ual

4

1 Gratification, clarification, notification, modification, identification, ramification, specification.

2 Authority, majority, austerity, sincerity, posterity, minority, popularity, charity.

3 Only, extremely, thoroughly, surely, gladly, flatly, clearly.

4 Ritual, mutual, conceptual, annual, factual, intellectual.

Building Transcription Skills

448 TRANSCRIPTION TYPING

13

23

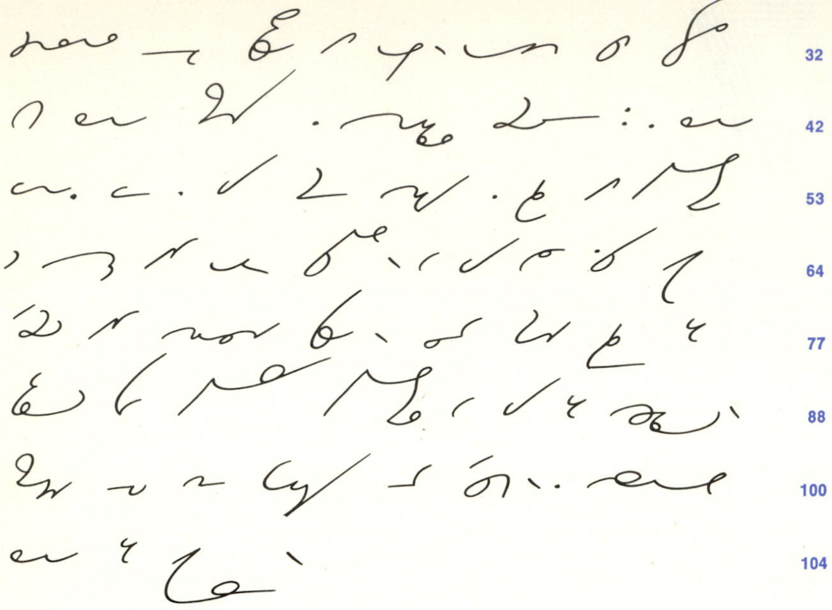

449 **Business Vocabulary Builder**

work load Amount of work done in a given amount of time.

revision A corrected version.

appraisals Expert or official valuations.

Stair-Step Dictation

450 **PREVIEW**

[451]

[452]

[453]

451 Session, clarification, prior, conceptual, minority, transparency, techniques.

452 Conservation, austerity, crucial, continually, ruined, to produce, usable.

453 Modifications, therefore, calendar, authority, transportation, majority, attending.

LETTERS

451 To: Edwin Bloom, Training Director Subject: Lecture on April 17 After visiting the session for[1] employees being trained for middle management, I should like to make some suggestions. First, there should have been[2] clarification of the technical terms used. It might be wise to prepare a manual defining these terms and[3] distribute it prior to the lecture. Although the majority of the listeners followed the conceptual[4] presentation, a minority were simply lost at the end of ten minutes. Probably you should develop[5] visual aids to accompany your presentation. You could write your outline on a transparency as you[6] lecture so that students can see it on the screen, or use flip charts of materials prepared ahead of time. As[7] my final suggestion, why not join the organization of training directors to pick up teaching techniques?[8]

452 To All Employees: Subject: Conservation of Supplies We have received notification that we are on an[9] austerity budget and must cut down on wasted supplies. Management has asked that we reduce our consumption[10] of paper by at least 5 percent, for the situation is extremely crucial. We have increased our use of[11] paper by 15 percent annually for the past two years at the same time that prices have risen continually.[12] I have three suggestions. First, use any ruined sheets for scrap paper. Second, ask yourself every time you[13] make an extra copy, "Is a need for this copy clearly established?" Some people are "copy happy." Finally,[14] evaluate your ability to produce usable work the first time you attempt it. Are you saving time and money?[15]

453 To: Ms. Adelaide Miller, Personnel Department Subject: American Management Association[16] Seminar We are planning some modifications in the hiring of management trainees from minority[17] groups. Therefore, I should like to invite you to accompany me to a seminar on this topic given by[18] the American Management Association in Cleveland on March 18–20. We would[19] probably get a lot of factual information about practices in other companies that would improve[20] our program. If it is possible for you to clear your calendar for this meeting, telephone me by Wednesday[21] so that I can get the authority for transportation and maintenance. The meetings will be held at the[22] Cascade Hotel, and I imagine that the majority of those attending this seminar will stay there.[23] [460]

Reading and Writing Practice

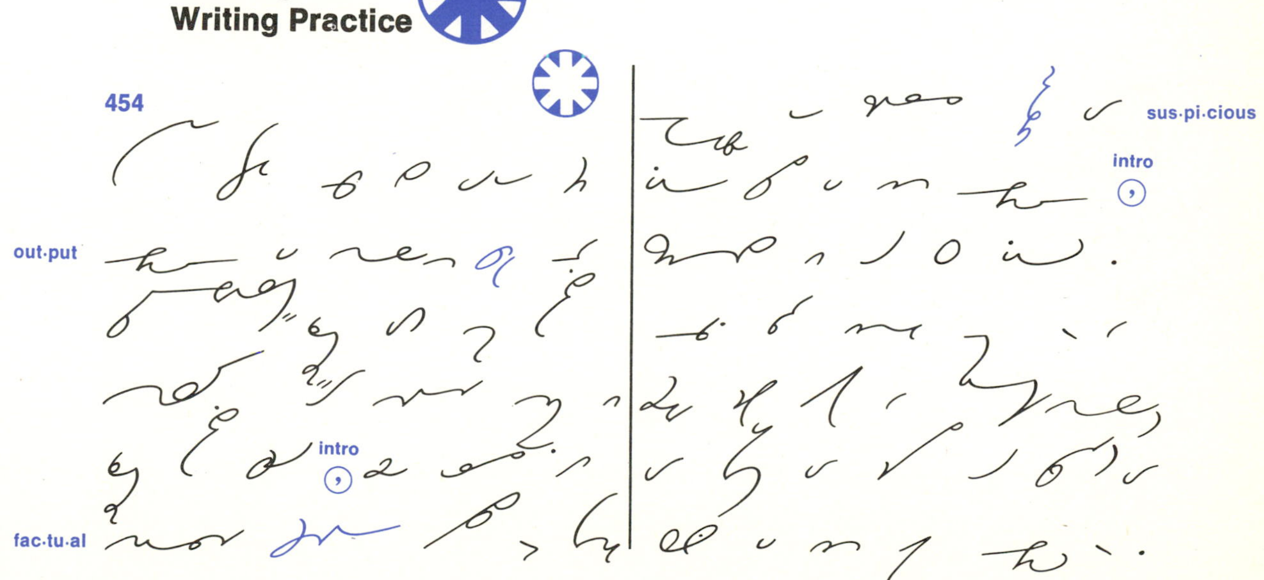

ap

[151]

455

ap

steno·graph·ic

con·tin·u·al·ly

conj

out·mod·ed

par

par·tic·i·pate

par

mo·rale

ap·point·ment

intro

de·sir·able

con·ve·nient

if

Transcribe: 10 a.m.

de·cide

[257]

456

ap

rit·u·als

con·cep·tu·al·ly

conj

ex·cel·lent

intro

or·di·nary

intro

Transcribe: 42 percent

10-hour *hyphenated before noun*

coun·sel·ing

conj

aus·ter·i·ty

[224]

tech·niques

Shorthand Vocabulary Builder

457 BRIEF-FORM POWER

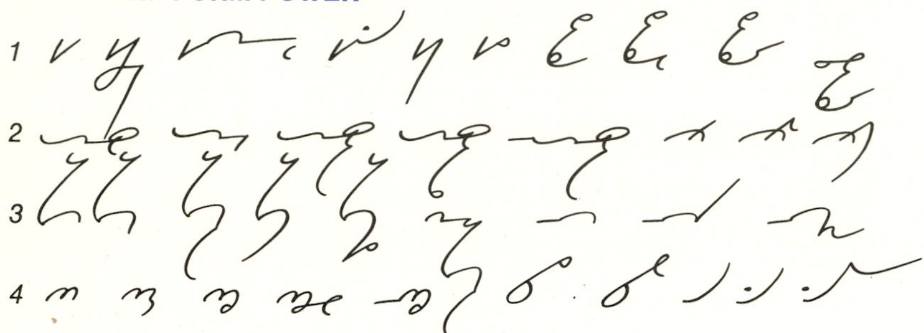

1 Short, shortchange, shortcomings, shorthand, shortage, shortly; experience, experiences, experienced, inexperienced.

2 Recognize, recognition, recognizable, recognizably, unrecognizable; quantity, quantities, quantitative.

3 Object, objection, objectionable, objective, objectivity, unobjectionable; enclose, enclosed, enclosure.

4 World, worlds, worldly, worldliness, unworldly; idea, ideas; and, hand, handle.

458 CITIES

-ville

Pleasantville, Greenville, Harrisville, Nashville, Louisville, Jacksonville, Gainesville.

Building Transcription Skills

459 SPELLING FAMILIES ■ dropping letters

In most cases, drop the final *e* of a word when adding a suffix beginning with a vowel.

make	mak*ing*	arrive	arriv*al*	force	forc*ible*
desire	desir*ous*	use	us*age*	judge	judg*ment*

Do not drop the final *e* of words ending in *ce* or *ge* when adding a suffix beginning with *a* or *o.*

notice	notice*able*	service	service*able*
courage	courage*ous*	manage	manage*able*

Check the dictionary to help determine the correct spelling of words.

460 Business Vocabulary Builder

shortsighted Lacking foresight.

feasible Possible.

immersed Engrossed.

Progressive Dictation [90–120]

461 PREVIEW

[462]
[463]
[464]
[465]

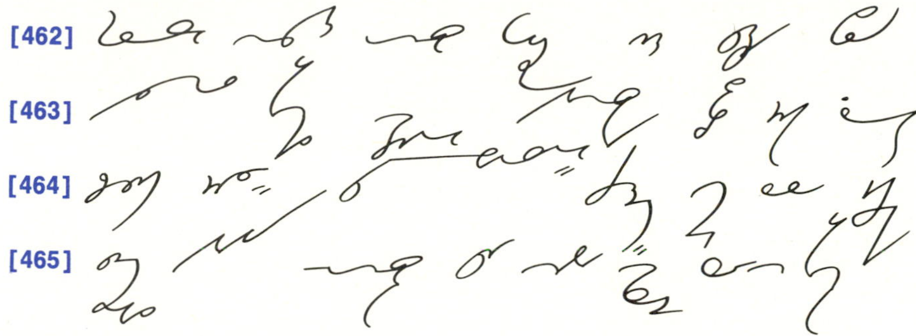

462 Free-lance, credentials, recognize, professional, worlds, outside, appoint.

463 Degree, objectivity, computers, described, especially, suitable, helpful.

464 Executive, Southern, Administrators, Jacksonville, convention, earlier, shortchanged.

465 University, distorted, unrecognizable, out of the, context, comparison, article, objectionable.

LETTERS

[1 Minute at 90]

462 Dear Miss Sweeney: Thank you for your interest in a free-lance job to revise our employees' manual. From your interview and/written credentials we recognize that you could do a very professional job. On the salary, though, we are worlds apart.//Unfortunately, we shall have to forgo using the services of an outside employee and appoint a writing committee/// consisting of the present staff. A check is enclosed to cover your expenses for the interview. Yours very truly, [1]

[1 Minute at 100]

463 Dear Mr. Ames: Thank you for the degree of objectivity you displayed in answering my questions about your experience with/VCB computers in your company offices. I recognize that we would have the same kinds of problems you described in your letter//of August 10, especially in providing room conditions suitable for operation. Many of our offices are not air-conditioned///either. If there is any way in which I can be helpful to you by sharing experiences, please let me know. Yours cordially, [2]

[1 Minute at 110]

464 Dear Jane: The executive board of the Southern Office Administrators Association will meet in Jacksonville, Florida, at 9 o'clock on/November 18 at the Early America Inn. The present agenda includes (1) a discussion of the site of the convention, either Nashville//or Louisville; (2) a proposal to begin the convention half a day earlier because some of the members have felt that they are now being///short-changed; and (3) a consideration of an increase in dues to $25 a year. Please send me any items that should be added. Yours cordially, [3]

[1 Minute at 120]

465 Dear Mr. Butler: I should like to raise a number of objections to your report of my lecture at the University of Virginia on Tuesday, April/21. In my opinion, the article completely lacked objectivity. It represented the views of your reporter, and my own statements were so distorted//as to be unrecognizable. A few remarks were taken completely out of the context in which they were spoken. I am enclosing a copy of the speech that///was actually delivered. A comparison of this text with your newspaper's account will indicate my reasons for finding the article objectionable. Yours truly, [4] [420]

466

writ·ing

ex·pe·ri·enc·ing

du·pli·ca·tor

short-cir·cuits

conj

intro

in-com·pa·ny *hyphenated before noun*

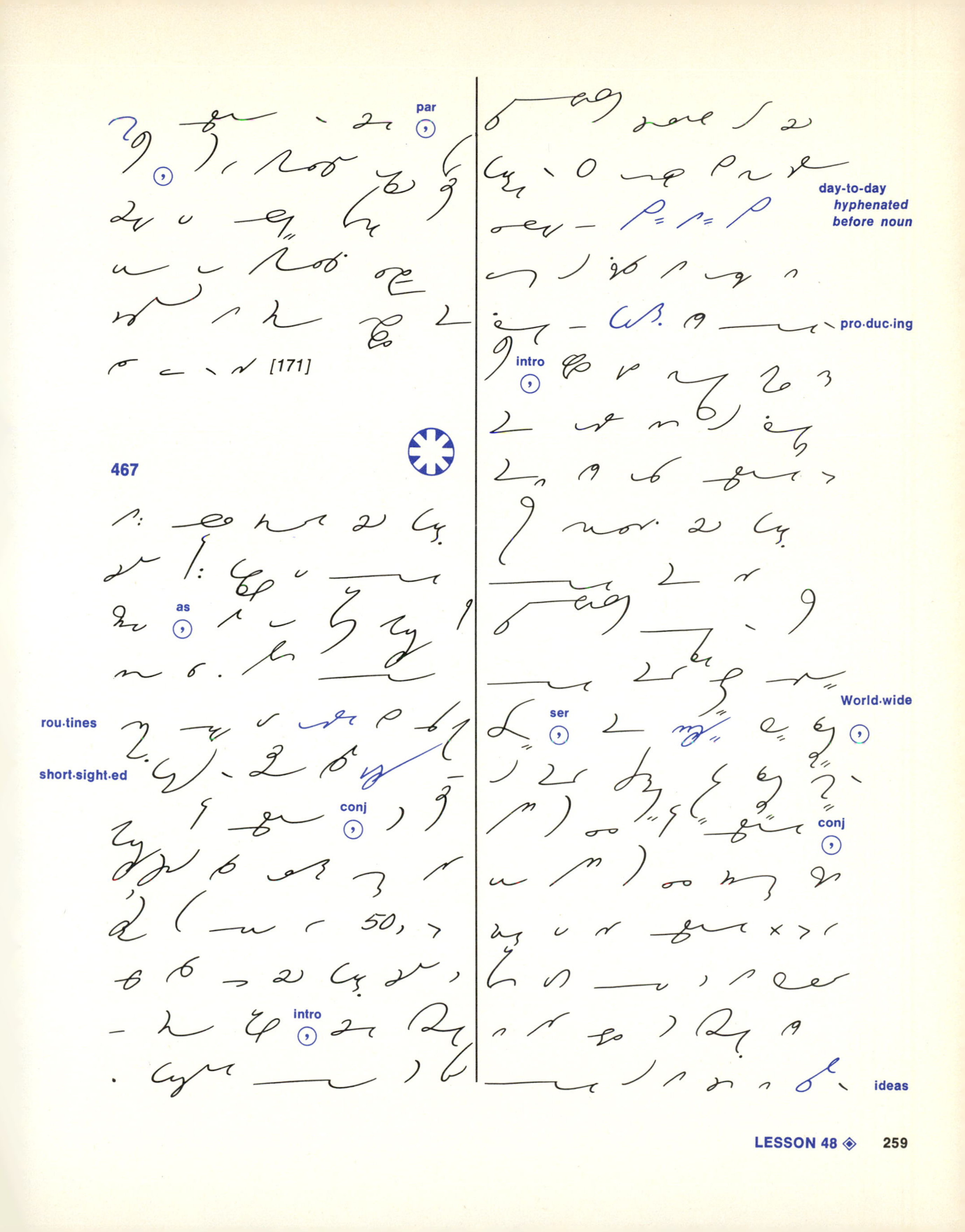

par

[171]

467

as

rou·tines

short·sight·ed

conj

50,

intro

day-to-day *hyphenated before noun*

pro·duc·ing

intro

ser

World·wide

conj

ideas

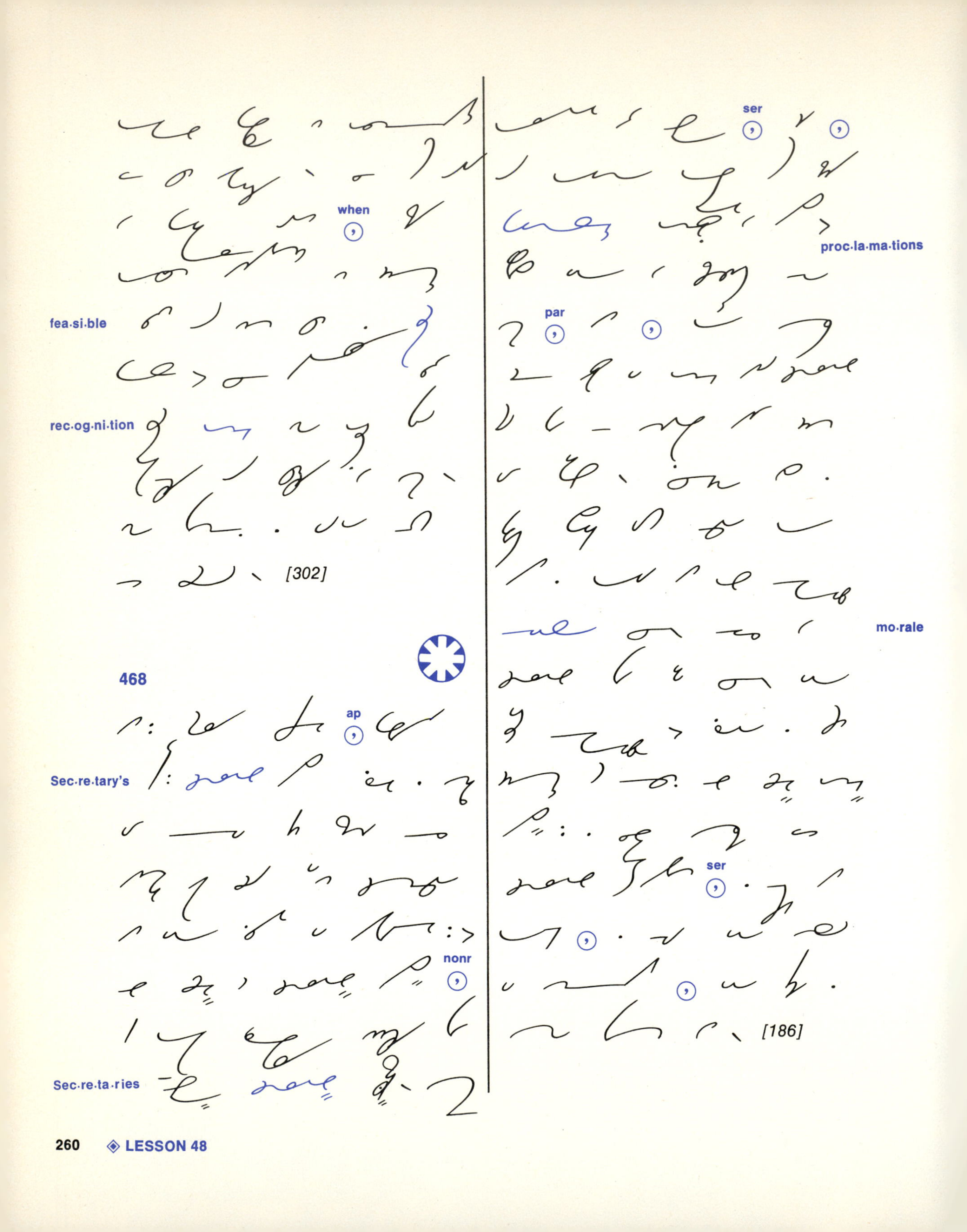

when

fea·si·ble

rec·og·ni·tion

[302]

468

ap

Sec·re·tary's

nonr

Sec·re·ta·ries

ser

proc·la·ma·tions

par

mo·rale

ser

[186]

LESSON 49

Shorthand Vocabulary Builder

469 WORD-BUILDING PRINCIPLES

Man, Men, Min

Oi

U

Omission of E From U

1 Manipulate, manager, menace, mend, nominal.
2 Boy, boiler, toil, join, enjoy, spoiled, annoy, annoyance, choice.
3 Unit, unite, view, refused, fuel, usual, utilize, unique.
4 Avenue, duty, continue, music, numerous, issue, reduce, induce, suit, pursue.

Building Transcription Skills

470 TRANSCRIPTION TYPING

12

24

38

51
60
69
81
94
104
117
128
139
146

471 **Business Vocabulary Builder**

output Production.

utilize To put to use for a purpose.

Stair-Step Dictation

472 PREVIEW

[473]

[474]

[475]

473 Annoyed, quality, deterioration, feather, excess, manuscripts, refuse.

474 Utilize, threatened, fiscal, administrator, submit, welcomed.

475 Participation, decisions, depart, manager, communicate, unique, implementation.

LETTERS

473 Gentlemen: We are very much annoyed that the quality of duplicating paper we have contracted for[1] with your company shows continual deterioration in quality with each new shipment. It is not[2] unusual for the ink to feather on the sheet if there is even the slightest excess of ink. The duplicating[3] unit tells me that it is humanly impossible to get clear copies unless the quality is[4] restored. The higher grades of paper seem to be all right, and the manuscripts produced on them are still excellent.[5] We will, however, refuse any future shipments of the present duplicating paper. I suggest that you[6] send one of your quality control engineers to discuss our problem and to do something at once. Yours truly,[7]

474 Dear Hubert: I enjoyed your talk at our convention very much and intend to utilize many of your ideas.[8] It is true that we are constantly threatened by other divisions as they demonstrate their direct[9] effect on profits. Your recommendations for communicating our monetary contribution to management[10] at the end of each fiscal period should be considered by every office administrator. The problem[11] now is that what you said was heard only by our own group. Why not submit a copy of this speech to a magazine[12] read by executives? A manuscript of this type would probably be welcomed. Very cordially yours,[13]

475 To All Unit Managers: Subject: Unit Committees on Budget In view of the request of certain employees[14] for greater participation in management decisions, we will depart from our usual practice this[15] year in developing our budget requests. Each unit will choose a committee of three whose duty it will[16] be to join with the manager in determining next year's needs. When each committee has completed its work, it will[17] communicate its recommendation to me in a meeting prior to November 2. Because this[18] approach is unique, ample time must be allowed for its implementation. Your planning meetings should begin soon.[19] [380]

Reading and Writing Practice

476

pro·ceed·ings

when

use·ful

out·put

elu·sive

com·pelled

uti·lize

par

conj

ques·tion-and-an·swer
hyphenated before noun

[177]

477

ma·neu·ver·ing

by·pass

as

var·i·ous

ac·quaint

intro

unan·i·mous

ma·nip·u·late

if

dem·o·crat·ic

at·mo·sphere

if

ser

[274]

478

par

as

men·aced

high-grade
hyphenated
before noun

intro

com·mu·ni·ca·tion

if

orig·i·na·tor

let·ter·heads

cir·cu·lar

us·able

req·ui·si·tion

week's

[252]

LESSON 50

Shorthand Vocabulary Builder

479 PHRASING FOR SPEED

Omission of Words

1

To Do

2

What

3

Such

4

Sure

5

1 One of our, in the future, in the past, many of those, every one of the, at a loss, glad to see, glad to have, in addition to this, in such a way, one of the best, day or two ago, brother-in-law, here and there.

2 To do, to do this, to do that, to do it, to do so, to do the, to do your.

3 What is, what is the, what is this, what was, what are, what will, what will be, what will be done.

4 In such, on such, with such, no such, from such, such matters, such a thing, in such a manner.

5 I am sure, we are sure, I feel sure, you may be sure, to be sure, you can be sure, he will be sure.

Building Transcription Skills

480 **Business Vocabulary Builder**

punched card A card with holes or notches representing letters or numbers.

analysis A statement of the results of a study.

Reading and Writing Practice

481

intro

buck·le

air-con·di·tioned

anal·y·sis

nonr

par

if

[120]

482

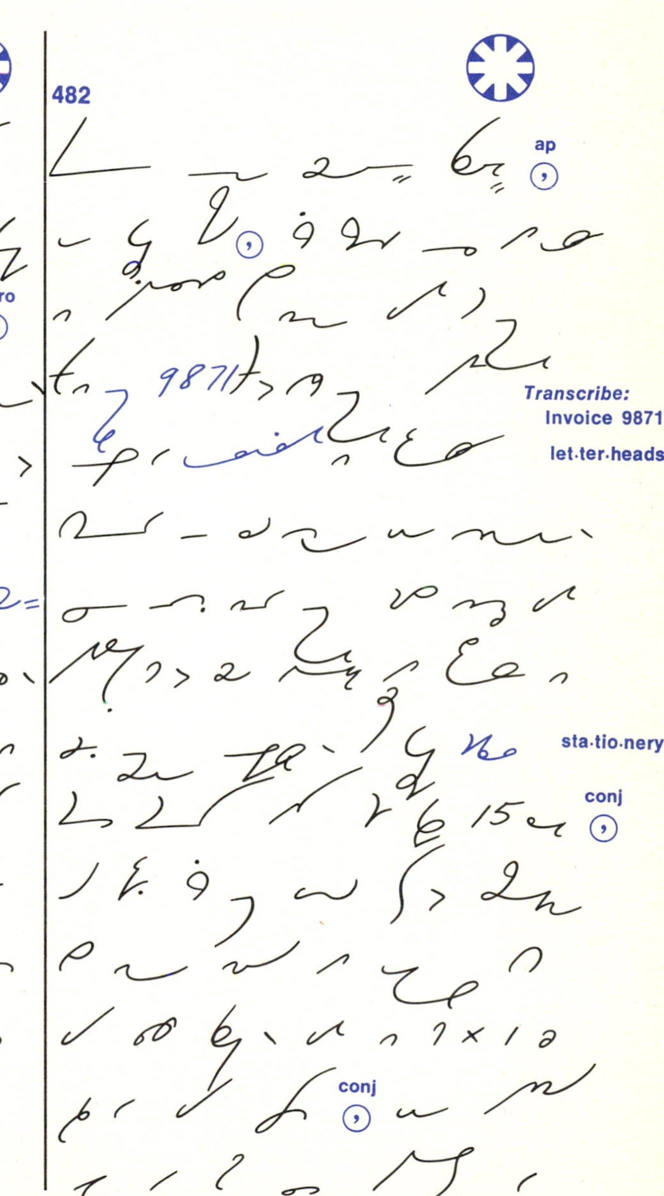

[156]

483

Ad·min·is·tra·tive

isq

Ev·ery·body's

iq

as

ev·ery·day

ef·fect

as

role

ini·ti·ate

[183]

484

ap

in-ser·vice
hyphenated before noun

prac·ti·cal·ly
su·per·vi·sors

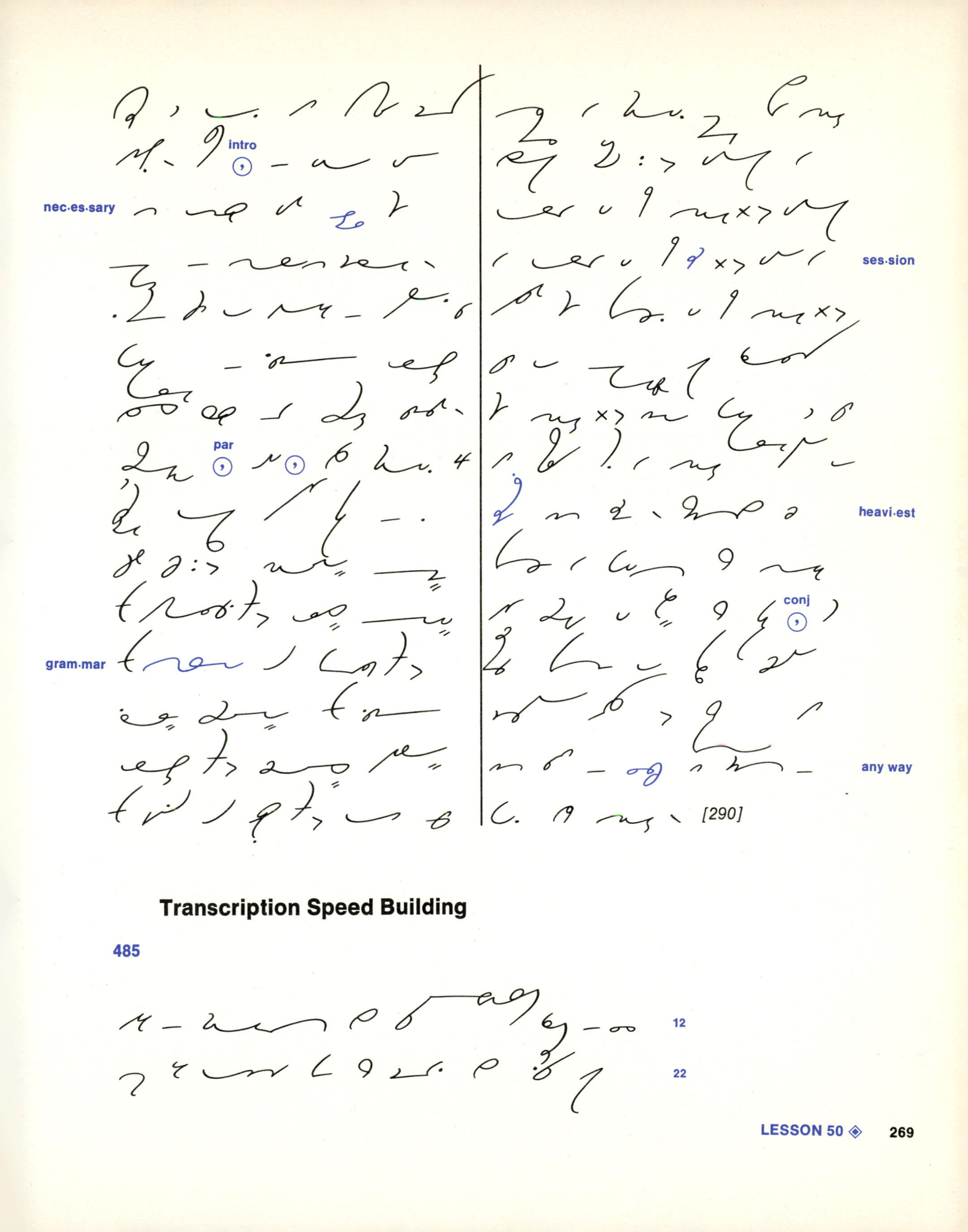

intro

nec·es·sary

ses·sion

par

heavi·est

conj

gram·mar

any way

[290]

Transcription Speed Building

485

12

22

34

45

58

70

83

97

110

20 25 124

137

148

160

172

183

195

206

219

228

239

251

260

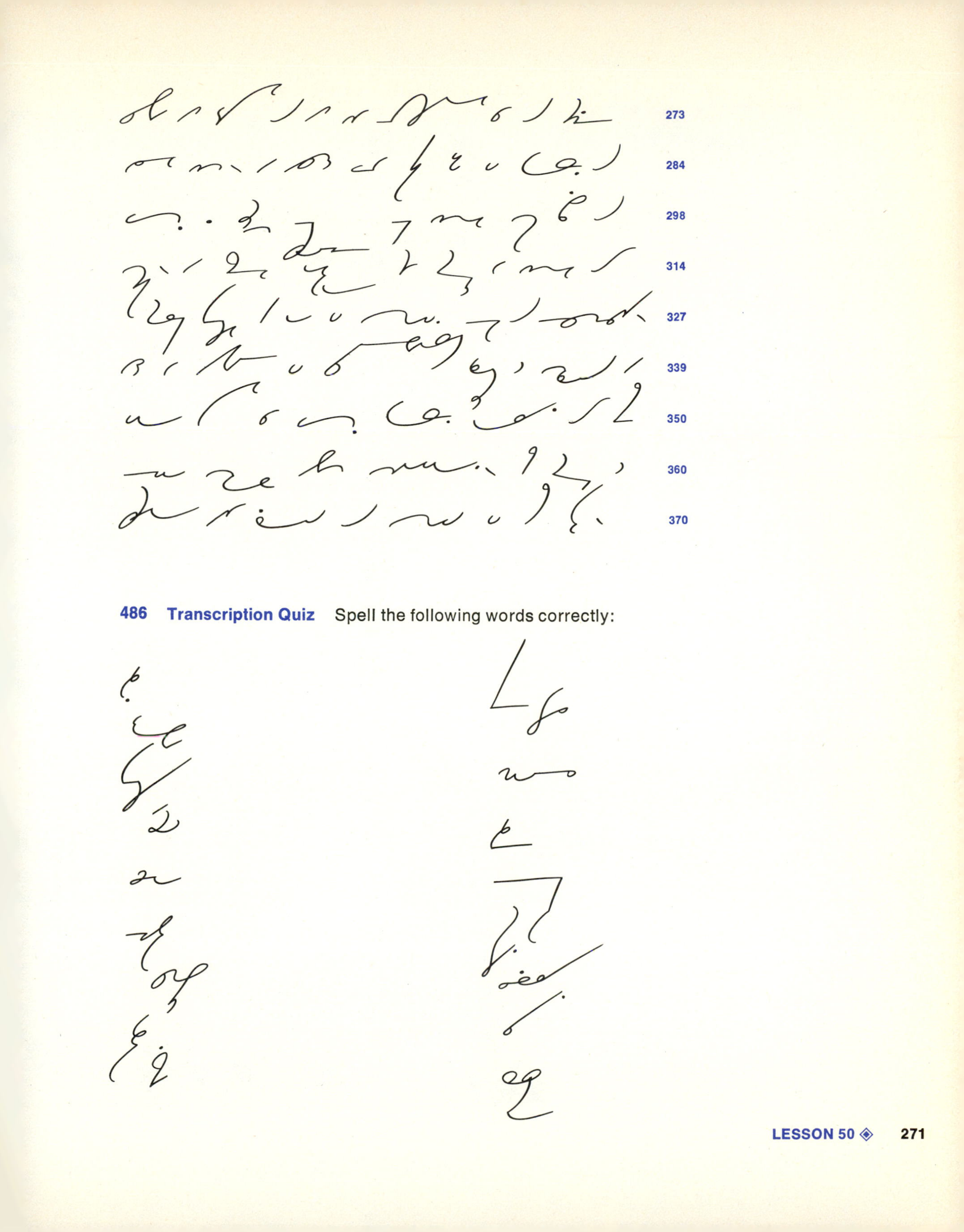

273

284

298

314

327

339

350

360

370

486 Transcription Quiz Spell the following words correctly:

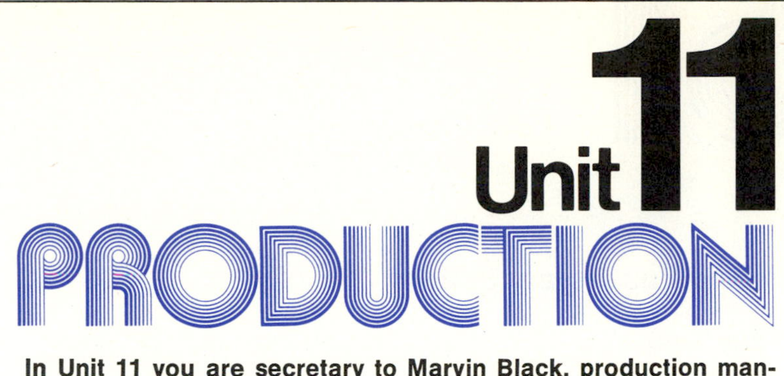

Unit 11 PRODUCTION

In Unit 11 you are secretary to Marvin Black, production manager of Continental Products, which manufactures metal products and children's clothing.

The Production Department schedules and maintains production to be sure that goods are available for sale at specified delivery dates. It works closely with the Purchasing Department so that raw materials of appropriate quality are available in sufficient quantity to ensure that manufacturing equipment is efficiently utilized. It recommends purchases of equipment and maintains present equipment. The Production Department trains and oversees supervisors in its factories.

LESSON 51

Shorthand Vocabulary Builder

487 WORD FAMILIES

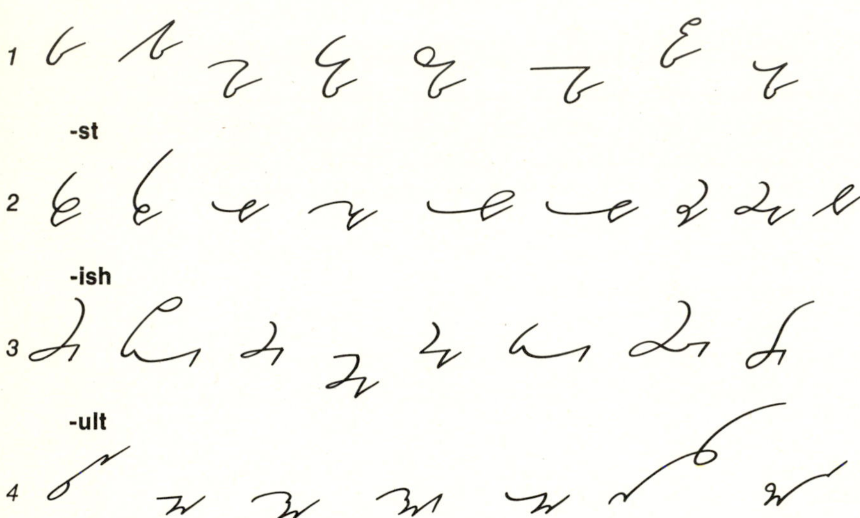

1 Port, deport, comport, purport, airport, import, export, report.
2 Past, best, rest, cost, last, list, fist, first, test.
3 Vanish, abolish, finish, unfinished, furnished, polish, varnish, banish.
4 Adult, insult, consult, consultation, result, ultimatum, exultant.

Building Transcription Skills

488 SPELLING FAMILIES ■ words ending in y

If a word ends in *y* preceded by a consonant, change the *y* to an *i* when adding any suffix except *ing.*

happy	happ*iness*	multiply	multipl*ier*	multiply*ing*
faculty	facult*ies*	bully	bull*ied*	bully*ing*

If a word ends in *y* proceded by a vowel, retain the *y* when adding a suffix.

		Exceptions	
attorney	attorney*s*	pay	paid
betray	betray*ed*	lay	laid
convey	convey*able*	say	said

489 Business Vocabulary Builder

staggering vacations The practice of having workers take vacations at different times so that the production of a factory or plant may be maintained.

ultimatum The final statement of terms.

Progressive Dictation [90–120]

490 PREVIEW

[491]
[492]
[493]
[494]

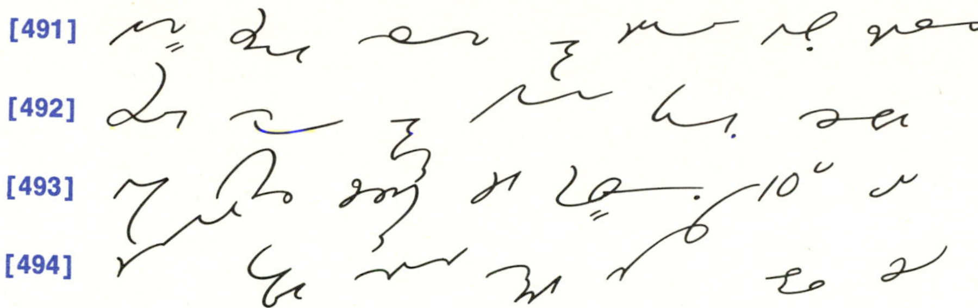

491 Tokyo, fasteners, cargo, newspaper, stolen, tracing, extremely.
492 Varnish, quality, inspections, duller, polishing, chemists.
493 Trouble, difficulty, executives, situation, Friday morning, 10 o'clock, although.
494 Standards, purports, contract, consultation, ultimatum, necessary, we want.

LETTERS

[1 Minute at 90]

491 Mailgram to Coastal Cargo Line, Inc. We have received invoices from Tokyo Steel Company indicating/that they shipped us 100 dozen steel fasteners on November 8 via your air cargo line. This morning's newspaper//reports large shipments from Tokyo have recently been stolen from your export-import center. Since this shipment should have been///received here in Hartford no later than November 12, please furnish us with complete details tracing this shipment. Extremely urgent. [1]

[1 Minute at 100]

492 To: Dan Matthews, Supervisor Subject: Varnish Used on Product 18 Our quality control inspections indicate that the varnish being/used on Product 18 is not measuring up to past performance. The finish is quite a bit duller than it usually is although//the same polishing process is being used. In the past you and I have taken samples of the finished product to the Best Paint factory///and consulted with their chemists. Possibly the quality of the unfinished wood is different on the new mill runs. What is your opinion? [2]

[1 Minute at 110]

493 To: Melvin Wright, Manager of Purchasing Subject. Product 18 Dan Matthews has been having trouble maintaining the quality of Product 18./At first we thought the problem was with the varnish, for he has not been getting the usual high finish after polishing. We have decided, though, that the//difficulty lies with the unfinished wood being furnished by First Lumber Company. Two of their executives will consult with us about this///situation here in my office Friday morning at 10 o'clock. Can you come? Although their flight is due at the airport at 9:11, they may be delayed. [3]

[1 Minute at 120]

494 To: Dan Matthews, Supervisor Subject: Product 18 After our discussion of the quality of the unfinished wood being used and an examination of/the samples you furnished, I am convinced that the wood does not meet the standards it purports to meet according to our contract. I have asked the First Lumber Company for// a consultation, and two of their executives will be here on Friday morning to discuss the situation. I am asking you and Mr. Wright, manager of///Purchasing, to join me for this meeting in my office at 10 o'clock. It will probably be necessary to issue an ultimatum to them as to what we want. [4] [420]

Reading and Writing Practice

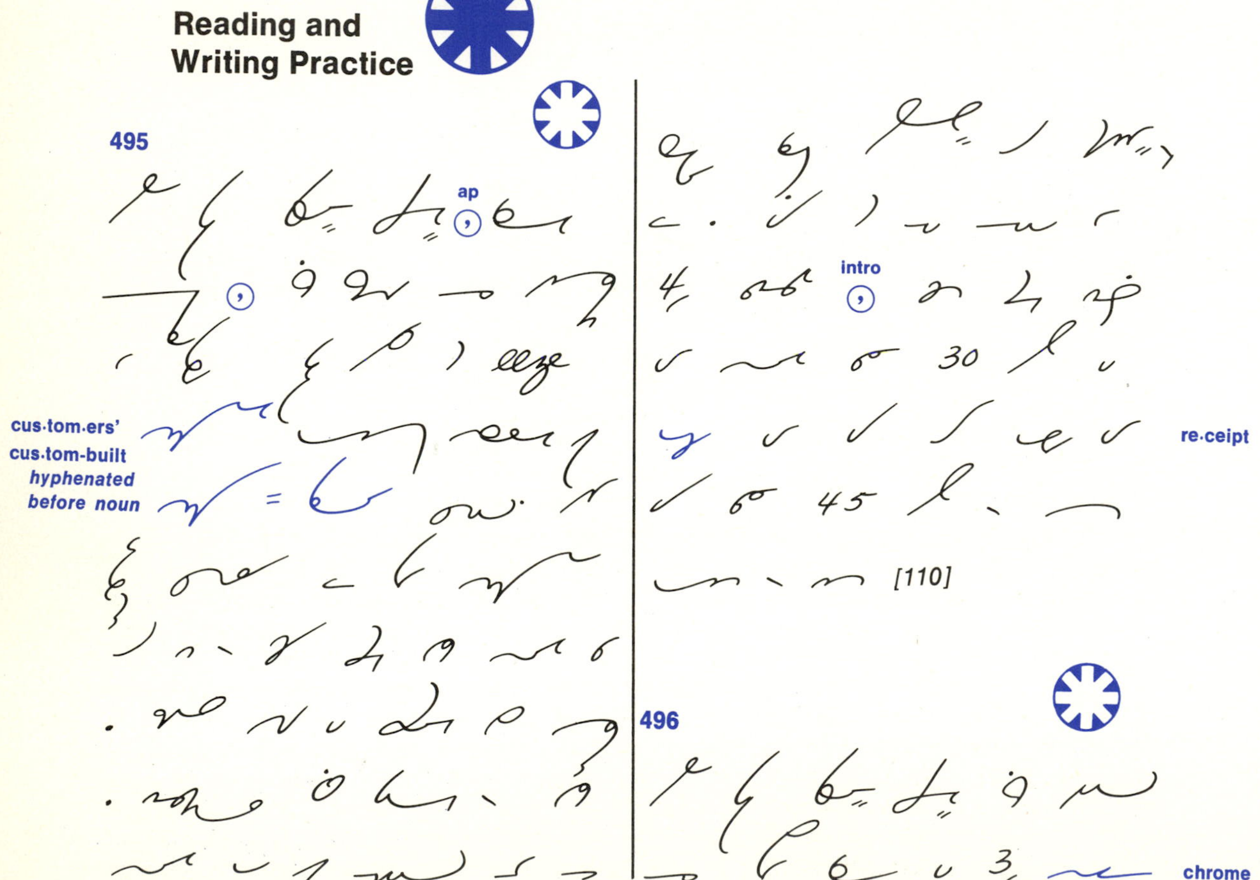

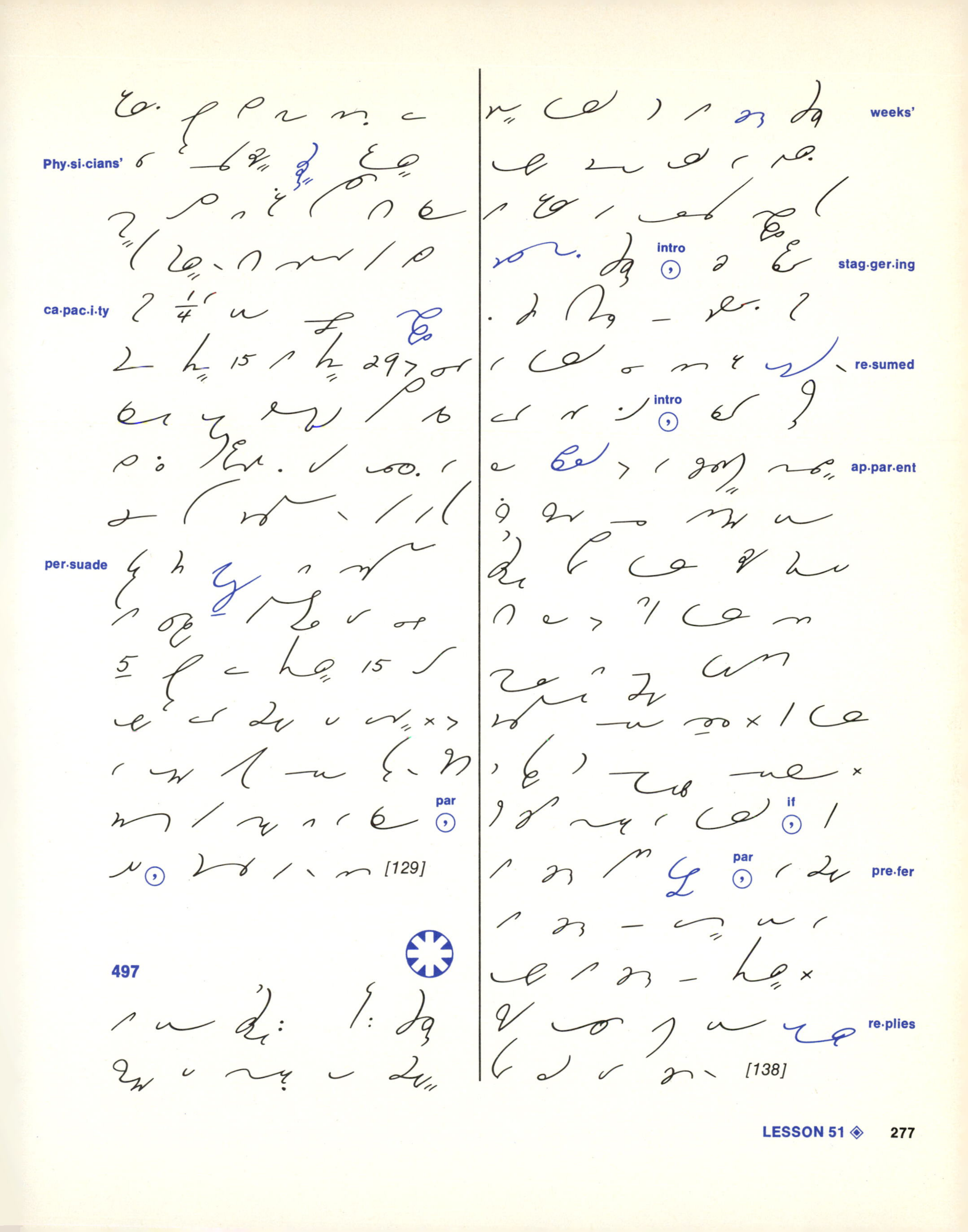

Phy·si·cians'

ca·pac·i·ty

$\frac{1}{4}$ 15 29 5 15

per·suade

par

[129]

497

weeks'

intro

stag·ger·ing

re·sumed

intro

ap·par·ent

if

par

pre·fer

re·plies

[138]

498

re·ceived

intro

shipped

as

con·sul·ta·tion

par

com·mit·ments

par

short·en

abol·ish

conj

par

fixed-cost *hyphenated before noun*

conj

al·ter·na·tives

sup·pli·er

[260]

Shorthand Vocabulary Builder

499 WORD BEGINNINGS

In-, En-

Self-

Un-

Post-

1 Incident, indefinite, increment; encounter, encouraged, enlighten.

2 Self-centered, self-command, self-defense, self-support, selfish, self-respect, unselfish.

3 Uncover, undecided, unfriendly, unfair, unlock, unless, uninterested.

4 Postage, postal, postbox, postpone, postmark, postmaster, posthaste, postpaid.

Building Transcription Skills

500 TRANSCRIPTION TYPING

10

22

37

50
60
71
82
93
105
116
126
135
139

501 **Business Vocabulary Builder**

inventory control The process of storing materials and supplies conveniently, locating them quickly, and ensuring that a quantity of all items consistent with needs or customer demands is maintained at all times.

increment An increase.

Stair-Step Dictation

502 PREVIEW

[503]

[504]

[505]

503 Encountered, insurmountable, postpone, copper, unquestionably, increments.

504 Engineer, specified, procedures, blueprints, proceed, require.

505 Kitchen, criticism, self-defense, impeded, workers, harassments.

LETTERS

503 To: Ed Enright, Sales Manager Subject: Product 118 We have encountered some difficulties with the[1] production of Product 118 that seem insurmountable. It is unlikely that we can adhere to our[2] schedule. It will be necessary for you to postpone indefinitely the sales campaign you have been developing.[3] Unless we can uncover another source of supply for copper, we may not be able to[4] continue manufacturing Product 118. Recent incidents in Chile will unquestionably bring[5] increments in copper prices, and they may cut off our supply entirely. Our Purchasing Department is[6] investigating several other possible sources, but up until today the prospects have not been encouraging.[7] We shall keep you informed of the results of our efforts and of the quantity that we can produce.[8]

504 Dear Dr. Wilton: We have uncovered more problems with the design of Product 32 and are undecided[9] about how to handle them. You were the engineer in charge in our Research and Development Department[10] when test runs were made and you specified that you preferred to handle any later problems personally. Can you[11] visit our factory at once, study our procedures, and then enlighten us as to our best procedure? We[12] have postponed further work on this item until we have had the benefit of your advice. It is our opinion[13] that the blueprints will require major revision before we can proceed. Very cordially yours,[14]

505 To: Herman Benson, President Subject: Delays in Production Schedules of Kitchen Furniture Since I feel[15] that your criticism of our department for failing to meet its production schedule for kitchen furniture[16] is unfair, I should like to explain in self-defense the reasons. Because of the threatened strike, several[17] unfriendly incidents have occurred that have impeded production. One cutting machine was purposely damaged and[18] required a day and a half for repair. Two workers locked up the supply of paint, and there was a delay of[19] four hours before the door could be unlocked and work resumed. These are only two of the petty harrassments we have had.[20] [400]

Reading and Writing Practice

506

In·ven·to·ry

spon·sored

fore·front

spe·cial·ists

if

de·ci·sion

ap

17. [144]

507

ten·ta·tive

intro

self-de·fense

ad·e·quate

conj

Un·cas

ap·prov·al

[144]

508

Re·jects

in·cre·ment

di·sas·trous·ly

75 88

in·ci·dence

par

sal·able

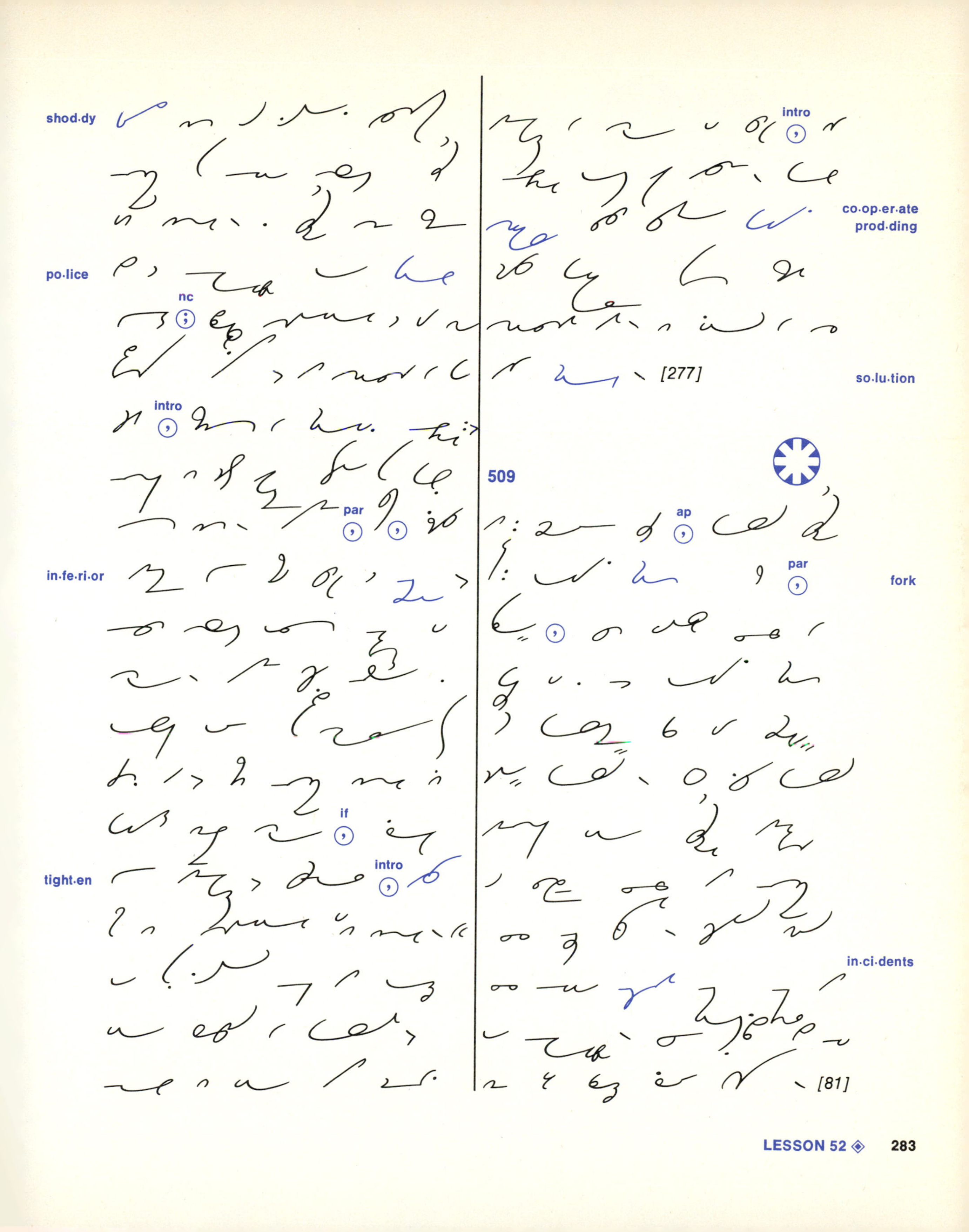

shod·dy

po·lice

nc

intro

par

in·fe·ri·or

if

tight·en

intro

intro

co·op·er·ate

prod·ding

[277]

so·lu·tion

509

ap

par

fork

in·ci·dents

[81]

Shorthand Vocabulary Builder

510 BRIEF-FORM POWER

1 Satisfy–satisfactory, satisfied, dissatisfaction, self-satisfaction, unsatisfied; speak, speaks, speaker.

2 Regular, regularity, irregular, regularly, irregularity.

3 Subject, subjects, subjected, subjective, subjectively, subjectivity; progress, progresses, progressive.

4 Organize, organizes, reorganize, organization, disorganized, organizer.

511 CITIES

-son

Madison, Harrison, Jefferson, Carson, Dawson, Atchison, Jackson.

Building Transcription Skills

512 SIMILAR WORDS ■ precede, proceed; biannual, biennial

Study the following words which are somewhat alike and which are sometimes confused.

precede To go before.

proceed To advance.

biannual Occurring twice a year.

biennial Occurring every two years.

513 **Business Vocabulary Builder**

subcontract A contract that assigns some of the obligations of the main contractor to another party.

breach of contract Failure to fulfill a contract.

deadline A time limit for completing an assignment.

Progressive Dictation [100–125]

514 **PREVIEW**

[515]

[516]

[517]

[518]

515 Bearings, reorganized, irregularities, accumulated, release.

516 Kansas, acceptable, vocabulary, qualification, candidate's, ability.

517 Department, applicants, demonstrate, necessary, premises, function.

518 Congress, paper work, legislation, irksome, potential, congressional.

LETTERS

[1 Minute at 100]

515 Gentlemen: We are, of course, dissatisfied that you cannot ship our orders for Jefferson ball bearings on the dates specified in our contract./We have, therefore, reorganized our production plans to provide for the irregularities in shipping schedules which you reported//in your letter of July 18. We shall plan factory runs only when we have accumulated a large enough supply to warrant///a start-up of equipment rather than organize an irregular schedule. Please ship any ball bearings that you can release. Yours truly, [1]

[1 Minute at 110]

516 To: Al Simmons, Director of Personnel Subject: Secretary to Director Mary Harrison, my secretary, is moving to Atchison,/Kansas, at the end of June, and I shall need a replacement. I hope you can send me someone like Miss Harrison, for she has been acceptable to our whole//staff. We need someone with an engineering vocabulary and an interest in production scheduling. The most important qualification,/// though, will be the candidate's ability to get along with the workers who visit my office. The workers need to deal with someone who knows their problems. [2]

[1 Minute at 120]

517 To: Al Simmons, Director of Personnel Subject: Assignment of a Member of Your Staff to the Production Department I am delighted, Al, that the reorganization/ of your department has been approved and that a member of your staff will be assigned to this department to handle our blue-collar workers. Since all applicants//must either demonstrate their skill on the machines or take tests that measure their ability to learn them, it is necessary that hiring take place on these premises.///Yes, indeed, I do have a staff member who could handle this function. I recommend Fred Dawson. He has done most of the hiring of new workers for the past two years. [3]

[1 Minute at 125]

518 To: Don Horn, Director of Finance
According to stories in the business newspapers, it appears that Congress is quite serious about taking a bit of the paper work burden/off the backs of small firms.

A bill to cut certain kinds of red tape has been introduced into the House by Representative John Frame. This bill may have started the ball rolling.//If the Senate agrees, legislation against the irksome problem may follow.

Those who support this bill see a great potential for savings. I believe we should help too. Would you///please call a meeting of the officers of the company and all division managers to discuss ways to encourage desirable congressional action. [4]
[455]

Reading and Writing Practice

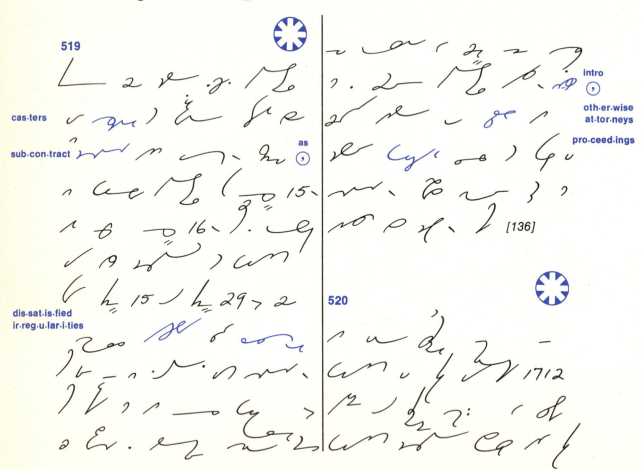

519

cas·ters

sub·con·tract

as

dis·sat·is·fied
ir·reg·u·lar·i·ties

intro

oth·er·wise
at·tor·neys

pro·ceed·ings

[136]

520

pat·tern

when

par

dead·line

if

[151]

521

Re·or·der·ing

in·fla·tion·ary

intro

stores-rec·ord *hyphenated before noun*

conj

stock·pile

intro

20, [121]

522

ap

con·fi·den·tial

su·per·in·ten·dent

bi·an·nu·al

self-sat·is·fac·tion

7, 17 3, 11 17

intro

nei·ther

2 20

dis·or·ga·nized

conj

[161]

523

nonr

4351

conj

fas·tened

intro

conj

sub·sti·tute

re·im·bursed

[121]

LESSON 54

Shorthand Vocabulary Builder

524 WORD-BUILDING PRINCIPLES

Th

1

Dem

2

OO on Its Side

3

Business Phrases

4

1 Bath, smooth, method, theater, clothing, growth, throat.

2 Demand, demonstration, freedom, medium, random, damage, domestic.

3 Moon, noon, move, removal, number, numerous, news.

4 Dear Miss, Dear Mr., Dear Mrs., Dear Ms., Yours very truly, Cordially yours, Very truly yours, Yours truly.

Building Transcription Skills

525 TRANSCRIPTION TYPING

14

27

40

49

62

74

87

97

108

117

127

138

149

160

526 **Business Vocabulary Builder**

telephone collect To make a call for which the receiver makes payment.

bolt of cloth A roll of fabric coming from the loom, usually containing 30 to 40 yards of material.

Stair-Step Dictation

527 **PREVIEW**

[528]

[529]

[530]

528 Theater, costumes, resemble, moonlight, discrepancy, intensify.

529 Newsprint, manuscript, celebrate, lunch, major, delight.

530 Interviewed, supplement, anecdotes, assembly, limited.

LETTERS

528 Dear Miss Carson: We are sorry to tell you that the materials we are producing for your theater costumes[1] do not exactly match the color specifications we agreed on. We used the method you observed in our[2] factory, but the gold thread does not dye quite as bright as expected. Since you indicated that the scene will be[3] lighted to resemble moonlight, we doubt that this discrepancy will make any difference. We are, however,[4] enclosing some of the dyed material for your inspection. Please try it under moonlight and let us know if[5] it is satisfactory. If not, perhaps you can suggest another dye that would intensify the shade. Yours truly,[6]

529 To: Harold Newman, Engineer, Research and Development Subject: First Runs of Newsprint and Manuscript Papers[7] We have finally set up all of the equipment for manufacturing our new newsprint and manuscript papers[8] and will start the machines on Monday, February 2. I should, however, like to hold a demonstration of[9] the first results that morning at 11 o'clock for you and the members of your staff who worked on the[10] development of these papers. If you have any suggestions after you have seen our first runs, you will be able to[11] help us smooth out any problems. Our demonstration should be finished by noon. If all goes as I expect it will,[12] perhaps we can celebrate by having lunch together. Working with you on this major project has been a delight.[13]

530 Dear Ms. Moon: Yes, I shall be happy to accept your invitation to be interviewed for your new book about[14] the future of women on the production line. I suggest that you come to my office at 10 o'clock on Tuesday,[15] October 8, with a list of questions to be discussed. (If I have the list before the interview, I might[16] be more helpful, since you asked that I supplement my answers with a number of anecdotes from experience.)[17] We will then tour the plant so that you can see for yourself the women on the assembly line. It is quite all right[18] if you ask them a limited number of questions. I hope that you will stay for lunch with me. Yours very truly,[19] [380]

Reading and Writing Practice

531

intro

some time

ap

Transcribe:
11 o'clock

ran·dom

[144]

532

ap

Re·or·der

intro

Transcribe:
1,250

ser

Swiss

iden·ti·cal

chil·dren's

mod·els

me·di·um-price
hyphenated before noun

conj

quar·rel

if

ex·er·cise

de·vi·a·tion

cri·sis

[276]

533

con·sul·tant

baf·fling

em·broi·der·ing

Transcribe: No. 43

43

par

ap

13

conj

some·times

suit·able

wax

if

anx·ious

[205]

conj

Shorthand Vocabulary Builder

534 PHRASING FOR SPEED

You

1

I

2

Able

3

They

4

1 You are, you will, you have, you can, you have been, you might, you may be, you know, you see, you say.

2 I would, I did, I could, I was, I should, I do, I do not, I made, I can.

3 Be able, has been able, has not been able, have not been able, he may be able, he should be able, he will be able, he would be able, I have not been able, I shall be able, I shall not be able, you may be able, you would be able, you could be able, you should be able, I will be able.

4 If they, if they are, if they are not, as they, as they are, they may be, if they can, they will, they will have, they will be, they can be, they might, they know, they want, they need.

Building Transcription Skills

535 Business Vocabulary Builder

allotment Apportionment; quota.

thread count Number of threads in a certain measure of cloth.

Reading and Writing Practice

536

ap

Transcribe: 5,600

al·lot·ment

par

le·git·i·mate

mem·o·ran·dum

par

conj

oc·cu·pied

qws

[166]

537

ap

Do·mes·tic

spec·i·fied

judg·ment

if

sup·pli·ers

[125]

quo·ta

out·dat·ed

scrapped

[127]

538

ap

par

539

ap

Work·shops

ad·vis·abil·i·ty

intro

al·ready

ini·ti·at·ed

intro

15-min·ute *hyphenated before noun*

in·ter·pre·ta·tion

neg·a·tive

sep·a·rate

the·ater

conj

aware

[302]

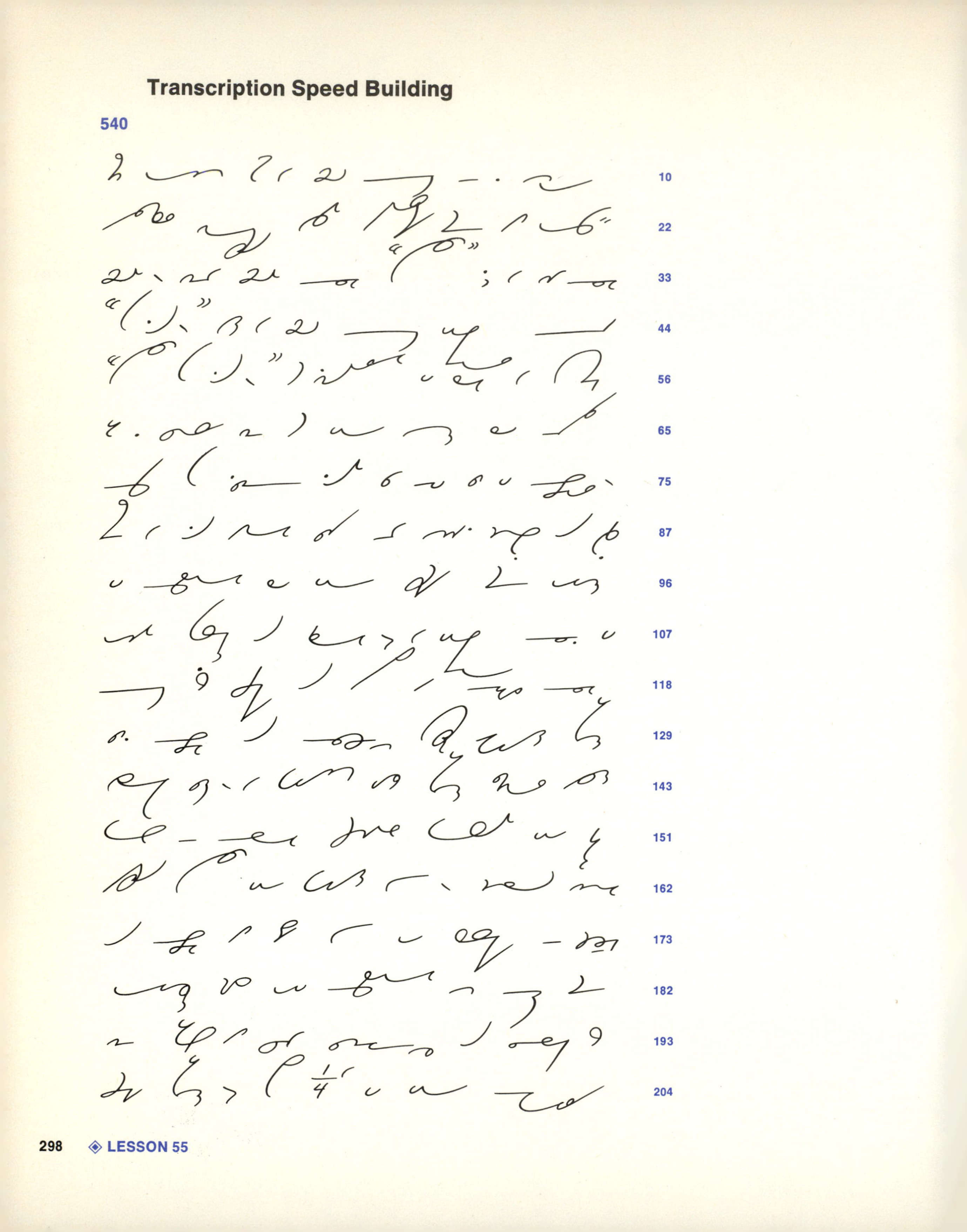

Transcription Speed Building

540

10
22
33
44
56
65
75
87
96
107
118
129
143
151
162
173
182
193
204

215
227
239
249
260
273
284
298
308
316

541 Transcription Quiz

[121]

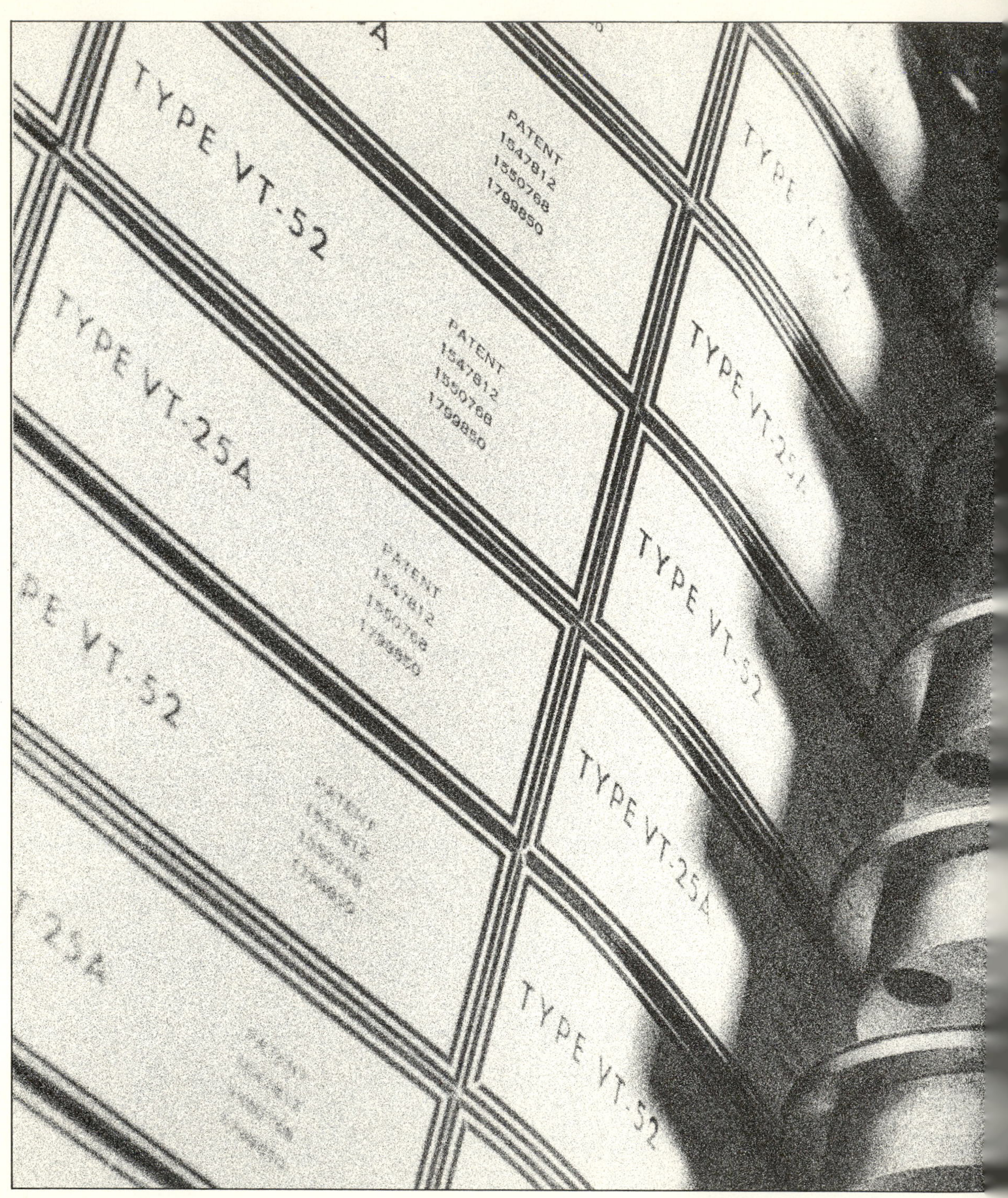

TYPE VT-52
PATENT
1547812
1550768
1799850
TYPE VT-25A
PATENT
1547812
1550768
1799850
TYPE VT-52
TYPE VT-25A
TYPE VT-52
TYPE VT-25A
TYPE VT-52

Unit 12

GENERAL COUNSEL

In Unit 12 you act as secretary to D. M. King, general counsel at the Lockwood Textile Company. Much of his time is spent in advising management on the legal implications of proposed or already completed actions. He examines all contracts and other legal papers the company is expected to sign or issue. He is responsible for all matters dealing with patents and other government contacts.

Mr. King does not, however, initiate legal proceedings. He turns that aspect of the legal work of the corporation over to a local law firm, Mastic, Jones, and Brownell, with whom he maintains a close relationship.

Another duty is to maintain good company relations with stockholders, and many of his letters are in answer to their inquiries.

You will learn a great deal about corporate operations if you keep your eyes and ears open while you are Mr. King's secretary.

LESSON 56

Shorthand Vocabulary Builder

542 WORD FAMILIES

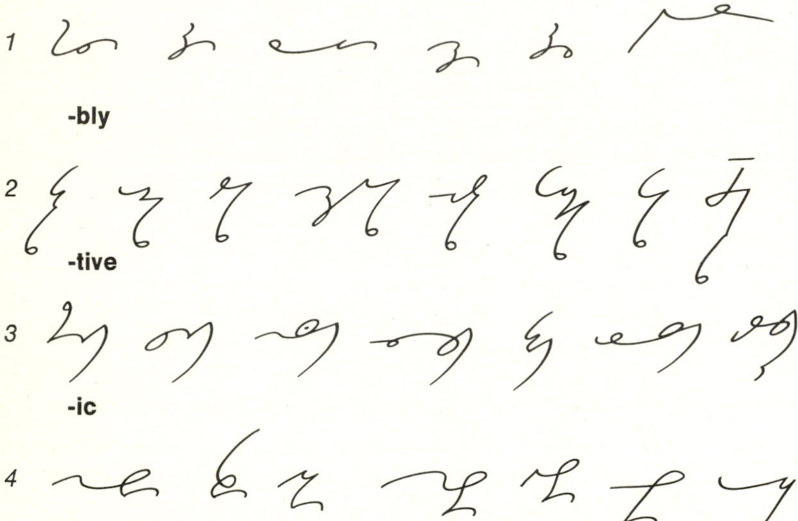

1 Frequent, subsequent, eloquent, consequent, subsequently, delinquent.

2 Possibly, reasonably, terribly, considerably, noticeably, profitably, probably, interchangeably.

3 Effective, active, creative, negative, positive, relative, alternatives.

4 Classic, basic, topic, graphic, traffic, magic, logic.

Building Transcription Skills

543 NOTEBOOK AND TRANSCRIPTION TIPS ■ changes

Classroom dictation is smooth, well-timed material read by an instructor at a planned speed to satisfy current learning requirements of students. In an office the dictation is given at varying speeds with corrections, deletions, and special instructions included. A dictator in an office adjusts the pace of speaking to the speed at which material can be composed to answer the correspondence at hand or to initiate new ideas to be communicated to other people. All thoughts of the dictator must be recorded clearly and correctly.

When a word or phrase is to be deleted, place a heavy downward line through it as in the example:

When a group of words or an entire sentence is to be deleted, place a wavy line through it thus:

If the dictator wants to change a word or two after completing a sentence, indicate the change in the following manner:

When the dictator makes a statement, changes his mind, then restates the original wording, indicate the changes thus:

Often during dictation the dictator will give special instructions such as *rush, transcribe first, carbon copy,* or *air mail.* To accommodate these, leave several blank lines between pieces of dictation as shown in the following illustration.

ILLUSTRATION OF OFFICE-STYLE DICTATION

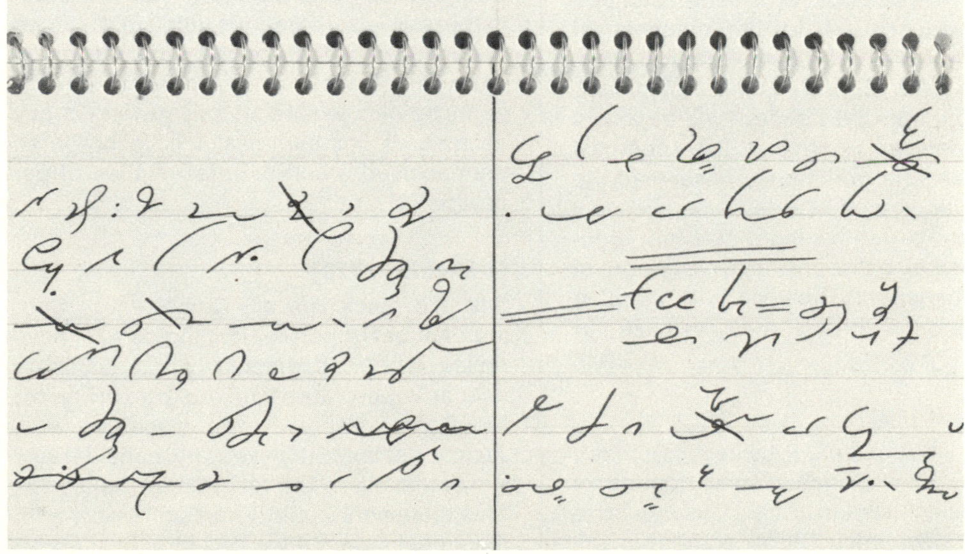

544 **Business Vocabulary Builder**

modular homes Homes made up of uniform structural components called *modules.*

write-off A cancellation from the accounts as a loss.

Progressive Dictation [100–125]

545 PREVIEW

[546]

[547]

[548]

[549]

546 Infringement, patent, preliminary, logic, support, defense.

547 Judiciary, signature, subsequent, graphic, investigation, representation.

548 Stockholders, optimistic, forecast, rosy, traffic, negative.

549 Employee, collided, although, sworn, injured, dismissal.

LETTERS

[1 Minute at 100]

546 To: Walter Cook, President Subject: Magic Cleaner Suit for Infringement of Patent No. 8,643,901 Since Magic Cleaner/is suing us for infringement of patent, I am preparing what I believe will be a very positive defense relative to the//charges. I shall have the preliminary case ready to discuss with you on Monday, when you will be able to follow the logic of///my arguments. I shall enlist the active support of Mastic, Jones, and Brownell in developing the topics on which we intend to base our defense. [1]

[1 Minute at 110]

547 To: Walter Cook, President Subject: Possibility of a Congressional Hearing I am enclosing a letter to the House Judiciary/Committee which I have drafted as you requested for your signature. Just because we operated more profitably than our competitors in//corporations relatively similar to ours during 1973 and the two subsequent years is no reason for an investigation./// In my opinion we are on safe ground in any defense of our earnings. I have prepared the enclosed graphic representation of our profits. [2]

[1 Minute at 120]

548 To: Jack Howell, Comptroller Subject: Annual Report to Stockholders I have reviewed your statements in the preliminary annual report that you are/preparing for Mr. Cook's approval and signature. Yes, Jack, I do think that you are considerably too optimistic in the forecast for next year. This statement could//hurt us terribly with the stockholders if we do not subsequently measure up. It is even possible that statements that paint too rosy a picture could possibly///involve us in litigation. I do not want to be too negative, but I do suggest that you tone down the whole piece noticeably before you submit it to Mr. Cook. [3]

[1 Minute at 125]

549 My dear Mrs. Miller: I have been authorized to offer you $2,500 in full settlement for the damage done to your knee when the delivery truck/driven by our employee collided with your car at the corner of Tenth Street and Fifth Avenue on Friday, November 30. Although the traffic police officer//has sworn that your car did not stop when the light changed, our driver was also possibly at fault. We appreciate the fact that your knee was slightly injured, but our doctor who///examined you at your hospital feels that there can be no possible injury subsequent to your dismissal. We feel sure that this settlement is a fair one. Yours truly, [3] [455]

Reading and Writing Practice

550

com·pa·ny's

mod·u·lar

write-off

af·fect·ed

par

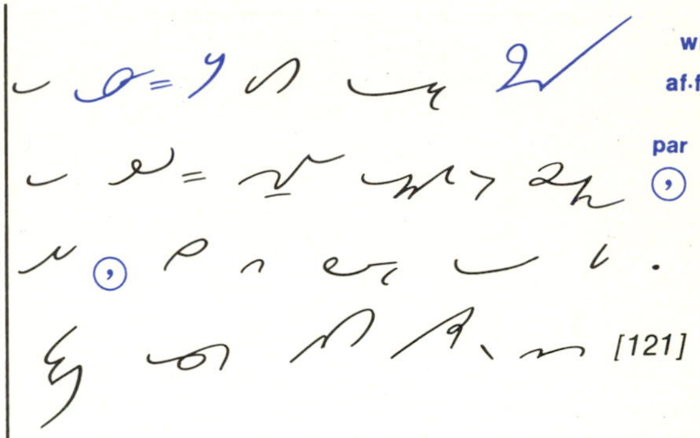

[121]

551

In·fringe·ment

nonr

43,222,221

par

Transcribe: No. 43,222,221

1971

ap

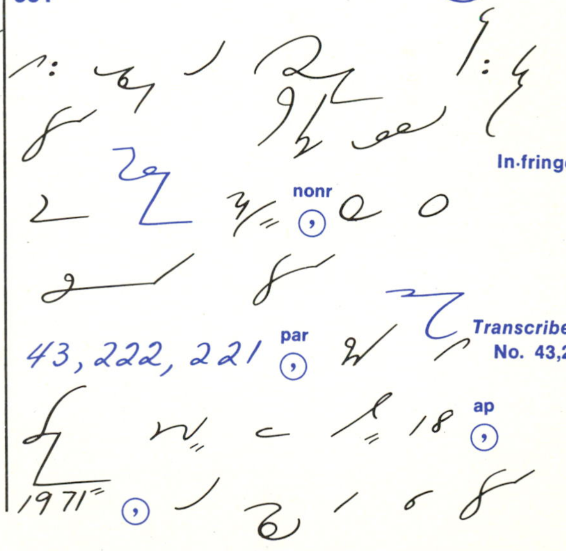

par

re·sem·blance

ap

Cre·ative

conj

[121]

552

le·gal

el·o·quent

par

sep·a·rate·ly

[138]

553

non·pay·ment

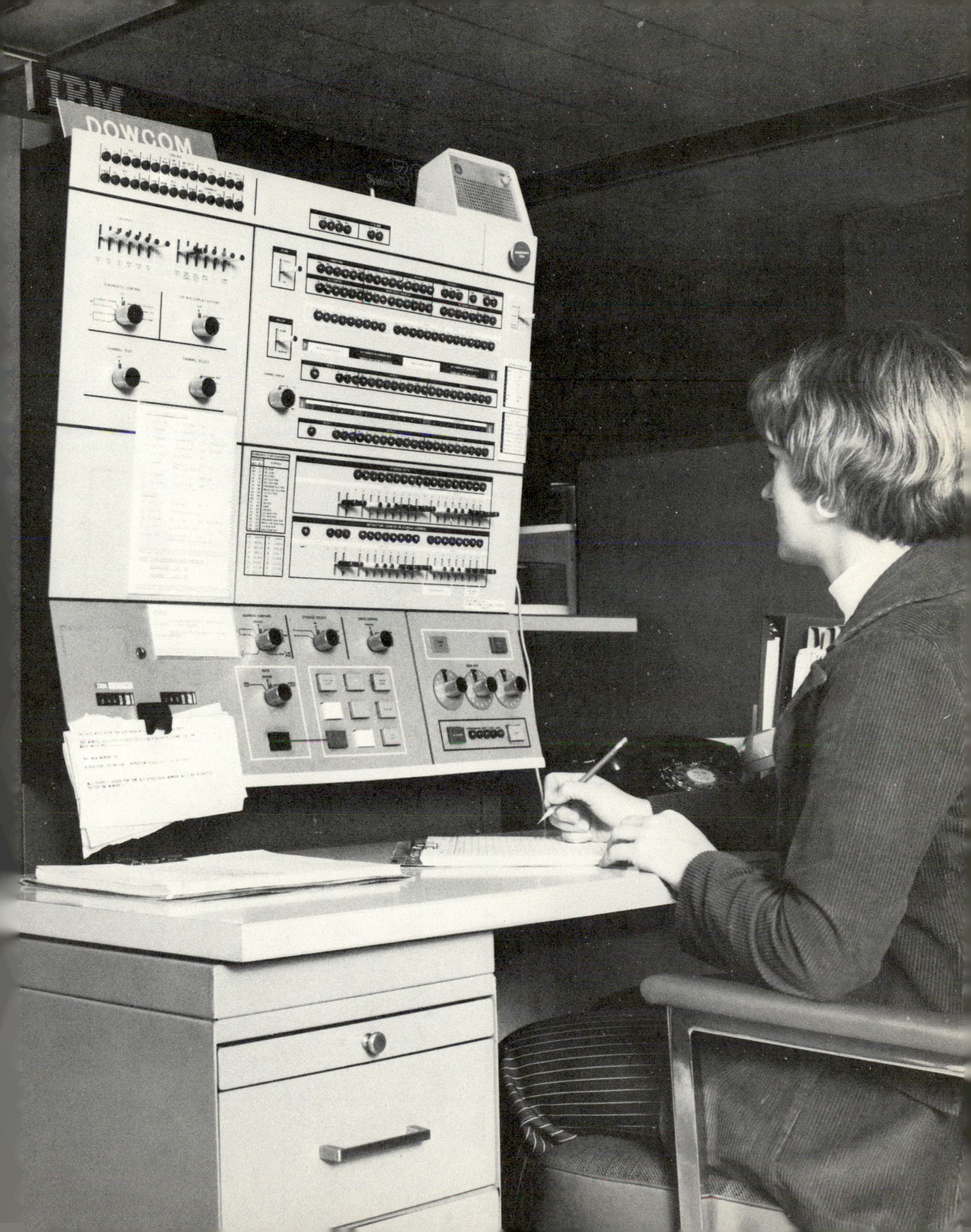
IBM
DOWCOM

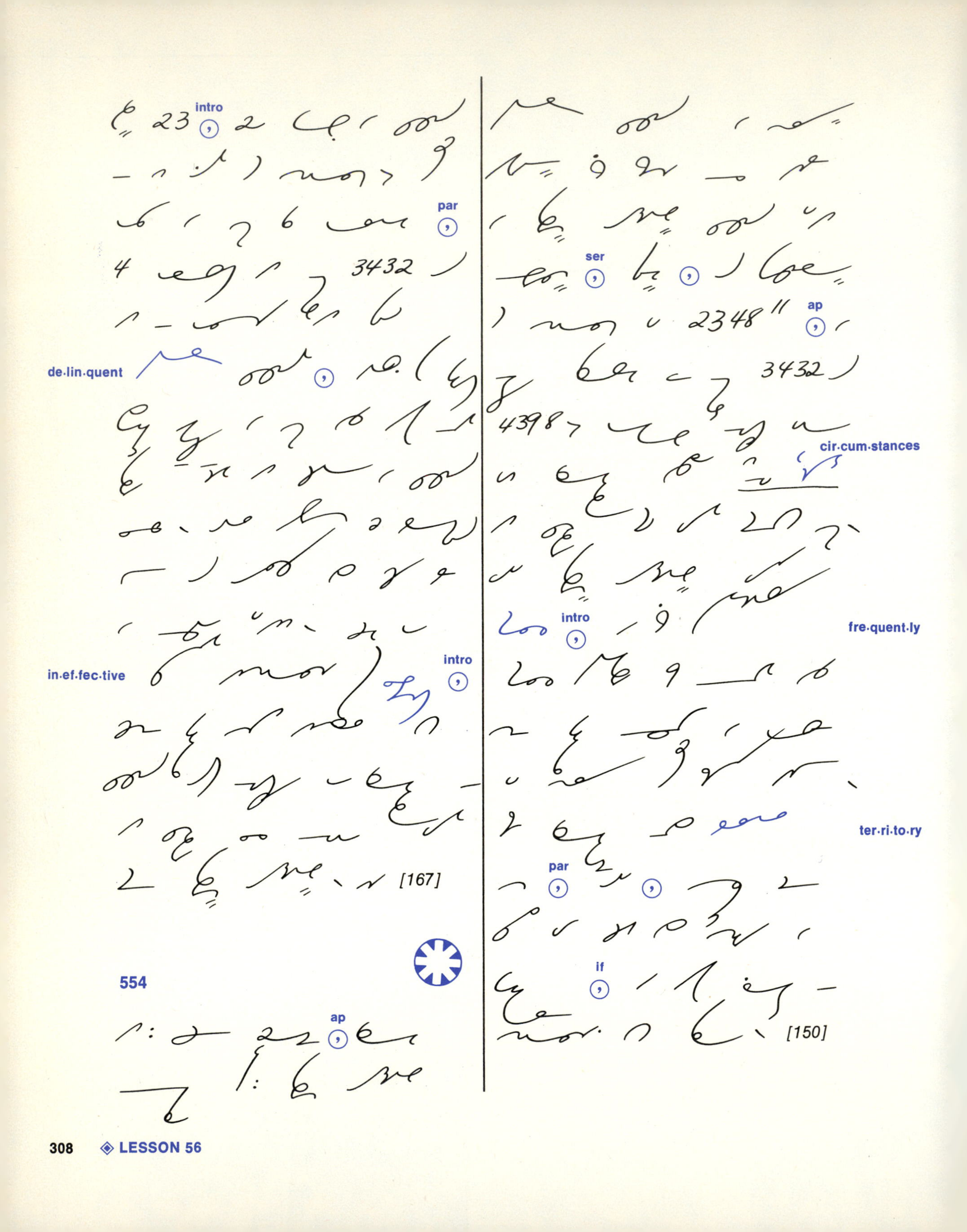

23 intro 3432

par

de·lin·quent

in·ef·fec·tive

intro

[167]

554

ap

ser 2348" ap 3432 4398

cir·cum·stances

intro

fre·quent·ly

ter·ri·to·ry

par

if

[150]

LESSON 57

Shorthand Vocabulary Builder

555 WORD ENDINGS

-sume, -sumption

1

-ort

2

-hood

3

-ship

4

1 Assume, resume, presume, presumption, consumption, consumer.

2 Sort, assort, sportsmen, resort, portable, quarterly, reportable, support, quart.

3 Falsehood, neighborhood, brotherhood, likelihood, boyhood, manhood.

4 Worship, championship, sportsmanship, professorship, kinship, statesmanship, warship.

Building Transcription Skills

556 TRANSCRIPTION TYPING

13

26

37

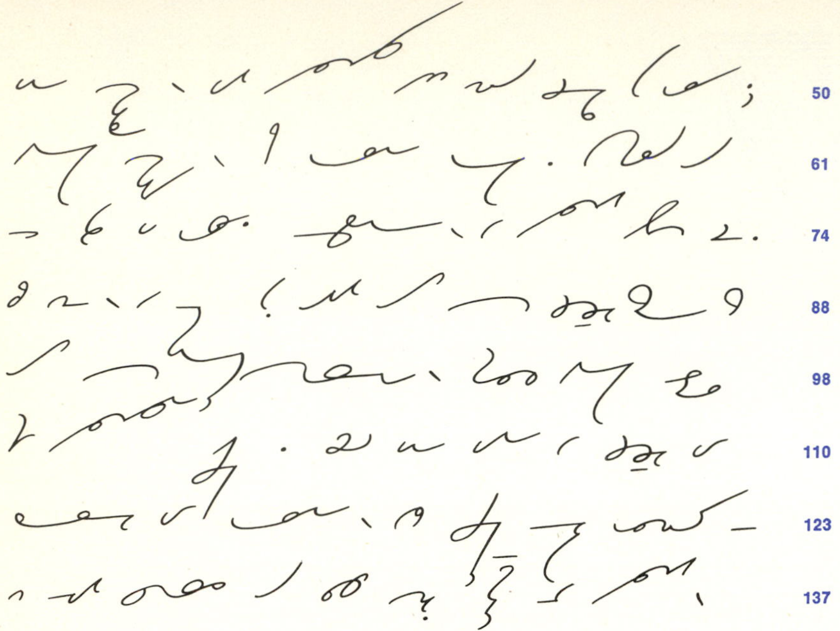

557 **Business Vocabulary Builder**

lease A contract permitting use of land and/or buildings for a specific period of time for payment of rent.

grievance suit A proceeding in court to settle a complaint of being wronged.

Stair-Step Dictation

558 PREVIEW

[559]

[560]

[561]

559 Resort, understand, portable, collapsed, incurred, questionnaire, details.

560 Preventive, basketball, championship, exempts, liability, playoffs.

561 Indicted, perjury, altered, presumption, discrepancies, client's.

LETTERS

559 To: Shirley Keller, Director of Administrative Services Subject: Claim Against Pine Valley Resort[1] Since you were injured at the Pine Valley Resort while you were on company business, I presume that you want me[2] to represent you in the company's case against the resort. As I understand it, you were injured when a[3] portable television fell on your foot when the table on which it was sitting collapsed. Please follow these[4] instructions carefully in preparing your claim and send it to me:

1. Get a statement from your family doctor[5] stating the condition of your foot.
2. Send me a copy of the paid bill for medical expenses incurred[6] at the resort.
3. Complete the enclosed questionnaire and be sure to give full details of the accident.[7]

560 To: Herbert Porter, Accounting Department, Manager of Company Basketball Championship Games Subject:[8] Liability of Company for Injuries During Sports Events This memorandum is written as a[9] preventive measure before the various department basketball teams start championship play. I am enclosing[10] a number of forms to be signed before any play is permitted on the court. The form exempts the company[11] from liability for any injuries incurred during the game. There is little likelihood that any[12] problem will arise, but last year during the championship playoffs of the Brotherhood of Railway Employees[13] a player lost an eye and subsequently sued the Brotherhood for damages. Please send the forms to me before the games.[14]

561 To: Walter Cook, President Subject: Litigation Against Kenneth Mann After studying the evidence in[15] the case against our corporation, I am convinced that Kenneth Mann's brief is shot through with falsehoods and that he could[16] be indicted for perjury. It looks to me as if the quarterly report of earnings has also been[17] materially altered. On this presumption I think that we will have no problem if this case is tried by jury.[18] It would be to our advantage, of course, if we could get a settlement out of court. I know the attorney[19] for Mr. Mann personally, and I shall attempt to arrange a consultation with him so that I can point out[20] the discrepancies in his client's case. Perhaps we can get him to talk Mr. Mann into dropping the suit.[21] [420]

Reading and Writing Practice

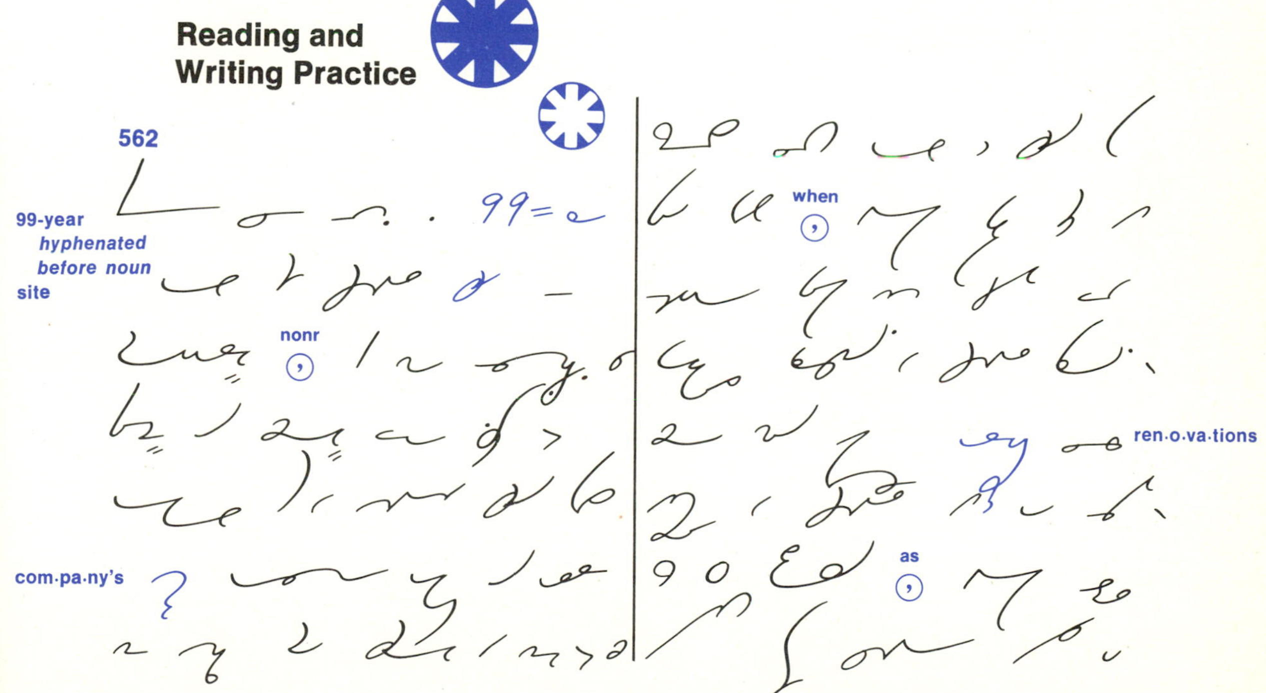

[133]

563

314[26]

Re·sort

ap as

par

12 12 24

re·frig·er·at·ed

when

thawed

us·able

intro

[125]

564

ap

Dis·miss·al

intro

par

ac·cused

pre·sume

al·ready

like·li·hood

griev·ance

[147]

565

ef·fec·tive

vi·o·la·tion

rem·e·dy

par

[127]

566

quar·ter·ly
Transcribe:
45 cents

ap

pos·si·bly

[118]

LESSON 

Shorthand Vocabulary Builder

567 BRIEF-FORM POWER

1 Ever–every, everlasting, whenever, however, whoever, everybody, everywhere, everything, everyone.

2 Time, times, timeless, timepiece, timetable, noontime, overtime.

3 Question, questions, questionable, unquestioned, questioner, questionnaire, questionably, questionless.

4 State, stately, restate, understate, statesman, overstate, stateroom.

568 CITIES

-ton

Riverton, West Newton, Galveston, Castleton, Evanston.

Building Transcription Skills

569 SIMILAR WORDS ■ principal, principle; emigrate, immigrate

Study the following words which are somewhat alike and which are sometimes confused.

principal Chief; leading.

principle A rule; a general truth.

emigrate To go away from a country.

immigrate To come into a country.

570 **Business Vocabulary Builder**

merger A union of commercial units or corporations.

Dun & Bradstreet A well-known credit-rating company.

Progressive Dictation [100–125]

571 PREVIEW

[572]

[573]

[574]

[575]

572 Corporation, breach, warranty, inferior, allegations, timetable.
573 Overtime, lunchroom, accident, explosion, whenever, everybody.
574 Noontime, affidavits, wet, companions, obstruction, negligence.
575 Legal, standpoint, questionnaire, invasion, privacy, returns.

LETTERS

[1 Minute at 100]

572 Gentlemen: Your letter to our sales manager stating that you intend to sue our corporation for breach of warranty for supplying/washing machines of inferior quality has been referred to me. It is our opinion that you overstate the case and make a number//of questionable allegations about this merchandise. Will you please delay, however, until our salesman Larry Pope, has adjusted///his timetable for calling on you. After he reports on his inspection, we will be in touch with you again. Yours very truly, [1]

[1 Minute at 110]

573 Dear Mr. Lamb: I learned only this morning about the accident you had while working overtime in the company lunchroom last Friday. Whenever/you are able, I should like to visit you in the hospital so that you can state for our records the conditions under which the accident occurred,//name everybody who saw the explosion, give the exact time when it happened, and supply any additional details that you feel are important.///Will you please inform my office whenever your doctor is willing for you to talk with me. Everybody hopes you are getting along well. Yours truly, [2]

[1 Minute at 120]

574 Dear Miss Berk: I have carefully examined your claim for $2,000 for damages suffered in a fall when you were on your way into the building on July/18 after a noontime appointment. We have sworn affidavits from three workers that they did not leave any wet rags on the mall. Indeed, they had not been working on//the mall that noon. We also have statements from two of your companions that the fall was not caused by any obstruction whatever in your path. Unless an accident outside/// the building is caused by negligence of our staff, the company cannot be held responsible in any way. Please reconsider your claim. Yours very truly, [3]

[1 Minute at 125]

575 To: Wilma Montrose, Director of Personnel Subject: Proposed Questionnaire to All Personnel Thank you, Wilma, for letting me review from a legal standpoint the proposed/questionnaire to be sent to all personnel. Two of the questions (Nos. 11 and 16) should be restated. They could be interpreted as an invasion of privacy.// You know how concerned everybody everywhere is about this point. I would be very careful not to open my department to question in this respect. The rest of the///questionnaire is excellent. The questions are clearly stated, and the results should provide you with data that will be very useful to your department. Good luck with the returns. [4] [455]

Reading and Writing Practice

576

merg·er

ap

intro

ev·ery·where

intro

opin·ion

intro

de·ci·sion

le·gal·ly

intro

ser

ap

spe·cial·iz·ing

Cham·pi·on

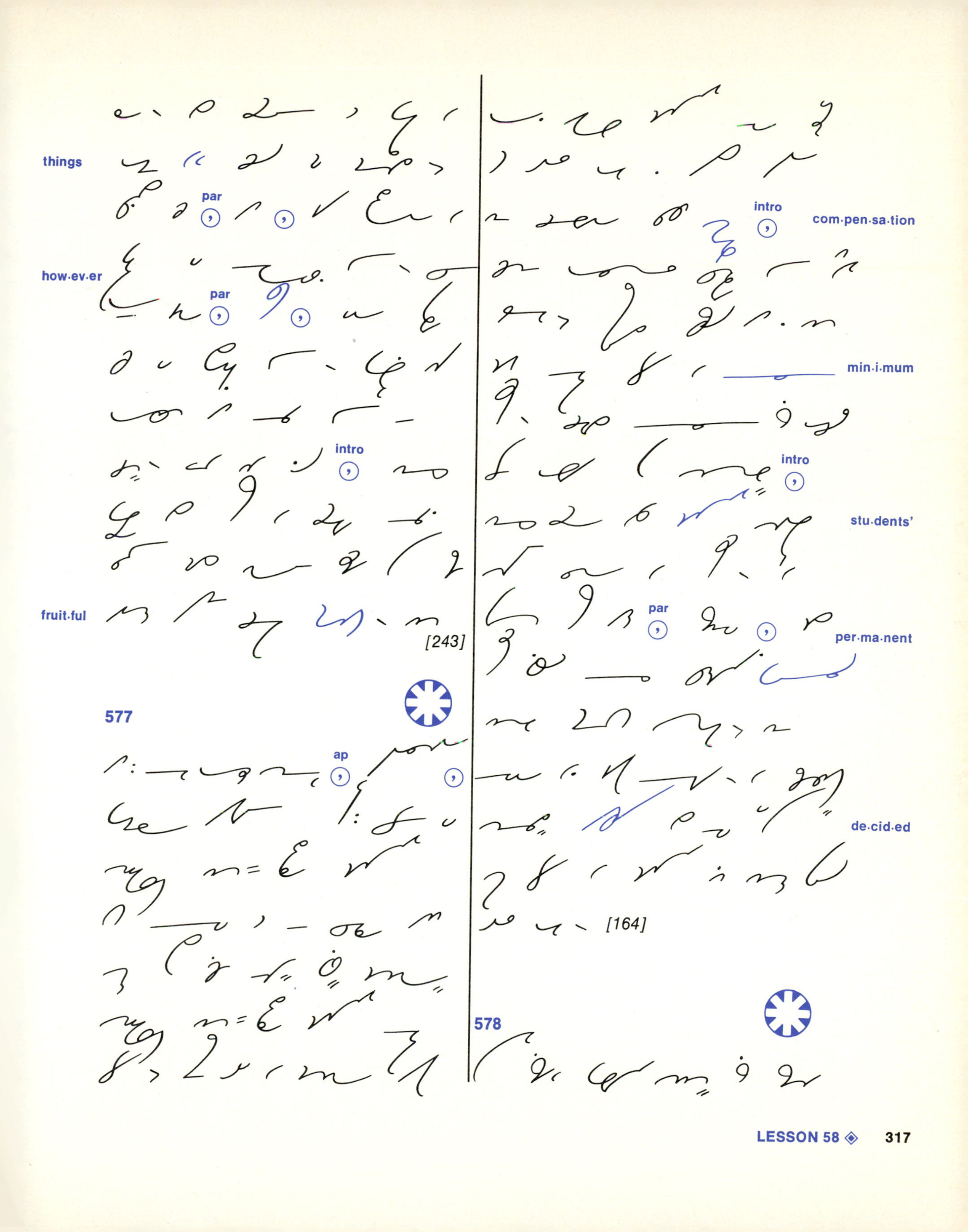

things

par

how·ev·er

par

intro

fruit·ful

[243]

577

ap

intro

com·pen·sa·tion

min·i·mum

intro

stu·dents'

par

per·ma·nent

de·cid·ed

[164]

578

re·states

kit

par

off·set

intro

[141]

579

nonr

es·tab·lish

when

re·course

par

at·tor·neys

ser

conj

pro·ce·dures

par

in·debt·ed·ness

[141]

LESSON 59

Shorthand Vocabulary Builder

580 WORD-BUILDING PRINCIPLES

Compound Words

1 

Tim, Tom

2 

Ah, Aw

3 

Y

4 

1 Anyhow, however, someone, anywhere, withstand, worthwhile, whatsoever, within.

2 Estimate, legitimate, timber, bottom, custom, customer.

3 Ahead, ahoy, away, awake, awakened, award, awarded, await.

4 Yacht, yawn, yield, yard, yardstick, young, barnyard, vineyard.

Building Transcription Skills

581 TRANSCRIPTION TYPING

12

23

35

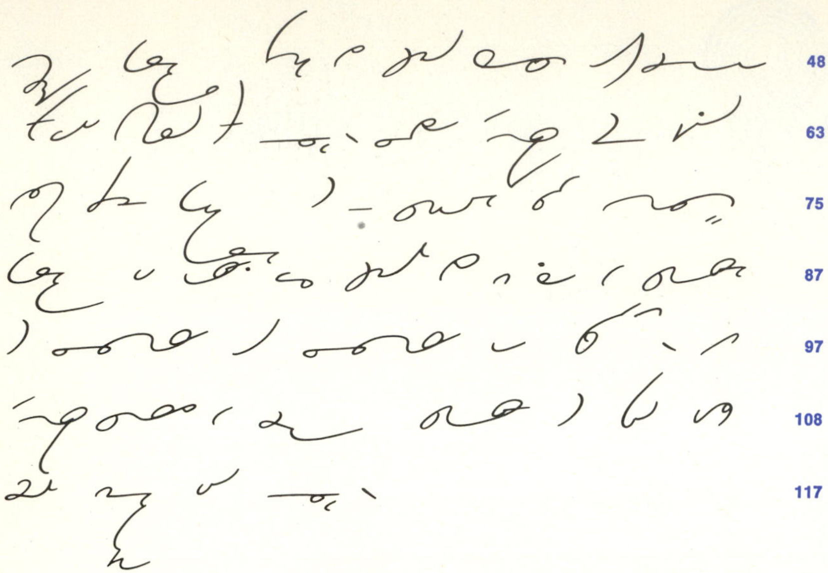

582 **Business Vocabulary Builder**

cost-plus Paid on the basis of a fixed rate of profit added to the cost of production.

5/10, n/30 An expression of terms which allows a 5 percent discount if an invoice is paid in 10 days; net amount must be paid in 30 days.

Stair-Step Dictation

583 PREVIEW

[584]

[585]

[586]

584 Liability, whatsoever, Yoder, legitimate, malfunction, barnyard.

585 Hesitate, appraiser, safeguards, notary, awarded, Riverton.

586 Luncheon, library, locate, shortages, terminate, co-workers.

LETTERS

584 To: James Downing, Sales Manager Subject: Your Letter of July 7 about Invoice 19865 It[1] is my opinion, Jim, that our company has no liability whatsoever on the warranty given[2] to Mr. Yoder. The one-year warranty expired at midnight on June

2, and the customer has[3] no legitimate claim for any malfunction that occurred the next day either in the barnyard or anywhere[4] else. Although the date when Mr. Yoder signed and mailed the warranty was June 6, the date the warranty is in[5] effect is determined by the date of purchase as shown in your sales invoice. In this case, that date is June 2. If[6] Mr. Yoder sues, as he threatens to do, he would not be awarded any damages in any court in the land.[7]

585 To: Walter Cook, President Subject: Contract for the 25-Year Lease of Georgia Timberland Today I received[8] the contract we have awaited so long. I have reviewed it carefully and find nothing whatsoever that would[9] cause you to hesitate to go ahead with the deal. It falls within the estimates made by the real estate[10] appraiser and contains the requested safeguards. Please sign it on the bottom line on page 3 in the presence of a[11] notary public and mail it directly to the Georgia Timber Company within business hours tomorrow[12] without fail. I would witness it myself, but I am leaving at 4 o'clock with Mr. Ahern to complete[13] the contract, which was awarded to us just this week with Riverton Manufacturing Company.[14]

586 To: Louise Cummings, Director, Personnel Department Subject: Termination of Howard Mann's Employment[15] I have thought very carefully about the situation as you described it to me yesterday during our[16] luncheon appointment. I have also consulted my library to locate similar cases, but I have not[17] yet found one anywhere exactly like this one. Since you have not yet been able to get to the bottom of the[18] story regarding the shortages, I agree that it would be best to terminate Mr. Mann's employment on[19] other grounds if possible. You have said that you have had numerous complaints that he is not carrying his part of[20] the work load. To protect yourself, why not set up a hearing on these complaints before a committee of his co-workers?[21] [420]

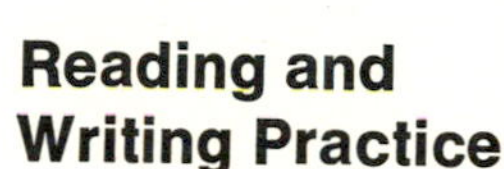

Reading and Writing Practice

587

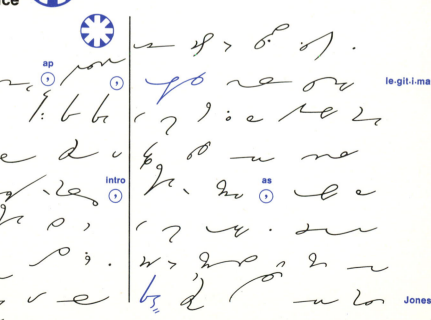

ap

intro

dis·rup·tive

le·git·i·mate

as

Jones's

in·sub·or·di·na·tion

when

[137]

588

ap

ware·house

as

cost-plus
hyphenated before noun

13.8,

par

if

in·dem·ni·fied

5/

as·sess

[166]

589

intro

45

ap

par

ex·ten·sion

worth·while

cus·tom-made *hypenated before noun*

[193]

590

ap

Ahoy

ap

intro

and o

par

and o

intro

usu·al

sup·pli·er

[120]

Shorthand Vocabulary Builder

591 PHRASING FOR SPEED

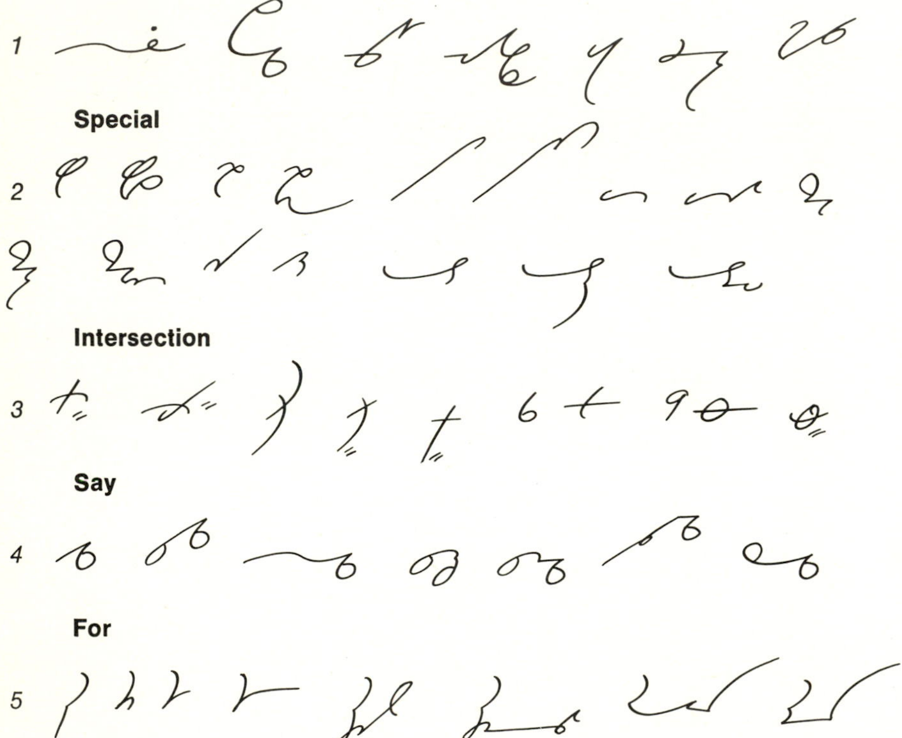

1 Glad to hear, able to say, in addition to the, in order to prepare, ought to be, seems to be, up to date.

2 I hope, I hope that, we hope, we hope you will, to do, to do this, of course, of course it is, as soon as, as soon as possible, as soon as you can, your order, to us, let us, let us have, let us know.

3 Chamber of Commerce, COD, vice versa, TV, New Jersey, 6 p.m., 9 a.m., Rhode Island.

4 To say, I would say, glad to say, I can say, I cannot say, did not say, I will say.

5 For which, for you, for the, for them, for a few days, for a few minutes, for a long time, for some time.

Building Transcription Skills

592 **Business Vocabulary Builder**

bankruptcy A judgment of insolvency with a legal distribution of all assets to creditors.

patent A grant by the government assuring an inventor of sole right to make, use, or sell an invention for a certain period of time.

Reading and Writing Practice

593

stock·hold·ers

par

div·i·dend

usu·al·ly

intro

if

oc·ca·sion·al·ly

sum·ma·ries

[178]

594

Transcribe: 37 cents

conj

bet·ter-than-av·er·age *hyphenated before noun*

intro

pru·dent [117]

595

Mer·can·tile

bank·rupt·cy

Transcribe: $3,022.09

3,022.09

[153]

596

TV

par

if

ap·pli·ca·tion

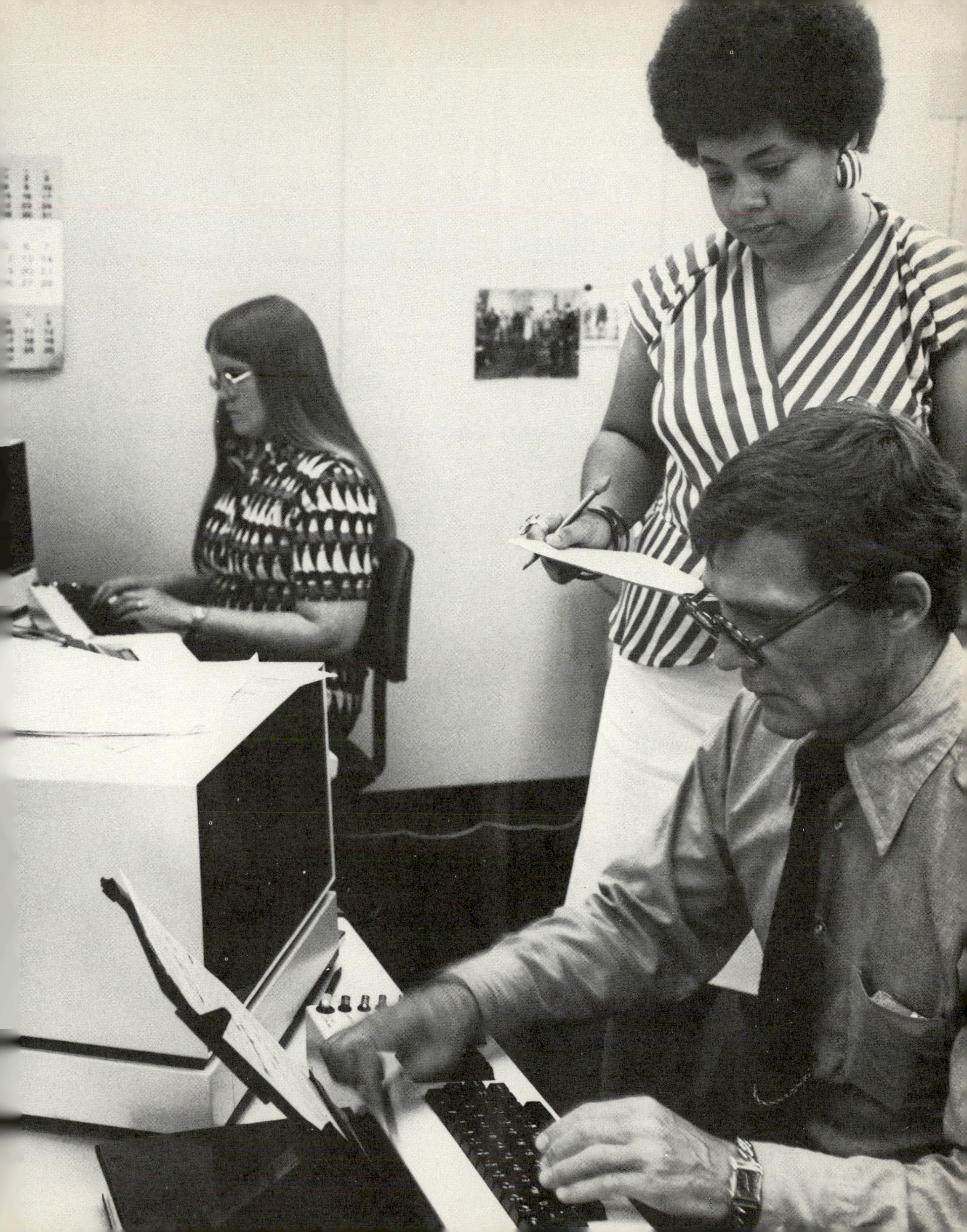

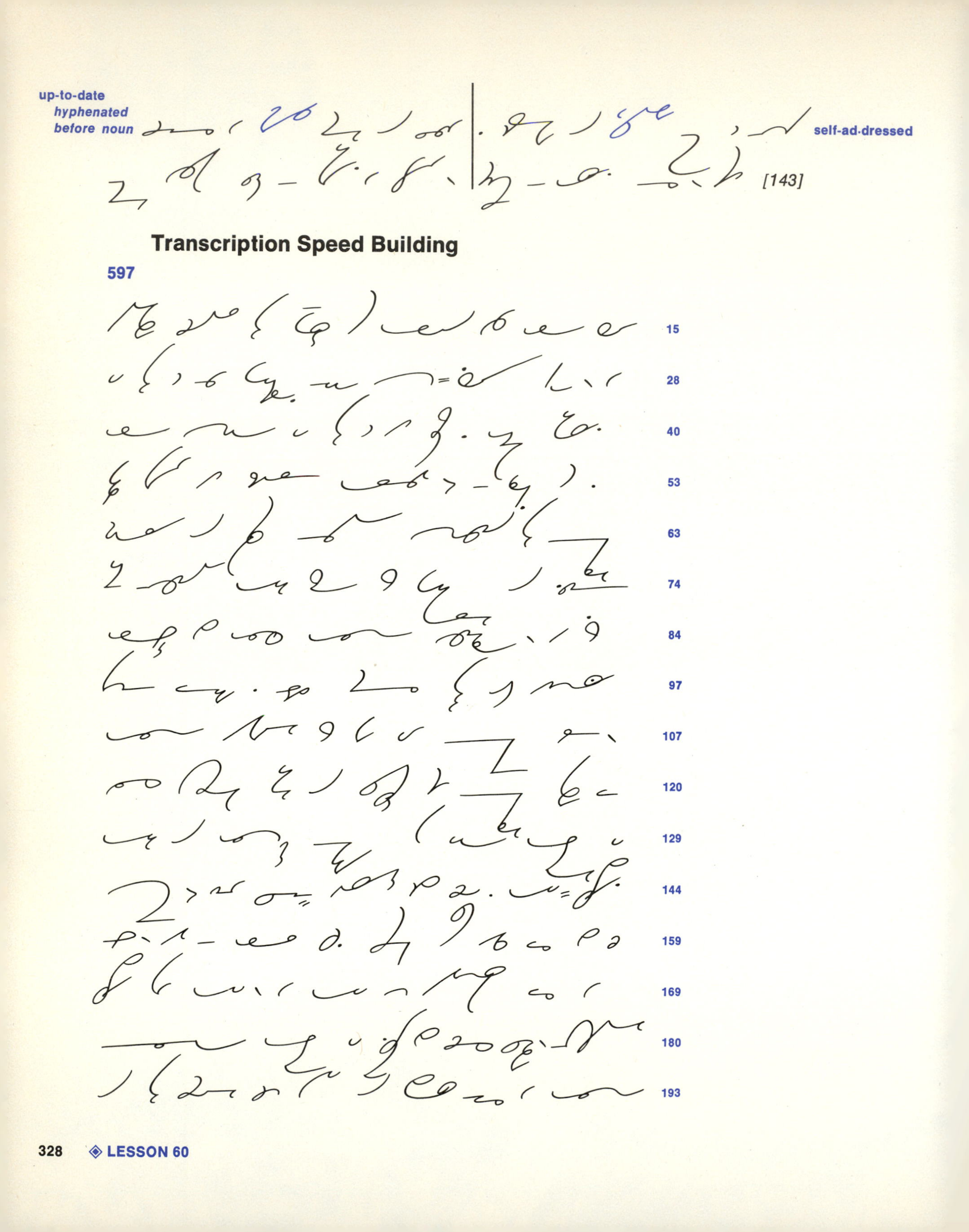

up-to-date *hyphenated before noun*

self-ad·dressed

[143]

Transcription Speed Building

597

15

28

40

53

63

74

84

97

107

120

129

144

159

169

180

193

206

218

229

243

257

270

280

292

304

316

327

336

598 Transcription Quiz

8 13

8½ 14

[92]

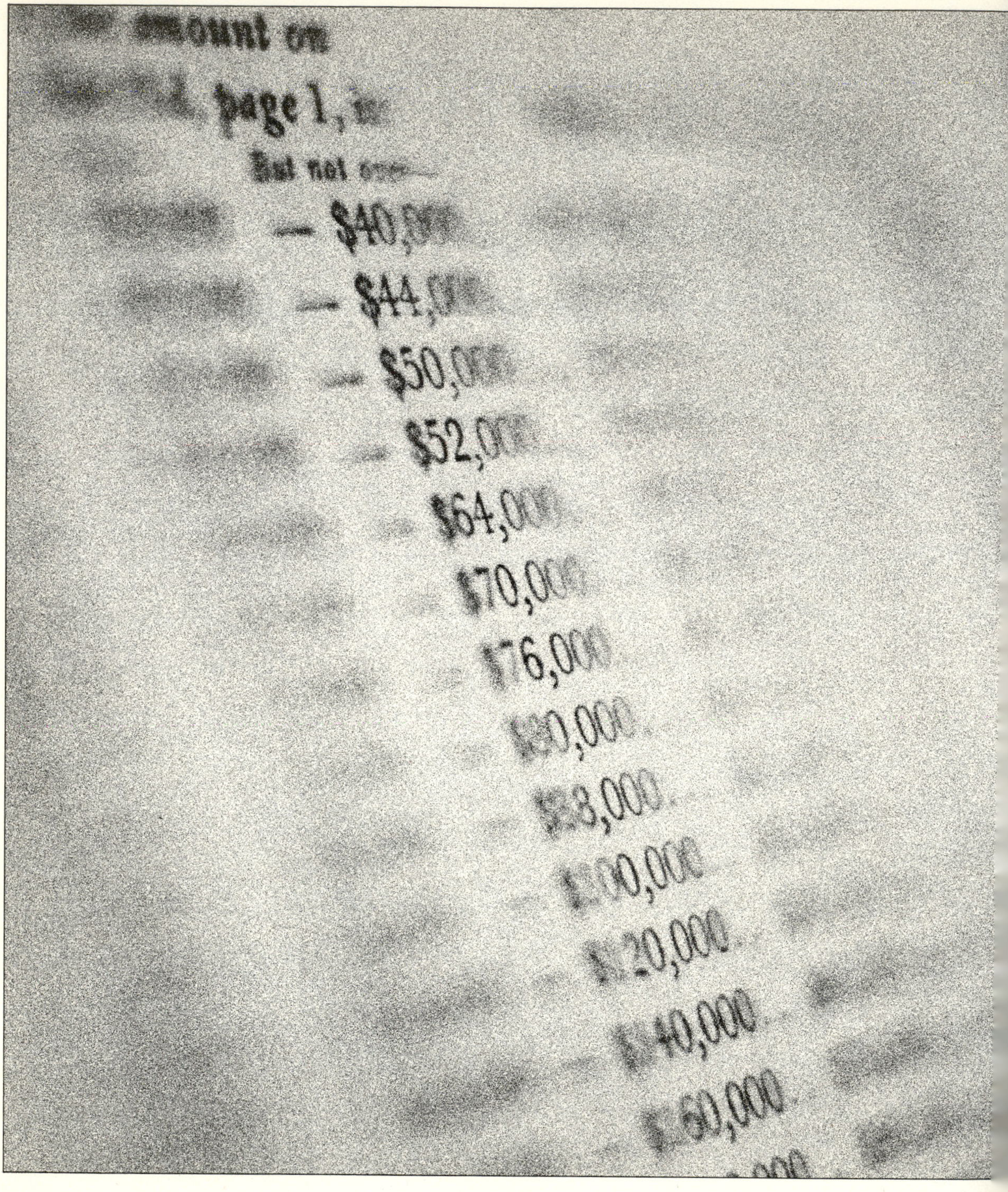

amount on

page 1,

but not over

— $40,

— $44,

— $50,

— $52,

$64,

$70,

$76,

0,000

8,000

00,000

20,000

40,000

60,000

Unit 13
FINANCIAL SERVICES

You have just been transferred to the Financial Division. Here you are secretary to Charles Sanford, chief financial officer, whose title you will use in signing his correspondence.

Your company is Great Industries, a conglomerate comprising a number of companies manufacturing a diversity of products from frozen foods to air filters to filing equipment.

Mr. Sanford is responsible for providing the money for carrying on the corporation's business, and he must be sure that the cash flow will provide ample funds for day-to-day operations. He recommends financial policy to the president and the board of directors for issuing bonds and for borrowing money in other ways as well as for arranging mergers with other companies.

He is watchdog over expenditures and constantly tries to keep expenses down throughout the organization. One of his duties is to represent his corporation's stocks and bonds as good investments before financial groups, such as financial analysts, who recommend securities to investors.

LESSON 

Shorthand Vocabulary Builder

599 WORD FAMILIES

-tate

1

-ify

2

-rity

3

-gate

4

1 Rotate, dictate, hesitate, imitate, irritate, facilitate.

2 Justify, classify, amplify, qualify, notify, simplify, verify.

3 Maturity, prosperity, security, authority, clarity, majority, charity.

4 Obligate, navigate, aggregate, delegate, interrogate, instigate.

Building Transcription Skills

600 NOTEBOOK AND TRANSCRIPTION TIPS ■ large insertions.

Office-style dictation presents problems which must be corrected quickly and clearly. When the dictator changes the order of words, sentences, or paragraphs, the changes must be marked so that the items will be transcribed in the correct order. When the dictator wishes to make a large insertion, it can be handled in this manner:

1 Write a large *A* in a circle at the point where the new material is to be inserted.

2 Draw two heavy lines after the last sentence that has been dictated to separate the insertion from the rest of the dictation.

3 Alongside the two heavy lines, write "Insert A" encircled; then write the insert below.

4 Draw two heavy lines to indicate the end of the insert.

Subsequent insertions in the same letter can be spotted and identified with *B, C,* and so on.

ILLUSTRATION OF OFFICE-STYLE DICTATION

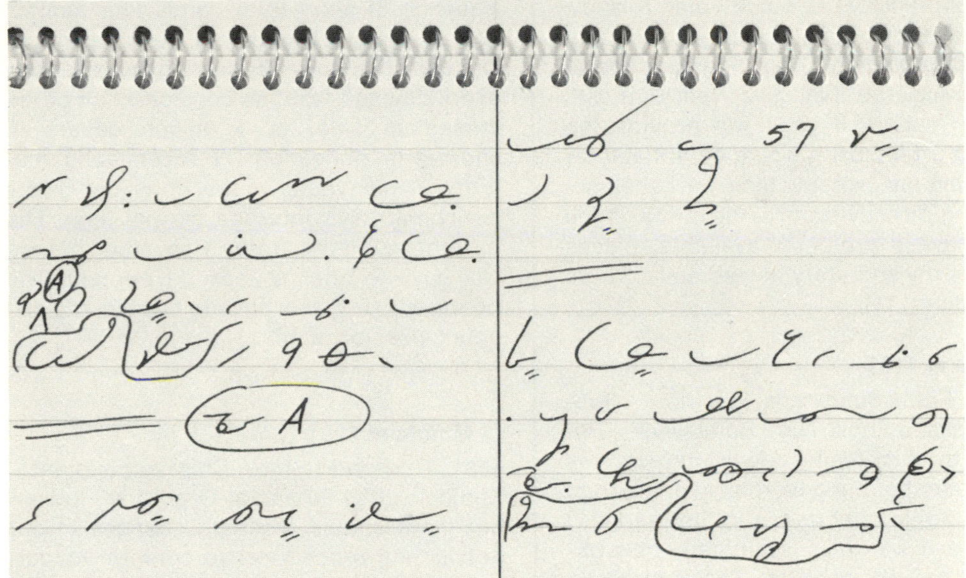

601 **Business Vocabulary Builder**

withholding tax A part of an employee's salary withheld by the employer to be paid to the government.

audit An examination of financial records to check their accuracy.

Progressive Dictation [100–125]

602 PREVIEW

[603]

[604]

[605]

[606]

603 Notifying, luncheon, clarify, during the last, facilitate, overhead, projector.
604 Short-term, frightening, antitrust, confidence, defer, austerity, expansion.
605 Reconsideration, issuance, obvious, serious, prosperity, discount, 11 percent.
606 Instigate, conform, adoption, corporations, analysts, Fortune.

LETTERS

[1 Minute at 100]

603 Dear Mr. Stack: Thank you for notifying me of the change of time of the luncheon on September 10. Since I plan to show some charts that should/clarify your members' understanding of our financial operations during the last five years, it will facilitate matters if you//will provide the overhead projector. It would be difficult for me to bring my own machine, for I shall not be coming directly from///the office. If you do not have a projector available, please telephone my secretary immediately. Yours very cordially, [1]

[1 Minute at 110]

604 To: Frank Simmonds, President Subject: Proposed Short-Term Bond Issue Because of the frightening rise in interest rates and the effect of the government's/antitrust suits on public confidence in the market, I suggest that we defer issuing any new obligations for six months. The majority// opinion seems to be that conditions will settle down by that time. I believe that we should operate on an austerity budget and delay expansion///during this period. I should like to amplify my reasons for this recommendation in a personal conversation with you. [2]

[1 Minute at 120]

605 To: Frank Simmonds, President Subject: Reconsideration of Short-Term Bond Issue Although we decided to defer the issuance of short-term bonds four months ago,/it is now obvious that we were wrong. Our cash position is becoming more serious every day and justifies consideration of the immediate sale//of 5 million dollars in short-term obligations. I recommend maturity in ten years in the hope that prosperity will have returned by that time. The current///interest rate is so high that we will have to offer at least 11 percent. The bonds will probably have to be sold at a discount, possibly at 97. [3]

[1 Minute at 125]

606 To: Robert Stacy, Chief Accountant Subject: LIFO Financial Reporting I wonder if we should instigate changes in our accounting procedures to conform to/current trends. The principal change would be the adoption of LIFO (Last In/First Out) inventory reporting. The authority for this new procedure is the//government itself. It is being adopted by many large corporations and is widely approved by security analysts as giving a better picture of a///company's operations. Although I am sure you are familiar with the plan, I am enclosing an article that appeared in *Fortune* magazine which you may not have seen. [4] [455]

Reading and Writing Practice

607

ap

with·hold·ing

intro

prep·a·ra·tion

par

year's
pay·roll

if

anal·y·sis

[225]

duties

608

Transcribe:
$150,000
90-day
hyphenated
before noun

Chat·ta·noo·ga

150

ABD

fi·nan·cial

fa·cil·i·tate

if

intro

ap

[164]

609

ap

sum·ma·rize

au·dit

cor·po·rate

par

del·e·gat·ing

intro

vouch·ers

clas·si·fy·ing

[154]

LESSON 62

Shorthand Vocabulary Builder

610 WORD BEGINNINGS

Per-, Pur-

Al-

Mis-

Circum-

1 Permit, perpetual, persistence, permeate, pursue, purvey, purport, purple.

2 Also, altered, alteration, alternate, alternative, although, altercation, altogether.

3 Mislead, miscellaneous, miscue, misfire, misspell, misunderstand.

4 Circumstance, circumvent, circumspect, circumference, circumvented, circumflex, circumstantiate.

Building Transcription Skills

611 TRANSCRIPTION TYPING

10

24

38

48

60

71

85

96

107

120

125

612 Business Vocabulary Builder

callable bonds Bonds issued by a government or a corporation which the holder must surrender for redemption (present for payment) at the request of the government or the corporation.

underwriters Corporate bodies (or individuals) who engage to buy, at a determined price and time, all or part of the stock in an enterprise or company that is not subscribed for by the public.

Stair-Step Dictation

613 PREVIEW

[614]

[615]

[616]

614 Prerecession, mature, possibility, circumvent, approximately, peruse, let us know.

615 Rebuilding, miscellaneous, quarter, upward, inflation, discount.

616 Current, circumstances, rigid, collection, altered, appropriate, schedule.

LETTERS

614 To: Frank Simmonds, President Subject: $150,000 60-Day Loan Because our inventories[1] must be built up to prerecession levels, we must immediately borrow $150,000[2] to mature in 60 days. I feel that tight money has driven city bank discount rates so high that we[3] should explore the possibility of getting this loan at a smaller bank than we have always used and thus[4] circumvent the high rates here. These small banks also apparently have larger deposits than they have demands for loans. Therefore,[5] I am writing five banks in cities with approximately 50,000 people. I am asking them[6] to peruse our financial reports and let us know if they are a possible source for such loans and what rate they would charge.[7]

615 Dear Mr. Winters: We are in need of a 60-day loan for $150,000 immediately[8] and other similar loans in the future for use in rebuilding our inventory levels to their[9] 1975 levels. I am enclosing some miscellaneous financial reports. You will see that[10] our performance over the past two years and during the current second quarter has shown improved profits. We would[11] mislead you, though, if we did not point out that some of the gains result from valuing our inventories upward[12] because of inflation. Our credit rating is excellent in all of the rating services. Please let us know[13] if you would be interested in making this loan and the discount rate you would charge. Yours very truly,[14]

616 To: Howard Payne, Credit Manager Subject: Alterations in Credit Policy Our loss on bad debts is running[15] altogether too high. To circumvent additional losses caused by current business circumstances, I[16] think we should pursue a more rigid policy. This would include more careful investigation of customers[17] before granting credit as well as following up on past-due accounts with greater persistence. My final[18] suggestion is that when we give up on an account, we turn it over to the collection agency at least ten[19] days sooner than we are now doing. This altered policy would improve our cash flow and would be altogether[20] appropriate under present business conditions. Please develop a definite schedule that follows these[21] suggestions. Can you have it ready to discuss with me over lunch next Wednesday, the 17th, at 1 o'clock?[22] [440]

Reading and Writing Practice

617

ap

cir·cum·spect

debts

com·par·a·tive

conj

cir·cum·vent

short-term *hyphenated before noun*

[157]

618

ap

as

Transcribe: 25 percent

conj

high·er-priced *hyphenated before noun*

al·to·geth·er too

as

me·di·um-priced *hyphenated before noun*

intro

high·est-priced
hyphenated before noun

if

idea
na·tion·wide

[264]

619

call·able

30-year
hyphenated before noun

Transcribe:
$1,200,000

Bel·gium

mis·cel·la·neous

intro

ap

if

al·ter

and o

[161]

LESSON 63

Shorthand Vocabulary Builder

620 BRIEF-FORM POWER

1 Character, characteristic, characteristically, characterize, characterization, uncharacteristic.

2 Advantage, advantages, advantageous, advantageously, disadvantage, disadvantaged; business, businesses, businesslike, businessman.

3 Out-how, outline, outboard, outdoors, outdistance, outpost, outlive, outfit.

4 Use, useful, useless, usable, user, usage, misuse, disuse, reuse.

621 CITIES

-ingham

Wilmingham, Birmingham, Buckingham, Nottingham, Cunningham, Shrevingham.

Building Transcription Skills

622 SIMILAR WORDS ■ sometime, some time, sometimes; choose, chose

Study the following words which are somewhat alike and which are sometimes confused.

sometime At an undefined time.

some time A period of time.

sometimes Now and then.

choose To select.

chose Did choose (past tense of to choose).

623 **Business Vocabulary Builder**

diversification The act of varying activities and investments.

savings bank A bank which receives and invests money from a private depositor and pays interest on the deposits.

Progressive Dictation [110–130]

624 **PREVIEW**

[625]

[626]

[627]

[628]

625 For some time, circumspect, capital, expansion, double-digit, criteria.

626 $100,000; certificates, deposit, tax-free, short-term, investments.

627 Headquarters, gasoline, fuel, excess, directive, characteristic.

628 Cashier's, canceled, outdistancing, useless, characteristically, courteous.

LETTERS

[1 Minute at 110]

625 Gentlemen: I have felt for some time that our company has been too circumspect in its investment of capital funds. They could be put to better use/until needed when starting a new plant or making some other type of costly expansion. With double-digit inflation we should be getting more for the//use of our money by choosing short-term investments that reflect the new higher interest rates. There are two criteria for our selections. First, we must///be able to get our money out when we need it. Second, the rate must be advantageous. Please send me a list that have these characteristics. Yours truly, [1]

[1 Minute at 120]

626 Dear Mr. Cunningham: This will confirm our order to buy $100,000 certificates of deposit when and if the interest is increased to the/advantageous rate of 9 percent. As you indicated during our telephone conversation, it would be useless to try to obtain any tax-free 11//percent bonds in the present market situation. However, if any such offering comes to your attention, please give me a call, for we are looking for short-term///investments that will put some of our available funds to use until we start building a new plant in Birmingham in October. Yours very truly, [2]

[1 Minute at 125]

627 To: Marvin Mayer, Sales Manager Subject: Curtailment of Automobile Rentals Unfortunately, we have had to make a decision here at headquarters that will be/disadvantageous to some of your sales force in remote areas. Because of the increase in the price of gasoline and the fuel shortage, we are forced to curtail the use of rented//automobiles for distances in excess of 100 miles from the sales representatives' bases of operations. If they travel beyond this limit, they are///to use public transportation. They may rent a car at the point of arrival if that will be useful. This directive is characteristic of our entire cost-cutting policy. [3]

[1 Minute at 130]

628 Gentlemen: I am enclosing our cashier's check for $18,916.25 in full payment of our 90-day 9 percent note for/$18,500. Please send us the canceled note for our records. Because interest rates are outdistancing profits, we have decided that it would be useless to follow our original// plans for expansion of our plant and for modernizing our equipment until conditions improve. We do not expect, then, to need additional short-term loans before springtime///unless the situation changes greatly. Thank you for the characteristically courteous way in which you handled this loan and others similar to it. Yours very truly, [4] [485]

Reading and Writing Practice

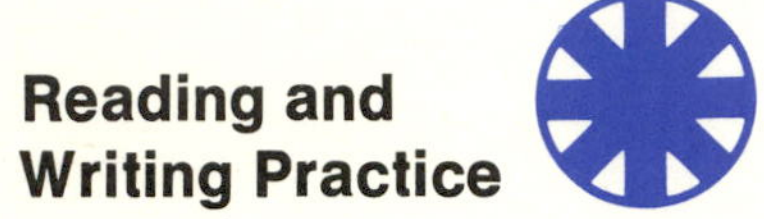

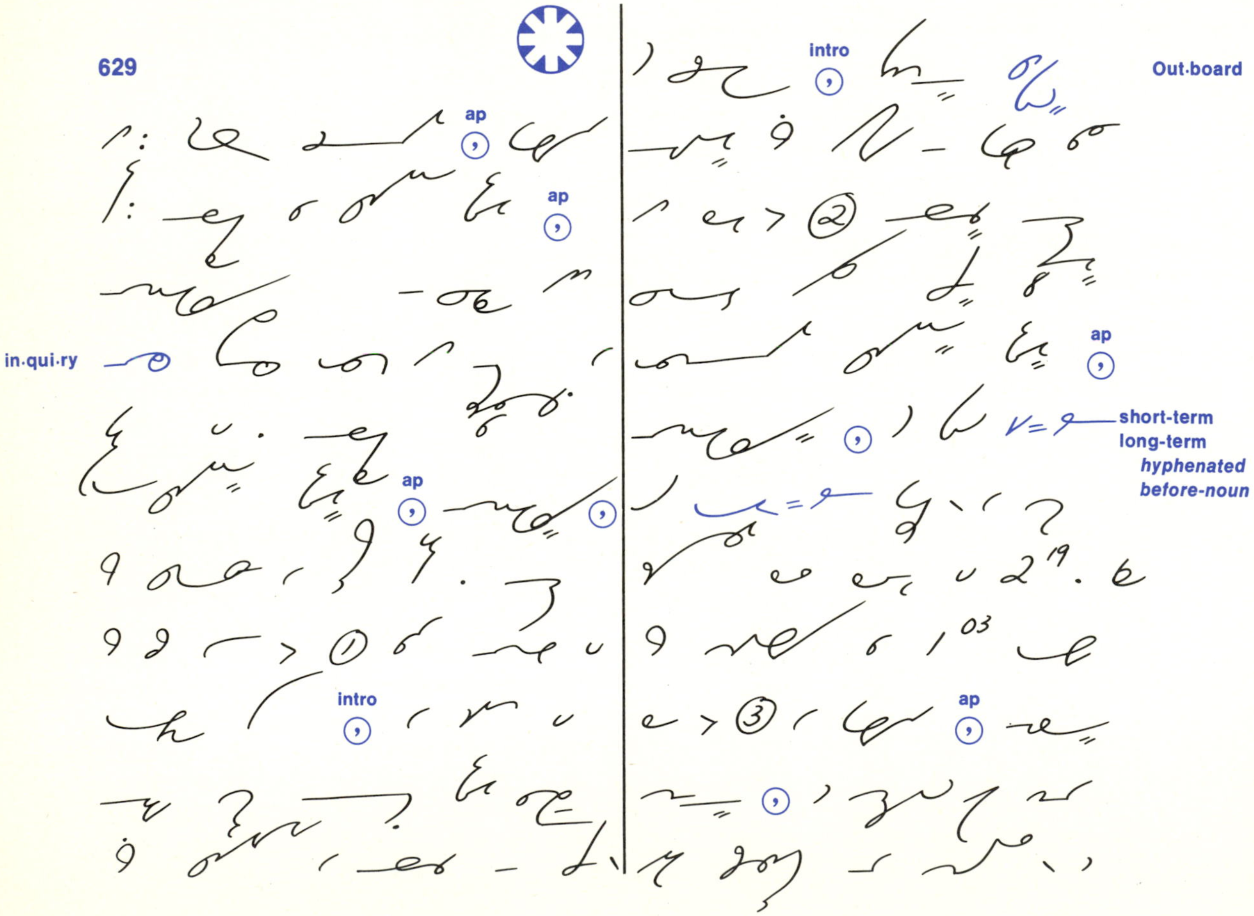

629

ap

ap

in·qui·ry

ap

intro

intro

Out·board

ap

short-term
long-term
hyphenated
before-noun

ap

ser

iq

di·ver·si·fi·ca·tion

if

ap

intro

much-needed
hyphenated before noun

boom

intro

de·sir·abil·i·ty

ap

par

[414]

630

ap

In·ven·to·ries

intro

if

com·pet·i·tors

intro

fore·cast

[158]

631

ex·pi·ra·tion

if

un·ex·pired

[130]

LESSON 

Shorthand Vocabulary Builder

632 WORD-BUILDING PRINCIPLES

Past Tense

1

Vowels Inside Curves

2

Vowels Outside Angles

3

OO-s

4

1 Heard, finished, filled, programmed, styled, seemed, passed, filed.
2 Bare, gave, given, bell, pair, pardon, search, church, hosiery.
3 Refer, trace, earnest, firm, felt, imagine, middle, rave.
4 Us, discuss, bus, gracious, conscious, continuous, customer, just.

Building Transcription Skills

633 TRANSCRIPTION TYPING

8

21

32

634 **Business Vocabulary Builder**

promissory note A written promise to pay on demand or at a fixed future time a sum of money to a specified person.

statute of limitations A law setting a time limit on the enforcement of a right.

Stair-Step Dictation

635 PREVIEW

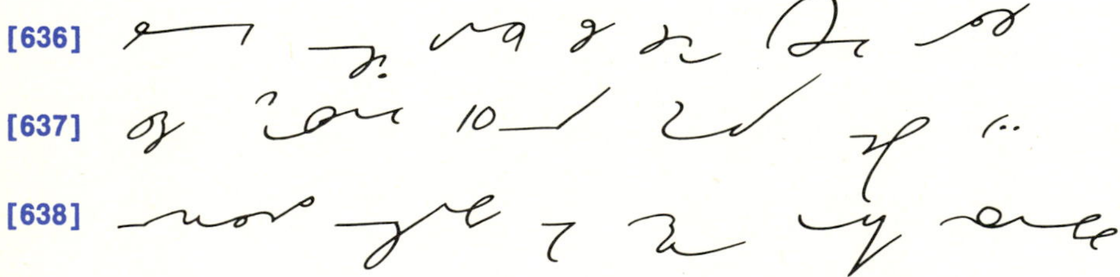

636 Termination, misusing, altercation, exit, security, defames, indicate.

637 Outset, underwriters, 10 million dollar, floated, unstable, thinking.

638 Incorrectly, misaddressed, input, console, lodged, carelessness.

LETTERS

636 To: K. L. O'Reilly, Director of Personnel Subject: Termination of John Cunningham Unfortunately,[1] John Cunningham has been found guilty of misusing the funds of the company, and his employment was[2] terminated today. He was asked to leave without seeing anyone in the company. There was quite an altercation[3] in my office, and he was in no frame of mind to be subjected to the exit interview that is[4] customarily held. I suggest that you outline the procedures he is to follow in collecting his salary[5] and completing his personnel records. He left his keys with me. So that he will have no opportunity to[6] misuse his experience record with the company, I suggest that under *Reason for Termination,* you[7] write *Security* and in the column for recommendations indicate *No Recommendations Available.*[8]

637 To: Frank Simmonds, President Subject: Underwriters of Bond Issue At the outset it seemed like a good idea[9] to secure as many underwriters as possible for our 10 million dollar bond issue. After discussing[10] the matter with several comptrollers whose companies have floated bond issues in a market of the[11] unstable character we have today, it seems advantageous to limit the number of underwriters to no[12] more than five. The general feeling is that they work much harder for you if they believe that they have a chance for[13] higher profits because they have the whole issue. The interest rate is high enough that the people I talked with[14] feel that there will be an active market for the bonds in any case. If you agree with my thinking, I will sound[15] out the three brokers with whom we do the most business: Buckingham, Cunningham, and Walker. Let me have your reaction, please.[16]

638 To: Mark Middleton, Purchasing Subject: Incorrectly Addressed Envelopes Used in Paying Bell Stores I have given[17] considerable attention to trying to place the blame for the misaddressed envelopes in which our checks[18] to Bell Stores were mailed. Our computer is programmed to give us a continuous update on customers' changes of[19] address just as soon as they are reported by our sales personnel. Although the new address was filed on[20] October 14, the change was apparently ignored by a new input clerk and the memorandum slipped down between[21] the top of the console and the shelf. During our search today we found it still lodged there. It is too bad that we[22] lost the $346.97 cash discount as well as much of Bell Stores' goodwill just[23] because of carelessness. A copy of this memorandum is being sent to the clerk who made this mistake.[24] [480]

Reading and Writing Practice

639

An.a.lysts'

ap

Transcribe:
10 a.m.

conj

re·search

[145]

640

intro

prom·is·so·ry

ap

1972

211

ap

Transcribe: 4336

intro

when

fu·tile

Ad·dress·ee

when

par

conj

stat·ute

out·lawed

pros·e·cu·tion

if

intro

[244]

641

ap

con·scious

par

es·pe·cial·ly

con·tin·u·ous

1910

conj

prep·a·ra·tion

conj

ideas

[212]

LESSON 65

Shorthand Vocabulary Builder

642 PHRASING FOR SPEED

Few

1

Thank

2

Us

3

Want

4

Glad

5

1 Few days, few days ago, few minutes, few months ago, few times, few minutes ago, few moments, few thousand dollars, for a few days, for a few minutes.

2 Thank you, thank you for, thank you for the, thank you for this, thank you for that, thank you for your, I thank you for your, thank you for your order, we thank you for.

3 By us, gave us, give us, before us, for us, on us, send us, with us, from us.

4 I want, I wanted, he wants, he wanted, they wanted, you wanted, if you want, do you want.

5 I will be glad, he would be glad, glad to have, I am glad to say, I should be glad.

Building Transcription Skills

643 **Business Vocabulary Builder**

New York Stock Exchange
American Stock Exchange } Associations of stockbrokers who buy and sell securities.

comptroller A controller; one who supervises the financial affairs of a business.

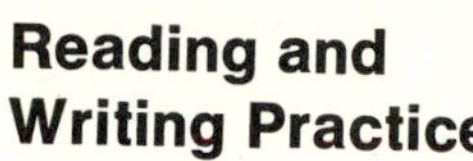

644

com·pa·ny's

el·i·gi·ble

par

de·ci·sion

Se·cu·ri·ties

ef·fect

if

choose

frank

fur·ther

comp·trol·lers'

[229]

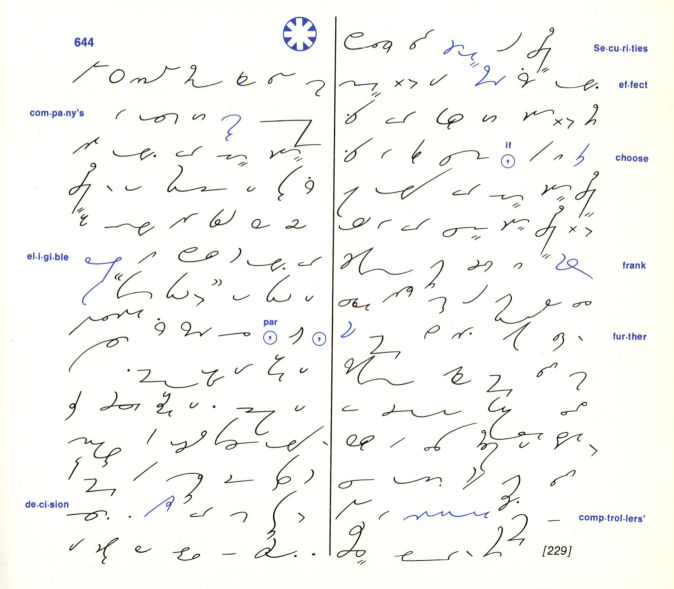

645

An·a·lysts'

conj

conj

fur·ther

au·di·ence

if

[130]

646

16

57

5½

60

par

month-end *hyphenated before noun*

5

ap

Teague

ap

with·draw·als

when

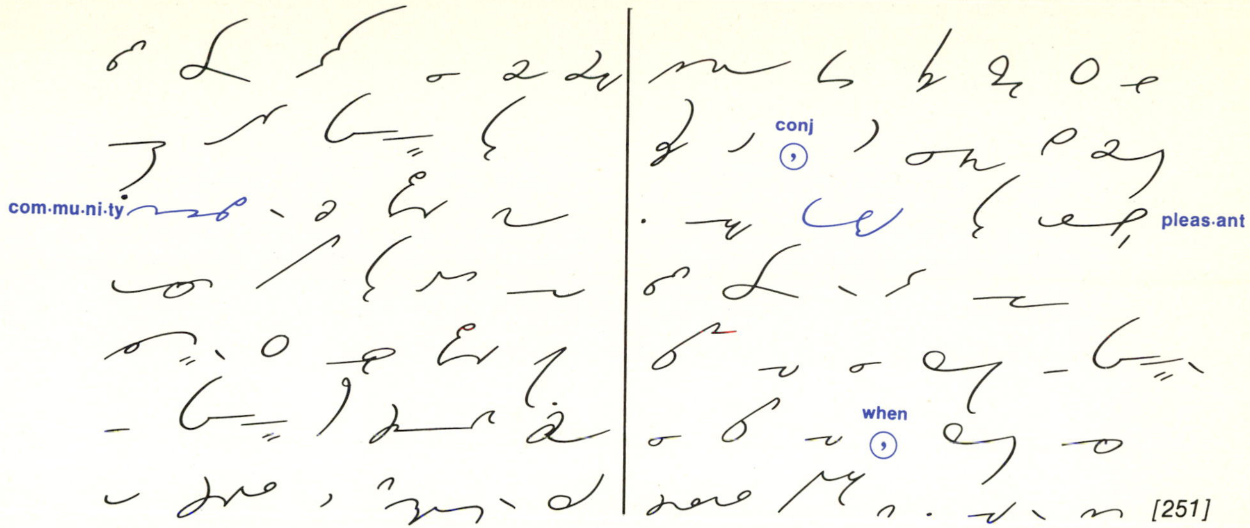

Transcription Speed Building

647

8
20
30
39
50
60
73
86
97
108

119
130
141
153
163
173
185
196
204
212
223
231
240
253
266
278
288
297
309
320

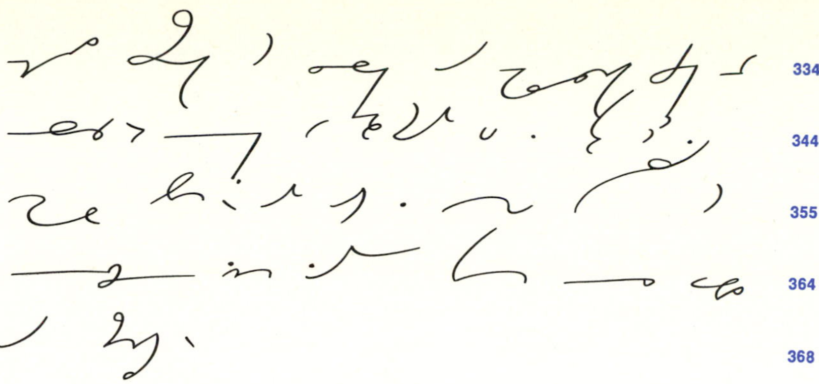

648 Transcription Quiz

[111]

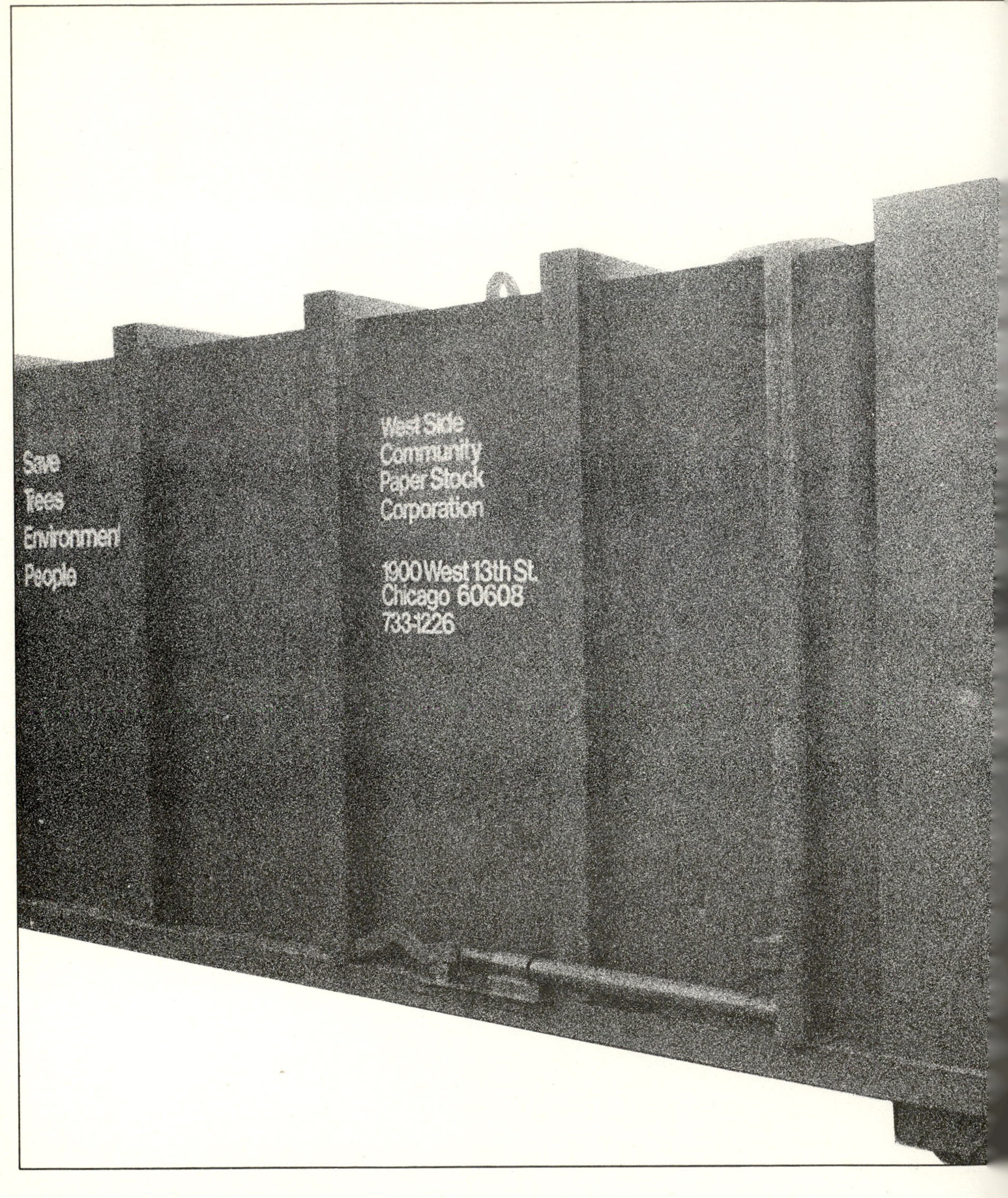
Save
Trees
Environment
People
West Side
Community
Paper Stock
Corporation
1900 West 13th St.
Chicago 60608
733-1226

Unit 14
ENVIRONMENTAL CONTROL

In Unit 14 you will enter a relatively new field, environmental control. You are employed by the Miller Paper Company as secretary to W. R. Jones, manager of environmental control. Because of recent legislation requiring strict controls over emission of pollutants to air and water, many corporations have created new positions for specialists who are assigned to antipollution control.

Mr. Jones and his counterparts in many companies select and supervise the installation of new equipment and the building of new plants that will enable their factories and mills to meet required standards. Much of their time is spent in answering criticisms of environmentalist groups and educating them about the measures being taken by American business to reduce pollution.

Shorthand Vocabulary Builder

649 WORD FAMILIES

-vity

1

-gent

2

-olve

3

-man

4

1 Activity, inactivity, brevity, gravity, productivity, captivity.
2 Agent, negligent, intelligent, diligent, urgent, stringent.
3 Solve, resolve, evolve, involve, involved, absolve.
4 Freshman, postman, foreman, newspaperman, workman, businessman.

Building Transcription Skills

650 NOTEBOOK AND TRANSCRIPTION TIPS ■ procedures

Proper shorthand notebook procedures should be developed to simplify transcription.

1 Before dictation begins, write the day's date (month/day/year) at the bottom of each page in the notebook. Estimate the number of pages to be used on that day. Dating additional pages can be done when necessary.

2 If the dictator frequently makes changes and additions while dictating, use the left column of the notebook page for writing notes and use the entire right column for corrections and additions.

3 Number the notes for each letter in the notebook and write the same number on the letter or other background material that is handed to you by the dictator.

4 Use a question mark to identify items that are to be verified or explained when the dictation is completed.

5 Draw a line through material which has been transcribed.

6 Place a rubber band around pages which have been transcribed.

651 **Business Vocabulary Builder**

pollution Contamination of air, water, or soil by the discharge of noxious substances.

stringent tight; strict.

Progressive Dictation [110–130]

652 PREVIEW

[653]

[654]

[655]

[656]

653 Recreational, adjoining, negligent, untidy, wastepaper, containers.

654 Temperature, stringent, wildlife, surrounding, Fahrenheit, monitor.

655 Destruction, destroyed, industrial, theater, urgently, nature.

656 Absolved, administer, questionnaire, environmental, brevity, hesitate.

LETTERS

[1 Minute at 110]

653 To All Employees: Subject: Cleanup of Parking and Recreational Areas Since most of you drive to work, you have a lot of reasons to take pride/in the appearance of the parking area. Many of you also bring your lunches and on pleasant days eat in the adjoining park which your company// provides for your enjoyment. Yet a few of you—a very few—are negligent about disposing of paper, bottles, and cans. You make your corporate///home an untidy place that neither you nor your co-workers can enjoy. Will you please pick up all wastepaper and put it in the containers provided. [1]

[1 Minute at 120]

654 To All Supervisors and Workers in Plant 11: Subject: Wastewater Temperature

Beginning on March 15 we are adopting the first of several stringent/measures to attempt to restore wildlife to the area surrounding the plant. In an effort to bring fish back to the river, we have resolved to cool all//wastewater from the factory to at least 60 degrees Fahrenheit before it is dumped back into the river. Just this simple activity is an important step///forward in restoring our environment; yet it will not reduce the productivity of our plant. I urge every supervisor to monitor this activity. [2]

[1 Minute at 125]

655 To All Employees: Subject: Movies About Environmental Restoration You, like many other Americans, are probably worried about the continuing/destruction of our natural environment. I am too. I have, therefore, scheduled a series of three movies showing how three different companies have brought back native//wildlife to areas that have been almost destroyed by industrial pollution.

These movies will run only 20 minutes each. They will be shown in the company theater on///Tuesdays at 12:40 starting next week, the 17th. I urgently invite you to see all of these beautiful nature pictures. I hope you will join me on the 17th. [3]

[1 Minute at 130]

656 Dear Mrs. O'Dea: For my talk before your club I have chosen the title, "No Person Is Absolved From the Responsibility to Maintain the Beauty of Nature." I will/ administer a short questionnaire to the group first to involve them in serious consideration of their own attitudes toward environmental control. After I discuss how they//can rate themselves on the basis of their answers, I plan to talk for only about 20 minutes; brevity is important in this type of presentation. The rest of the hour/// will be devoted to questions from the floor. If you have any suggestions for improving my presentation, please do not hesitate to offer them. Yours very cordially, [4] [485]

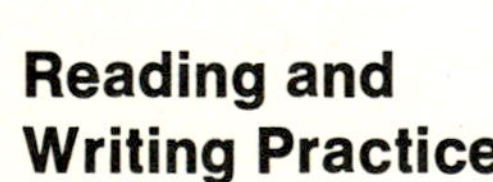

Reading and Writing Practice

657

ap

if

sym·pa·thet·ic

par

in·tel·li·gent·ly

[115]

658

ap

ap

ap

strin·gent

1970 1971

mod·i·fi·ca·tions

ma·chine·ry

Transcribe:
5½ million dollars

wa·ter-qual·i·ty
hyphenated before noun

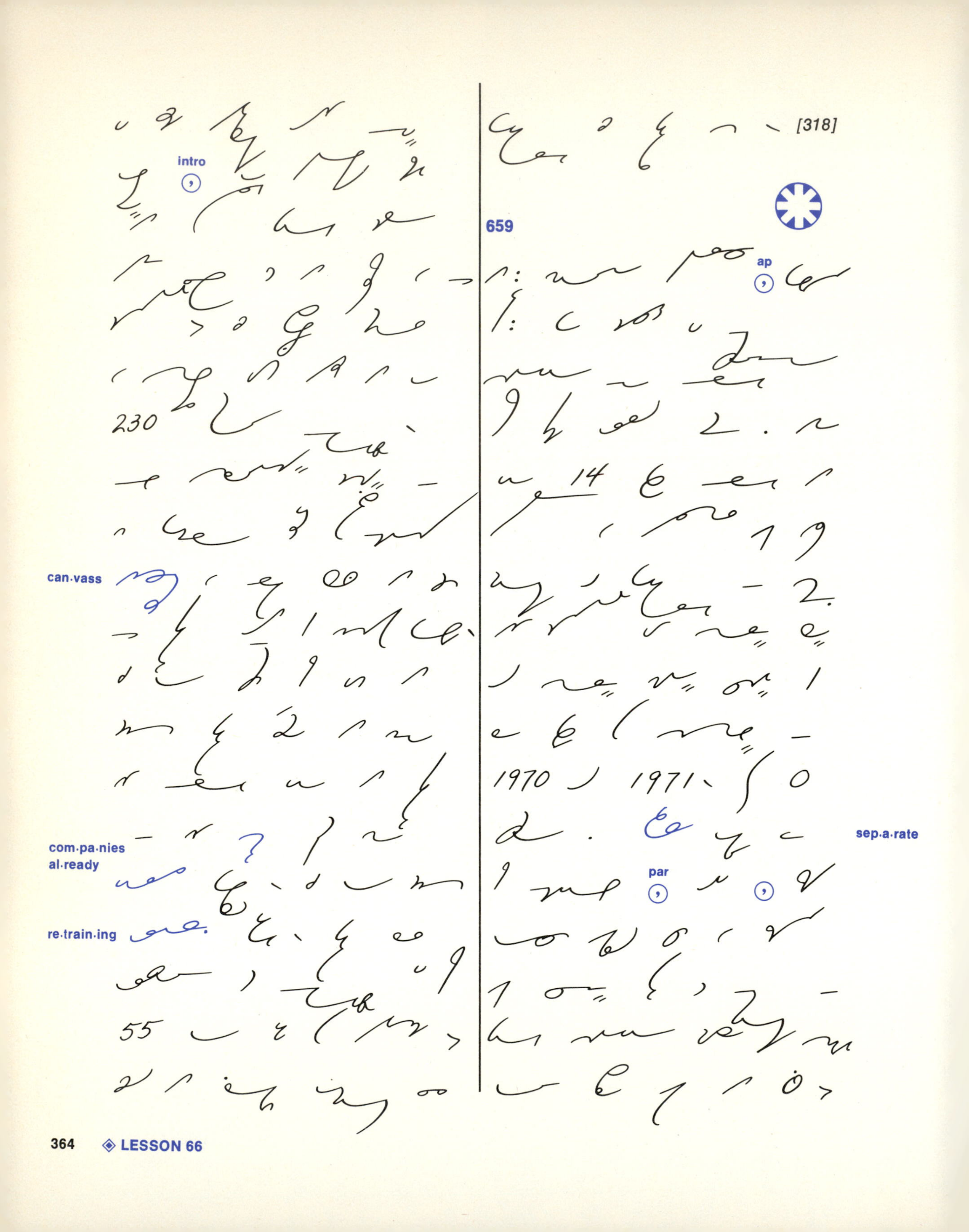

intro

230

can·vass

com·pa·nies
al·ready

re·train·ing

55

[318]

659

ap

14

1970 1971

sep·a·rate

par

intro

Transcribe: 6 billion dollars 1973

Transcribe: 38 percent

1971

Transcribe: 515 million dollars 1973

par

pro·duc·tiv·i·ty 12,

par

to·day's

conj

law·suits

[312]

Shorthand Vocabulary Builder

660 WORD ENDINGS

-cient, -ciency

1

-ily

2

-ingly

3

-lity

4

1 Efficient, deficiency, patience, impatience, quotient, proficiency, insufficiency, inefficient.
2 Happily, angrily, easily, shakily, necessarily, family, heavily, steadily.
3 Surprisingly, willingly, astonishingly, disgustingly, smilingly, knowingly.
4 Ability, credulity, reliability, illegality, feasibility.

Building Transcription Skills

661 TRANSCRIPTION TYPING

12

24

40

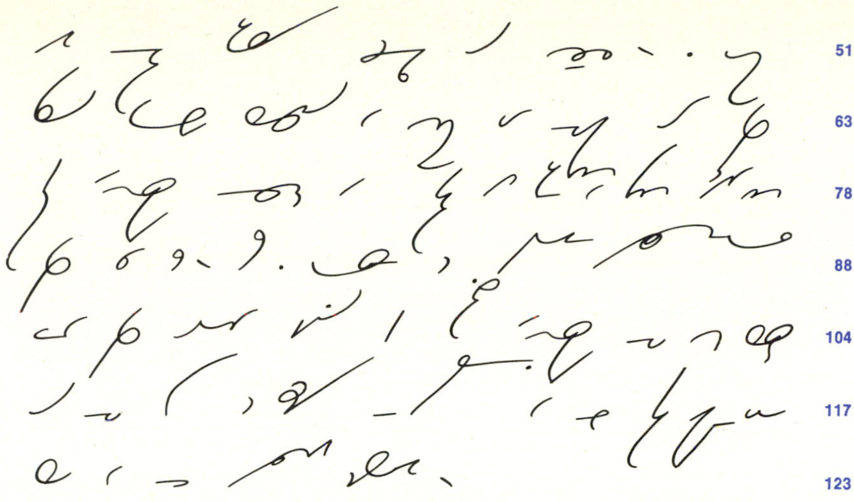

662 Business Vocabulary Builder

feasibility study A study to determine the possibility of accomplishing a goal in a practical manner.

image The concept of someone or something that is held by the public.

Stair-Step Dictation

663 PREVIEW

[664]

[665]

[666]

664 Pollution, Long Island, astonishingly, reuse, marine.

665 Police, river, illegalities, totally, valid, assistance.

666 Patience, amendments, debated, defeating, naïve, refuted, within the.

LETTERS

664 Gentlemen: We can readily appreciate your concern over the possibility of pollution problems[1] when we open our new plant on Long Island Sound. We are well aware of such a possibilty and want[2] to assure you that we are installing a water treatment plant that produces astonishingly good results.[3] In fact, we will be able to reuse the wastewater one time and thus reduce the amount of waste going into[4] the Sound.

There is a strong probability that we may be able to reuse it two times when we get our[5] plant in operation. We have also installed equipment that will cool any waste before it is dumped to a[6] temperature that will support marine life. We are patiently working on other pollution control measures[7] and invite your inspection. We can easily arrange a tour for your committee. Yours very truly,[8]

665 To: Paul Gentry, Chief Engineer Subject: Police Inspection of Waste From Mill This morning I received a telephone[9] call from the police stating that they plan to take samples of the water just below the point where our waste enters[10] the river. I assured them that we are free from any illegalities in the quality of the waste and[11] told them that both you and I would willingly assist them in taking samples. They said that they would prefer to work alone.[12] I doubt if they totally understand what they are trying to do or have the ability to make valid[13] tests of this nature, but what can we do? They said that the present plan is for two of them to be here early Wednesday[14] morning to start taking samples. Perhaps we can just happen by and offer our assistance. What do you think?[15]

666 Dear Senator Alcott: I appreciate your patience in listening yesterday to my reasons for voting[16] against the proposed amendments to the Clean Air Bill. In all probability, it will be reported out of[17] committee next week and debated on the floor within the next three weeks. I am enclosing copies of several[18] studies made in our own company that may help you in defeating the amendments. Some of the arguments being[19] used in support of the legislation are naïve and should be strongly refuted. Our research figures on[20] the costs of complying with this bill may seem surprisingly high, but I can assure you that they are totally[21] within the realm of possibility. Miller Paper Company will appreciate any effort made. Yours truly,[22] [440]

Reading and Writing Practice

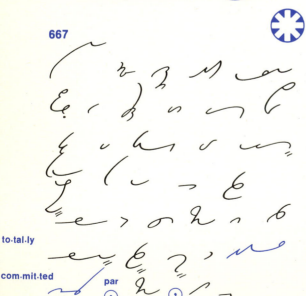

667

to·tal·ly

com·mit·ted

par

intro

fea·si·bil·i·ty

some·times

ac·cept·able

18–24

14

5

if

2

[281]

pri·vate·ly

668

odors

kraft

conj

par

conj

odor-con·trol *hyphenated before noun*

intro

if

in·stalled

when

su·per·in·ten·dent

ap

[245]

669

Wom·an's

as

crit·i·cism

im·age

aware

intro

good·will

[97]

LESSON 68

Shorthand Vocabulary Builder

670 BRIEF-FORM POWER

1 Think–thing, thinking, thinkable, unthinkable, unthinkingly, thinks–things, thinker; enclose, enclosing, enclosure.

2 Where, everywhere, somewhere, anywhere, whereabouts, whereas, whereby, whereupon.

3 Business, businesses, businesslike, businessman, businesswoman, unbusinesslike.

4 Circular, circulars, circularize; particular, particulars, particularly, subject, subjects, subjected.

671 CITIES

-ington

Washington, Downington, Bloomington, Burlington, New Kensington.

Building Transcription Skills

672 SIMILAR WORDS ■ farther, further; eminent, imminent

Study the following words which are somewhat alike and which are sometimes confused.

farther At a greater distance.

further In addition; moreover; to a greater degree.

eminent Important.

imminent Impending.

673 **Business Vocabulary Builder**

environmentalist One who is interested in the surroundings that influence the growth of an organism.

scrap iron Leftover pieces of metal suitable for reprocessing.

Progressive Dictation [110–130]

674 PREVIEW

[675]

[676]

[677]

[678]

675 Circulating, recleaned, circularized, blueprints, unthinkable.

676 Whereabouts, antipollution, converted, federal, environmental.

677 Advisor, Burlington, university, flexible, expertise.

678 Contemplate, expansion, acquired, Silverlake, locations.

LETTERS

[1 Minute at 110]

675 Gentlemen: We have been looking everywhere for a company that will produce a custom-built machine for circulating recleaned water through the/sheet-metal unit in our new plant in Charleston. We have even circularized the custom engineers listed in their professional directory. Finally//somebody gave us your name. Have you had any experience in building such equipment? If you do such work, would you be willing to visit our plant///to study our problem? We shall, of course, be able to provide the blueprints, but it would be totally unthinkable to work from blueprints alone. Yours truly, [1]

[1 Minute at 120]

676 Dear Ken: I wonder if you can tell me the whereabouts of Warren Pollard, who worked with you on installing the antipollution equipment in New Kensington Mills./ After he completed that project, he wrote me a letter requesting a job in our company. Since I had already completed hiring my staff, I unthinkingly//destroyed the application. We have recently acquired two old mills that will have to be converted to meet the new federal and state standards, and I am///searching everywhere for people with some environmental control experience. They are hard to find. If you have Warren's address, please call me collect. Yours cordially, [2]

[1 Minute at 125]

677 Dear Dr. Washington: I have been thinking about a possible arrangement whereby you could act as adviser on the project in Burlington. If you retain your full-time/position at the university, the only businesslike arrangement would be to hire you as a consultant at a flexible rate whenever we need your services//and you are free. That would not give us anywhere near the help we need, but it would be better than nothing. I unthinkingly told our chief engineer that I am negotiating///with you. Of course, he had at least two full-time people to suggest. I would much prefer you even on very limited terms to someone without your expertise. Yours truly, [3]

[1 Minute at 130]

678 Dear Mr. Pollard: I recall that you applied to me for a position involving environmental control after you had completed the project at New Kensington Mills./At the time our staff was complete, and we did not contemplate any expansion. Surprisingly, though, the corporation has acquired two old mills that will have to be converted//to meet national and state standards. One is in Silverlake, Washington, and the other one is in Burlington, Kansas. Would you be interested in a position with us in either/// one of these locations? If so, the company would willingly pay your expenses for an interview here in my office with our hiring committee. Yours very truly, [4] [485]

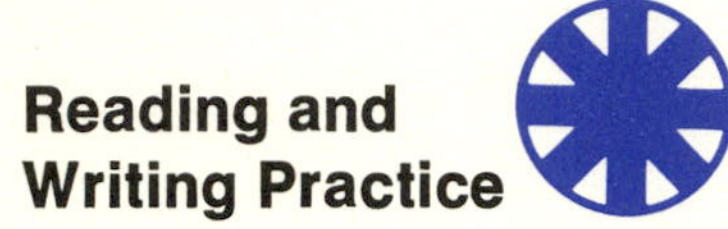

679

ap

waste·wa·ter

stud·ies

hence

if

pro·ceed

intro

lit·er·al·ly

un·think·able

fea·si·bil·i·ty

nonr

[176]

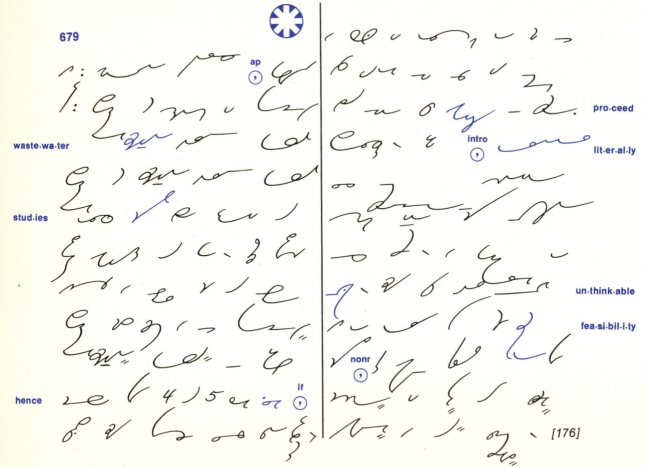

680

de·sir·abil·i·ty

any·where

par

intro

an·ti·pol·lu·tion

KLX

sim·i·lar

cir·cu·late

4-page hyphenated before noun

[265]

681

en·vi·ron·men·tal·ists

[168]

682

re·use

found·ry

[118]

ap

cost-shar·ing
start-up
hyphenated before noun

par

ser

par

Des Moines

fo·cus

LESSON 69

Shorthand Vocabulary Builder

683 WORD-BUILDING PRINCIPLES

Abbreviated Words

1

Ol, Or

2

Mon, Min

3

Past Tense

4

1 Privilege, reluctant–reluctance, philosophy, significant–significance, convenience–convenient, atmosphere.

2 All, recall, ball, oral, sore, sorrow, restore, chore.

3 Money, harmony, month, minute, prominent, eliminate.

4 Hoisted, soiled, voiced, remembered, betrayed, traded, past, faced.

Building Transcription Skills

684 TRANSCRIPTION TYPING

12

24

39
53
65
78
87
102
114
127
135

685 **Business Vocabulary Builder**

wastewater treatment plant A plant that cleans the water after use in the manufacturing process and recycles it through the factory.

Wall Street Journal A daily newspaper discussing the financial interests of the United States.

Stair-Step Dictation

686 PREVIEW

[687]

[688]

[689]

687 Secret, classifications, confidential, reluctant, divulge, deleted.

688 Conversation, credentials, significant, outstanding, variety, interview, 10 o'clock, out-of-date.

689 Moral, harmony, graduating, philosophy, reaction.

LETTERS

687 Dear Monroe: If it would not betray a secret, I would appreciate knowing the approximate monthly salaries[1] and the classifications and titles used by your staff in environmental control. I assure you that[2] the information about individual companies would be kept confidential, but it would be helpful[3] if we had a bit of background about what other companies are doing. Please do not use any names. I am[4] asking nine other people in jobs similar to ours in pollution control administration for the same[5] information. If you are reluctant to divulge this information, I shall, of course, understand. However,[6] maybe I can encourage you to share this information with others if I promise to send you a copy[7] of the replies—naturally with the names of the companies deleted. Will I see you at the conference? Yours truly,[8]

688 Dear Miss Baldwin: I received your application this morning for a position with our company as soon as[9] you have completed your degree. I am glad you remembered our conversation at the spring meeting and followed[10] up with your credentials. As I told you, I thought the student paper you presented makes a significant point.[11] Your university has a fine record for an outstanding course in our field. We have nobody employed in[12] environmental control from Illinois, and it is our policy to select our staff from a variety[13] of colleges. We should like to invite you for an expense-paid interview at my office on June 18[14] at 10 o'clock. I wonder if the interest you voiced in an opening in Burlington, Kansas, is still alive.[15] We are trying to staff a unit in Burlington, for our company has bought an out-of-date mill there. Sincerely,[16]

689 To: Sam Bates, Director of Personnel Subject: Helen Baldwin's Application For some time I have felt that we[17] have a moral obligation to add a woman to our staff. I have been looking for someone who would work in[18] harmony with the rest of the staff and could make a significant contribution. I found the person who I[19] think meets my standards, Helen Baldwin. She is graduating from the University of Illinois in June[20] with a double major, philosophy and environmental control. I have eliminated two other[21] possible candidates and have asked Miss Baldwin to come in for an interview on June 18 at 10 o'clock.[22] Please study her credentials, which are enclosed, carefully before you interview her. She would probably be assigned[23] to the pollution problem at the mill in Burlington, Kansas. I shall be awaiting your reaction.[24] [440]

Reading and Writing Practice

690

waste·wa·ter

intro

re·ver·sal

an·ti·pol·lu·tion

alu·mi·num

prom·i·nent

par

cus·tom·ary

sore·ly

as

sig·nif·i·cant·ly

[257]

691

re·cy·cling

ap

pro·hi·bi·tion

make·shift

as

var·i·ous

ad·min·is·tra·tors

ap

[251]

692

ap

En·vi·ron·men·tal

gov·ern·ment's

intro

for·mer

ad·e·quate

intro

[153]

Shorthand Vocabulary Builder

693 PHRASING FOR SPEED

Omission of Words

1

Special

2

Days

3

Month

4

To Do

5

1 One of our, one of the, in the past, in the future, some of the, some of them, none of the, none of them.

2 Your order, your orders, as soon as, as soon as possible, of course, of course it is, let us, let us have, to us.

3 Friday morning, Friday night, Saturday morning, Saturday night, Wednesday morning, Tuesday morning.

4 Each month, this month, several months, few months, every month, in a few months.

5 To do, to do it, to do the, to do so, to do this, to do that, to do your, to do these, to do those.

Building Transcription Skills

694 Business Vocabulary Builder

agenda *(Plural, used with a singular verb.)* A list of things to be done at a meeting.

key role Crucial part.

Reading and Writing Practice

695

waste·wa·ter

con·tin·u·a·tion

fa·cil·i·ties

sew·age

equal·ly

leg·is·la·tion

nonr

month's

Coun·cil

intro

ben·e·fit

intro

whether

[279]

696

ap

long-dis·tance *hyphenated before noun*

ac·com·pa·nied

par

conj

if

en·gi·neers

Lynch·burg

[138]

697

en·vi·ron·men·tal

intro

tech·niques

intro

9 7:30

per·ma·nent

intro

iden·ti·fy

par

co·op·er·ate

par·tic·i·pants

par

par

ex·plor·ato·ry

ap

[251]

Transcription Speed Building

698

14

24

36

48

57

68

77
92
102
115
125
136
147
158
169
182
191
202
214
226
235
249
263
273
286
298

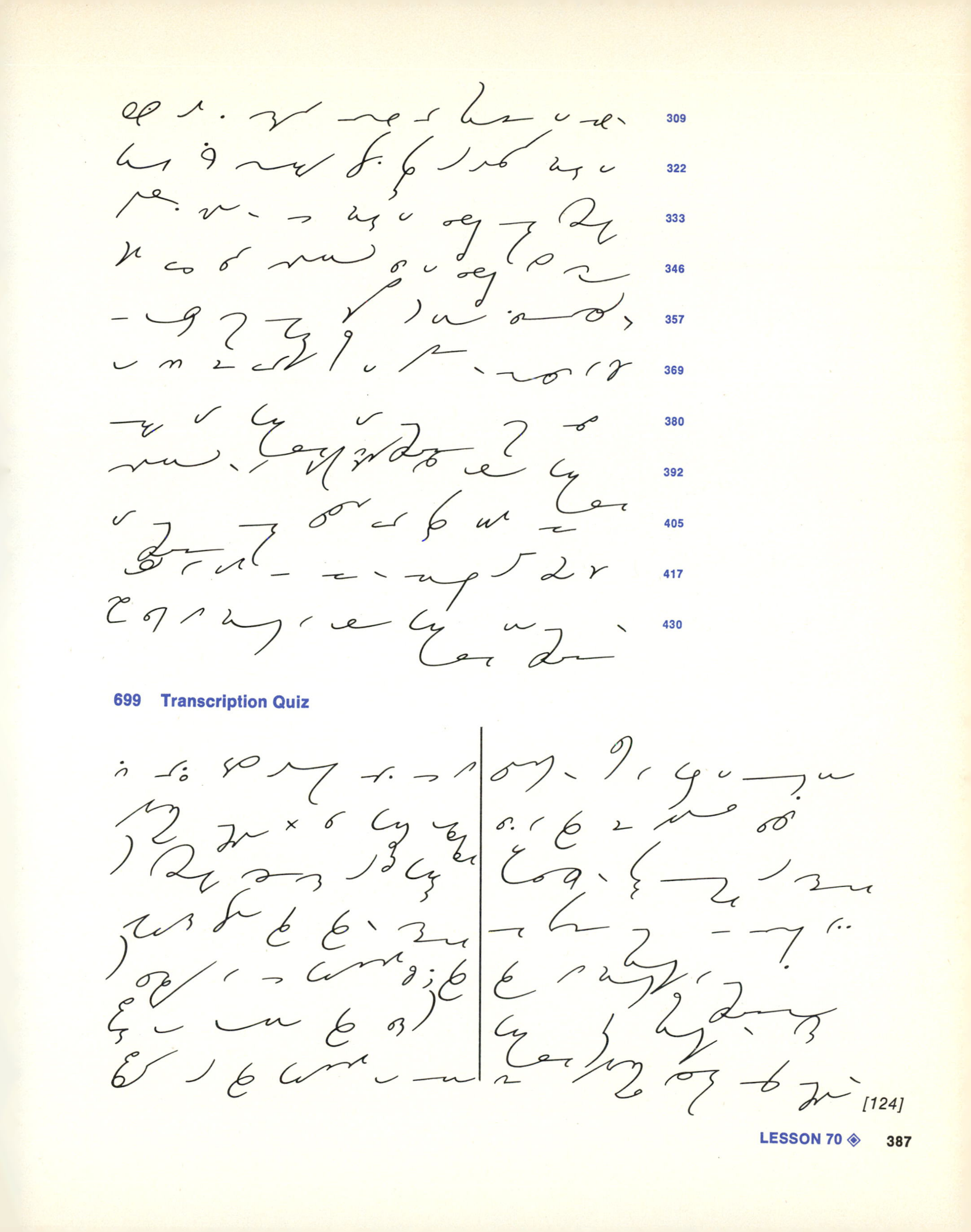

309

322

333

346

357

369

380

392

405

417

430

699 Transcription Quiz

[124]

PAN AMERICAN

Unit 15
TRANSPORTATION SERVICES

In this unit you are secretary to W. A. Saunders, manager of Transportation Services. Mr. Saunders and his staff see that goods are properly packaged for safe shipment. They must choose the most expeditious method of shipment. Mr. Saunders also arranges transportation for executive employees when they make business trips and controls issuance of credit cards for travel. He must issue the proper legal papers to accompany goods, or if the customer has not established credit, he must forward these papers to the bank at the destination for collection before goods are released to the buyer.

He must file claim for goods damaged in transit. He protects his company's interests so far as rates are concerned.

Your work with Mr. Saunders will require close attention to detail and an understanding of transportation terms and procedures.

Shorthand Vocabulary Builder

700 WORD FAMILIES

-sist

-pend

-tract

-eous, -ious

1 Assist, insist, resist, persist, desist, resistance, assistance, insistence, subsistence.

2 Pending, spend, happened, depend, suspend, expenditure, impending, dependent.

3 Attract, contract, distract, detract, protract, abstract, retract.

4 Courteous, various, serious, furious, studious, industrious, obvious, previous.

Building Transcription Skills

701 NOTEBOOK AND TRANSCRIPTION TIPS ■ procedures *(continued)*

Transcription can be more quickly and accurately completed if good procedures are developed.

1 Before leaving the dictator's office, ask all questions you may have about the dictation.

2 Check your shorthand notebook for special instructions before beginning transcription.

3 Estimate the length of the letter before starting to type.

4 Consider the manner of expressing numbers included in the material and check the spelling of unfamiliar words before starting transcription.

5 Have a good dictionary handy.

6 Proofread before removing the page from the typewriter.

702 **Business Vocabulary Builder**

act of God Unforeseeable occurrence caused by nature, not by human beings.

sight draft A draft or a bill payable on demand or on presentation.

bill of lading A notification to a purchaser that a shipment has been made which specifies date, carrier, and the route.

Progressive Dictation [120–135]

703 **PREVIEW**

[704]

[705]

[706]

[707]

704 Pending, inquiring, renewal, various, discourteous, sullen, expenditures.

705 Protracted, shortage, availability, crisis, concede, railway, suspend.

706 Excessive, forced, reminding, emergency, authorized, strictly, regulations.

707 Interstate, Association, highways, proposal, inadequate, opposed, deterioration.

LETTERS

[1 Minute at 120]

704 Dear Mr. Tanner: Subject: Pending Contract Thank you for your telephone call this morning inquiring about our renewal of our contract with your company. Today/I contacted our sales manager and various supervisors in the shipping department to inquire about your service. They tell me that in//various instances your service could not be thoroughly depended upon and that your drivers are frequently discourteous and even sullen. Because of these reports, it seems///obvious that we should spend some time searching for a trucking company that more nearly meets our needs and possibly involves lower expenditures. Yours very truly, [1]

[1 Minute at 125]

705 To: Willard Pickett, Sales Manager Subject: Effect of Oil Shortage It seems obvious that a protracted oil shortage will seriously affect our transportation of/goods to our customers. I not only expect an increase in delivery costs in the coming year but am even more concerned about the availability of//adequate carrier space during the crisis. As you know, railroads are a much cheaper mode of shipping than trucks. Although we concede that they are usually slower than other///methods, beginning on June 15 we shall use railway express or freight whenever possible. We hope to suspend this directive just as the pending oil shortage eases. [2]

[1 Minute at 130]

706 To: Mary King, Supervisor of Travel Arrangements Subject: Excessive Number of First-Class Airline Tickets In reviewing your report for June, I find that our expenditures/for air travel are much too high. You are being forced to provide first-class ticketing much too often because coach seats are not available. It is obvious that persons//traveling on company business need reminding that their requests must be made at least three days prior to the trip unless emergency travel is called for. Will you please contact all persons///authorized to travel and courteously insist that they adhere more strictly to our travel regulations. Perhaps you should enclose an abstract of the rules for them to review. [3]

[1 Minute at 135]

707 To: H. W. Smith, President Subject: Interstate Commerce Commission Hearings on Increasing Load Capacity of Trucks On behalf of our National Transportation Managers'/Association, I plan to appear tomorrow before the Interstate Commerce Commission's hearings to protest against increasing the size of trucks permitted on interstate highways.//Our group resists the proposal because it will reduce service that is already inadequate and believes that deliveries will be further slowed down because fewer express routes will///be maintained. The various state highway commissions are also opposed to larger trucks and insist that approval will bring added loads that will cause more rapid highway deterioration. [4] [510]

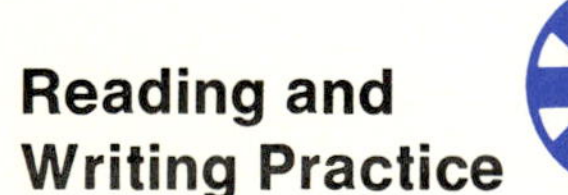

Reading and Writing Practice

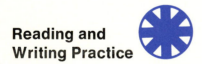

708

in·curred

oc·curred

intro

pro·tract·ed

iq

par

af·fi·da·vit
at·test·ing

if

de·pend·abil·i·ty

intro

se·ri·ous

ap

re·open

[248]

709

Cit·i·zens

Du·buque

intro

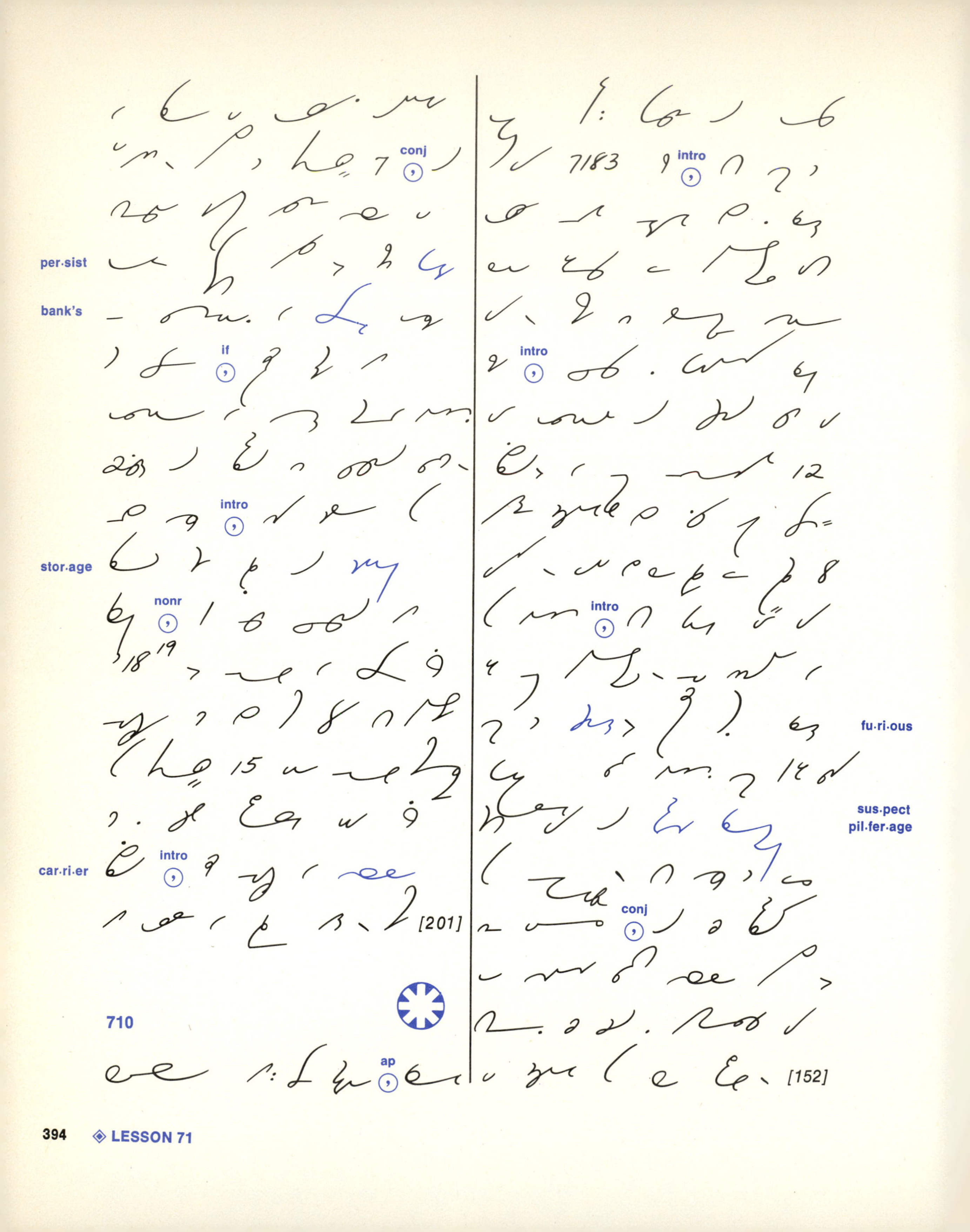

conj

per·sist

bank's

if

intro

stor·age

nonr

intro

car·ri·er [201]

710

ap

intro

intro

intro

fu·ri·ous

sus·pect
pil·fer·age

conj

[152]

Shorthand Vocabulary Builder

711 WORD BEGINNINGS

For-, Fore-

1

Fur-

2

Be-

3

Electr-, Electric

4

1 Fortune, forgive, forfeit, forgotten, foremost, foreman, foresee, foretold.
2 Furnish, furnishings, furniture, furnace, further, furthermore, furtive, furlough.
3 Betray, belong, behind, behave, because, belittled, beneath, began.
4 Electric, electrical, electricity, electron, electrometer, electronic, electric fan.

Building Transcription Skills

712 TRANSCRIPTION TYPING

11

23

713 **Business Vocabulary Builder**

railway express A method of shipment that transports material by rail with truck pickup and delivery.

air express A system for the transportation of packages by airplane with truck pickup and delivery.

Stair-Step Dictation

714 PREVIEW

715 Reservation, interconnecting, exhibited, availability, issuance, one of the, justified, gathered.

716 Insistence, 10 percent, investigating, Minneapolis, discovered, Oklahoma, liable.

717 Plaintiff, baggage, unpatented, devices, suitcase, in the future, guarded.

LETTERS

715 To: Jack Lewis, Purchasing Agent Subject: Electronic Reservation System At the National Electronic[1] Show last week three different electronic systems for interconnecting with airlines were exhibited.[2] This equipment furnishes immediate information about the availability of space and permits[3] immediate issuance of tickets in our office. Later I made a behind-the-scenes inspection of[4] one of the systems in operation at Foremost Industries. In my opinion the volume of company[5] travel has grown to such a point that the purchase of such a system would be justified, especially since the[6] expenditure is not as large as you might expect. If you would be interested in learning more about such[7] equipment, I should be glad to furnish you with the advertising material I gathered up. Furthermore,[8] I am sure that Will Beamer would be glad to show you the installation there and discuss its proven advantages.[9]

716 Dear Mr. Yancy: Mr. Pickett told me of the insistence of the Big Spring Furniture Company that we[10] allow a 10 percent discount on their Order 45810 because the goods did not arrive in time for[11] their advertised sale. After spending considerable time in investigating what happened that could cause an[12] eight-day delay between Minneapolis and Big Spring, I discovered that the truck was involved in a serious[13] accident in Oklahoma. Repairs were necessary that caused a protracted delay while parts were obtained[14] from Detroit. Our company was not told anything about this problem. It is obvious that the trucking[15] company is liable. When you get to Big Spring on Thursday, May 5, please grant the discount. Very truly yours,[16]

717 To All Personnel Traveling for the Company: Subject: Company Property Is Not Baggage A recent[17] case against an airline which was lost by the plaintiff corporation should be of interest and concern to all of[18] you. A company representative had checked as baggage some samples of unpatented electronic[19] devices designed to improve the flow of heat from furnaces. The suitcase containing the samples was lost, but the[20] company could not collect because electrical materials cannot be classified as baggage. In the future[21] be sure of two things: (1) that whenever possible you carry small devices on board and keep them carefully[22] guarded and in your possession at all times and (2) that you ship such devices by air express so that they travel[23] with you on the same plane. This warning is especially important to members of the Research and Development[24] Division, but it could easily apply to a number of other company travelers.[25] [500]

Reading and Writing Practice

718

ap

past

par

cal·cu·la·tors

nonr

fore·most

ex·hib·it·ed

mi·cro·scopes

elec·trom·e·ters

[305]

719

re·ex·am·i·na·tion

For·tune

ap

ours

re·quire

par

ap

ap

pur·chas·er

elec·tri·cal

[137]

720

Christ·mas

304

19

304

19

304

15

nonr

20

4

if

Transcribe: 9:15 a.m.

56

9:15

ap

23

23

for·feit

4

[143]

Shorthand Vocabulary Builder

721 BRIEF-FORM POWER

1 Thank, thanked, thankful, thankfully, unthankful, thankless, thanksgiving, thanking.
2 Order, ordered, orderly, orderliness, disorder, disorderly, disorderliness, reordered.
3 Value, valued, valueless, valuable, invaluable, revalued, unvalued.
4 Year-were, years, yearly, midyear, yearling, yearbook, yearlong.

722 CITIES

-ford

Stamford, Oxford, Bedford, Bradford, Hartford, Westford, Brantford, Stanford.

Building Transcription Skills

723 SIMILAR WORDS ■ allowed, aloud; all ready, already

Study the following words which sound alike and which are sometimes confused.

allowed Permitted.

aloud Audibly.

all ready All prepared.

already Previously.

When in doubt, check a good dictionary for correct spelling and usage.

724 **Business Vocabulary Builder**

spur track A short branch of a railroad connecting with the main line.

siding A short section of railroad track beside the main track.

Progressive Dictation [120–135]

725 PREVIEW

[726]
[727]
[728]
[729]

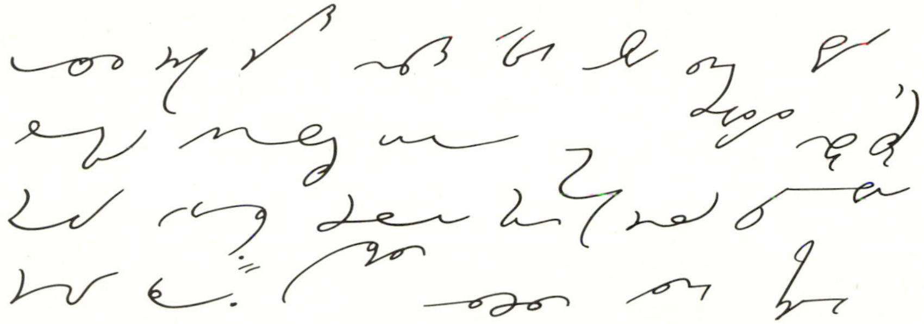

726 Likely, suitable, studious, credentials, transportation, enticed, university, assistant.

727 Telephoned, to clarify, oral, invaluable, orderly, chaos, supervises.

728 Furloughed, Thanksgiving, familiar, fork, screened, administer.

729 Forgotten, sealing, domestic, mechanic, technician, adjustments.

LETTERS

[1 Minute at 120]

726 To: Lola Davis, Director of Personnel Subject: My Replacement on June 1 As you requested, I have been trying to contact all likely sources for a/suitable replacement when I retire on June 1. After a studious appraisal of credentials, I suggest two possible candidates for interviews as a//starter. Martin Bedford now heads the transportation department at CMS Company but could probably be enticed away from a company of its size. He is///a recent graduate of the School of Business at Stanford University. My other suggestion is my assistant, Betty Bradford. She knows the work thoroughly. [1]

[1 Minute at 125]

727 To: Lola Davis, Director of Personnel Subject: Application of Martin Bedford As you requested, I telephoned Harvey Barnes in Stamford to clarify several/ points about his rather vague recommendation of Martin Bedford. Actually, his oral statements were far more glowing than the earlier comments led us to expect. He// said that Mr. Bedford has made an invaluable contribution to the orderly reorganization of a unit that was in utter chaos when he took over///the job ten years ago. He said that Mr. Bedford has the complete respect of the people he supervises. In his opinion, we would be fortunate to have him on our staff. [2]

[1 Minute at 130]

728 To: Lola Davis, Director of Personnel Subject: Shipping Supervisor Replacement I received approval this morning for employing a new supervisor for the unit/ responsible for shipping home furnishings. He is to replace Herman Blake, who is being furloughed at Thanksgiving time until he reaches retirement age at the end of// the year. The candidate should be familiar with the operation of the electrically controlled loading fork. After you have screened several applicants, I can administer a///test to check their competency for this requirement. We could promote one of the clerks in the department. Will you please review the personnel records of the two enclosed applicants. [3]

[1 Minute at 135]

729 Gentlemen: I have forgotten the name of your representative who installed our new machine for sealing the tape on packages in our shipping room, so I cannot write directly to/him. A number of both our domestic and foreign customers have reported recently that the tapes are not secure when they are delivered. Our mechanic does not feel that a minor//adjustment would correct the difficulty and insists that the machine is defective. As he is an excellent technician, I am inclined to agree. Will you, therefore, send a///troubleshooter to check this equipment and make any adjustments. You will remember that a one-year guarantee accompanied this machine and that we have had it only seven months. Yours truly, [4] [510]

Reading and Writing Practice

730

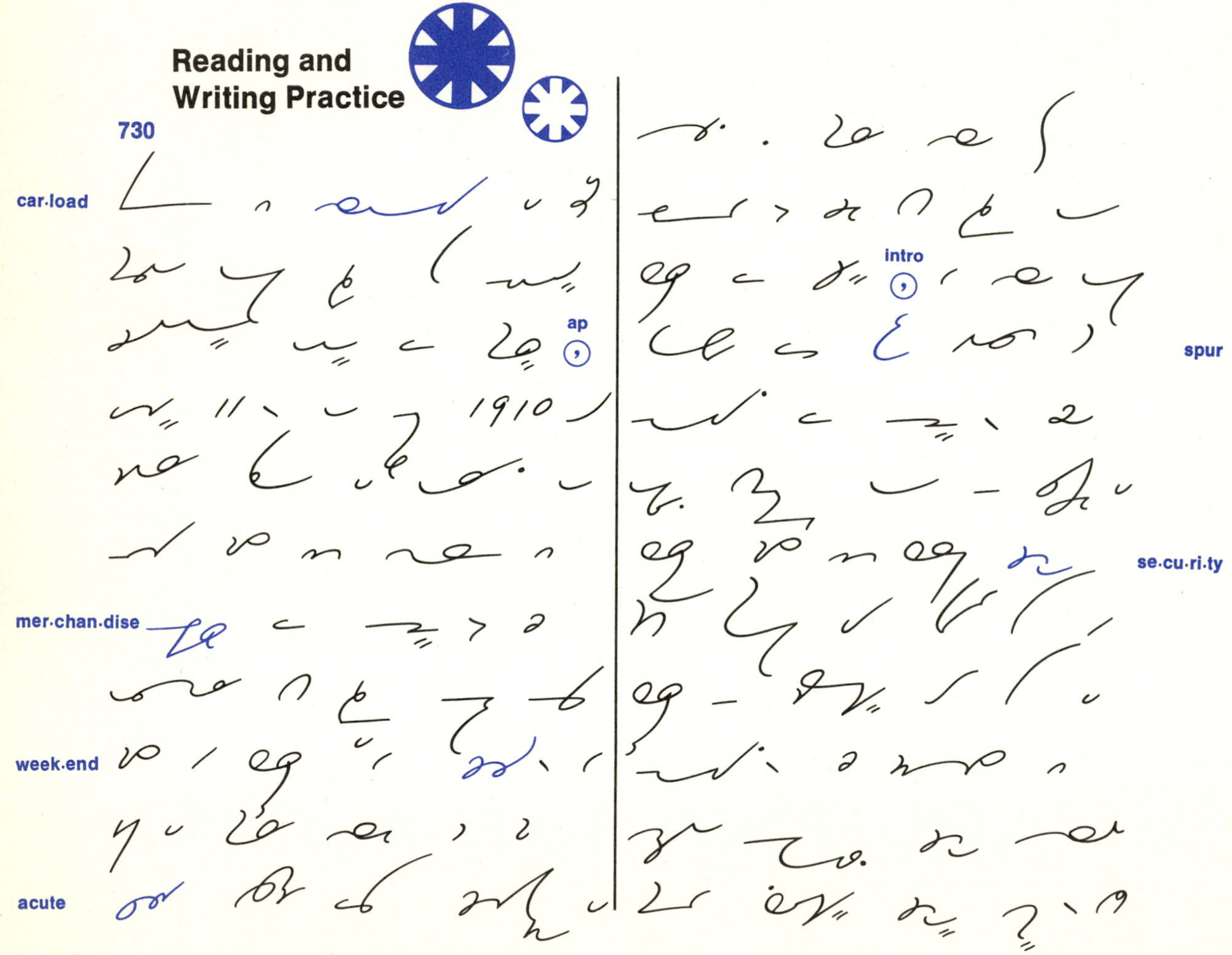

past

Con·nect·i·cut

spe·cial·izes

rail·road

par

fourth

par

[280]

731

9762

ap

barge

15,

un·as·sem·bled

intro

mode

ap

par

knocked-down *hyphenated before noun*

as·sem·bly

Man·u·fac·tur·ers'

[287]

732

042-347-872

172[45]

14

ap·par·ent·ly

sup·port·ing

ac·com·pa·nied

conj

intro

[110]

LESSON 74

Shorthand Vocabulary Builder

733 WORD-BUILDING PRINCIPLES

Omission of Minor Vowels

1

Circle Vowels on Straight Lines

2

Circle Vowels on Opposite Curves

3

-er, -or

4

1 Genuine, graduate, millions, miscellaneous, auditorium, previous, theory.
2 Tight, tide, main, name, deed, died, dietary, minimum.
3 Rack, leg, pave, behave, February, lack, crack, cricket, vapor.
4 Speaker, worker, sender, greater, governor, taller, error, honor.

Building Transcription Skills

734 TRANSCRIPTION TYPING

9

19

32

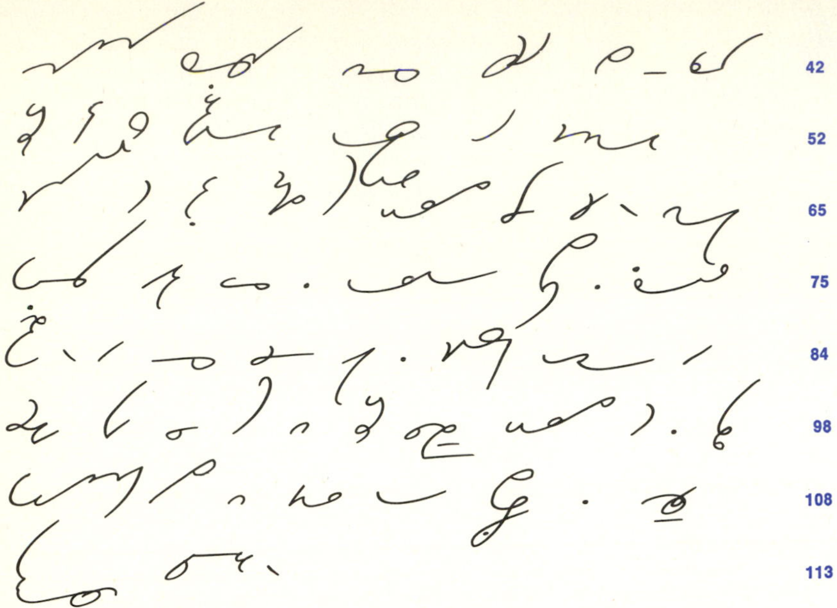

735 **Business Vocabulary Builder**

LCL shipments Less than a full carload.

honorarium Monetary reward for a service on which a price cannot customarily be set.

Stair-Step Dictation

736 PREVIEW

[737]

[738]

[739]

737 Fragile, thank you for, tomorrow, in addition, corrugated, cardboard, apologies.

738 Shipping, demonstration, auditorium, theory, include, packing, overcome.

739 Lecture, 4 o'clock, I suggest that, discuss, tight, previous, honorarium.

LETTERS

737 To: Willard Pickett, Sales Manager Subject: Breakage of Fragile Shipments Thank you for telling me of the complaints[1] from our customers about receiving fragile shipments in damaged condition. We have just been in touch with the[2] manufacturer of our new electric tape-sealing machine, which we have been using for only seven months.[3] After receiving our letter, their representative telephoned that a person to do repairs will arrive[4] tomorrow. Either this machine will be removed and replaced with another one, or it will be adjusted[5] satisfactorily. In addition, we have just contracted for a more heavily corrugated cardboard box.[6] Will you please send our apologies to your sales representatives and ask them to explain the difficulty[7] to their customers. Assure them that we have taken steps to improve our packing, especially for fragile shipments.[8]

738 To: Harry Wilson, Manager of Shipping Department Subject: Demonstration for Shipping Room Employees In[9] an effort to achieve greater efficiency in the Shipping Department, I have arranged for Ted Mansfield to[10] give a demonstration lecture for all employees in that department. The meeting will be held in the[11] auditorium on Monday, February 16, at 4 o'clock. He was the main speaker at the January[12] meeting of the Transportation Club, where I heard the talk I have asked him to repeat here.

It is my theory that[13] we can achieve better performance from our employees if we include them in such programs occasionally.[14] They will learn a great deal about developments in packing our products. I hope they will overcome the feeling[15] that their company lacks interest in their development and that opportunities for advancement are limited[16] for them.

Will you please use the enclosed press release to inform your employees about the speaker at this meeting.[17]

739 Dear Ted: I have completed all arrangements for your lecture demonstration before the workers in our shipping[18] department on Monday, February 16, at 4 o'clock. The meeting will be held in the auditorium.[19] I suggest that you come to my office in the main building by 1 o'clock so that we can have lunch and then[20] visit our shipping room. In the shipping room you can see our present methods and supplies and discuss our special[21] problems. I am asking the manager, Harry Wilson, who runs a tight ship, to join us for lunch.

Please follow the[22] general outline used in your previous lecture. Be sure to bring along ample materials for your[23] demonstration. Plan to submit your travel expenses on the day of your appearance so we can pay them promptly.[24] As I told you, we shall pay an honorarium of $100. We are indeed looking forward to your visit. Cordially yours,[25] [500]

Reading and Writing Practice

740

Carr

odd-shaped hyphenated before noun

1-inch hyphenated before noun

par·ti·tions

[73]

741

intro

ap

aide

Gov·er·nor

less-than-car·load *hyphenated before noun*

intro

ex·ces·sive·ly

In·ter·state

if

con·ve·nience

some·time

ap

intro

[207]

742

ap

Transcribe: No. 106-457-872

106-457-872

RTA

ap

re·cord·ed

18 19

par

trans·por·ta·tion

[126]

743

78-357 19

rip·tide

ap Hawaii

mis·cel·la·neous

Ma·nila

intro

Tel·ex

[172]

Shorthand Vocabulary Builder

744 PHRASING FOR SPEED

We

1

Think

2

Been

3

Ago

4

Be

5

1 We made, we can be, we can have, we can say, we cannot be, we did not, we have not been able, we shall be able, we are not.

2 If you think, as you think, I do not think, do you think, I think, I think that, if they think, to think, we think, they think.

3 Who have been, you have been, I have been, have not been, would have been, he might have been, there might have been, there has been, it has been, we have not been, they have not been.

4 Week ago, several months ago, some time ago, months ago, years ago, days ago, several days ago, day or two ago, few minutes ago.

5 To be, to be sure, he must be, I must be, has to be, she must be, they will be, I will be, can be.

Building Transcription Skills

745 Business Vocabulary Builder

demurrage charge A charge made for delaying a vehicle during loading or unloading.

tariffs Duties imposed by a government on imported or exported materials.

Reading and Writing Practice

746

is·sued

pos·si·bly

par

bank·rupt·cy

as

stor·age

de·mur·rage

intro

par

re·serve

[164]

747

ap

Sum·mers'

tour·ist-class *hyphenated before noun*

nonr

Trans-Ocean

17 14

Mar·seilles

312

17

Zu·rich

102 19

15

20

par

RKA

if

21

wait-list·ed

20 [172]

748

tar·iffs

par

con·fu·sion

Com·mis·sion

ser

pipe·line high·way

par

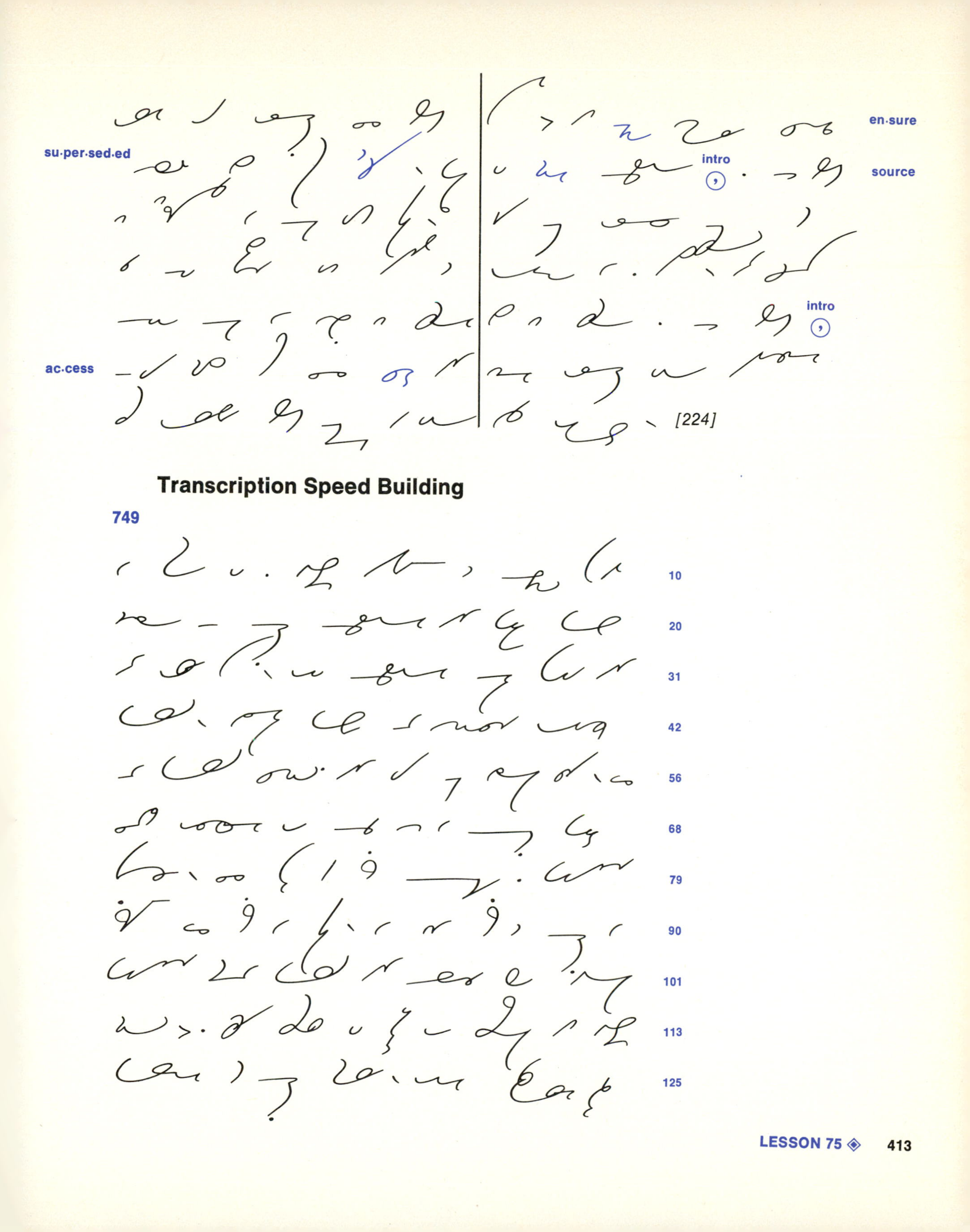

su·per·sed·ed

en·sure

intro

source

intro

ac·cess

[224]

Transcription Speed Building

749

10

20

31

42

56

68

79

90

101

113

125

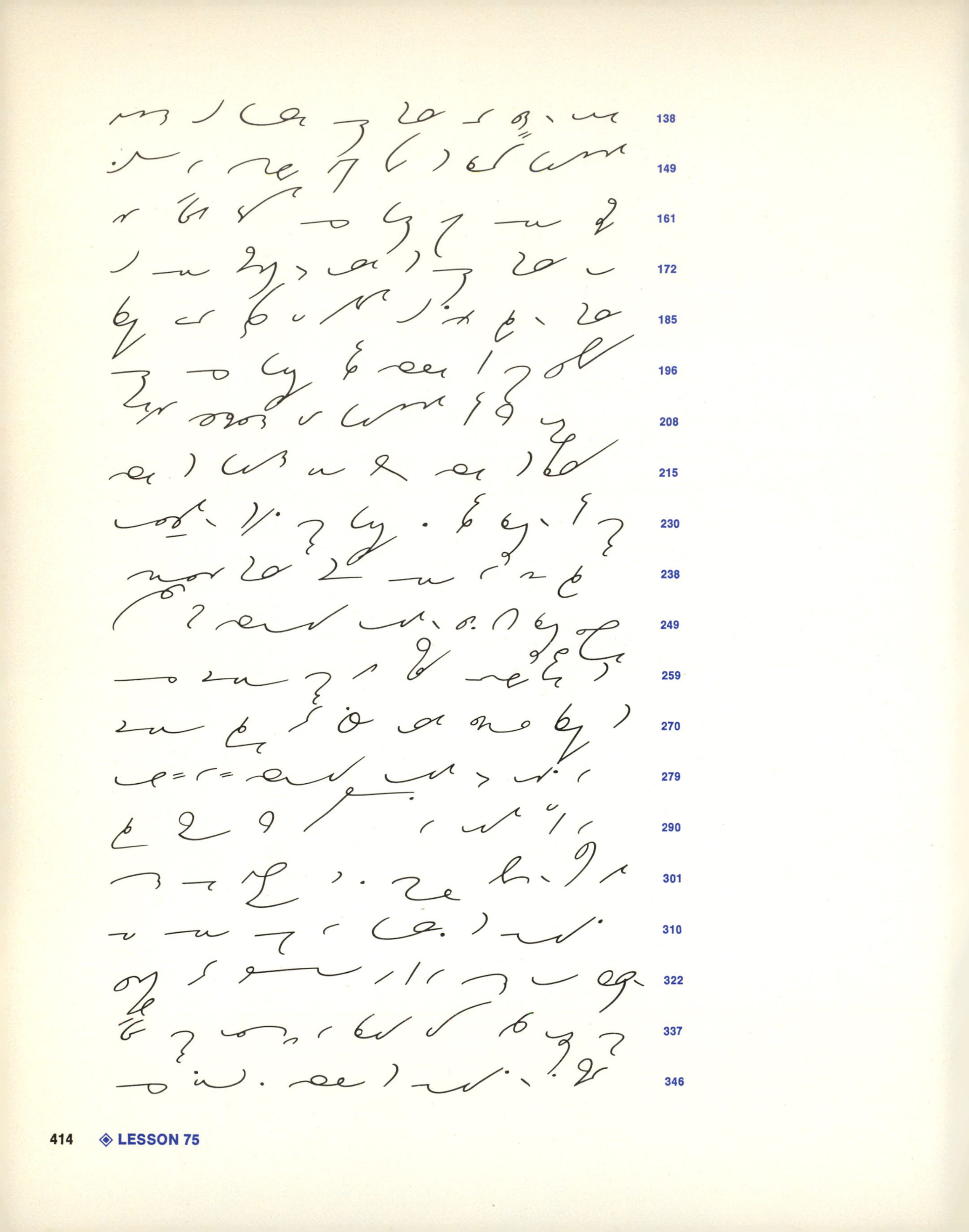

138
149
161
172
185
196
208
215
230
238
249
259
270
279
290
301
310
322
337
346

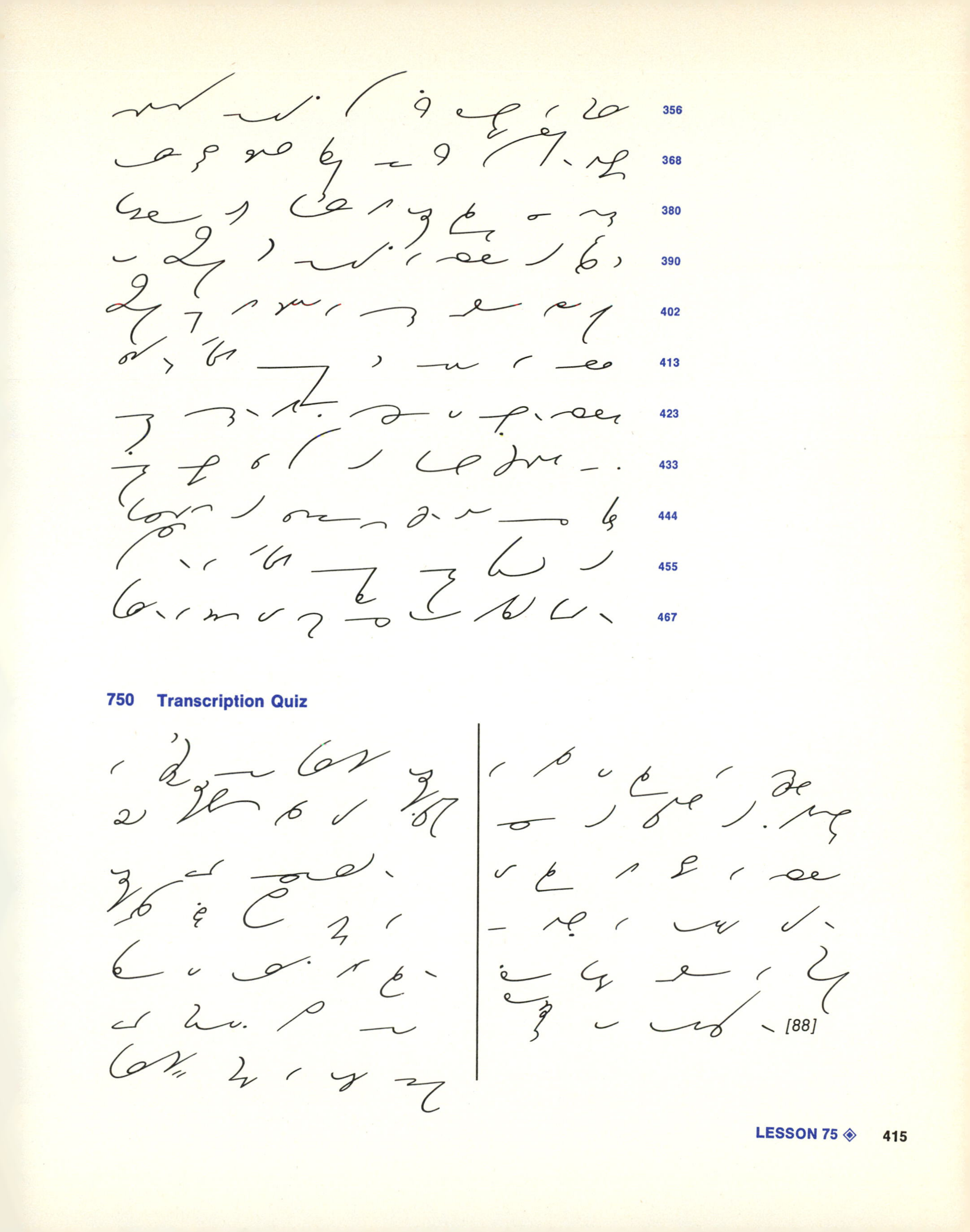

356

368

380

390

402

413

423

433

444

455

467

750 Transcription Quiz

[88]

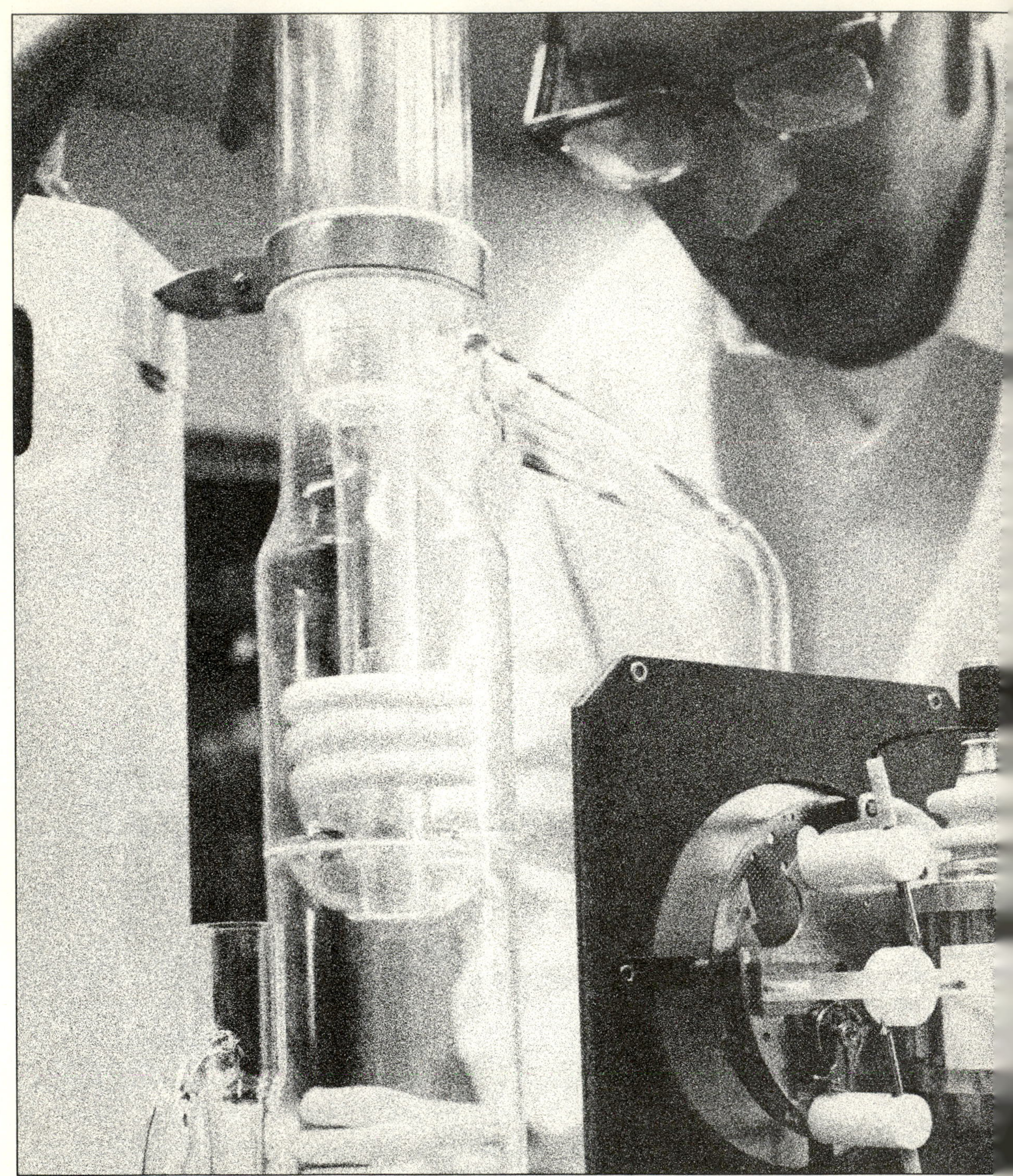

Unit 16
RESEARCH AND DEVELOPMENT

At your last work station, you are secretary to Dr. Douglas French, director of Research and Development. This is an exciting job, for experiments undertaken here lead to the manufacture of new products and the modification of old ones. Its discoveries are the basis for the expenditure of millions of dollars. The work done here can make a company move forward or fall behind its competitors. Its mistakes are costly. If Research and Development is not progressive, the whole organization is in trouble.

Shorthand Vocabulary Builder

751 WORD FAMILIES

-side

1

-cation

2

-sure

3

-dent

4

1 Side, inside, outside, decide, aside, reside, subside, preside.

2 Indication, vacation, location, allocation, complication, dedication.

3 Sure, pressures, measured, pleasure, assured, assurance, reassure.

4 Evident, incident, diffident, president, confident, accident, resident.

Building Transcription Skills

752 SIMILAR WORDS ■ compliment, complement; therefore, therefor

Study the following words which sound alike and which are sometimes confused.

compliment *(noun)* A flattering remark.
(verb) To praise.

complement That which completes.

therefore Consequently.

therefor For that thing.

753 **Business Vocabulary Builder**

to pool To group resources for the common advantage of those participating.

R and D A popular short form for research and development indicating an activity as well as a department or division engaging in these functions.

Progressive Dictation [125–140]

754 PREVIEW

[755]

[756]

[757]

[758]

755 Whiteside, reassure, remeasured, screws, deterioration, difficulties.

756 Accident, rearranged, outside, mobile, unfamiliar, prevalent.

757 Summarizes, identify, incurred, interviewees, radius, required.

758 Patents, electronically, motorist, preliminary, entrance, percentage.

LETTERS

[1 Minute at 125]

755 Dear Mr. Whiteside: Let me reassure you about the specifications for Product 17. We have remeasured the screws and retested the required pressure for/manufacturing the threads required. You can proceed confidently with production of this item so far as specifications are concerned.

It is our opinion that any//complications during the trial run result from deterioration in the quality of metals available today. We understand your difficulties in///the location of materials that meet our quality-control standards in the present market. Unless we obtain these materials, we cannot produce a good product. Yours truly, [1]

[1 Minute at 130]

756 To: James Morrison, President Subject: Reducing Accidents in Our Mobile Homes We have rearranged our schedule to include research on accident prevention both inside and/outside the mobile homes we manufacture, as you requested in your memorandum of July 16. We should be able to comply with your request for a report by October 1.//

One of the reasons for so many accidents is that these homes are usually used for vacations. Since the residents are in an unfamiliar environment, accidents are/// naturally more prevalent than if they were living in their regular homes. Features can be included in our advertising and should greatly increase the sales of our vacation homes. [2]

[1 Minute at 135]

757 To: Nancy Wexford, Project Manager Subject: Interviews With Owners of

Mobile Homes This memorandum summarizes our discussion yesterday of the project to identify/causes of accidents incurred by residents of our mobile vacation homes.

You will interview 50 present owners of these homes between September 1 and 15. To choose interviewees,//you will consult records in the Sales Department both of sales made and of accidents reported.

You will try to locate owners residing within 100 miles of our///headquarters. If travel expenses beyond this radius are necessary, my approval is required prior to the interview. It will be a pleasure to work with you on this project. [3]

[1 Minute at 140]

758 Dear Dr. Watson: In examining the patents recently issued, I noticed that you have developed a light that turns on electronically when someone approaches a dark area/in much the same way that a door can be opened by a motorist nearing his or her garage.

We are considering new safety devices for making mobile homes more safe for residents.//Preliminary research indicates that a frequent cause of accidents is a fall as the resident approaches the dark steps at the entrance. Would your invention be helpful as standard equipment///for mobile homes? Would you be interested in a contract for a percentage of sales rather than your selling the patent outright? May I come to see you if you are interested? Yours truly, [4] [530]

Reading and Writing Practice

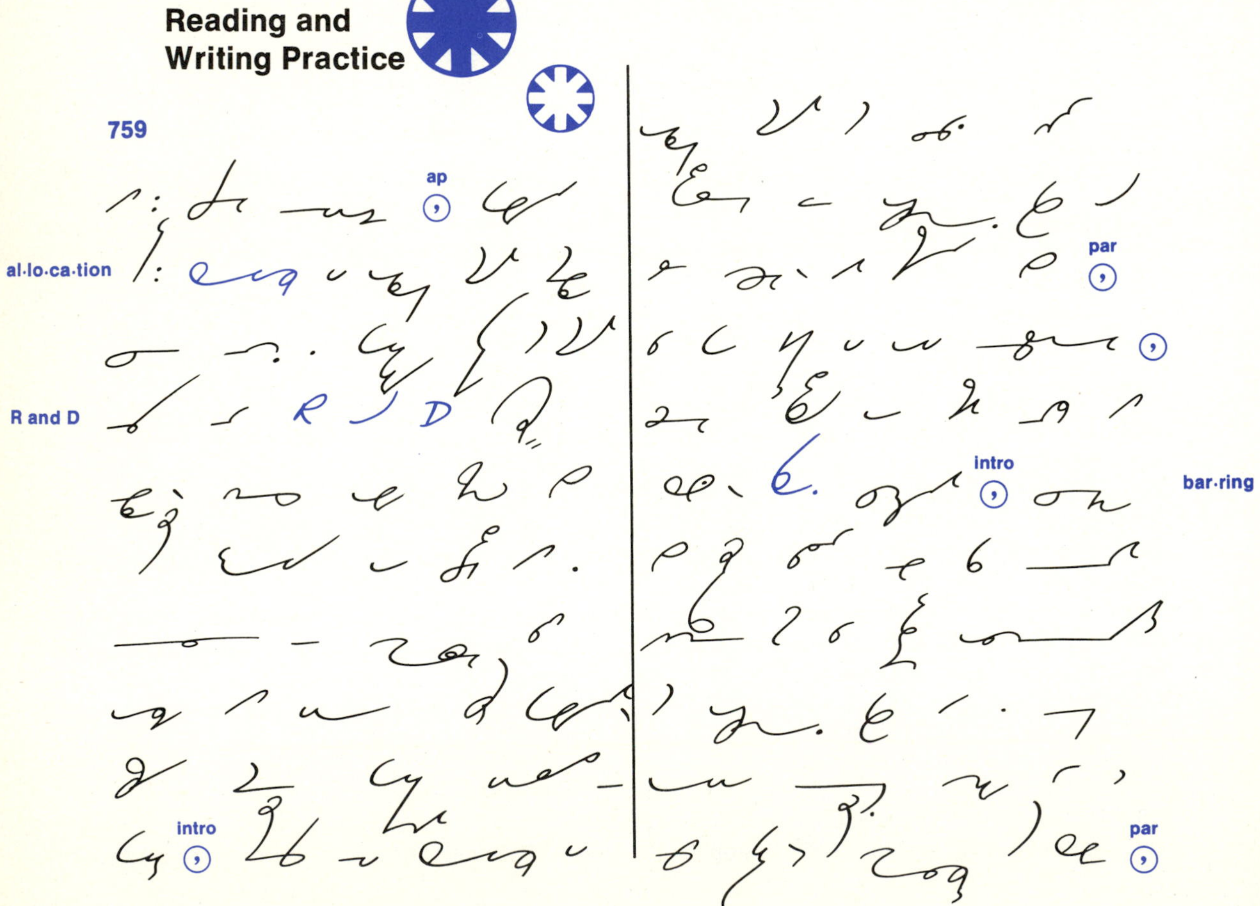

con·sul·tant

par

guid·ance

intro

par

[263]

760

par

su·per·i·or·i·ty

there·fore

ap

au·di·to·ri·um

if

com·pe·tent

intro

ef·fec·tive·ly

if

[171]

co·op·er·ate

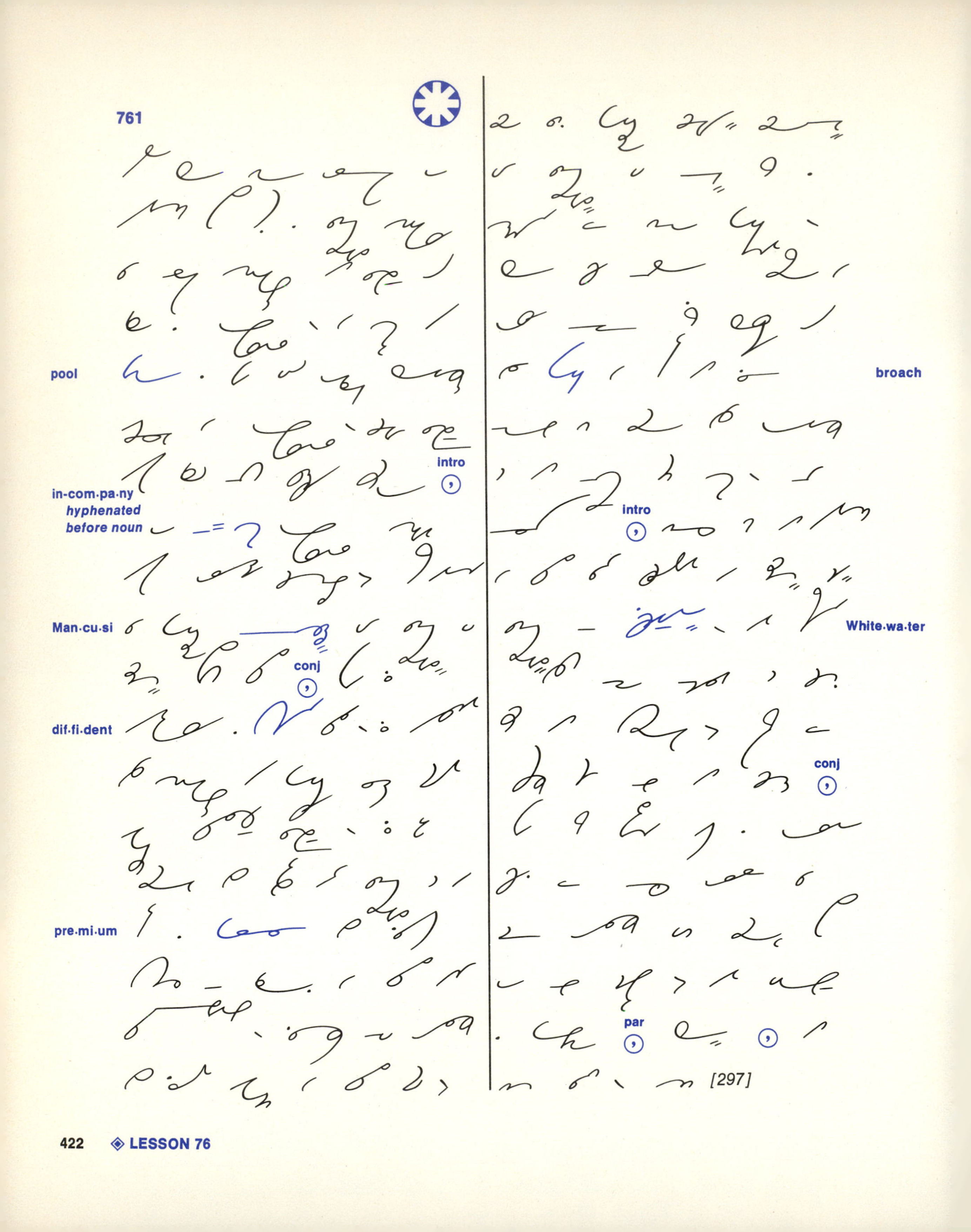

761

pool

in-com·pa·ny *hyphenated before noun*

intro

Man·cu·si

conj

dif·fi·dent

pre·mi·um

broach

intro

White·wa·ter

conj

par

[297]

LESSON 77

Shorthand Vocabulary Builder

762 WORD ENDINGS

-tain

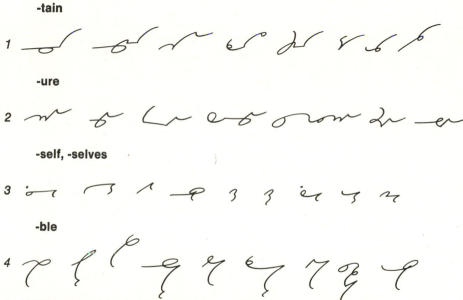

1

-ure

2

-self, -selves

3

-ble

4

1 Maintain, mountain, container, certainly, fountain, sustain, retain, detain.

2 Culture, nature, puncture, armature, agriculture, fixture, mixture.

3 Himself, themselves, itself, myself, yourself, yourselves, herself, ourselves, oneself.

4 Cable, tables, sable, marbles, terrible, syllables, trouble, acceptable, liable.

Building Transcription Skills

763 TRANSCRIPTION TYPING

10

22

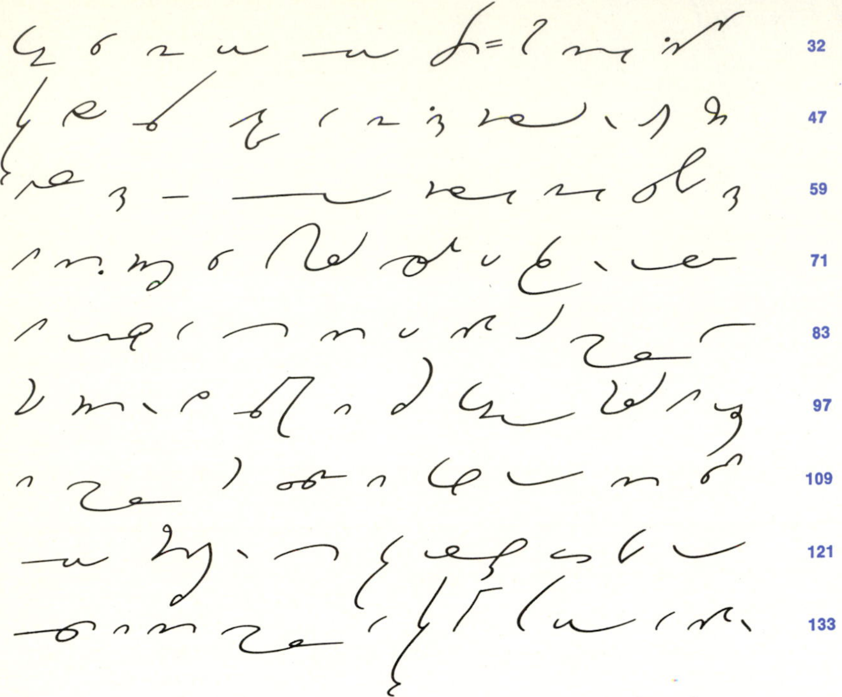

764 **Business Vocabulary Builder**

chemically stable Not easily decomposed.

armature The rotating part of a motor or generator which consists of an iron core around which are wound many loops of copper wire.

Stair-Step Dictation

765 PREVIEW

[766]

[767]

[768]

766 Gladly, redesign, delicate, puncture-proof, experiment.

767 Requests, during the past, Vincent, diffident, modifying, negative.

768 Fertilizers, agricultural, India, Pakistan, enrichment, projections.

LETTERS

766 To: W. A. Saunders, Transportation Manager Subject: Redesign of Shipping Containers Yes, our[1] division will gladly undertake the redesign of the containers used in the Shipping Department. Because of[2] the delicate nature of many of our electronic products, we must improve these containers so that they[3] are more nearly puncture-proof. Our chemists are analyzing the mixtures used in the present containers to try[4] to determine for themselves their present composition. Later they will experiment with new mixtures and new[5] shapes and processes. If you would like for us to analyze containers other than those we are currently using,[6] please send along samples. Such analyses may prove the key to the improvement in packaging fragile items.[7]

You can certainly depend on us to make recommendations by January 18, the date named in[8] your memorandum. As our research develops and results emerge, I shall myself report to you on our progress.[9]

767 Dear Vincent: I am sorry that you have found it necessary to write me twice before I got around to[10] reporting to you, but we have been extremely busy here in R and D on two urgent research requests during[11] the past two months. I want to assure you, Vincent, that I am not diffident toward our research on your proposal[12] for modifying Product 76. Our results do not, however, sustain further expenditure of[13] funds in the light of our negative findings. The construction of the armature you propose is a much more[14] complicated process than building the present one and would increase the price of the finished product out of proportion[15] to the benefit gained.

Of course, we want to use the ideas submitted by our employees whenever possible.[16] Please, therefore, continue to give us your suggestions for improving our products. Very cordially yours,[17]

768 To: James Morrison, President Subject: Leave of Absence for James Winthrop As you know, James Winthrop is a research[18] scientist working on the development of our fertilizers for increased production of agricultural[19] products. Mr. Winthrop has been invited to join a team of agricultural specialists touring India[20] and Pakistan for two months to study their needs for soil-enrichment materials.

I am enclosing[21] a letter from this valued employee asking for two months' leave of absence to accept this invitation. It[22] is a great honor not only to him but also to our company.

I strongly support his request. Our market[23] projections indicate that more than half of our fertilizer sales will be made abroad during the next five[24] years. This trip will give us the opportunity to examine for ourselves the needs and the problems of the two countries.[25] [500]

Reading and Writing Practice

769

ap

In-Ser·vice hyphenated before noun

R and D

as

conj

intro

specialists

conj

intro

40

intro

polymerization

8-week hyphenated before noun.

8-week

intro

satisfactorily

par

[289]

770

ap

Dougherty

strength·en·ing

as ,

intro ,

stur·dy

sta·ble

af·fect·ed

intro ,

anx·ious

[169]

771

ar·ma·ture

mag·net·ic

$\frac{1}{64}$

par ,

,

de·cid·ing

intro ,

[127]

Shorthand Vocabulary Builder

772 BRIEF-FORM POWER

1 Good, goods, good-bye, goodness, goodwill, good-natured.

2 Their–there, thereafter, thereby, therefore, thereupon, therewith, thereabouts; order, orders, orderly, ordering, ordered.

3 Work, workable, worker, workman, framework, patchwork, homework.

4 By, bylaws, byplay, byword, bypass, by-product, standby, byway.

773 CITIES

-field

Westfield, Springfield, Garfield, Plainfield, Greenfield, Fairfield.

Building Transcription Skills

774 SIMILAR WORDS ■ lead, led; respectively, respectfully

Study the following words which are somewhat alike and which are sometimes confused.

lead *(noun)* Metal.
(verb) To guide.

led *(verb)* Past tense of *to lead.*

respectively In the order given.

respectfully In a courteous way.

775 **Business Vocabulary Builder**

bylaws Rules governing internal affairs of an organization.

industrial chemistry A branch of general chemistry that is devoted to the development of new products from organic raw materials and/or the recycling of used materials of organic composition.

Progressive Dictation [125–140]

776 **PREVIEW**

[777]

[778]

[779]

[780]

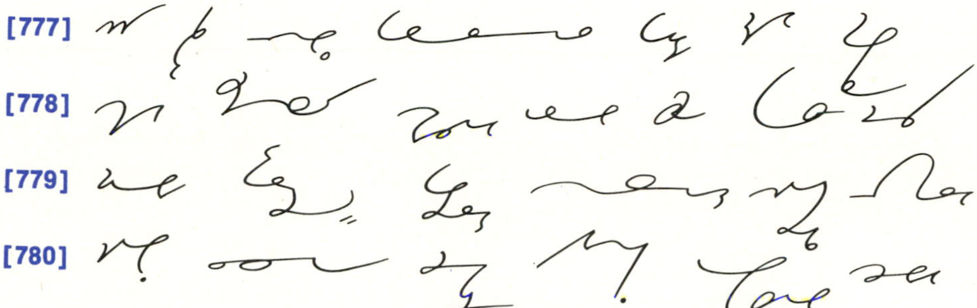

777 Wooden, chips, increasingly, preliminary, processed, substance, fragile.

778 Confidential, safeguarded, competitors, release, wire, by-line, submitted.

779 Solicit, Springfield, preferences, glamorous, controversy, indifference.

780 Stripping, enamel, symposium, discouraging, laboratories, chemists.

LETTERS

[1 Minute at 125]

777 To: W. A. Saunders, Transportation Manager Subject: By-Product From the Manufacture of Product 9 Our division has been trying for some time to develop/a workable plan for manufacturing a by-product from the wooden chips now being wasted while making Product 9. As the price of paper increases every week, the//importance of such a by-product becomes increasingly apparent.

We now have some preliminary results that look exciting to us. These chips can be processed into a substance///that could be used as a filler around fragile goods by our shipping room. We have a sample that we would like to show you while we discuss the possibilities. [1]

[1 Minute at 130]

778 To: Andy Garfield, Public Information Subject: Publicity About Product XX Yes, Andy, I did make a presentation before the Executive Committee about/Product XX, which will go into production within the next six months. The discussion was, however, confidential, for the processes we have developed must be safeguarded//from our competitors. It is all right for you to prepare a very general report for release to the wire services immediately over your own by-line, but I///must insist that the article be cleared by me before it is submitted.

Please come to my office for an interview with Hank Byram and me after you have prepared the release. [2]

[1 Minute at 135]

779 Dear Hal: I should like to solicit your support of John Westfield as president of our regional research association next year. The voting will take place in Springfield, but we should give/thought to our preferences before we arrive.

John is really the good old standby of our group, always willing to fill in for the more glamorous member who sometimes fails to "come through." He is//a hard worker for improved research. He is always good-tempered even when controversy develops.

I feel that he has not received the recognition he deserves and has been passed over///in favor of less dedicated members. Speaking for myself alone, I would like to see our indifference to his worth reversed. May I count on your support. Yours cordially, [3]

[1 Minute at 140]

780 Dear Dr. Greenfield: I understand that your division has recently developed a process for removing the guesswork from stripping enamel from furniture. If this is not a trade secret,/I should very much appreciate your sharing the results of your research with us. I assume that it is not, for I have read very carefully your discussion in the February issue//of *Chemistry Today*. I note also that you are giving a talk on the topic at the symposium in Houston on March 29.

We have been working on the same problem for some time but///have had most discouraging results. I should like to visit your laboratories to observe your chemists at work if that would be possible. When may I visit your laboratories? Yours truly [4]

[530]

Reading and Writing Practice

781

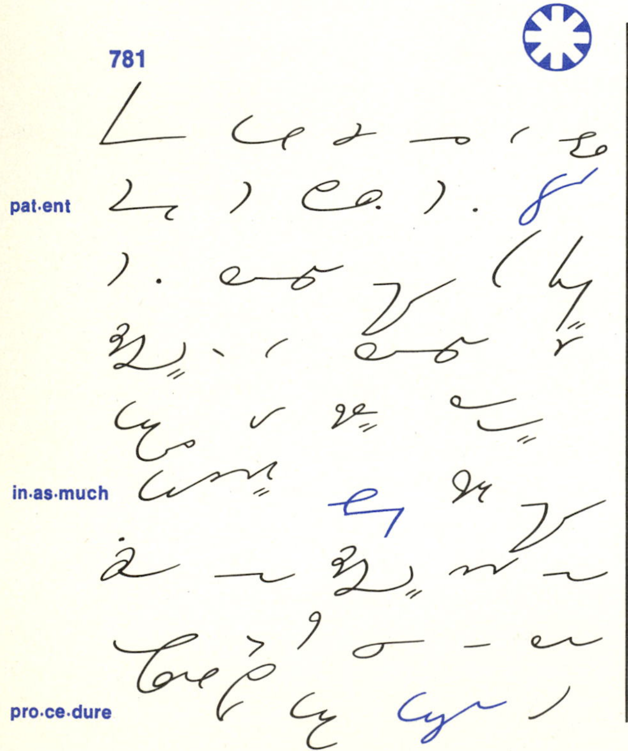

trade·mark

[157]

782

in·qui·ry

pos·si·bil·i·ty

grad·u·ate

dis·ser·ta·tion

phd

intro

as

par

com·pet·i·tors

by·laws

mon·e·tary

vi·o·lat·ing

par

[186]

783

par

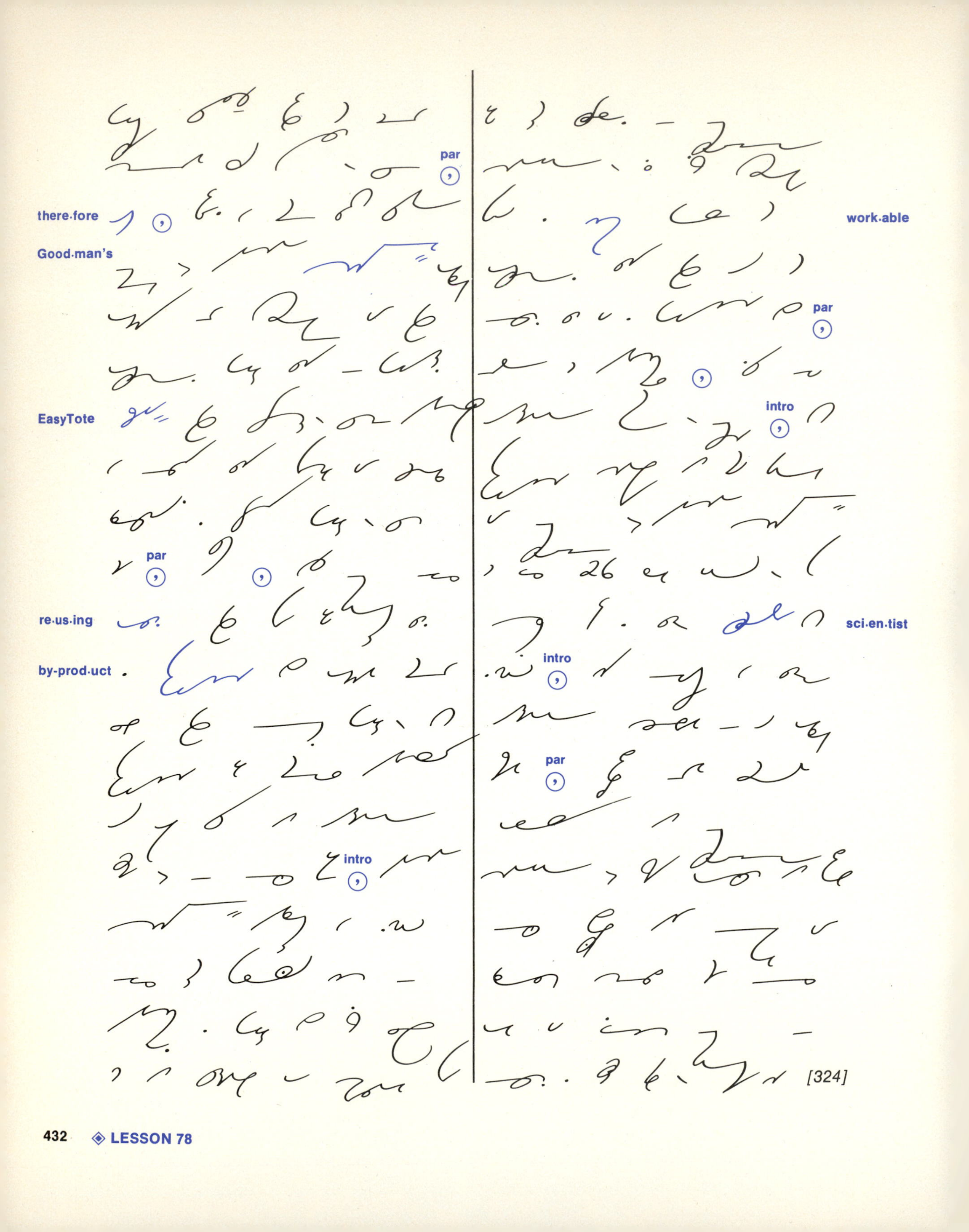

par

there·fore

Good·man's

EasyTote

par

re·us·ing

by-prod·uct

intro

work·able

par

intro

sci·en·tist

intro

par

[324]

LESSON 79

Shorthand Vocabulary Builder

784 WORD-BUILDING PRINCIPLES

Omission of Vowels

1

Ness Joined With a Jog

2

Single Stroke for Double Consonants

3

Omission of Unaccented Diphthong U

4

1 Carpet, landscape, obituary, petroleum, petition, occur.
2 Meanness, suddenness, openness, sullenness, plainness, calmness.
3 Bookkeeper, roommate, earrings, storeroom, penknife, nighttime.
4 Formula, popular, accurate, singular, ambulance, vocabulary.

Building Transcription Skills

785 TRANSCRIPTION TYPING

10

23

34

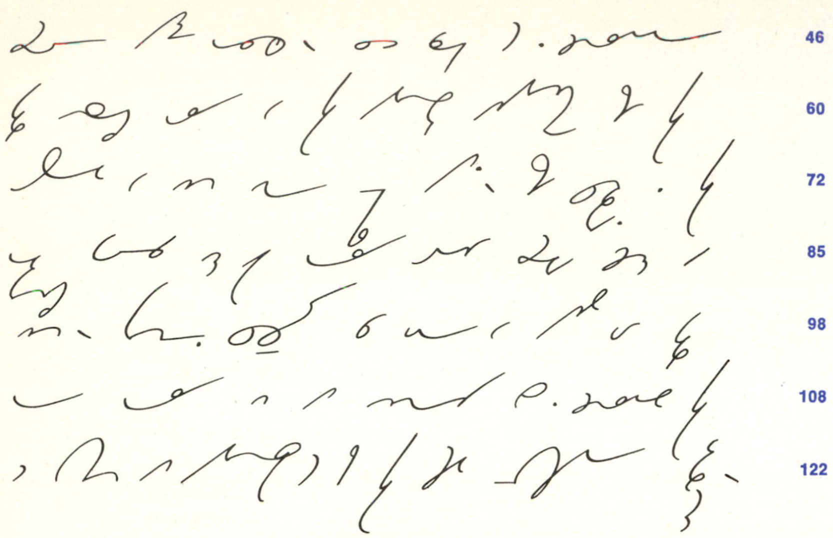

786 Business Vocabulary Builder

nonallergenic cosmetics Cosmetics in which the chemical components have been selected and blended to prevent hypersensitive or pathological reaction.

liters Metric units of volume.

notarized Authenticated.

Stair-Step Dictation

787 PREVIEW

[788]

[789]

[790]

788 Slashed, postponed, petroleum, inaugurate, automobiles.

789 Obituary, organ, stricken, ambulance, peers, calmness, shock.

790 Delighted, highly, transcript, scientific, vocabulary, notification.

LETTERS

788 To the Staff: Subject: Economies Our budget for research and development has been slashed 26 percent[1] for next year, and the building of our new laboratory has been temporarily postponed. Because of the[2] petroleum shortage, we shall have to inaugurate small economies all along the line. For instance, all[3] buildings will be kept at 65 degrees during the week. Over the weekends the temperature will be reduced[4] to 55 degrees with the exception of Storeroom 26, to which all experiments requiring[5] higher temperatures will be transferred on Friday afternoons. Provision of staff automobiles will be[6] limited to three small cars—one for the manager and two for a pool of engineers and chemists.

Fortunately,[7] we do not anticipate having to reduce our present staff, for we have been operating with three fewer[8] members than needed. We shall have a staff meeting next week to plan additional economies.[9]

789 To: Andy Garfield, Public Information Subject: Obituary for Henry Carpenter These notes can be[10] used in the obituary for Dr. Henry Carpenter to be published in our house organ immediately.[11] Additional information can be found in his file in the Personnel office. Dr. Carpenter[12] was stricken with a heart attack while in his laboratory on Friday morning and was taken[13] immediately to Memorial Hospital by ambulance. He was pronounced dead on arrival at the[14] hospital.

He was one of the most popular members of the research staff and was often praised for his openness[15] in dealing with those above him in command, with his peers, and with those he supervised. He usually displayed[16] calmness under pressure and was unusually good-natured and supportive of his colleagues. The suddenness[17] of his death is a great shock to the entire company. His temporary successor is Dr. John Franklin.[18]

790 Dear Ms. Wilkins: I am delighted to invite you to join my staff as my[19] secretary starting on February 1. My decision to offer this position to you is based on the highly accurate transcript you made[20] of 160-word dictation during your test in the Personnel office. Your performance is all the[21] more satisfactory because of the rather scientific vocabulary used in the letters dictated.[22] It is typical, though, of the vocabulary you will be expected to use in this position. Both the[23] Personnel office and I were pleased with the calmness and openness you displayed in answering our questions during[24] your interview.

All arrangements for starting to work should be made with Mildred Brown in Personnel, who will also[25] be writing you. This letter is merely notification of appointment. I think—and hope—that you will find this[26] appointment as exciting as I myself think it is. We look forward to having you join our staff. Yours truly,[27] [540]

791

obit·u·ary

when ,

in·ad·e·quate

intro ,

as

di·ver·si·fied

due

Toi·let·ries

intro

nonr

non·al·ler·gen·ic

cos·met·ics

in·au·gu·rat·ing

intro

par

ser

intro

dim·ness

intro

wind·fall

ap

Transcribe:
11 o'clock

[351]

792

Car·pen·ter's

ap

,

,

li·ters

store·room

conj

,

am·bu·lance

intro

,

sec·ond-de·gree
hyphenated before noun

par

,

,

room·mate

if

,

[224]

no·ta·rized

Shorthand Vocabulary Builder

793 PHRASING FOR SPEED

Quantities

1

Contractions

2

In Addition

3

I

4

We

5

1 Per hundred, per dollar, per pound, several hundred, several dollars, several thousand dollars, a million, a thousand, a hundred, a billion.

2 We couldn't, I couldn't, I don't, you don't, we shouldn't, we aren't, we didn't, they didn't.

3 In addition, in addition to the, in addition to these, in addition to those, in addition to that, in addition to them.

4 I know, I knew, I wish, I think that, I remember, I cannot, I wanted, I was.

5 We are, we have been, we should, we would, we have, we could, we cannot, we shall, we will, we can't.

Building Transcription Skills

794 **Business Vocabulary Builder**

mass production The manufacture of goods in large quantities.

guarantee To assume the responsibility for payment, quality, execution of.

Reading and Writing Practice

795

Transcribe: No. 81

high·way

par

com·pa·ra·ble

if

intro

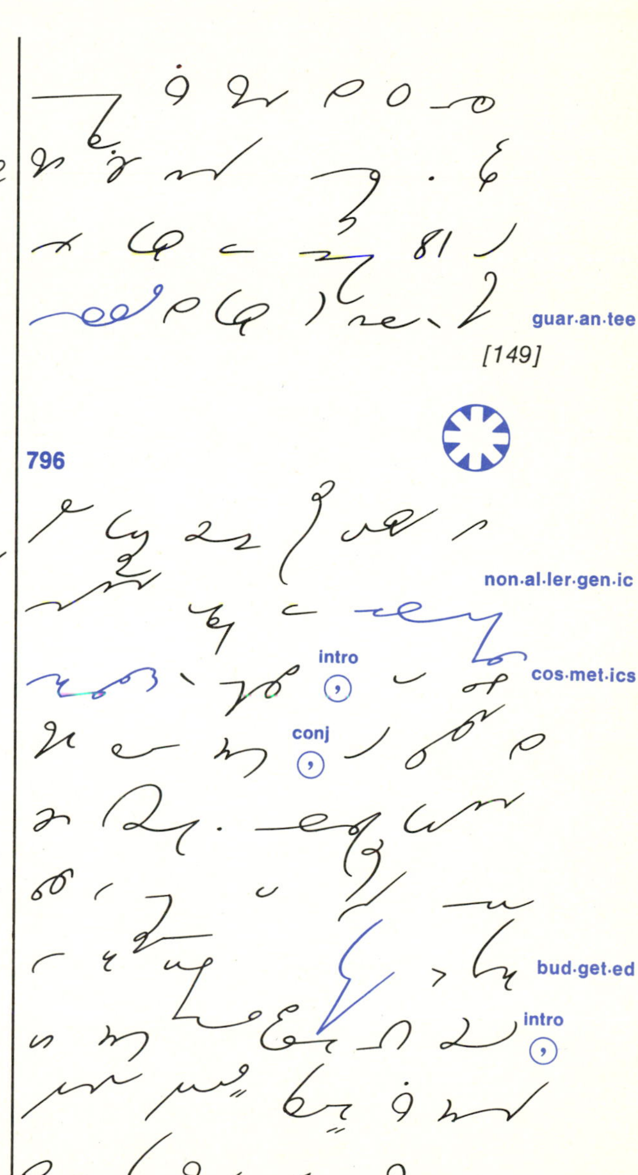

guar·an·tee

[149]

796

non·al·ler·gen·ic

intro

cos·met·ics

conj

bud·get·ed

intro

con·sul·tant

lab·o·ra·to·ry

if

[134]

797

ap

as

in·au·gu·rat·ed

nonr

dol·lars'

intro

pat·ent

conj

nonr

dis·ser·ta·tion

intro

al·ler·gies

par

15

nonr

cru·cial

conj

intro

Transcribe: Inc.

CNL

[316]

Transcription Speed Building

798

14

30

40

52

64

77

87

96

105

117

128

142

154

164

175

186

196

207

223

232

245

258

270

281

293

306

318

330

342

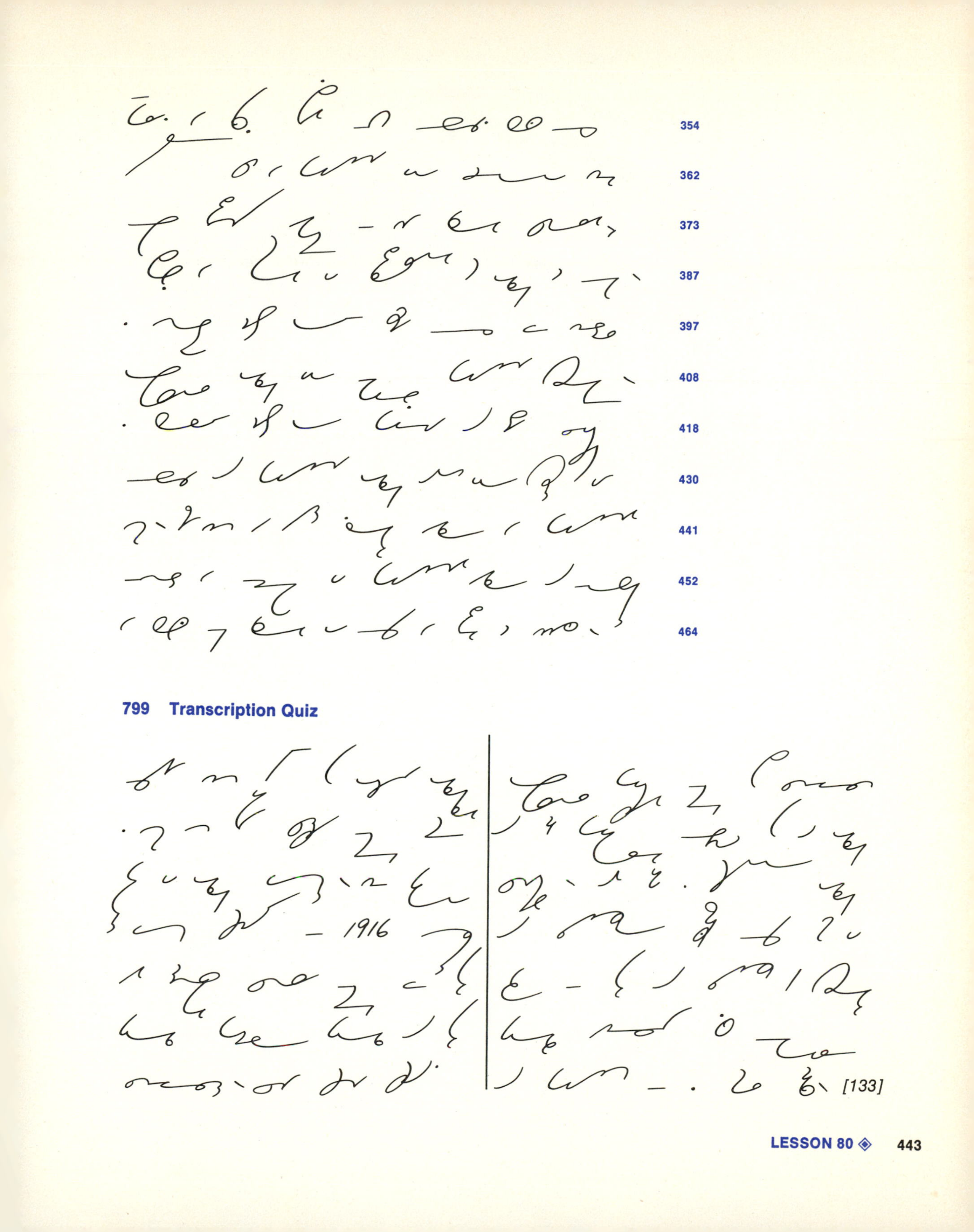

354
362
373
387
397
408
418
430
441
452
464

799 Transcription Quiz

1916

[133]

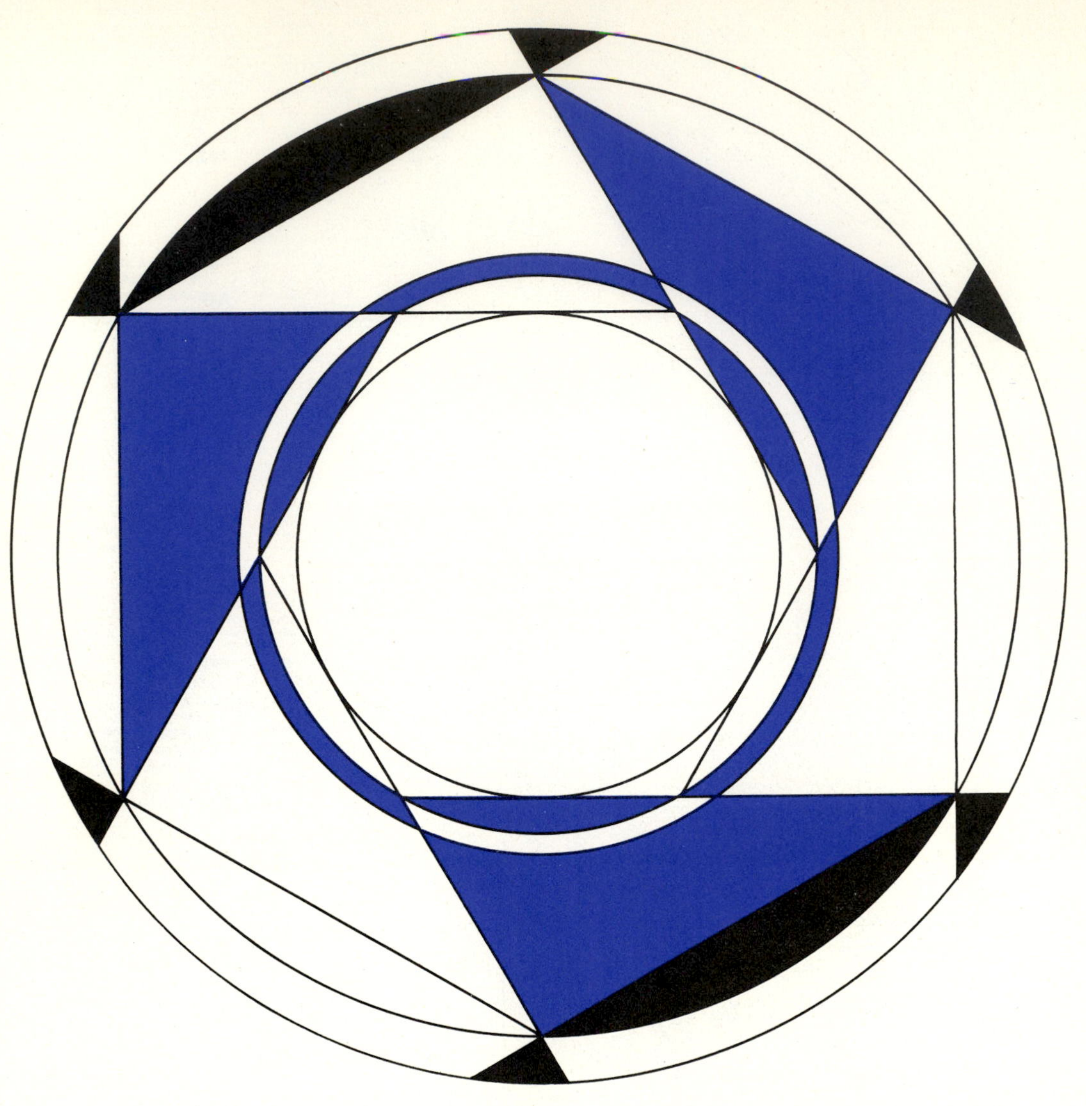

APPENDIX

ADDRESSES FOR TRANSCRIPTION

(The numbers of the following names and addresses correspond to the lesson numbers of the supplementary letters in the *Instructor's Handbook for Gregg Shorthand for Colleges, Speed Building, DJS.)*

UNIT 1

1 General Printing Company, 9219 Howard Street, Chicago, Illinois 60626
2 Overton Brothers, 541 Water Street, Providence, Rhode Island 02914
3 Miss Ethel Percy, 549 Lewis Street, Albuquerque, New Mexico 87101
4 Mrs. Mary Underwood, 119 Washington Street, Fargo, North Dakota 58102
5 Black and Carter, 1611 East Carondelet Street, New Orleans, Louisiana 70113

UNIT 2

6 Miss Betty Shore, Raleigh Telephone Company, Raleigh, North Carolina 27602
7 Memorandum to All Sales Employees
8 Mr. Conrad Jones, Manager, National Commercial Insurance Company, 545 State Street, Chicago, Illinois 60607
9 Mr. Leonard Carlin, Personnel Manager, AMG Industries, Airport Road, Mansfield, Ohio 44901
10 Mrs. William March, Chairman, Parks and Recreation Department, San Jose, California 95125

UNIT 3

11 Jones Mercantile Company, 911 South Street, Springfield, Massachusetts 01101
12 Mr. Albert Harding, Harding Stores, 32 Congress Street, Portland, Maine 04101
13 New Stanton Publishing Company, 43 Elm Street, New Stanton, Pennsylvania 15672
14 Mr. James Newsome, Chairman of Corporation Gifts, Community Fund, First National Bank, 515 State Street, Orlando, Florida 32802
15 Mr. Harold Brown, Brown and Hodges, 511 Hudson Street, Union Square, New Jersey 07201

UNIT 4

16 Memorandum to the Sales Staff
17 Mr. William Seagram, Pine Cliff Inn, 816 Gulf Drive, Biloxi, Missouri 39530
18 Mr. Alan Dewar, 411 East Sixth Street, Fort Necessity, Louisiana 71243
19 Mr. Glenn Wright, Regency Hotel, Atlanta, Georgia 30304
20 Memorandum to Our Sales Staff

UNIT 5

21 Mr. Ronald Harris, Henry Phipps Dormitory, University of Missouri, Columbia, Missouri 65201
22 Memorandum to All Applicants for Clerical Positions
23 Mr. Sam Sweeney, Director of Personnel, Montana Manufacturing Company, Great Falls, Montana 59401
24 Memorandum to All Department Heads
25 Memorandum to Frances Martin, Employee-Evaluation Unit

UNIT 6

26 Braun and Braun, 53 Alleestrasse, Düsseldorf, Germany Airmail
27 Associated Mills, 12245 Sedgefield Road, Charlotte, North Carolina 28202
28 Pittsburgh Coal Company, 112 River Front, Pittsburgh, Pennsylvania 15219
29 Plattsburg Optical Manufacturers, Inc., Albany Road, Plattsburg, New York 12901
30 Electro Thermal Products, Springfield Road and Wilson Avenue, Eugene, Oregon 97401

UNIT 7

31 Mr. Harry Lennox, City Desk, Chicago Tribune, Tribune Tower, Chicago, Illinois 60607
32 Mr. Martin Ames, Program Director, Station KJK, Oklahoma City, Oklahoma 73100
33 Memorandum to Jim Bolton, Sales Manager
34 Memorandum to Franklin Norton, Vice President
35 Dr. Thomas Devery, 811 Fourth Avenue, Fort Lauderdale, Florida 33310

UNIT 8

36 Ms. Helen Westerly, 1945 Park Lane, Topeka, Kansas 66603
37 Dr. Myron Baker, c/o Mr. Henry Stanford, Lake of the Ozarks, Camdenton, Missouri 65020
38 National Insurance Company, 1415 High Street, Columbus, Ohio 43216
39 Memorandum to All Department Heads
40 Memorandum to Lawrence Botsford, President

UNIT 9

41 Mr. Fred Weaver, Advertising Manager, Chico News, Chico, California 95926
42 Mr. Robert White, White Advertising Company, John Hancock Plaza, Boston, Massachusetts 02109
43 Mr. Ben Bates, Bates Public Relations, 237 249th Street, White Plains, New York 10602
44 Mr. Elwood Forbes, Forbes Printing Company, 113 Harper Street, Boise, Idaho 83707
45 Mr. Elmer Spottswood, Manager, Thompson's, Paducah, Kentucky 42001

UNIT 10

46 Memorandum to All Department Heads
47 Memorandum to Adele Schroeder, Supervisor of Stenographic Services
48 Miss Wilma Sweeney, P.O. Box 861, Myrtle Beach, South Carolina 29577
49 Shreveport Office Papers, Inc., Davis Road, Shreveport, Louisiana 71102
50 New Era Business Equipment Manufacturers, 1345 Elm Street, Hartford, Connecticut 06101

UNIT 11

51 Mr. Robert Kelman, Sales Engineer, Rancher Hotel, Dallas, Texas 75221
52 Mr. Henry Taylor, Production Manager, Uncas Manufacturing Company, 411 Ninth Street, Akron, Ohio 44309
53 Dawson and Hodges, Inc., Railway Street, Atchison, Kansas 66002
54 Miss Mary Carson, Carson Theater Costumes, 745 Seventh Avenue, New York, New York 10001
55 Memorandum to Monroe Moon, Director of Research and Development

UNIT 12

56 Mrs. Marcia Summerville, 743 Magnolia Drive, Natchez, Mississippi 39120
57 Mr. Robert Merton, 566 Monument Drive, Richmond, Virginia 23219

UNIT 12 (Continued)

58 Ms. Alma Billings, 1818 South Harrison Street, Durham, New Hampshire 03824

59 Custom Carpet Company, Kinston, North Carolina 28501

60 Mastic, Jones, and Brownell, Attorneys-at-Law, Brown Building, Charleston. South Carolina 29401

UNIT 13

61 Memorandum to Frank Simmonds, President

62 Mr. Martin Berger, President, The Security Bank, Ottumwa, Iowa 52501

63 Mr. Benjamin Cunningham, Birmingham State Bank, Birmingham, Alabama 35203

64 Mrs. Helen Newcomb, Newcomb Enterprises, Middlebury, Vermont 05753

65 Mr. Dan Woodworth, Boston Trust Company, State Street, Boston, Massachusetts 02109

UNIT 14

66 Mrs. Edna O'Dea, President of Federated Women's Clubs, Kensington Lane, Birmingham, Alabama 35203

67 Mr. John Swann, Secretary, The Sierra Club, One River Road, Grants Pass, Oregon 97526

68 Dr. Roger Washington, Deparment of Engineering, Indiana University, Bloomington, Indiana 47401

69 Mr. Monroe Harper, 814 Adams Street, Huntington, West Virginia 25704

70 Memorandum to Walter Drennan, President

UNIT 15

71 The Dependable One, 414 First Street, Alton, Illinois 62002

72 Furbush Hardware Store, Fortuna, California 95540

73 Kane Electric Sealing Machines, Inc.,118 Cypress Road, Oxford, Mississippi 38655

74 Mr. Ted Mansfield, Transportation Manager, Lake Manufacturing Company, 118 Lake Superior Drive, Duluth, Minnesota 55801

75 Memorandum to Harold Gentry, Sales Manager

UNIT 16

76 Mr. Al Goodson, Director of Research and Development, GHI Pharmaceutical Company, Flint, Michigan 48502

77 Mr. James Winthrop, Maidens Hotel, Delhi, India Airmail

78 Dr. Wilma Franklin, First Chemical Company, 1989 Park Boulevard, Wilmington, Delaware 19899

79 Memorandum to Andy Garfield, Public Information

80 Martin Manufacturing Company, 102 Fifth Street, Springfield, Arkansas 72157

INDEX

The number next to each entry refers to the page in the text in which the entry appears.

MODEL LETTERS

Average letter 36
Interoffice memorandum 37
Long letter 37
Short letter, double-spaced 36
Short letter, single spaced 36
Two-page letter 37

NOTEBOOK AND TRANSCRIPTION TIPS

Changes 302
Large insertions 332
Procedures 360, 390

PROGRESSIVE DICTATION

Dictation speeds
- 50 - 60 - 70 - 80 58, 67
- 60 - 70 - 80 - 90 83, 93, 109
- 70 - 80 - 90-100 118, 135, 145, 163
- 80 - 90-100-110 174, 191, 201, 219
- 90-100-110-120 229, 247, 257, 275
- 100-110-120-125 285, 304, 315, 333
- 110-120-125-130 343, 361, 373
- 120-125-130-135 391, 401
- 125-130-135-140 419, 429

PUNCTUATION PRACTICE

Apostrophe 228
Direct quotation 218
—COMMAS
- *And* omitted 109
- Apposition 67, 117
- *As* clause 57
- Conjunction 57
- *If* clause 57
- In numbers 118
- Inside quote 219
- Introducing short quote 219
- Introductory 57
- Nonrestrictive 82
- Parenthetical 66
- Questions within sentences 92
- Series 108
- *When* clause 57

Hyphens 134, 144
—PUNCTUATION WITH QUOTATION MARKS
- Colon outside quote 219
- Comma inside quote 219

—PUNCTUATION WITH QUOTATION MARKS *(continued)*
- Comma introducing short quote 219
- Period inside quote 219
- Question mark inside and outside quote 219
- Semicolon outside quote 219

—SEMICOLONS
- No conjunction 200
- Series 201

SHORTHAND CHARTS

Brief-form review 14, 17, 20, 24, 27; Inside back cover
Frequently used phrases Inside back cover

SHORTHAND THEORY

Principles 32, 38
Principles of joining 41, 45, 50

SHORTHAND VOCABULARY BUILDERS

Brief-form power 66, 92, 117, 144, 173, 200, 228, 256, 284, 314, 342, 372, 400, 428
Cities 66, 92, 117, 144, 173, 200, 228, 256, 284, 314, 342, 372, 400, 428
Phrasing for speed 75, 101, 127, 155, 183, 211, 239, 266, 294, 324, 352, 382, 410, 438
Word beginnings 62, 108, 168, 223, 279, 337, 395
Word-building principles 71, 96, 122, 150, 178, 205, 233, 261, 289, 319, 347, 377, 405, 433
Word endings 87, 139, 195, 251, 309, 366, 423
Word families 56, 82

Word families *(continued)* 108, 134, 162, 190, 218, 246, 274, 302, 332, 360, 390, 418

SIMILAR WORDS

adverse, averse 190
advice, advise 190
affect, effect 173
allowed, aloud 400
all ready, already 400
biannual, biennial 284
choose, chose 342
compliment, complement 418
council, counsel 173
emigrate, immigrate 314
eminent, imminent 372
farther, further 372
lead, led 428
precede, proceed 284
principal, principle 314
respectively, respectfully 428
sometime, some time, sometimes 342
therefore, therefor 418

SPELLING FAMILIES

Double letters 246
Dropping letters 256
Words ending in *y* 274

STAIR-STEP DICTATION

63, 72, 88, 97, 113, 123, 140, 151, 169, 179, 196, 206, 224, 234, 252, 262, 280, 290, 310, 320, 338, 348, 367, 378, 396, 406, 424, 434

TRANSCRIPTION SPEED BUILDING

78, 104, 130, 158, 186, 214, 242, 269, 298, 328, 355, 385, 413, 441

TRANSCRIPTION TYPING

62, 71, 87, 96, 104, 122, 139, 150, 168, 186, 195, 206, 223, 233, 251, 261, 279, 289, 309, 319, 337, 347, 366, 377, 395, 405, 423, 433

TYPING STYLE STUDY

Amounts 163
Commas in numbers 118
Numbers written as figures 163
Numbers written as words 163
Time 163

Frequently Used Phrases

of Gregg Shorthand

	A	B	C	D	E	F	G
1							
2							
3							
4							
5							
6							
7							
8							
9							
10							
11							
12							
13							
14							
15							
16							
17							
18							
19							